D1558842

VENETIAN PHOENIX:
PAOLO SARPI

VENETIAN PHOENIX:
PAOLO SARPI

And Some of
His English Friends
(1606-1700)

BY

JOHN LEON LIEVSAY

THE UNIVERSITY PRESS OF KANSAS
Lawrence, Manhattan, Wichita

© 1973 by the University Press of Kansas
Printed in the United States of America

Designed by Fritz Reiber

Library of Congress Cataloging in Publication Data
Lievsay, John Leon.
   Venetian Phoenix.
   Bibliography: p.
   1. Sarpi, Paolo, 1552-1623. I. Title.
BX4705.S36L53   282′.092′4 [B]   73-6818
ISBN 0-7006-0108-2

For

Louis B. Wright

whose generous assistance to scholars,
whose own numerous and distinguished publications,

> *and*

whose lively interest in humane studies
have been prominent redeeming features of a
sick century

Preface

THE PRESENT STUDY is the middle volume in a projected series of three works designed to examine selected aspects of the cultural relations between Italy and England during the period, roughly, between 1550 and 1650. The first member of the series, *Stefano Guazzo and the English Renaissance* (Chapel Hill, N.C.: University of North Carolina Press, 1961) has already been published; the third, presently in preparation, will concern itself with the historical and literary reflections of Pope Urban VIII's efforts to regain England for the Roman Catholic faith.

Active—although lamentably desultory and protracted—collection of the materials for this volume began in the summer of 1952, while I was holder of a fellowship at the Newberry Library, in Chicago. A Fulbright Research Fellowship to Italy in 1953–1954, while directed primarily at other ends, enabled me to begin examining Sarpiana in Venetian and other Italian libraries and archives; and this was more vigorously renewed in the summer of 1958, when I again visited Italy under a special grant from the Folger Library. Thereafter, for almost a decade, I slowly acquired a moderately adequate collection of basic Sarpiana, the Folger meanwhile obligingly purchasing items beyond my reach. Then, in 1968–1969, as recipient of a John Simon Guggenheim Fellowship, I was enabled once more to visit England and Italy, to refresh and complete my notes, and to enjoy a period of uninterrupted writing amid the conveniences and attractions of the Folger Library.

Without this generous and continued support from the sources named and without the advice of, and the advantage of constructive discussions with, numerous interested individuals, this book could scarcely have been written. That it escapes numerous inconsistencies incident to piecemeal composition, I owe to the vigilant editorial eye of Mrs. Virginia Seaver; that it has avoided at least some of its original infelicities of organization and phrasing, I owe to the perceptive comments of the readers for the University Press of Kansas. I offer to each and all of them my heartfelt thanks; and I hope that they may find in the finished product some return, however inadequate, for their trust and concern.

—J. L. L.

Durham, N.C.

Contents

1 --- A Quiet Glory

NO RECORDED PORTENT announced the birth of one of the most portentous figures of the late Renaissance. He had as illustrious coevals in the year of his birth Alberico Gentili, Edmund Spenser, Richard Hakluyt, Sir Walter Raleigh, and, through one of those ironic quirks of destiny arranged by the gods for their private entertainment, Camillo Borghese, later to become Pope Paul V. In that year, 1552, the Council of Trent entered upon its longest period of suspension; and in that same year died St. Francis Xavier, the most rigorous missionary of that Jesuit order which the wondrous newly born child would live (and rejoice) to see banished from his native Venice. It was a year to be remembered.

And it has been. The birth of Pietro Sarpi, son of Francesco Sarpi, a choleric Friulian merchandising in Venice, and of a pious mother, Isabella Morelli, was duly (and anonymously) recorded in *La Vita del Padre Paolo*, now known to be the work of Fra Fulgenzio Micanzio, the inseparable companion and admiring Boswell of his later years.[1] Upon the early death of the father, Isabella placed her young son under the tutelage of his clerical maternal uncle, Ambrogio Morelli. This worthy—"uomo d'antica severità di costumi, molto erudito nelle lettere d'umanità"[2]—conducted a small *studium* where, among others later distinguished, one of his pupils was the future historian of Venice, Andrea Morosini.[3] The young Pietro was so apt a pupil, so gifted in memory and judgment, that he soon outstripped his master's capacity to instruct him; whereupon Ambrogio, following the larger dictates of those "lettere d'umanità," passed him along to a second master, Gian Maria Cappella, resident nearby in the convent of the Servi. With the change of masters the young Pietro's studies assumed a graver, more philosophic cast. And, if possible, so did the young Pietro.

Fra Fulgenzio describes his subject's customary sobriety at this period of his development:

1

His carriage of himselfe even at that age, gave a true presage of his future deportment, which wee will rather call naturall inclinations, the better sort whereof he hath since raised to a great perfection, having corrected the rest which were more imperfect by vertue, being in himselfe a meere retirednesse, and of a semblant or meane, alwaies thoughtfull, and rather melancholique then serious, of a continued silence even with those of his owne age: alwaies in quiet, without being addicted to any of those exercises, wherewith children are by nature most pleased, (though but in a gentle motion, and only for preservation of health).[4]

"A notable thing," adds the admiring biographer, "and never observed in any other."

This preternatural owlishness of the young Sarpi and his abstraction from the ordinary frivolities of youth—or of manhood, too, for that matter: he touched no wine until he was past thirty—placed a stamp of singularity upon him. His schoolmates, when he was by, were mindful of their noise and language, as if he were a second nobly censorious Cato. When against the wishes of his mother and uncle he entered the Order of the Servites on 24 November 1566, he continued his studies under the Servite Cappello, changing his manners not a whit. One of his fellow novices recalls that "in his childhood he was of great retirednesse, silence and quietnesse, and that hee was wont to withdraw himselfe from every childish sport. And they spoke it of him as a common by word. All we are for trifles and pamphlets, but *Fryer Paul* is for Bookes."[5] It goes almost without saying (although Fra Fulgenzio says it) that "he was never reprehended for speaking an undecent word, nor doing an unbeseeming act."[6]

In these student years knowledge and virtues proceeded *pari passu* until, continues Fra Fulgenzio,

the accumulation of sciences, and probity made this religious young man so venerable, and (I may say) so majesticall, that as it is a custome in *Venice* among the noble, and ingenuous youth, that if any of them be not so decent in their habite, or that they be of a lesse modesty in discourse or cariage, then they ought to be, yet when they appeare before the first Senator, they are carefull to put themselves into their best habite and posture, so in this order of the religion of *Servi* (for even among the religious, especially those of the younger sort, are not alwaies under rule, nor as wee say with their bowes bended,) yet at the appearance of *Fra. Paolo* they were al' composed reducing themselves to a more seriousnes of behaviour, setting aside both sport and Joviality, as if his onely presence had been the black rod; whereupon it became a proverbe among them, whensoever he was present or appeared. *E qua la sposa mutiamo proposito*, let us change our discourse, here comes the bride.[7]

Does one catch in these sketches a suggestion of another virtuous and learned young paragon—"The Lady of Christ's"—at least as he later recalled his own impeccable youth?[8] Akin they were, no doubt, in spirit; and John Milton was to become, in any event, one of Fra Paolo's sincerest English admirers.

What studies did the young Sarpi pursue? Beyond those that constituted the routine curriculum for cloistered persons—grammar, logic, rhetoric, letters, philosophy, divinity—his bent led him particularly towards mathematics, law, medicine, anatomy, architecture, and the physical sciences. To these he added "a sufficient understanding of divers tongues, beside the latine, the Greek, the Hebrew, and the Caldean."[9] Being endowed with a quick perception, a photographic memory, an insatiable curiosity, and an indefatigable industry, he soon became (and small wonder) a prodigy of wide and accurate learning.[10] So startling was his proficiency that, later, specialists talking with him each came away with the impression that his own particular interest had been the Friar's exclusive concern.[11] The course of busy and unremitting study which he undertook in these tender years he maintained throughout his life. His mathematical wizardry, his inventions, his original discoveries in physics and the biological sciences (he is said, for instance, to have anticipated Harvey in discovering the circulation of the blood) have probably been exaggerated by those enthusiasts who have written most about them;[12] but his later correspondence with various learned men in several countries and the respectful terms in which he is mentioned by some of the most eminent scientists of his day are sufficient evidence that all the smoke was not without some fire.

In 1570, when he was eighteen, Pietro (in religion thereafter, Paolo) engaged in a theological disputation at Mantua, where in the presence of the reigning Gonzaga Duke, Guglielmo III, he sustained with great applause no fewer than 318 theses. As a result of this spectacular performance the Duke forthwith named him Court Theologian, and the bishop, Gregorio Boldrino, appointed him Reader in Positive Theology. Such a double vote of confidence in one so young might ruinously have swelled a head less humble than Sarpi's. He remained in Mantua for four years under favor of the Duke, continuing his studies of mathematics and languages and continuing to stupefy all with the range and precision of his learning, so that when he left the court there arose a common saying, "There will never come more among us another frier *Paul*."[13] At Mantua he also formed a close alliance with the unfortunate Camillo Olivo, who had been secretary to Cardinal Gonzaga at the Council of Trent. This marks, perhaps, the genesis of his enduring interest in that great event. It was, in any case, a fabulous opportunity for him to gather first-hand information about the inner workings of the Council, which had come to its close while he was still a child of eleven.

His reasons for leaving the Duke's service are not entirely clear, but his biographer says that they were in no way discreditable: "The true cause of his departure (which he made with the Princes favour and approbation) was, because that a court life was so absolutely averse to his Genius, and his fame in religion made him to be perpetually importuned by his friends and superiours, who had a design to make use of his labours in their profession."[14] In 1574, at the age of twenty-two, Fra Paolo was ordained a priest. Thereafter, through a succession of increasingly important offices and onerous duties, he rose rapidly to a position of prime authority and significance within his order—not without some trials and contretemps arising from the envy of his fellow friars.

Among the first of those "who had a design to make use of his labours in their profession" was the famous reforming Cardinal Carlo Borromeo, now sainted. The Cardinal sent for him

> and against his inclination made him heare confessions [the number of confessors, because of abuses of the confessional, being rigorously reduced], making use of him not onely in the Church of his own order, but in others (as it was needfull) and tooke great affection in him, being much pleased with his company. He would alwaies be present at the most difficult discussions of cases of conscience & other consultations upon divers accidents, where the opinion of the most learned divines were had, and would often make him stay to dine with him in his refectory.[15]

Fra Fulgenzio does not specify the length of Sarpi's stay in the Cardinal's service, but he does spell out in some detail the nature of the distressing physical weaknesses which were to plague the Friar for the rest of his life:[16] constipation, hemorrhoids, *prolapsus ani*. And he records the unsuccessful attempt of an envious fellow friar, Maestro Claudio of Piacenza, to entrammel him in the toils of the Inquisition.[17]

At some indefinite moment during this period, however, his biographer records that

> the affaires of his own province, and the instance of his friends, were able to cal him backe to his owne Country in *Venice*, & his province, where immediately, al those that were of greater yeares giving place to an eminency of vertue, and integrity, more to be admired then related; he being already gone through all those degrees which the lawes of his order had appointed; of student, of Bachelor, of master, (which is the title of the Doctorates in *Theologie*) and being a yeare before that,

aggregated to that most famous Colledge of *Padua,* was with universall applause 1579. created Provinciall,[18] (with this addition that he should governe the studie as regent) for so they call the readers of the sacred Theologie.[19]

In the exemplary execution of this office, adds Fra Fulgenzio, "*Padre Paolo* chalkt out a way to his successours, by which they might arrive at their end with great reputation."

Never before in the 340 years since the founding of the Servite Order had one so young—he was twenty-six—been named to a provincialship, which was a wonder in itself. In the same year (1579) at a general chapter of the order, which was meeting at Parma, Sarpi was named one of a committee of three to revise "the constitutions and rules for the government of the whole order." This exceptional circumstance was not lost upon Fra Fulgenzio, who observes that Sarpi "was but a youth in respect of the venerable and hoarie haires of the other two."[20] Such a revision, necessitated by the recently published decrees of the Council of Trent, led Fra Paolo to spend a certain amount of time in Rome. In the process he was thrown much into the company of Cardinals Alessandro Farnese, Protector of the order, and Santa Severina, Vice-Protector, as well as, occasionally, the Pope himself. The Jesuit Bellarmino, Sarpi's admirer and future opponent, not yet a cardinal, was in Rome at this period. It is not clearly established that Sarpi met him so early; but the period and the task in hand provided excellent opportunity for the observant Servite to see at close range the operations of the Curia and to leave behind him in the Eternal City "a great fame of his knowledge, and prudence."[21]

Upon the termination of Sarpi's three-year appointment as Provincial, writes Fra Fulgenzio, "he entered into some more quietnesse, which he said was all the repose he enjoyed in the whole course of his life . . . so for three whole yeares he gave himselfe to nothing but speculations of naturall things."[22] This was the sort of life for which Fra Paolo was by temperament and inclination most suited. The "speculations" and experiments in botany, mineralogy, and especially anatomy at this time were such as to earn him the respect of Girolamo Fabrizio d'Acquapendente, of Santorio Santorio, and of Pierre Asselineau.[23] For similar reasons other distinguished names would later be added to the list.

This "garden of spiritual delights" was too good to last. Thereafter, though in a less secular theater of activity, Padre Paolo continued his rise to eminence. In 1585 at a general chapter of his order, "he was by common consent created Procurator of the Court called Proctor generall."[24] As Provincial, his authority had been regional and Venetian only. As Procurator-General he was, with much more singular distinction, next in authority under the

General of the whole order; and the juridical obligations of the new post summoned him again to Rome for the next three years. Here, with an irony that only the future would reveal, he hobnobbed on terms of easy familiarity with the great and the near great of the ecclesiastical hierarchy. And here, in addition to performing the regular legal activities of his post,

> by order from the Pope himselfe [Sixtus Quintus] he entred into divers congregations, where there was occasion to discourse in occurrent actions upon important difficulties of doctrine. At which meetings he came to know and take intimate acquaintance with father *Bellarmine*, who was often present, and was afterwards a Cardinall, whose friendship continued even to the end of his life.[25]

Others of the Lords Spiritual he also met, including the future Urban VII, who "was infinitely pleased with him."[26] During this period he also "had once occasion to goe to *Naples* to sit President as Vicar Generall at the Chapters, and to make the Visitation, where hee grew acquainted with that famous witt *Gio. Battista Porta*, who in some worke of his that came to light makes honorable mention of *Padre Paolo* as of no ordinary personage, and particularly of his specular perspective."[27] But the great moment, apparently, in this part of Fra Fulgenzio's artless narrative—a moment ridiculous in its aftermath but rich in its humorous undertones—came when

> upon a time the Pope being in the street in his Litter, called the Father unto him, holding him a good while in discourse, which was nothing else but of certaine memorials that were come to his hands against the Generall of that time. This unwonted passage, and observ'd by the Court that used to make observations upon all things, was presently divulged abroad how much the Father was in the Popes favour; what would you have more? The vanity had already made him a Cardinall. But the favour which was neither sought nor desired by him, cast him into a most troublesome persecution.[28]

We need not enter into the messy intricacies of that "troublesome persecution," which involved the ambitious intrigues of a fellow Servite, Gabriele Collisoni, to secure for himself the generalship of the order and—fortunately without success—to discredit Father Paul. Nor need we follow the other petty bickerings and factious commotions that swirled about the Father as he fulfilled his duties. Suffice it to say that he *did* fulfill them, and with such aplomb and distinction that, as his biographer remarks, "it was well worth observing, that in all the controverted *Points*, the opinion of the father was ever approved of."[29]

The year was now 1588, and Father Paul was back once more in Venice.

6

Edmund Spenser, having with the publication of his *Shepheardes Calender* (1579) become England's "New Poet," was now buried in the obscurity of an Irish secretaryship. Hakluyt, after his collection of 1582 (*Divers Voyages*), was about to issue the first form of his *Principall Navigations* (1589). Raleigh, now Lord Lieutenant of Cornwall and Warden of the stannaries, was scurrying about the west country levying men against the expected Spanish invasion. And Camillo Borghese, not yet a cardinal, was Vice-Legate of Bologna. It was a moment of something like calm before a storm.

"The father being come back to *Venice*, resumed the course of his former studies, and of his retirednesse from businesse frequenting his accustomed vertuous conversations,"[30] and especially those intellectual gatherings at the home of Andrea Morosini, where the best wits of Venice and any notable visiting virtuosi were wont to congregate. Fra Fulgenzio gives an ecstatic account of these meetings:

> In my life I have not seene more vertuous exercises, and I wish it had pleased God that as the vertues of those two *Andria* and *Nicolo* the uncles (which discended by inheritance unto their nephews) so there might have been in *Venice* such another meeting, where there were met at sometimes five and twentie or thirtie men of rare endowments. At this meeting the ceremony (which is a thing so much affected in our times and so superfluous) had no countenance which tries the braines of the wiser sort, & vainely spends so much time in an artificiall kind of lying, that signifies nothing because it signifies so much, but a civill and free confidence was onely there in use. It was allowed every man to make his discourse of whatsoever pleased him best, without restriction of passing from one subject to another, provided it were alwaies of new matter, and the end of their disputation was for nothing else but to finde out truth. But the felicitie of our father was rare, who upon any subject that was propounded did not onely discourse without premeditation; but made no difference of sustaining or impugning any proposition in a scholastique way. All which he did with so much facilitie that it raised a wonder in all men. And afterwards in his riper age, when he was put in minde of those exercises, he would smile at them as puerilities.[31]

Very far from being "puerilities" were the conversations which our Friar held at another of his favorite meeting places, the "Golden Ship" in the *Merzeria*, a shop owned by Bernardo Secchini and the common resort of seamen and travelers. Here Father Paul gathered news of events and manners of the outside world, storing his mind with the exotica which he had the skill to draw from the least able conversationalist. And occasional meetings with a more learned set of *dottori* in Padua at the home of Vincenzo Pinelli

VENETIAN PHOENIX: PAOLO SARPI

were no doubt given over to weightier matters. Pinelli's estimate of Sarpi—"I relate it in his owne words," says Fra Fulgenzio—was that he was *"il miracolo di questo secolo."*[32]

In the midst of this period of unmixed felicity, the Father thought he saw an opportunity to render his present happiness permanent. In 1591 there occurred a vacancy in the bishopric of Caorle, a small and unimportant place within the Venetian territory. The appointment was a virtual sinecure and would permit the incumbent to pursue his studies and experiments in peaceful content. Sarpi asked for it, was supported by the Venetian authorities, who had the right of nomination—and was refused at Rome. He was disappointed, but not overwhelmed. When another vacant bishopric, that of Nona, came up in the following year, he again asked for the appointment, was again backed by the Venetian authorities, and was again rejected. It became apparent to him that he was not destined to be a bishop. Unembittered and unambitious, he went about his daily concerns. The later Romanist charges that he opposed the curial policy of Pope Paul V out of resentment for these rebuffs, given the nature of the man, are wildly improbable.

These happy, quiet times when the Father devoted his mornings to his religious offices and his evenings to his studies and "vertuous conversations" lasted about six years, into the mid nineties. Then, because Envy never sleeps, the Father's troubles were renewed. Partly they stemmed from the power struggle within the Servite order, involving that Maestro Gabriele of whom mention has been made; and partly they arose out of laughably frivolous charges of misconduct leveled against Sarpi, one of which (though never proved, "that he had held commerce with the *Hebrewes*") was afterward remembered against him by Clement VIII and cost him the bishopric of Nona, to which, as was mentioned above, the Venetian Republic had commended him.[33] The split within the order, in which the peaceable Father Paul was sure to be a loser because he did not actively support either faction, lasted until 1597. It was then so complicated by collateral squabbles that Sarpi determined to go to Rome in an effort to resolve the bitternesses. In Rome he dealt directly with Cardinal Santa Serverina,[34] Protector of the order and, through his stubborn support of Maestro Gabriele, one of the chief fomenters of strife within it. Eventually he was able to convince Santa Severina of his own integrity and to return once more to Venice with some of the rancors abated.[35] The restoration of a modicum of peace within the order was accompanied by some welcome relief from his physical ailments, especially the prolapsus, for which he had at last found an instrument capable of making the condition endurable.[36]

The six years that followed were devoted to the exercise of divine offices, the continuance of "vertuous conversations," the intensified study of moral philosophy—ancient and more recent—and the repeated perusal of the New Testament, both the Greek and the Latin texts. During these relatively placid years Sarpi entered into correspondence with various learned men, lay and religious; and during these years he was repeatedly urged to return to Rome, where his talents might have had a broader scope. He was destined, however, never again to set foot within that city—though most earnestly summoned. And just as well!

One episode that followed (in May 1605) on the heels of these quiet years is so grotesque that its recital cannot be spared. Although the scheming Gabriele and the persistent Santa Severina had succeeded in 1603 in getting the former created General of the order, they were outmaneuvered by fate: the new General was barely in office before he was summoned by that fell sergeant, Death. In Gabriele's place, though operating under diminished authority, there was "supplyed" a nephew of his, a certain Maestro Santo, as ambitious and unprincipled as his uncle but somewhat more feather-witted. Like Gabriele, he understood that the chief obstacle to any high-handed skulduggery which he might attempt in office would most likely be Fra Paolo. Nothing to do, then, but to involve Fra Paolo in trouble with the chapter, on whatever trumped-up or ridiculous charges. Fra Fulgenzio relates the story with a certain grim gusto:

> So *Maestro Santo,* and *Maestro Arcangelo* stood up, and to doe nothing with much diligence, and with power to make a conspicuous buffonery; they oppos'd three heads of exception or reproach against father *Paul,* with the indignation and derision of all the Chapter, and they were these. That he wore a hat upon his head contrarie to a forme that had beene lately published under *Gregory* the fourteenth. That he wore pantables [=pantofles, slippers] that were hollowed in the soles of the *French* fashion (alledging falsly) that it had beene decreed otherwise upon paine of deprivation of their votes. That at the end of Masse he did not use to repeate the *Salve Regina.* Things that were no sooner heard then resolved by the Vicar generall, the President and the Provinciall into nothing, and exploded by all the assembly, being rejected and kickt out. And because his pantobles were taken off by order from the Judge, and caried to the Tribunall, it became a proverb which is yet in use. *Esser il Padre Paolo cosi incolpabile & integro che sino le sue pianelle erano state canonizate.* The father Paul is so blameles and pure that his very pantobles were canonized.[37]

Saint and *Archangel* argued against him, who said not a word in his own defense, and were hooted down! It was an emblem of things to come.

"By this time," says Fra Fulgenzio, "(wee may say) that the fathers quiet studies and his private life were come to their period, and that from hence till the end of his life, he entred upon another world; or rather came into the world, wherein it pleased God to call him into employments, which he had never thought he should have applied himselfe to."[38] Fra Fulgenzio goes on to paraphrase Plato about man's not being born for himself alone, and so forth—a timeless truth; but we, who are concerned more with time than with Plato, had better look at the calendar.

It was now late in the year 1605. Except for the *Cantos of Mutabilitie*, all Spenser's great poetry had been published, and the piping of Colin Clout, whether from hunger or from heartbreak, had ceased forever. Hakluyt had published his *Principall Navigations* in their definitive collection. The ill-starred Raleigh lay prisoner in the Tower, the victim of his own restless ambition and of the meanest-minded king in Christendom. England had had a change of monarch, and the horrid Gunpowder Plot—Jesuit-inspired, it was thought—had shaken the minds, if not the halls, of Parliament. Cardinal Camillo Borghese, of Siena, sweet of face and bitter of heart,[39] assuming the name of Paul the Fifth, had come to the Chair of St. Peter. And Sarpi had come to the end of a chapter in his career.

2 --- Crisis in the Serenissima

PINELLI'S ASSESSMENT of Sarpi as "the miracle of this century" notwithstanding, and della Porta's even warmer encomium of him as "the splendor and ornament not of Venice only, or Italy, but of the world,"[1] published in a book widely circulated, up to this point Sarpi remained, remarkable as indeed he was, simply a peninsular figure. He was not to remain so much longer. His alter ego, Micanzio, who thus far has obligingly carried our narrative for us, but whose encomiastic view remains limitedly Italian, or even almost exclusively Venetian, must now be abandoned for other voices. With the coming of Sir Henry Wotton to Venice as the first resident British ambassador in 1604, the fame of Sarpi begins to be known even in distant England. And that is the strain we must henceforth pursue.

It is a mistake, doubtless, to speak of the "troubles" that were in store for Sarpi; for few things ever deeply troubled that serene spirit. Troubles there were, however, and he was in the midst of them. They were the troubles that have crept into the history books under the rubric, generally, of "The Quarrels between the Most Serene Republic of Venice and the Sanctity of Our Lord, Pope Paul V," 1605–1607. They ended in complete discomfiture for the papal pretensions, a defeat of which the Servite friar was the principal engineer. To this day, in Rome, that ignominious collapse has been neither forgotten nor forgiven.

The issues leading to the famous (or infamous) interdict were not matters merely of secular or ecclesiastical jurisdiction, although they may seem to point to a continuance of the long struggle between church and state. Back of the immediate and ostensible points of conflict were causes involving the history, politics, and especially the economics of the Venetian Republic. And

11

on the papal side there were the problems of solidifying the Counter Reformation spelled out in the decrees of the Council of Trent, the tricky personality of an individual pope, and the unrelenting pressure exerted upon the papal temporal ambitions by the all-enveloping Austro-Spanish hegemony in the Italian peninsula. These must now be summarily examined.[2]

After her long centuries of growth in wealth and power, and her established position of proud independence (the famed "Venetian liberty"), the republic at the end of the sixteenth century was entering upon a period of decline which marked the prelude of her final dissolution. She had lost effective control over shipping from her ports in the Levant. The development of new trade routes around Africa had robbed her of her spice trade through the established eastern routes. The Uskoks, covertly supported by the Austrians, and other pirates (including some Englishmen), were making the Adriatic less and less a Venetian sea.[3] Every hand seemed to be lifted against Venice. Her military and commercial fleets were sadly shrinking, and she was ceasing to build her own shipping. Outside her territory an ever-threatening Spain and the States of the Church ringed her round; and within, year by year more of her revenue-producing land slipped into the hands of the church. Diminished at sea, and with a quarter of her richest land producing no contribution to the treasury, she was short of cash and short of friends. The *Serenissima* had reason to be a little less than serene.

These, however, were bread-and-butter matters, with no savor of "the spiritualities." Venice tried to meet or solve them by legislation, by political alliances, and by the subtleties of a long-experienced diplomacy. Her success was only indifferent. Under such pressures tempers grew short, and traditional practices and ancient "rights" were guarded more jealously than ever before. Any invasion of territory, any attack on ancient prestige, or any diminution of authority was doubly galling to the Senate and the people of Venice. The Venetian clergy, almost wholly drawn from the territories of the republic, though faithful sons of the church and respectful toward Rome, had long enjoyed a degree of administrative autonomy equaled elsewhere only in the Gallican Church. They were inclined to be, as someone has observed, "Venetians first and churchmen afterwards." Further, through long use and wont, they had reached their own comfortable working arrangements between church and state. Dictation of policy from without was therefore not only unacceptable; it was well-nigh unthinkable.

On the other hand, the new pope—once he had freed himself of the silly, not to say superstitious, notion that he was destined to an early death, as astrologers had predicted[4]—proved himself by native bent, by education, and by curial function (he had long exercised the office of Auditor of the Apostolic Chamber) to be an extreme stickler for the "rights" of the church. He

12

was, moreover, something of a bully; and from vicariously thundering forth the blasts of another, he turned with gusto to performing in his own behalf. As a papal aid for the directing of his bolts he had an infallible nose for *heresy*, which he tended to define as anything running counter to his will.[5]

Here, then, ready-made, were the conditions for fireworks. The first explosions were not long in coming. One of the ancient customs of the republic was, upon naming a Patriarch for the state church, to have him go to Rome for the receiving of the pope's blessing—a sort of official announcement of the appointment. When the Senate on 28 January 1600 elected Matteo Zane to replace Lorenzo Priuli, Cardinal Patriarch of Venice, who had died two days earlier, the new Patriarch made the customary courtesy call upon the Pope, Clement VIII. After greetings, a few polite questions, and the departure of the Patriarch, the Pope began to let creep abroad insinuations that he had "examined" in theology (and therefore *approved*) the elected official. On 13 July, angered at this presumption on Clement's part, the Senate rejected any papal claim to a right to subject its appointee to an examination in theology.[6] To avoid any opportunity for renewal of the papal claims, when Zane died and Francesco Vendramin was elected (24 July 1605) to replace him, the new Patriarch did not make the usual visit to Rome. It was not exactly a flattering salute to Pope Paul V, who had been recently elected (16 May 1605).

Other actions of the Senate, both before and after the accession of Pope Paul V, had to do more directly with money matters and the economy of the land. A minor but potentially irritating act was the Senate's placing of a strict limit (26 July 1602) upon the amount of dowry a nun about to take the veil could bring to the church. On the tenth of January 1604, a much more touchy law was enacted—or, rather, reenacted: no further churches, hospitals, schools, or monasteries were to be built without permission from the Council of Ten. But the decree that was really aimed at effectively plugging the hole in the bottom of the public purse was enacted on 26 March 1605. This provided that the alienation of real estate to ecclesiastics through testamentary legacy or other form of gift must be approved by the *pregadi*—the members of the Senate. It, too, was merely an extension of a law already of long standing. A further provision was that any real property thus coming into the possession of the church must upon the expiration of a two-year period be turned into cash, which would remain with the church, the property reverting to secular possession.[7]

The Pope had had time to brood but a little on these and other similar vexations when there came to his attention two further "outrages" perpetrated by those villainous (and probably heretical) Venetians. For certain gross offenses against public order and decency, and particularly against a woman who had repulsed his unwelcome attentions, Scipione Saraceno—a canon of Vicenza, which was in Venetian territory—was summoned before the Council of Ten and summarily committed to their prison (secular, of course). While the Pope was fuming over this violation of "ecclesiastical liberty" and insisting that the prisoner should be turned over forthwith to the ecclesiastical tribunal, these being crimes too trivial for the secular arm, the Venetians apprehended and incarcerated another ecclesiastical libertine. This one was Count Marcantonio Brandolino, Abbot of Nervesa, in Friuli. The crimes with which he was charged were so horrendous as to make the blood of normal human beings run cold: repeated attempts at parricide, actual fratricide, numerous "just plain old murders," incest, rape, robbery, and general unrestrained hell-raising. But the Pope did not boggle at pleading ecclesiastical exemption for even this depraved man and insisting that he be turned over to ecclesiastical judgment.[8]

When the Pope could not persuade or cajole the Venetians to see reason, he lost patience with them. Under his own firm resolve, supplemented by the incitements of some of his consistory ill affected towards the Venetians, he sent two papal briefs to his nuncio in Venice on December tenth. In one of them he demanded release of the two prisoners; in the other, the repeal of the laws limiting church properties and inheritances. If these conditions were not met, the state would be liable to interdiction.[9]

The issuing and delivery of these briefs was a comedy of perhaps not entirely undeliberate errors. For one thing, in the haste and confusion with which they were drawn up and dispatched from the papal secretariat, not two different briefs but two copies of a single one (the second) were sent to the nuncio. In the second place, the nuncio, using his own judgment (for which the Pope could willingly have flayed him), held up delivery for a moment *he* judged more propitious. Then, instead of being able to deliver them to the Doge and Senate while they were in session, on Christmas morning as the Council members were on their way to Mass, he turned over the briefs to them—and scampered. Knowing or suspecting their contents, he could already see his hide nailed to the door of his residence.[10]

It was not the propitious moment he had waited for. Even while the senators were in St. Mark's, the Doge, Marino Grimani, was reported to be lying at death's door. The following day his death was officially announced.[11] In the temporary suspension of business the Pope's briefs remained unopened. Meanwhile, on 10 January 1606 Leonardo Donato (or Donà) was elected Doge. On the fourteenth the briefs, opened at last, were found to be duplicates concerning the repeal of the laws against alienation of property to ecclesiastics. On the twenty-third, preachers were warned not to treat of politics in their sermons; and the Pope's brief, after the Senate's consultation

14

with various theologians and learned doctors of Venice, of Padua, and of other parts of the Venetian territory—Sarpi among them—was rejected on the twenty-eighth of January. On that same day the Senate named as its *Consultore* and *Teologo* Fra Paolo Sarpi.[12]

The gauntlets were down.

It was a matter of some days before the Pope's second brief was read (25 February) in the Senate and likewise rejected. Though affairs were moving towards the inevitable clash, it was still delayed. Not until 17 April did the Pope, in full consistory, breathing fire against the recalcitrant Venetians, lay down his final terms: surrender of the prisoners and repeal of the offensive laws within twenty-four days (with an added three days of ultimate grace) or imposition of an interdict.[13] The possibility of negotiations seemed to be at an end. Unperturbed, the Venetians made their anticipatory response the very next day, as it happened: they required their clergy to submit to the Council of Ten, unopened, any bull, summons, or other writing emanating from Rome. The Senate did not propose to be caught unprepared. When the days of grace were past, the interdict, so far as Rome was concerned, was a *fait accompli*. Not so at Venice, however, where the Senate on 6 May, following the opinion rendered by their Consultore, declared the interdict to be illegal and invalid and ordered their clergy to disregard it and to continue uninterrupted the performance of the religious duties which Rome forbade them to perform.[14] A ticklish situation, this, and one which at another time or place could have led to infinite trouble.

But this was Venice, and in Venice, as the whole world knew, they did things differently. Most of the clergy, Venetian-born and Venetian in sympathies where conflicts of interest arose, at ease in their lagoonal Zion, went calmly about their business. A few protested, and a few, with the State's permission but not the blessing of the populace, left Venetian territory. No doubt the ordinary single protester, thinking to escape the Senate's edict through flight, was somewhat deterred by the knowledge that the borders were being watched and that ecclesiastics leaving illegally were liable to hanging on the spot. One protester proclaimed firmly that he would not say Mass on a certain important occasion. On the eve of the occasion a representative of the Council asked him how he intended to act on the morrow. He replied that he would not at the moment give a decisive answer but would act next day as the Holy Spirit prompted him. When this was reported to the Council, their representative was immediately sent back to convey a message. His answer, they told the priest, was in good spirit; but they, too, had been instructed by that same spirit, who had told them something that they thought might be of interest to him: they were instructed, they said (in something like papal overtones), to inform him that if he failed to perform every tittle of his expected service, they would *infallibly* hang him at the door of his own church. He said the Mass.[15]

The Jesuits, who were committed to an absolute fealty to the pope, were nevertheless willing, after their crafty manner, to make some compromises.[16] They would not agree to say Mass, but they were willing to continue certain other of their ministrations—particularly the hearing of confessions. The Venetians, however, had already penetrated the Jesuit politic and feared that if the order remained in Venetian territory, the pope would have a Trojan horse in the stronghold of his opponents. The compromises offered were unacceptable, and on the ninth of May the Jesuits were given a day's time in which to pull themselves together and absent themselves (a later decree said "forever") from Venetian felicity. When it became apparent that they planned to leave next morning in solemn procession, carrying the sacred symbols at the head of their ranks and striking the pose of martyrs, the Senate quietly advanced the time of their departure—no use to keep the martyrs waiting. At midnight they were rousted from their quarters, halted in their packing and hiding of church valuables, restrained from further hurried destruction of secret papers, and ushered, not always in decent array, out of the city. Such citizenry as were still afoot at that late hour greeted them with a cry that the martyrs could hardly have mistaken for uncontrollable grief: *andè in malora!*—"Go, in the devil's name."[17] A few days later, on 15 May, two other orders were permitted to leave the state—the Capuchins and the Theatines. With the dissidents out of the way, any further opposition to the stance taken by the Venetian government would have to come from without.

It came, and promptly. But though there were threats and intimations of violence and some arming for downright war, the principal form the warfare took was that of a massive pamphlet dueling between the opposed forces.[18] The penwork was waged furiously, and much ink was spilled. All Europe looked on, some cheering one side, some the other. And, to his own surprise, at the forefront of those writing on the Venetian side was Paolo Sarpi, Consultore to the Serenissima.[19] In the midst of battle and even more when it was over, Sarpi could have said accurately, as Milton was to say of himself with much less propriety in a later fray, his fame was something "of which all Europe talks from side to side."

The pamphlets poured out, literally, by the score. Sarpi's own contemporaneously published contributions began with his translation of the *Trattato et resolutione sopra la validità delle scommuniche di Gio. Gersone Theologo e Cancelliero parisino* (Venice, 1606).[20] Although Gerson may have been known to others as "il Dottore Christianissimo," Sarpi could hardly have lighted upon a name that would have been more repugnant to Pope

Paul V: Gerson was one of those "heretics" who maintained the supremacy of councils over popes! The *Trattato et resolutione* was followed by *Considerationi sopra le censure della Santità di Papa Paulo V. contra la Serenissima Republica di Venetia. del P.M. Paulo da Venetia dell'Ordine de'Servi* (Venice, 1606). Next, announced on its title page as the work of seven theologians (including Sarpi) but actually in its entirety or at least in great part Sarpi's own, came the *Trattato dell'Interdetto della Santità di Papa Paulo V. Nel quale si dimostra, che egli non è legittimamente publicato, et che per molte ragioni non sono obligati gli Ecclesiastici all'essecutione di esso, nè possono senza peccato osservarlo* (Venice, 1606).[21] Meanwhile, Cardinal Bellarmine having been stirred by the Pope to answer the odious translation from Gerson in his *Risposta ad un libretto intitolato Trattato et resolutione sopra la validità delle scommuniche* (Rome, 1606), Sarpi, toward the end of the year, made reply to his friend the Cardinal in an *Apologia per le oppositioni fatte dall'Illustrissimo, et Reverendiss.ᵐᵒ Signor Cardinale Bellarmino alli trattati et resolutioni di Gio. Gersone sopra la validità delle Scommuniche. Del Padre Maestro Paulo da Venetia dell'Ordine de'Servi* (Venice, 1606).

These were the Sarpian publications during the interdict. Afterwards, at the request of the French historian Jacques-Auguste de Thou (Thuanus), he composed a retrospective survey of the whole course of events during the struggle. The document which Sarpi proceeded to prepare for use by de Thou was essentially completed by the end of 1607; but for reasons of caution about transmitting it, Sarpi's account, now grown fuller, was not sent until 1617.[22] Unfortunately, de Thou died in Paris, 7 May 1617, without ever seeing the long-promised manuscript. And Sarpi himself had died before it was published (in Geneva, 1624) as *Historia particolare delle cose passate tra'l Sommo Pontefice Paolo V e la Serenissima Republica di Venetia gl'anni MDCV. MDCVI. MDCVII. Divisa in Sette Libri Viva San Marco*.[23] This, no pamphlet but a substantial volume, was the most memorable piece of writing to issue from the conflict.

Among other writers on the Venetian side were the senator Antonio Querini (or Quirino), author of the *Aviso delle ragioni della Serenissima Republica di Venetia* (Venice, 1606),[24] who was several times attacked or "answered" by writers of the Romanist party; the ex-Jesuit Neapolitan canonist Giovanni Marsilio; and Fra Fulgenzio Micanzio, Sarpi's right-hand man. On the Roman side, among many largely—and understandably—drawn from the ranks of the Jesuits, the great names were those of Cardinal Bellarmine, Cardinal Baronio, and Antonio Possevino, who wrote under many pseudonyms and was judged by Sarpi to be the most insidious of all.[25] The Carmelite Giovanni Antonio Bovio also played a prominent role with several of his pamphlets. Most temperate and reasonable among them was

Bellarmine, the tireless (but tiresome) controversialist; most irrational, bitter, and intransigent, for all his vast learning, was Cesare Baronio, the great Baronius of the *Annales Ecclesiastici*. In his angry response to the Venetian challenge to papal authority, Baronio behaved like a madman—little better, in fact, than the Pope himself.[26]

When all the ink had been squirted and the compromise had been reached which led to the lifting of the interdict on 21 April 1607, Sarpi stood out clearly established in the affection of the Senate and the Venetian people as their favorite and incomparable spokesman. The laws on ecclesiastical building, goods, and inheritance stood where they had stood at the commencement of the strife; and although the Venetians, through the intercession of the special French ambassador, Cardinal de Joyeuse, surrendered their two cleric-prisoners to his royal master to dispose of as he saw fit, they did not surrender their right to judge and punish such offenders. Very little of the Pope's face could be saved. It was manifestly a costly lesson for Rome; no later pope has had the hardihood or arrogance to make such a hazardous trial of his absolute powers. But in the process, on 5 January 1607, Sarpi, having refused to comply with a citation to appear in Rome and justify his conduct, was excommunicated. This action of the Pope's, another of his infallible mistakes, prepared the way for an event which was to rouse among Venetians an even fiercer pride in their champion and to center upon him the sympathetic attention of much of the rest of Europe.

On the evening of 5 October 1607, when Sarpi was returning from San Marco to his friar's cell in the Servite convent accompanied only by a servant and by the elderly patrician Alessandro Malipiero, he was set upon by a band of assassins. One of these wounded and overpowered the servant, another restrained Malipiero, and a third, armed with a stiletto, repeatedly stabbed Fra Paolo about the head and shoulders. Three of the strokes actually wounded the victim, two in the neck and the third and most serious in the head. Fortunately the last was an ill-aimed blow, the blade entering at the right ear and the point lodging in the right cheek. There it remained firmly fixed in the bone; and some women in houses nearby having witnessed the attack and summoned help with their cries, the assassins, firing harquebuses to frighten off any aid, made their escape. Sarpi, meanwhile, had fallen and lay apparently dead. The frightened servant, once released, took to his heels; and Malipiero, running to Sarpi and extracting the weapon, had the friar conveyed the short remaining distance to the convent.[27]

In Venice the response to this atrocity was instant and furious. Whether rightly or wrongly, at the time no one (including the victim) doubted that the attack was of papal inspiration.[28] Angry crowds, hearing that the would-be assassins had taken momentary shelter in the residence of the papal nuncio, had to be restrained by soldiers from burning it to the ground—and the nuncio with it. The five perpetrators of the attack, whose identities were known, fled into the States of the Church; and the Council of Ten, unable to apprehend them, decreed enormous rewards for their capture, alive or dead. If taken alive, they were to be carried to the scene of the crime, to have their right hands chopped off and suspended about their necks, and thence to be dragged at horse's tail to the pillars of San Marco, where they were to be decapitated and quartered,[29] the parts to be distributed in the usual manner: cruel and excessive punishment, by modern standards, but paralleled in England and elsewhere in those days, even in the Christian charity of Holy Mother Church.

The Senate immediately ordered for their Consultore the best of medical care, voted to increase his salary, and took steps to provide him greater security in the future. Sarpi meanwhile, fevered and hovering between life and death, remained immobilized in bed for days from shock and loss of blood. It was months before he could be pronounced cured and resume his regular attendance upon the pregadi. When he did return in mid 1608, he was no longer merely a local hero. His writings in defense of Venice in the continuing struggle for power between church and state had been read (and translated) in countries all over Europe. The attempt on his life rendered his name legendary as a defender of more than "Venetian liberty."

It was in these years that the English first began to be aware of Father Paul. The first English resident ambassador to Venice, Sir Henry Wotton, arrived in September 1604; and this, the first of his two embassies there, did not end until late in 1610. He was thus an interested spectator to all the quarrel between the republic and Pope Paul V, knowing and reporting the activities of Father Paul.[30] After the conclusion of that strife and the arrival in 1607 of his new chaplain, William Bedell, the English embassy was never unaware of the ideas and plans of Sarpi and Micanzio. If the new chaplain arrived too late for the prime fracas, he was still in ample time for the events of 5 October 1607. In a New Year's letter (1608) to his friend Adam Newton (who was later to be involved in the translation of Sarpi's greatest work) concerning Venetian religious affairs, Bedell indicates his own acquaintance with Sarpi and includes something of the Venetian reaction to the attack on the Servite:

> On the other side hath been the barbarous attempt against ye person
> of Father Paulo; whereof I know you have heard all-ready very particu-
> larly. Many remarkeable circumstances accompanied it. For the time;
> it was done the very next day that Perron, the French Cardinall, came

hither from Rome returning to France; the persons dwelt hard by the Nuncio his house, (who became by this means not lightly sprinkled with the suspition of being privy hereto): they fled to Ancona, the Popes towne, and a few days after were seen at Rome: where (as some think), they are entertain'd as souldiers in the Popes pay in the Castle of St. Angelo; others say, they were made Jesuits. But to have seen how this matter was taken were admirable. The whole City was in a broile; the Councell often called in the night; the chiefest of the senate flock'd to the monastery, where the wounded Father lay; the next day the people every where in clumps and clusters talking of this matter; the professor of Anatomy and Chiururgery, Aqua-pendente, a man of great age, learning, and experience, sent for by public counsell to Padua, and joyned with other physicians to the cure of the wounds; an edict published against the cut throats, with a strange tally sett on their heads; and which is specially to be marked therein, they are expressly stiled the ministers of this conspiracy, as if others were the authors and contrivers. Besides, the Priest's[31] head is sett in it to sale as well as the rest without reserving him to the Pope's correction. Not many days after, when the Father's recovery was certain, which for a good while for his great loss of blood, and an inflammation succeeding was doubtfull in such sort, as almost for a moneth he kept his bed; his pension was encreas'd to 600 Ducats: and an other edict set forth for the asseration of his person in time to come: and now by reason of the escape of those who attempted soe foul an enterprize, this day a third more generall to prevent the like, which you shall receive herewith.[32]

Venetian law, which did not permit unauthorized or private consultations between ambassadors and senators or other high officials of the state, prevented Wotton, at least technically, from having direct communication with Sarpi.[33] Bedell, on the other hand, was not thus restricted and was soon on intimate terms with Padre Paolo. In this manner he could serve as intermediary between the two principals, even though jealously watchful eyes were constantly upon them. Inasmuch as the chief end of all Wotton's diplomacy was to further the division between Venice and Rome and to introduce the reformed religion into Italy, he saw in the anti-Curial attitudes and activities of Sarpi the earmarks of a potential ally.[34] Despite Sarpi's extensive later correspondence with numerous non-Catholics in France, Germany, and England, the precise degree and nature of his alleged "protestant" sympathies is extremely difficult to ascertain. But however uncommitted and political, rather than religious, Sarpi's true position may have been, Bedell read it through spectacles provided by the embassy. From the same letter to Adam Newton, quoted above, here is his preliminary estimate:

All changes in religion seem to me to come from reasons of conscience, or of state. For the former, it should be necessary thereto that the magistrate, and people in some regardable number, should be informed of the present abuses, as they offer, or these call for redress. A great worke, and whereto much time and many instruments would be requisite; save that some times the dexterity and excellency of a few work more than the number of many. Some there are here as admirably fitted thereto as could be wish'd: Maestro Paulo, and his scholler Fulgentio, Serviti, both of great learning, piety, humility, discretion, and integrity of life; and which is especially to be consider'd as to our purpose, in great account with all sorts, and deservedly; haveing, in the late controversy serv'd their country soe faithfully, as the Pope conns them little thanks for their labour. The former for a long time liv'd in Rome, and is holden for a miracle in all manner of knowledge divine and humane; the chief counsellor of this signory in their affairs Ecclesiasticall. The other was sometimes reader of Schoole-Divinity in Bononia, the Pope's university: out of which place he was called home, or turn'd out, when the quarrell begun, his books still detain'd. He is said to be an excellent preacher: and of his sermons, I think, came the report, which I have seen sent out of England in print, of certaine preachings here the last lent. *These two I know (as haveing practic'd with them) to desire nothing in the world soe much as the reformation of the Church: and in a word, for the substance of religion they are wholly ours.*[35]

Bedell's description of Sarpi as "a miracle in all manner of knowledge divine and humane" accords well with Wotton's contemporaneous assessment (less commonly quoted than that of the famous letter to Dr. Collins, of Cambridge)[36] of him as "the most deep and general scholar of the world."[37] As time went on, Bedell became much more intimately acquainted with the two friars, teaching (or pretending to teach) them English, translating the *Book of Common Prayer* into Italian for them,[38] reading the Scriptures with them, and introducing them to English books of controversy.[39]

Wotton's own letters of 1606–1607—to James I, to Sir Thomas Edmondes (ambassador at Brussels), and especially to Robert Cecil—also carry occasional news of Sarpi and his activities. Various ones of them mention the Ambassador's plan to send to the King copies of all the books that had been written on both sides of the quarrel, and also to send a portrait of Sarpi.[40] Eventually he did send both, although on his first effort the messenger bearing them was intercepted at Milan and thrown into the prison of the Inquisition. Upon his release, however, undaunted, he returned to Venice, secured another portrait and other copies of the books, and this time managed to elude interceptors.[41] Such violations of the post, private or governmental, were of course as reprehensible and unethical then as the wire-tapping and "buggings" of today, but they were an expected hazard of the time. Wotton himself was delighted when he managed thus to lay hands on some piece of Jesuit correspondence.

These books were intended primarily, of course, for the King's eyes. But the public was not neglected. In 1606, even while the quarrel was still in progress, John Bill, the King's Printer, published in London *A Full and Satisfactorie Answer to the late unadvised Bull, thundred by Pope Paul the Fift, against the renowned State of Venice: Being modestly entitled by the learned Author, Considerations upon the Censure of Pope Paul the Fift, against the Common-wealth of Venice: By Father Paul of Venice, a Frier of the Order of Servi. Translated out of Italian.* There is no dedicatory epistle, no preface, no indication of the identity of the translator; but it is a moderately safe guess that the volume came into the hands of the royal printer by way of His Majesty's Embassy in Venice. Interestingly, a copy of this seventy-six-page quarto in the British Museum carries on its title page the ownership designation "Roger Twysden 1627," the significance of which will presently become apparent.[42]

Another work, of unknown authorship, in two parts, was printed in London in the same year: *A Declaration of the Variance betweene the Pope, and the Segniory of Venice . . . Whereunto is annexed a Defence of the Venetians* (= *STC* 19482). This provided Englishmen with a just statement of the grounds of difference between Venice and Rome, of the steps taken on both sides, and spelled out for them the role of Father Paul in the quarrel. After mentioning the "generall liberty given for divulging of Discourses and Translations; amongst which is put in print the judgement of *Gerson* the Chancellour of *Paris*, upon the invaliditie of the Popes Excommunications,"[43] of Sarpi's doing, it will be recalled, the anonymous writer goes on to say that once the floodgates are open,

> it is strange to see what sundry sorts of gybing and biting *Pasquils* were let fly abroad in derision of his Holinesse. But, amongst the workes Apologeticall sagely and judiciously written, Frier *Paulo* hath in a set Treatise composed by him, not onely defended the *Venetians* from this Excommunication and demands, but also in many points lessened the Authoritie of the Pope, by sound allegations, & by the proofe of privileges appertaining of right and in dignity unto the State: whom it is said, that this Commonwealth hath rewarded for his labour with a good pension yeerely during life. And I have likewise met with another intelligence, That there is on the other side made out a secret processe against him, by the Church, for his infidelitie and treachery therein. Nay, a later newes hath here arrived, That this Frier *Paulo* hath bene

since solemnly (by his image or picture) burned at *Rome*, and reproached also by a scornefull appellation of a *mezo Lutherano*; Such and so hote a fire of the Popes wrath, hath blazed foorth against him. But the *Venetians*, on the other side, (to uphold him in comfort, and make him amends in glory,) have out of their grace and contemplation of his well deserving, dignified him with a better chosen title of *Theologo designato*; Expressing thereby the nature of his merite to have beene this, Even the opening unto their darkened understandings, some necessary trueths in Divinitie, tending to the discovery of the false pretences of the Roman Supremacie. This high Attribute, from so Judicious and Illustrious a Senate, is (in the stead of his image reported to have beene consumed with flames) like to a goodly or gilded statue, which shall preserve his name and memory, in all succeeding times.[44]

From the evangelical note that pervades the little volume, one might well believe that it came either from Wotton himself or from some member of the Ambassador's household who was well informed of the temper prevailing there.[45]

In addition to these two works, the next year saw the translation and publication in England of Sarpi's own longer *Apologia* in answer to Bellarmine's first anti-Venetian tract.[46] Since this followed the familiar controversial method of stating both argument and answer, the margins carried the name of "Frier Paolo" a score or more times as confuter of the renowned Bellarmine, thus giving him at the same time an extra publicity and a certain elevation of status. By the end of 1607 the name of Father Paul was beginning to have a familiar sound, even to the man in the London streets.

Other works relevant to Sarpi and the Venetians appeared shortly. Two composite volumes, swamped under interminable titles, bear witness to the contemporaneity of the English response—and, in the first collection, of the response elsewhere as well: *Concerning the Excommunication of the Venetians. A Discourse against Caesar Baronius Cardinall of the Church of Rome. In which the true nature and use of Excommunication is briefly and cleerly demonstrated, both by Testimonies of Holy Scripture, and from the old Records of Christs Church. Written in Latine by Nicholas Vignier, and translated into English after the Copie printed at Samur 1606. Whereunto is added the Bull of Pope Paulus the Fift, against the Duke, Senate and Commonwealth of Venice: With the protestation of the sayd Duke and Senate. As also an Apologie of Frier Paul of the Order of Servi in Venice* (London, 1607).[47] Sarpi's "Apologie" (sigs. I2–K2) is last in the volume and consists of nine pages. The heading (sig. I2) reads: "Father Pauls Apologie for his not appearing at Rome, being called thither by citation." His reasons for not appearing are said to be

1. that his writings, past and future, are condemned unjustly and ambiguously;
2. that Bellarmino, against whom he has written, is to be a judge in the case;
3. that there is no hope of obtaining a "safe" safe-conduct;
4. that the Doge has prohibited the departure of ecclesiastics from the realm;
5. and that he has "others in their due place and time to be alledged."[48]

The fact that the volume was issued by the publicizing Cuthbert Burby indicates that it was considered "newsworthy."

The second of these made-up volumes (=*STC* 24635) is entitled *A True Copie of the Sentence of the high Councell of tenne Judges in the State of Venice, against Ridolfo Poma, Michael Viti Priest, Alessandro Parrasio, John of Florence the sonne of Paul and Pasquall of Bitonto: who of late most trayterously attempted a bloudy and horrible Murder upon the person of the reverend Father D^r. Paolo Servite, Theologue of the common wealth of Venice. Faithfully translated out of Italian* (London, 1608).[49] In addition to the *True Copie* (sigs. A2–B3) this thin quarto contains other Sarpiana:

1. "A Proclamation made for assecuration of the person of the R. Father Doctour Paolo Servite, Theologue of the Noble Common weale of Venice; In execution of a decree accorded in the most Excellent Councell of the Pregadie upon the 27 of Oct. 1607" (sig. B3 verso).
2. "A Decree made in the highest Councell of tenne, 1607. the 9. of Januarie: Touching those that commit offences and make assaults with intention to murther, with the penalty of Barge-men for transporting the Offenders from one place to another, or conducting them out of Venice . . ." (sigs. C1–C3 verso).

The English friends of the Venetians were left in no doubt that the republic meant business.

Wotton was not the only one to whom the idea of collecting the pamphlets of this paper war occurred. Such collections began early, both on the Continent and in England.[50] It is not always—in fact, it is seldom—possible to date exactly the time of their formation, but surviving records of public and private libraries indicate clearly the interest for Englishmen of this Venetian struggle. Thomas James's first *Catalogus* of the Bodleian, published in 1605, came too early to record the just-beginning turmoil; but his second catalogue, published in 1620, reflects a substantial accession of these pamphlets in the intervening years.[51] Other catalogues and booklists reflecting this interest, coming later in the century and including Sarpi's *Historia particolare*, which was only published posthumously, may more conveniently be left for treatment in a subsequent chapter.

In yet another way, also, Wotton must have helped to form his country-men's ideas of the Venetian situation and of Sarpi. Casual visitors to Venice, then most admired of Italian cities, and the less casual English students at the University of Padua, which sat next to the capital, would have been under his special care. Indeed, set off as he was from direct association with the Venetian nobility, such visitors and students would have been especially welcome reminders of home, looked upon almost as members of his English "family." How he affected at least one of them was very soon recorded for all to see.

Thomas Coryat ("Odcombian Tom")—the great walking tourist, who visited Venice for a month and a half in 1608 (24 June to 8 August) and received "many great favours" at the hands of the Ambassador at his house "in the streete called St. Hieronimo"—was among the first of those English and other visitors for whom the Queen of Cities took on an added luster as the home of Padre Paolo.[52] Having mentioned Wotton's residence, he adds:

> In this street also doth famous Frier Paul dwell which is of the order of Servi. I mention him because in the time of the difference be-twixt the Signiory of Venice and the Pope, he did in some sort oppose himselfe against the Pope, especially concerning his supremacy in civill matters, and as wel with his tongue as his pen inveighed not a little against him. So that for his bouldnesse with the Popes Holynesse he was like to be slaine by some of the Papists in Venice, whereof one did very dangerously wound him. It is thought that he doth dissent in many points from the Papisticall doctrine, and inclineth to the Protestants re-ligion, by reason that some learned Protestants have by their conversation with him in his Convent something directed him from Popery. Where-fore notice being taken by many great men of the City that he beginneth to swarve from the Romish religion, he was lately restrained (as I heard in Venice) from all conference with Protestants.[53]

Conference with Catholics, however, was another matter. And to one such "conference," extended over many years, we must now turn our attention.

3 --- Enter the Fat Bishop

MARCO ANTONIO DE DOMINIS was not a lovable man. He was born with a beautiful knack for irritating his fellow men, and he worked hard all his life perfecting the gift. Eventually it proved his undoing.

A sharper contrast than that existing between Paolo Sarpi and the Archbishop of Spalato (modern Split) would be hard to imagine. Where Sarpi was quiet, modest, and without personal ambition, de Dominis was rowdy, sought the limelight, and was consumed by a passion for authority. Where Sarpi's thought and expression were clear and incisive, bare and unadorned, exemplifying that *lumen siccum* praised by Bacon, the Archbishop tended to be butter-witted and rhetorical; he was also less variedly learned than he esteemed himself. And whereas Sarpi was of slight build, almost frail—in Wotton's phrasing, "one of the humblest things that could be seen within the bounds of Humanity," of "weakly and wearish Body"[1]—de Dominis was a robustious, handsome, Falstaffian mass of flesh. Perhaps even a little too much given to the delights of the flesh, as contemporary charges sometimes ran. In one respect, nevertheless, these two Venetian disparates saw eye to eye: each grew restive under the rod of papal authority. It is here, where their paths begin to cross and interweave in the tangle of history, that we must begin to follow the affairs of the Fat Bishop, interesting enough in themselves, but peripheral as at times they may seem to the story of Paolo Sarpi.

De Dominis was born in 1560 in the little town of Arbe on the island of Arbe (Yugoslavian Rab), which was then Dalmatian territory in the upper Adriatic and thus of immediate concern to Venice.[2] His family, it is said, had connections with that of Gregory X and were of some standing in Dalmatia.[3] He studied at the seminary in Loreto and at the University of Padua, was drawn into the Jesuit ambit, and was much admired and made over, being sent by his Jesuit masters to teach for them in various important centers—mathematics at Padua; rhetoric, logic, and philosophy at Brescia. But he was of too unruly and haughty a disposition to submit to the rigid discipline and unquestioning obedience demanded by the order. Consequently (whether at his own or the Jesuits' instigation is not clear), he withdrew in 1596 from the order, secularizing himself and becoming—slightly later and with powerful assistance from the emperor Rudolph and the Doge of Venice —Bishop of Segna. Here shepherd and flock could not agree, and after two years he was transferred to Spalato, where from 1602 to 1616 he was Archbishop and Primate of Dalmatia. It is as *Archiepiscopus Spalatrensis* that he is most commonly referred to—though other hard and unflattering names were devised for him—in the controversial literature of the seventeenth century.[4]

At Segna the new bishop had followed a Venetian policy of vigorous opposition to the piratical activities of the Uskoks, which, while making him *persona grata* to the Serenissima, had understandably not endeared him to his spiritual sons. A threat from some of them to hang him in his own see— one of their principal strongholds—may have encouraged his transfer to Spalato.[5] In any event, he proved to be a disquietant also at his new post, where members of the nobility and members of his own cathedral chapter were presently charging him with holding and propagating heterodox ideas. Reports of these differences filtered into Rome, and the Archbishop began to receive invitations to lay his case before the lords spiritual of that city—invitations which the Archbishop somehow managed to side-step. Then, while the quarrel between Venice and Pope Paul V was in full swing and the Archbishop, being in Venetian territory, cast his lot with the Serenissima, suspicions were redoubled on both sides. In one of his letters Sarpi indicates that de Dominis performed some unspecified service to the state in the war of propaganda,[6] and it has been suggested that he may have written, or helped to write, the *Aviso,* which passed under Querini's name.[7]

In this period, it may be, or very shortly afterwards, he began that acquaintance with Sarpi about which he later writes in the dedicatory letter to King James printed in the first edition of the *Historia del Concilio Tridentino.* And perhaps about 1609 or 1610 he began in some way to move into the circle of Bedell and Wotton. He was in any case acquainted with his fellow Dalmatian Giovanni Francesco Biondi, who was in England in 1609 with messages for James from Sarpi and the Ambassador's circle.[8] De Dominis, incidentally, is said to have influenced Biondi's conversion to Protestantism.[9] The publication in Venice (1610) of his *De radiis visus et lucis in vitris perspectivis et iride* would also have served as a likely point of contact between him and Sarpi, for among his other pretensions he had some claims to scientific knowledge. Bishop Burnet, writing long after the event and offering no exact dates, says that during Bedell's Venetian stay (1607–December 1610),

> the famous *Ant. de Dominis* Archbishop of *Spalato* came to *Venice*; and having received a just character of Mr. *Bedell*, he discovered his secret to him [that is, his disaffection toward Rome],[11] and shewing him his ten Books *De Republica Ecclesiastica*, which he afterwards printed at *London*: *Bedell* took the freedom which he allowed him, and corrected many ill applications of Texts of Scripture, and Quotations of Fathers. For that Prelate being utterly ignorant of the *Greek* Tongue, could not but be guilty of many mistakes both in the one and the other; and if there remain some places still that discover his ignorance of that Language too plainly, yet there had been many more, if *Bedell* had not corrected them: but no wonder if in such a multitude some escaped his diligence. *De Dominis* took all this in good part from him, and did enter into such familiarity with him, and found his assistance so useful, and indeed so necessary to himself, that he used to say he could do nothing without him.[10]

Possibly also about this time he made the acquaintance of the renowned Neapolitan canonist and arch-Romanist, Dr. Jacopo Antonio Marta, recently (1611) appointed Professor of Canon Law at the University of Padua, a figure like himself of unsettled religious mind and devious dealings, cloak-and-dagger fashion, with James I and his ministers.[12]

Whatever his acquaintanceships and movements between 1611 and 1614, de Dominis continued to be unhappy at Spalato and increasingly suspect at home and at Rome. Several letters of 1614 from the nuncio in Venice, Berlinghero Gessi, to Cardinal Borghese tell of the Archbishop's wish to resign and of the nuncio's unsuccessful attempts to persuade him to go to Rome and justify himself directly.[13] Gessi indicates that he is keeping a watchful eye on the malcontent. In September 1615, without further notice or official approbation, he abandoned his post at Spalato and came to Venice, determined to flee to England. What encouragement he received from the English Ambassador at this juncture, or from Sarpi and Micanzio, remains obscure—as does the date of his departure. But some preliminary agreement must have been reached earlier: a letter from the Archbishop of Canterbury (George Abbott) to Carleton in Venice, dated 15 December 1614, must have sounded slightly discouraging to de Dominis. Under its terms he was not to look for preferment in England to match what he now enjoyed; but he was to have £200 per year and some university post.[14] A confirming letter followed on 16 February 1615;[15] so that de Dominis knew he was not fleeing to abject poverty. By the late autumn of 1616 he was en route, passing through Coire (in the Grisons) and, more leisurely, through Germany, where he stopped at Heidelberg long enough to publish the brief and biting *Profectionis consilium*, written in Venice and dated 20 September 1616. Thence he proceeded to The Hague, where he was received by Dudley Carleton, the English Ambassador. On June 10 1616 Carleton had written (in anticipation?) a letter of recommendation or introduction for him to Sir Ralph Winwood, Secretary of State for Foreign Affairs. The Archbishop, escorted by one of the warships of Count Maurice, arrived in England on 16 December 1616.[16] He had barely set foot on English soil when, on 20 December, Latin and English versions of the *Profectionis consilium*, no doubt through the direction of the court, were entered to John Bill in the Stationers' Register and printed in time, one is tempted to say, for the Christmas trade.[17] But trim and expeditious as Bill's footwork had been, the cardinals of the Sacred Congregation of the Index had already stolen a march on him. By special decree of 12 November 1616, both the *Consilium* (or *A Manifestation of the Motives*) and the as yet unpublished ten Books of the Archbishop's *De Republica Ecclesiastica* were already forbidden fruit to all faithful sons of the church.

At this point, before pursuing further the career of de Dominis in England, it may be well to skim lightly through *A Manifestation of the Motives*. Lest his defection from Rome be misinterpreted, he proposes to set down the reasons for his departure, which he has been considering for ten years or so (pp. 1–4). His decision is based on his quest for the Truth, and has not been influenced by heretical protestant writings, but by reflection, reading of the Scriptures, and studying of the Fathers (pp. 5–6). He "thirsted not after Ecclesiastical promotions" (p. 6), being content with Spalato. "And if I had longed after any of the Romane dignities," he says, "there was a faire way open for mee toward them: But the distast, which I tooke against the corruptions of the Court of Rome, made me still to abhor it" (p. 7). In view of his later reputation, incidentally, it is amusing to hear him declare, among his other virtues, "Neither was I greedy of worldly pelfe" (p. 8). He was brought up in the study of divinity, "and that mostwhat among the Jesuites" (p. 8), long remaining an unquestioning learner, until he began to have a few doubts (p. 10). He does not think it amiss that some control be exercised over the reading of the common people; but something must be wrong when seasoned learned men need such curbs (pp. 10–11). He has long been interested in the reconciliation of the Eastern and Western churches, and of Protestant and Catholic (pp. 12–13).

30

He relates his teaching services among the Jesuits before he was "plucked away from them by advancement to a Bishopricke" (pp. 13–15). His preaching, he found (for he was a preaching bishop), gagged at the "Postillers, and Lenten-homelists" (p. 15) used by most pulpit-men; in their stead he began to rely upon the ancient Fathers (pp. 16–18), questioning by their light also the hodgepodge of modern church discipline. These new insights he carried with him from Segna to Spalato; and there, during the interdict, when he and his bishops were under fire, with "the vast omnipotencie of the Court of Rome daily encroaching, and eating upon [his] Metropoliticall rights" (p. 18), he began, "poore worme" (p. 19), to seek assistance from his books, wherein it appeared to him that the "sects" attacked by Rome were nearer to the ancient models of the church than Rome herself, and that much was corrupt under the pope (pp. 20–23). He does not here list the numerous faults of Rome, he says, because he has written and has ready to turn over to a suitable printer a "booke concerning the *Ecclesiastique Common-wealth*" (p. 24), the contents of the ten Books of which he then proceeds to epitomize (pp. 24–28)—a sly bit of advance publicity.

With the veil lifted from his eyes, "what then," he asks, "should I doe tarying any longer in the midst of a crooked and perverse nation?" (p. 29). Rome would never have permitted his reform of even his own see—in fact, was so suspicious of him that he had already been "divers times convented before the Popes *Nuncio*, residing at Venice" (p. 30). He resolved "therefore to take the wings of a Dove, and by a far flight to retire [himself] into the wildernes"—of England. He grows a little warm when he considers how the power of bishops "is fled from home, and wafted over to the seven-hilld Citie. The Bishoppes themselves what are they, but (and scarce that) Vicars, and Servitors to our good Lord and Master the Pope; subject, abject, vile, servile, over-awed, over-trampled wretches" (p. 31), and so forth. *He* was called to teach, not to be a dumb dog, as other bishops were; under the restrictions imposed on him by the Roman tyranny, he had no freedom to spread the Truth; ergo, over the hills and far away. Furthermore, infected with light as he was, he would be daily exposing his "life to the hazard of poyson," his "throate to the poignard of an Assassine, the ordinary meanes now adayes to silence controversies: Whereof the Church of Rome hath found out a most compendious meane, by referring the decision and maintenance of their Doctrine, not (as our simple forefathers were wont) to learned Divines, and free Councels, but to tormenters, to hangmen, to hireling stabbers [*testè* Sarpi], cut-throats, and bloody parricides" (pp. 32–34).

Thinking these thoughts, though subtly tempted by the fleshpots of the Roman Egypt, the good bishop left his own country and his secure emoluments for the uncertainties of that "safe place, where the true Catholique

Religion holdeth up her head, and taketh free breath" (pp. 34–39; quotation on p. 39). Others support him in this decision (pp. 39–43)—the ancient Fathers. He would gladly have stayed at his post in Spalato, but that usurping Bishop of Rome would have made his voice ineffective there. Abroad, perhaps, he will be able to rouse others to a sense of the right and to a humbling of that proud prelate brother of theirs (pp. 43–46). In any case, when his "tenne forenamed Books of *Church-weale*" are published, pointing out the errors of Rome and indicating the right path to be followed by all true "Catholique Christians," he hopes that all present differences will be reconciled in "the essentials of our Faith" (p. 49) and that in matters indifferent each individual church may be allowed its own idiosyncratic position without persecution from that BABLYON from which *he* has departed, escaped, or fled (pp. 48–56).

Such was the footing upon which matters stood when England welcomed to her shores the most conspicuous of renegades from Rome.

The story of de Dominis's arrival and reception in England can be documented from many sources, in whole or in part.[18] But since the Scottish craftiness of King James I quartered him, at his first coming, upon the borrowed hospitality of the Archbishop of Canterbury (George Abbott), the Archbishop seems best entitled to throw the first stone. I abstract from his longish and querulous letter to Sir Thomas Roe, dated 20 November 1622, only some remarks relevant to the *character* of de Dominis:

> The archbishop of Spalato at his first comeing into England lying long in my house, and hearing of the intercourse that was betweene that patriarke [that is, Cyril, Patriarch of Alexandria] and mee, would needs write unto him; and sent him one of his bookes against the pope. This man, when you departed out of England, appeered to bee no otherwise but sound; but since, hee hath shewed himselfe such a bestaccio, as that I thinke fitt to give you, in particular, some account concerning him: Hee was in England honorably provided for, as having the mastership of the Savoy, the Deanry of Windsor, one benefice, and another donative, besides plate given him every yeere from the kinge, to the value of 200 marks; and wee of the clergy gave him 200 *l.* a yeere, which, for my part, I continued untill Christmas last.

There follows a brief account of the manner in which de Dominis fell from grace, and then a devastating thumbnail estimate:

> One great reason that wrought upon him was his pride, who magnifyed himselfe, and disesteemed all other men, expecting that he should

32

have had the highest regiment of ecclesiasticall thinges in England committed unto him; yea, supposing that his owne worth and wisdome was such, that hee merited at least heere to have bene a privy counsellor. Another thinge that transported him, was his inestimable avarice beyond the degree of an Italian, raking to him hee cared not what, and living so sordidly and basely as was a shame for any man of quality: besides, he was by nature and practise, a man so ungratefull, as that neither to the kinge, nor to mee, nor to any other person in England, hee did returne as much as thankes, or a good worde, for all the benefitts that were bestowed upon him: these thinges are evident in him.[19]

Pride, hauteur, self-esteem, ambition, avarice, ingratitude—these were the unlovely aspects of his character which reappear time after time in most English accounts of him.

One of the longest of these, and one written by the most charitable of men, is that in Fuller's *Church-History*.[20] In Book X, Section iv, paragraph 45, under date 6 December 1616, Fuller says: "*Marcus Antonius de Dominis*, Archbishop of *Spalato*, came over into *England*, was here courteously welcomed, and plentifully preferred, of whose *hypocrisie* and *ingratitude* largely hereafter." That "hereafter" promise is amply fulfilled in Fuller's main account of the Archbishop, Book X, Section vi, paragraphs 1-19, from which I lift the following nuggets:

It is almost incredible, what flocking of people there was to behold this old Archbishop, now a new Convert; Prelates and Peers presented him with Gifts of high valuation. . . . He was feasted wheresoever he came, and the *Universities* (when he visited them) addressed themselves to him in their solemn reception, as if he himselfe alone had been an University. [P. 94]

King James, says Fuller, treated him bountifully,

was most munificent unto him. . . . The KING consigned him to the Archbishop of *Canterbury*, for his present entertainment, till he might be accommodated to subsist of himself: and, as an earnest of his Bounty, sent him to *Lambeth*, a fair *bason*, and *bolle* of *silver*. Which *Spalato* received with this complement, *Misit mihi REX Magnae Britanniae polubrem argenteum ad abstergendas sordes Romanae Ecclesiae, & poculum argenteum ad imbidendam Evangelii puritatem, The KING of Great Britain hath sent me a silver bason, to wash from me the filth of the Roman Church; and a silver cup to minde me to drink the purity of the Gospel.* [P. 94]

33

Then follows the account of his preferments and of "his great avarice" (margin). His greed is said (pp. 94–95) to have prompted him to attempt raising rents and changing lease-terms for several tenants who held under him in the Savoy and at Windsor. He is, nevertheless, praised for "his learned Writings against Romish errour" (p. 95, margin), though the praise is somewhat reduced by the observation that "among other of his ill qualities, he delighted in *jeering*, and would spare none who came in his way" (p. 95) —among whom, to the jeerer's later cost, was Gondomar, the Spanish ambassador. Much else of interest follows, but must be passed over for the present while we proceed directly to Fuller's final paragraph (p. 100) on de Dominis, a "character" of the man:

> He was of a comely personage, tall stature, gray beard, grave countenance, fair language, fluent expression, somewhat abdominous, and corpulent in his body. Of so imperious, and domineering spirit, that (as if the *Tenant* were the *Land Lord*) though a stranger, he offered to controll the Archbishop of *Canterbury* in his own house. An excellent Preacher (every first Sunday in the moneth to the *Italian* Nation at *Mercers-Chappel*) as his Sermon called *Scopleos*, or the *Rocks*, doth plentifully witnesse, wherein he demonstrates, That all the Errors of the *Roman Church* proceed from their *pride* and *covetousness*. And (under the Rose be it spoken) if the great ship of *Rome* split it self on these *Rocks*, *Spalato* his own pinnace made *shipwrack of the faith* on the same, which were his bosome-sins. In a word, he had too much Wit, and Learning, to be a *cordial Papist*; and too little Honesty, and Religion, to be a *sincere Protestant*.[21]

Fuller's estimate of de Dominis as a preacher is not completely corroborated when one turns to an examination of the Archbishop's first sermon preached in England: *A Sermon Preached in Italian, by the most Reverend Father, Marc' Antony De Dominis, Archb. of Spalato, on the first Sunday in Advent, Anno. 1617.* This sermon, on a text from Romans (13:12), was issued immediately in its original tongue, as preached before a congregation of Italians and curious English auditors in the Mercers' Chapel, then in English, under the title given above—both by the royal printer, John Bill.[22] It begins with complimentary words, a denial of rhetorical ornament, the announcement and division of the text, a pious hope for the reunification of the church, prayers for various members of the royal family and for "those wise and Grave Senatours" of the Venetian state, and a recitation of the Lord's Prayer—in short (but not very short) with all possible preambulatory tedium and pomposity. When he gets to the exposition of his text, we are already at page seven; unless he padded it after delivery, the Archbishop held

34

his audience through seventy-four more mortal small-quarto pages of sermon while he proceeded to ring all the changes on the theme of the contrast between light and darkness as found in the Old Testament, the Apocrypha, the New Testament, and some of the outlying provinces of St. Augustine. Nor was he above lifting a remark or two from his own *De radiis visus . . . iride*:

> The Rainebow maketh a goodly shew being guarded, and striped with so many, and so amiable colours, which in truth are nothing els, but the light of the Sunne reflected from dewie clouds, and by divers composures of more, or lesse opacity reduced to such variety of colours. And generally al colours, which cloath with such beauty the best visible bodies, and represent them to the eie with delight, what are they else, but mixtures of the lightsome elements with the obscure.[23]

No doubt his audience felt greatly edified. With much truth (and modest restraint) he declares at one point, "Too tedious should I bee, if I should heere propound all the divers opinions of the holy Fathers upon those words."[24] Restraint, however, is not the chief characteristic of the central portion of his sermon (pp. 30–55), where he begins by developing the metaphor of the church as a ship, contrasts the Reformed and Roman vessels, lambastes the irresponsible and arrogant pilot-pope, indicates the numerous errors (shoals) into which the Romanists have fallen, and glories in the collapse of the pope's wicked weapon of excommunication (pp. 52–55).

One begins to get the idea, eventually, that de Dominis has departed out of the Land of Darkness and emerged in the Kingdom of Light—and, to the satisfaction of his smug audience, he says so explicitly:

> Here (beloved brethren) heere in this Kingdome wee have the hill of God, which is raysed up towards heaven, and standeth discoasted farre enough from the sinke, and myre of the Papall corruptions. Here are the tabernacles, and tents of the armies of the Lord of hosts pitcht in goodly aray, and furnished for the confronting all opposite forces. Heere the light of the trueth is freely, and openly let in. Heere the holy scriptures are most exactly studied. Here are great multitudes of learned men, and above all, the most learned the Anoynted of the Lord, a King, who is the wonder of the Kings of the earth, a matchless paterne of all the Kings and Princes of Christendome, of great zeale in purging, advancing, and mainteining Christs holy Religion. Heere the sincere word of God is taught plentifully. Here the Bishops are very learned, religious, and vigilant over their flocks. Here the Priests are every way sufficient, and very skilfull in the cure of soules. Heere the people are very zealous, and fervently addicted to holy and spirituall dueties. Thanks

therefore be to God, who after the night of so many errors, hath sent foorth his light and trueth, which have led me, and brought me into his holy hill, and to his tabernacles. And so rejoycing in the Lord, I say againe to my selfe, and to you, my brethren, *The night is passed, and the day is at hand*.[25]

Here was indeed a way to win friends and influence people. In a land flowing with milk and honey, the Archbishop's lips flowed with the oil of court flattery. Had he continued to sing in this key, he might have lived to die an even fatter bishop. It was not to be.

More particularized accounts of his visiting the universities, of his personal tastes, and of his extortionary proceedings with his tenants may be found in other writers. Bishop John Hacket, for instance, in his biography of Archbishop Williams, recalls that in July of 1617, when Williams was to stand for his D.D. degree at Cambridge, and when the newly arrived nine days' wonder of renegades from Catholicism was to be present to witness the university's commencement exercises, Williams was by the King's appointment named to be both the principal disputant and the host to His Eminence of Spalato. The disputations came off splendidly and much impressed de Dominis. But the biographer records one detail in the entertainment which was rather comically less than a staggering success—though probably of staggering expense:

> One thing deserves a Smile, That the Doctor was at no little Cost to send to the *Italian* Ordinaries at *London*, and to ransack the Merchants Stores for such Viands as might please Arch-Bishop *Spalato* out of his own Country. To which accates he was observ'd, that he never put his Hand towards them, but lik'd our Venison and *English* Dishes a great deal better, he Thank'd him. But enough of this; for many do not love the smell of a Kitchin.[26]

The Archbishop was not one of this "many."

Skipping over a few years in the indecorous antics of the "somewhat abdominous" de Dominis, Hacket recalls a jest that exhibits him in what the English must by then have considered a characteristic Spalatensian pose: "I shall not lose my Thanks, I hope," says Hacket,

> if I add my Observations, with a little more than hath already been discovered. *First*, About the middle of *Autumn, Ann.* 1621, *Ant. de Dominis* besought the King to confer the Arch-Bishopricke of *York* upon him. A hasty Suitor, for the Place was not void. The Error came about thus: The Arch-Bishop then in being (called familiarly *Toby Matthew*) was ever pleasant, and full of becoming Merriment; and

36

knowing that his Death had been long expected, was wont every year, once, or oftner, to cause Rumours to be raised that he was deceased. And when he had put this Dodgery strongly upon those at *London*, that gap'd for the Vacancy to succeed him, it was a Feast of Laughter to him, to hear what Running and Riding there was to fill up his Room, who jear'd them behind the Lattuce.[27] No wonder if *Spalat.* a Stranger, were catcht in this Trap; but he had worse Luck than to be derided for his Forwardness, for the King bade him sit quiet, and seek no further. It was not now as in *Lanfranke* and *Anselm's* Days, to make a Stranger a Metropolitan of *England*. The Man, impatient that his Request had so large a Denial, offers his Departure, as 'tis said before, not distrusting, but that the King would bid for such Ware, as much as the Man thought himself to be worth. But being over-shot, and laid aside with Scorn, he would have eat his Words, and cast out Speeches in oblique before some of the Council, that whatsoever he had uttered, he was dispos'd more to please the King, than to please himself. But he found no Place for Repentance. And of all this the Lord Keeper [that is, Williams] is my Author.[28]

Probably the harshest words to be uttered against de Dominis—*after* his defection from Anglicanism, it is true—and certainly the most sustained attack upon his ideas and conduct, came from Richard Crakanthorp, whose *Defensio Ecclesiae Anglicanae*, published posthumously, charges insatiable greed against de Dominis as one of the causes of his return to Rome and his attack on his erstwhile English hosts. And yet, says Crakanthorp, he fared well in England: "Tu certè egenus non fuisti, qui cùm unam domum Windsorae, alteram Londini, amplam satis splendidámque haberes, volebas tamen senex, ac peregrinus tertiam struere."[29] This mild-as-milk approach to the topic doesn't last long. A few pages later, when Crakanthorp has worked up a full head of righteous steam, the blast comes:

O hominem vilissimum, Apostatam, Atheum, Omnifidium, Nullifidium, bipedum omnium miserrimum, cuius cordi ac fibris plus fraudis & fellis inest, quàm Magi Simonis: qui fidem ac religionem non aliter quàm marsupio tuo meteris: cui non lingua solùm, & stilus, & manus, & mens, sed religio, fides, etiam & Deus ipse vaenalis est. Vident verò nunc omnes, quid te in Romanam reduxit Ecclesiam, non ulla fidei sinceritas, non religionis ullus amor, non ulla vitae sanctitas, non denique Deus alius, nisi *Deus venter & Deus Lucrio*; nec Diva alia, nisi *Diva Volupia, & Diva Moneta.*[30]

A man might be a little embarrassed to find that inscribed on his tombstone. On the other hand, not all the unlovely traits of de Dominis's character were at first revealed. For several years after his arrival he enjoyed a vast reputation for learning and for effective attacks upon the papacy.[31] Besides the works already mentioned, John Bill printed or published for him his *Papatus Romanus* (1617),[32] his much admired *De Republica Ecclesiastica* (in two parts, 1617, 1620), and his *The Rockes of Christian Shipwracke* (1618),[33] a translation from his *Scogli del Christiano naufragio*. His *A Manifestation* was republished in Edinburgh, 1617, as *A Declaration of the Reasons* . . . (= *STC* 6999); and John Harding, a converted Catholic, professed that he was led to Protestantism partly by reading the godly de Dominis.[34] Even Sarpi's earlier letters concerning de Dominis speak of him without rancor, one with praise.[35] Certainly he was still in the good graces (however frayed his welcome) of Lambeth and the court when, in 1619, he edited for John Bill the book which was to have such resounding acclaim in England and elsewhere, Paolo Sarpi's *Historia del Concilio Tridentino*.

But thereby hangs a tale which must be told in its own chapter.

4 --- Four Pounds of Dynamite

TWO OF SARPI'S mighty contemporaries, Cervantes and Shakespeare, completed all their writings during the lifetime of the Venetian friar. In our admiration for the *Don Quijote* of the former we sometimes forget that he also wrote the *Novelas ejemplares*, enough to have immortalized a lesser man; and swayed by the majesty of Shakespeare's finest dramas, we tend to forget the *Sonnets* and other poems. With Sarpi the case is not dissimilar: when he is remembered, the mind turns mainly to his *History of the Council of Trent*. It is good, therefore, to be reminded by Horatio Brown of the importance of Sarpi's writings on the interdict,[1] and of those numerous other writings, published and unpublished, that followed in the twelve-year interval between the ending of the quarrel at Venice and the publication, in a far country, of his chef-d'oeuvre. But if Sarpi's "lesser" writings first brought him to the attention and affection of the English, the publication of the *Historia del Concilio Tridentino* forever solidified his position.

And this, more or less, is how it came about.

Ordinarily, unless it is pornographic, of resoundingly scandalous content, concerns the latest events in a charged situation, or is the project of some greedy publisher intent upon "making a killing" by crashing the Book-of-the-Month-Club ready-made sales, a book will come to the attention of the public only when it achieves publication. Ordinarily, too, its existence, prior to publication, will be known to but a few—the author, an agent, the publisher, a "house" editor, and a handful of mechanics who see it through the printing shop. With respect to the first set of circumstances, in 1619, the English *public* was unprovided with the least intimation. With respect to the second, few books could have been "secretly" born while so many, and such important, persons were privy to the blessed event. Besides Sarpi and Fra Fulgenzio there were to be counted Wotton and Bedell, Sir Dudley Carleton and his cousin, Sir Nathanael Brent, Daniel Niis, the Archbishop of Canterbury, King James—and, of course, de Dominis. Let us begin with de Dominis.

The book appeared with the following title page: *Historia del Concilio Tridentino. Nella quale si scoprono tutti gl'artificii della Corte di Roma, per impedire che né la verità di dogmi si palesasse, né la riforma del Papato, & della Chiesa si trattasse. Di Pietro Soave Polano. In Londra, Appresso Giovan. Billio. Regio Stampatore. M.DCXIX.* A glance at the title in Sarpi's original manuscript, preserved in the Biblioteca Marciana in Venice, will show the extent of the scandal-stirring additions made by de Dominis.[2] Sarpi's title reads, simply, *Historia del Concilio Tridentino.* Subsequent editions of the work in Italian omitted these offensive and tendentious additions, and Brent's English translation somewhat softened them. Generally omitted also in later editions and translations was the dedicatory epistle, which de Dominis directed to King James. Because it will be necessary for us to examine closely the terms of this dedication, and because—so far as I know—it has not hitherto appeared in English, I subjoin a full translation.

> To the Most Serene and Most Powerful Prince, James, First King and Sole Ruler of Great Britain: King likewise of France, and of Ireland, Defender of the Faith, etc.
>
> Sacred Majesty,
>
> In departing from Italy to place myself under the August mantle of your Clemency, I attempted to secure a copy, in so far as it was possible for me, of various compositions by the most elevated spirits who flourish in great number in that most noble Province—of those, however, which appertain chiefly to my profession and which might be pleasing to your Majesty as True Defender of the True Catholic Faith. There are not lacking in Italy, Sire, lively Wits, free under God and with spirits unshackled from wretched captivity, who with clear and pure eyes perceive the pitfalls which are there laid for the things of holy Religion: they are all too well aware of the frauds and deceptions with which, to maintain itself in its temporal grandeur, the Court of Rome oppresses the true Christian doctrine, brings in falsehoods and lies as articles of Faith; and the arms once given by the spirit of Christ to His Holy Church to serve for her defense and for the extirpation of heresies and abuses, the Court perverts to the oppression of that Church to make her a slave under foot.
>
> Formerly, sacred Councils served to expose errors, abuses, and falsehoods; but, during the last centuries, since the Roman Pontiffs have so

aggrandized themselves, transforming themselves from ministers and
servants into Lords and Monarchs of the Church, fearing—precisely—to
be revealed in the Sacred Councils for what they are and even to be reformed and reduced to what they ought to be, with inventions and with
devilish stratagems they have either shoved aside and extinguished the
true Councils or have spoiled and corrupted, or even oppressed those
which, with their forced consent, have sometimes been convened; avoid-
ing, with marvelous skills, fakeries—and even violence—that such Councils might be able to seek out the Truth, but instead that they might
serve them as a means to increase their own greatness so much the more,
and, indeed, to restrict the liberty of Holy Church.

This was clearly seen in the most recent Council of Trent, which is
peddled off to us as so legitimate, faultless, and holy—and yet was so full
of frauds, human devisings, passions, pressures, violence, and deceits
diligently revealed and minutely related in the present History. It ought,
in truth, to be attributed rather to the great power of the Truth, and to
the disposition of Divine Providence, than to human devising, that such
a work should come from the hands of a person born and educated
under obedience to the Roman Pontiff. I have known the Author, a person truly of much Learning, of great judgment and integrity, and of
most upright intention. He manifested in himself a most sincere zeal
that ecclesiastical discords should be resolved; and in that Captivity he
served, however, in such manner that he regulated himself by an un-
blemished conscience rather than by common practice. And if he did
not willingly listen to the over-severe censurings of the Roman Church,
nevertheless he abhorred also those who defended her abuses as holy
institutions. And for the rest, he was a singular friend of the Truth,
and most tenacious of it; whereof he avowed without any reservation
that wherever it were, it should be received and embraced.

This Work of his, known to me and to a very few of his intimates, I
adjudged worthy to be guided into the light of day, wherefore I labored
not a little to get a copy out of his hands; and this precious jewel obtained (by him little regarded), I have not judged that it should any
longer remain hidden, even though I knew not what that Author
might think nor how he might have to construe this resolution of mine
to publish it. But I am well convinced that for our mutual responsibility
toward Truth and zeal for purity of Religion against depravations so
inexcusable, he will have been content with it. I never doubted that he
was fully aware of the supreme qualities which render Your Majesty
conspicuous to the whole World, whence he must have been a most devout observer of your Heroic Virtues, have relished greatly that you

should become Patron of the pious labors by him performed; and, in consequence, to approve as a thing well done and to rejoice that those labors were by my means fallen into the most noble and worthy hands that Europe, nay, the whole world, has; into the hands of a King the Wonder of the present World, in doctrine, in wisdom, in valor, in piety and Religion second to none and first before all. May your Most Serene Majesty take note that I present you a Moses rescued from the waters, by miracle of God not submerged (and yet on point of being submerged by his begetter, either for the honor of the Papacy, whose inmost secrets he saw there uncovered, or because of the usual perils and terrors). Behold him safe in Your Majesty's arms, to the end that, tutored by your piety and holy zeal, he may issue forth to the World to aid in liberating the children of God from the tyranny of that Pharaoh who also with the chains of so irregular and deceiving a Council holds them bound in harsh servitude.

With that most refined judgment of yours, may Your Majesty enjoy this truly honored work, with which it will pierce the deep mystery, why the Roman Curia has never been willing to permit human eyes to see the Acts of that Council, but keeps them hidden under a thousand locks—after having with most clever artifices destroyed in great part the records of this Council which were to be found in the hands of individuals and in many old libraries of the Prelates and others who took part in it; whereas the Acts of practically every other general Council are laid open in every historical detail. And of this Council nothing is published save the bare decrees, fashioned in Rome rather than in Trent. Your Majesty will perceive by means of this most noble and penetrating History many deep secrets of the Papacy. And I, who am the bearer of this so prized a gift, shall go about rejoicing that there has been presented to me so fair an occasion of showing to Your Majesty that not only with my own but with the works of others I desire to employ myself completely in serving you. May you receive consolation that in Italy, wholly oppressed by the Papacy born and rooted there, nonetheless are to be found brave minds inimical to the base flatteries of the Pope and friends to the Truth, which, in this work concerning the holding of the Tridentine Council, is with such sincerity revealed.

May God preserve Your Most Serene Majesty to your Kingdoms, and to the Holy Universal Church for many years, in health, prosperous, and happy; and may He grant you the power and the opportunity to demonstrate yourself in His affairs and in His true Faith, a true and zealous Defender.

From the Savoy, the First of January, 1619.
Your Majesty's Humblest Servant,
M. Ant. de Dominis,
Abp. of Spal.

Stripped of its rhetoric and flattery, what does this epistle tell us of the way in which this famous Italian book came to have its first edition in England? Looked at closely, the language is seen to be studiously ambiguous. De Dominis does not *say* that while in Venice he secured a copy of the book from Sarpi.[3] What he *says* is that he "attempted to secure a copy" —*procurai d'havere copia*—not of the *Historia* in particular, but "of various compositions"—*di varie compositioni*—by prime Italian wits. And he repeats the formula: "I labored not a little to get a copy out of his hands"—*m'affaticai non poco per cavargliene copia dalle mani*. This does not say that he got a copy; it says merely that he *tried* to get a copy. When he continues with "and this precious jewel obtained" (*& havuta questa preciosa gioia*), he does not say when, nor how, nor by whom a copy was obtained. What the words may legitimately be made to spell out is that at some time before it was published, a copy was in his hands. Nothing more. Nor does his description of himself as the "bearer" (*portatore*) of the gift now being laid before James necessarily mean any more than that he is about to set his name to the dedicatory epistle.

It is easy to see, nevertheless, how a quick reading of the epistle, especially by someone impatient with the magniloquence of de Dominis's buttery approach to King James's Most Serene Majesty, could leave the impression that the Archbishop had secured his copy directly from Sarpi during his stay in Venice and had brought it with him to England.[4] De Dominis was putting his best foot forward with the King—or thought he was. This overesteemer of himself and disesteemer of others was quite willing to let it appear that he had had a primary role in the securing of this "preziosa gioia," this "preggiato dono." Some crafty readers, looking past the unlikelihood of the name on the title page, might even jump to the conclusion that the epistle was a blind to cover de Dominis's own authorship of the work:[5] let them, and so much the better. The epistle is loaded with the arch Bishop's Intimations of his own Immortality.

But it may not have happened in just the way he tells it. Whatever the exact sequence of details in the intricate story of the publication of the *Historia del Concilio Tridentino*, we now know, or think we know, that de Dominis was in no important sense the "onlie begetter," even if we mean by that term nothing more than *portatore*.

43

Nathanael Brent's translation, *The Historie of the Councel of Trent. Conteining eight Bookes*, published in 1620 by Robert Barker and John Bill, "Printers to the Kings most Excellent Majestie," makes no mention of de Dominis. It does, however, make additions of its own to the title: "In which (besides the ordinarie Actes of the Councell) are declared many notable occurrences, which happened in Christendome, during the space of fourtie yeeres and more. And, particularly, the practises of the Court of *Rome*, to hinder the reformation of their errors, and to maintaine their greatnesse." It also has a dedicatory epistle directed to King James, which echoes here and there the phrasing in the de Dominis epistle. We learn from it one further fact—if it is a fact—that the author "was moved to write it, as for the common good of all Christendome, so *particularly in contemplation of your Majesties service.*"[6] This is followed by a brief epistle "To the Reader," and this, in turn, by a third epistle, directed "To the most Reverend Father in God, my singular good Lord, the Archbishop of Canterburie his Grace, Primate of all England, and Metropolitane, and one of His Majesties most Honourable Privie Councell." Here, too, are echoes of the epistle by de Dominis, though these are of small concern to us. What is of prime importance is the content of the penultimate paragraph:

> This Booke I have translated out of Italian into our vulgar language, presuming to commend it to the royall protection of his sacred Majestie, for whose sake (as some reasons induce me to beleeve) it was principally composed. And because I undertooke this worke at your *Graces* command, who have beene the chiefest cause why the originall crossed the Seas before the just nativitie of it, and saw the first light within his Majesties dominions, as also in regard of the high place you most deservedly beare in the Church of God, I thought it my dutie to crave your favour likewise; that as the birth of it hath beene happie by your *Graces* meanes, so the growth may accordingly proceede, and the fruit of both (which is to remoove an erronious opinion of the infallibilitie of this pretended Councell) may constantly endure untill the worlds end.[7]

Four points or propositions are to be observed here: (1) Brent has reason (reiterating the epistle to James himself) to believe that the *Historia* "was principally composed" for the sake of the King of England; (2) the English translation is a command performance to please the Archbishop of Canterbury; (3) the Archbishop of Canterbury, and not the Archbishop of Spalato, was the "chiefest cause why the originall" came to England; and (4) "the birth of it [that is, the publication] hath beene happie by your *Graces* meanes," not by the means of that portatore, de Dominis. If these assertions are true, and if James had any inkling of the facts they allege, he must have read de Dominis's epistle with a mixture of amusement and high wonder. And James, as it turns out, did have more than an inkling of what was going on.

When the fog of de Dominis's ambiguities (or prevarications) had lifted somewhat, the essentials of the operation whereby a manuscript of Sarpi's work could be provided the King's Printer became fairly well known even to the seventeenth century—the essentials, not the details. But in the long interval between the early eighteenth century and the twentieth, much even of what was once known slipped back into limbo. Only in recent years has a firm recovery been made.[8] David Lloyd's *The Statesmen and Favourites of England* (London, 1665), in its sketch of the life of Sir Henry Wotton, declares a bit exaggeratedly that at Venice Wotton "had such interest, that he was never *denied any request*; whereby he did many services to the Protestant interest (with his Chaplain Bishop Biddle, and *Padre Pauloe's* assistance) during the Controversie between the Pope and the *Venetians*, especially in transmitting the History of the Councel of *Trent*, sheet by sheet to the King and the Arch-Bishop of *Canterbury* as it was written."[9] His notion of the time and manner of the transaction is nebulous and incorrect, though the general pattern—sans the intermeddling de Dominis—accords well enough with the now-accepted version. Probably Lloyd picked up his basic statement from Izaak Walton's *Life of Wotton*, first published in 1651. Here is Walton's statement:

> These contests [papal-Venetian] were the occasion of Padre Paolo's knowledge and interest with King James; for whose sake principally, Padre Paulo compiled that eminent *History of the remarkable Council of Trent*; which history was, as fast as it was written, sent in several sheets in letters by Sir Henry Wotton, Mr. Bedel, and others, unto King James, and the then Bishop of Canterbury, into England, and there first made public both in English and in the universal language.[10]

Again, de Dominis is conspicuously uninvolved.

Some unpublished evidence, deriving from an even earlier source, confirms this general pattern, omits de Dominis, and adds some more precise information. A large-paper copy of the *Historia del Concilio Tridentino*, first edition, now in the Folger Library, once belonged to Roger Twysden, whose signature and the date 1627 it bears on the title page.[11] Both the title page and the margins throughout the book bear copious notes in Twysden's neat and microscopic hand. On the title page, just below his name, this former owner, one of England's distinguished antiquarians, has written: "Editio prima authoritate regiâ publicata, reliquis omnibus anteponenda." Just opposite the cut of the royal arms he has de-anagrammatized the pseudonym Pietro Soave Polano as "Paolo Sarpio Veneto" and given the dates of Sarpi's birth and death. Beneath the imprint are other longish notes, apparently written in or shortly after 1632, in the first of which we read the following very specific and unexceptionable information:

> Atque eundem Paulum fuisse authorem huius Historiae mihi saepe affirmavit Nathaniel Brent legum Doctor et Eques Auratus seque Venetiis iussu regis ab Archiepiscopo Cantuariensi missum ut exemplar transcriberet et in Angliam mitteret, quod fecit, ab ipso authore exemplaris ei Copiâ factâ, non tamen ante plenam inquisionem ab ipso Paulo factam qualis erat iste Brentius cuius fidei committeret, quem etiam phrasis, et Modus loquendi authorem fuisse prodeunt.

But the fullest account, the one which has led to the modern reconstruction of events and which all but annihilates the claims (or insinuations) of de Dominis, is found in a collection of letters published in 1705. These, says the editor,

> when carefully perused . . . will be found useful to discover some Truths which otherwise might have been conceal'd, to clear up some Transactions which have not been well understood, to rectify some Mistakes, and to set us right in several material Passages relating to the *History of the Council of Trent.* They will give us a taste of the Management of the Inquisition; they will inform us at whose Costs this useful Work was procur'd, by whom translated, and how agreeable to the Original, by what means transmitted to us, and with what Prudence and Conduct the whole Affair was managed; and what Danger Sir *Nathaniel Brent* expos'd himself to for the Service of the Church, and to advance the interest of the Protestant Religion.[12]

One of the letters is addressed to Basil Brent, son of Nathanael, thanking him for sending papers relating to the Council of Trent and regretting that there are not more of them.[13] Basil Brent's reply to his correspondent, while misinformed on some points—especially concerning Sarpi and Fra Fulgenzio —is of distinct bearing on our problem:

> What I can say of Father *Paul* is but little material; however, to satisfie your desire, I send you this Account, *viz.* That my Father (having been once before at *Venice*) was sent by *George Abbott* Arch-Bishop of *Canterbury,* a second time, on purpose to procure the History of the Council of *Trent,* where he fell into Acquaintance with *Padre Paulo* and *Padre Fulgentio* (two famous Fathers who sat in that Council) who were the Persons who compos'd the History of that Council, and my Father sent it over weekly as they compos'd it, to the Arch-Bishop in

46

Italian; to whose hands it came after five or six Superscriptions to other Persons for the greater Security: And when he had sent it all over, he came over himself, and translated it out of *Italian* into *English* and *Latin*. My Father sent to them to desire the Favour of them to send him their Pictures, which they did accordingly, drawn upon Canvas half way; and my Father put them into plain black Frames. I had them in my possession some time, but they were burnt in my Lodgings in *Fleet-street*, in the great Fire at *London*, I being then in the Country. I've heard my Father say, that he believ'd they were Protestants in their Hearts, tho' they durst not own it, or else they might have discover'd [= revealed] the Business he came about, which might have cost him his Life in the Inquisition.[14]

Beginning on page 6 there follows a series of letters, dated from Lambeth or from Croydon, from Archbishop Abbott to Nathanael Brent in Venice. In the first of these, dated from Lambeth, 21 June 1618, and addressed to Brent "at the *House of Mr.* Daniel Nice" (= Nis, or Niis), the Archbishop thanks his emissary for certain letters and "the *Canzoni* inclosed, which are twelve in number, whereof I shall make use as is fit" (p. 6). There is much secrecy and indirectness in the language: the *canzoni*, obviously, refer to installments of the *History*. Other letters follow, dated 15 July, 10 August, and 9 September. In this last one, still addressed to Brent in care of the merchant Nis, Abbott says, "The *Canzoni* which be come unto my hands at this present Day, are 154; and I do find by them, that there is no Musician which is skilful in his Art, but must give great Approbation to them. Commend me to the Compositors" (p. 9). The final letter in the Abbott-Brent series is dated from Croydon, 24 September 1618, again in care of Nis, and reads in its entirety:

> I have received all the Packets which you have sent unto me, so that there is in my hands the full Story [no need now to talk of canzoni], with the End and Conclusion thereof, being within three of 200 Speeches; so that you shall not need to make any longer stay about that Matter, the Packets coming most happily from the beginning to the end without Impeachment. The Old Man, which was my Guest [that is, de Dominis] when you departed, doth tell me that there be some other things in the hands of our two good Friends [that is, Sarpi and Micanzio], that are worth the transcribing. You shall do well to learn what they be, altho' not to stay for any of them, unless it should be some small things which might be writ out in a very few Days: For I would have you to return with the best and first Commodity, unless some Occasion of your own do detain you there or elsewhere. I pray you commend my

love to those two honest Men, and let them know, that as I hold this a great Work for God's Glory, so I shall be ready to serve them upon all occasions, and will take care that this Business shall be dexterously handled, according as it is fit. So commending me unto you, and hoping to see you here shortly, I leave you to the Almighty.[15]

With this much of the evidence before us, together with a little more to be supplied along the way, we may perhaps now begin to weed out the errors and false assumptions and construct something like a sequence of facts and probabilities.

FACT: Sarpi had long been interested in the history of the Council of Trent and had collected materials to write such a history long before de Dominis left Italy. King James had also known of this interest of Sarpi's before the arrival of de Dominis in England.[16]

FACT: Brent was sent to Italy by the Archbishop of Canterbury, under order from the King, for the specific purpose of securing a transcription of Sarpi's manuscript *Historia*. This transcription Brent sent back, piecemeal, to Abbott.

FACT: Brent's visit to Venice for this purpose took place in 1618, not in 1613–1614 (as Sir Sidney Lee, following Anthony à Wood, writes).[17]

FALSE: That the *Historia* was "composed" in 1618 by Sarpi *and* Fra Fulgenzio, and shipped to England as they finished installments. False also that either of them ever "sat in that Council" at Trent.

POSSIBLE: That de Dominis saw Sarpi's manuscript, or even borrowed it; probable, at least, that he knew of its existence before leaving Italy in September of 1616.

IMPROBABLE: That de Dominis made or had made for him a copy which he then carried to England. Otherwise, with "Spalato" under his own roof, why would Archbishop Abbott need to send a special agent to Venice to secure a copy? Or, for that matter, if de Dominis, alert to every opportunity for self-promotion, had a copy of his own, why didn't he make use of it at once to ingratiate himself with James?[18]

IMPROBABLE: That Sarpi did not know of the intended publication of his *Historia*, or that he did not approve.

POSSIBLE: That Sarpi did not know the work was to be edited by de Dominis or that it was to appear at exactly the moment when it did.

At this point we must pause to examine another document, one bearing directly on the last two sets of conjectures. This is a letter to de Dominis, dated 11 November 1619 and said to have been written by Fra Fulgenzio at Sarpi's request. Translated, it runs thus:[19]

> *Most Reverend* Sir,
> I give your Most Reverend Lordship this title because, although you

48

have placed yourself among the number of the Protestants, nevertheless the episcopal and sacerdotal imprint remains forever in your soul, of which you did not fear to wish to deprive yourself. My Padre Maestro Paolo complains much of this excess; and even more because, having lent to your Most Reverend Lordship to read his manuscript of *The History of the Council of Trent*, which he guarded so jealously, you had a copy made of it and have abused him not only by causing it to be printed without his permission, but also by interposing that most improper title and that terrible and scandalous dedication—and that, as we are well informed, out of motives of [self-] interest, not of honoring the modest author. And I tell you on this score, Milord, that these are not the ways to gain credit for yourself, and that my Padre Maestro Paolo and I did not believe you such, not even in that moment when, about two years ago, the news was spread of your deserting the Church governed by you in Spalato, and afterward was read that *Manifestation* which you scattered through Europe concerning your conduct and misguided way of thinking.

Praying the Lord, then, that He illumine you, I subscribe myself, etc.

Now this document, which fits in perfectly with the older (that is, "Spalatensian") version of the story, makes little sense in the Brent-Abbott scheme of things. To my ear it sounds suspiciously like an invention concocted by his enemies to throw further discredit upon de Dominis. Since the Spalatensian case rests upon the dubious readings of de Dominis's dedicatory letter in the *Historia* itself, the indisputable fact of his editorship, and, for the rest, upon a series of unsupported and questionable assumptions, whereas the external and authenticated evidence of the Brent-Abbott version is overwhelming—we must, I think, Griselini and Bianchi-Giovini notwithstanding, throw out the letter as spurious.[20]

Another matter calls for a brief review. We have already seen on several occasions that James I was reputed to have been the person for whose perusal Sarpi most particularly designed his *Historia*. But there is another English claimant—if not precisely to this distinction—at least to the distinction of having determined or helped to determine the form taken by Sarpi's finished manuscript. In the interval between Wotton's first Venetian embassy (1604–1610) and his second (1616–1619), Sir Dudley Carleton was England's ambassador to the Serenissima. Like his predecessor he, too, somewhat slowly established his connections with Sarpi. On 25 June 1612 King James wrote to Carelton requesting him to offer, in his name, English sanctuary to Sarpi. Although Sarpi (unlike de Dominis and some others who had dealings of this sort with James at this same period) did not accept, relations between him and the Ambassador improved.[21]

We do not know how or when Carleton became aware of Sarpi's interest in the Council of Trent (Cozzi, p. 573), but as an ardent Calvinist (and thus opposed to Lancelot Andrewes's Arminian and conciliatory position in the England of 1611–1612) he was interested in promoting a work of interpretation which would put the council in a bad light. It was not easy for him to persuade Sarpi, argues Professor Cozzi, to turn from his original idea of merely printing the *documents* he had gathered to writing an argued *history* of the council (p. 575); but Carleton finally succeeded. And the clincher was a book[22] written by his cousin George Carleton and sent by the latter to Sarpi with an accompanying letter, dated from London 23 December 1613 (pp. 576–77).[23] In any event, Cozzi believes, it was the working of the two Carletons that pushed Sarpi into writing his *Historia del Concilio Tridentino* in the form it took—of attacking Romanism (pp. 578–79). Carleton, says Cozzi, was sure that a work of the sort Sarpi now contemplated would work wonders in the Protestant world and would be well accepted, especially in England (p. 578). The event was to prove him an inspired prophet. Almost as soon as Sarpi had made his decision, Carleton wrote to the Duke of Somerset, telling him of his success in getting Sarpi's agreement and noting the Friar's qualifications to write such a *History*—this even before he had written to George Carleton to tell him that, unconsciously, *he* had been the moving cause of Sarpi's decision (p. 578). James, naturally, was delighted with this turn of events and again, somewhat later (in 1618), urged Sarpi to come to England (p. 581).

Other considerations must be involved, eventually, in rounding out the full story of the publication of the *Historia del Concilio Tridentino*. But for the present we may postulate some such sequence as the following.

As early as his years in Mantua, Sarpi was curious about the Council of Trent and began collecting documents and information concerning it. He had proceeded so far in this direction that when Sir Henry Wotton was recalled to England in 1610 and stopped briefly en route in Geneva, he was able to tell an Italian Protestant there that the most outstanding fact in Venetian religious life at that moment was Father Paul's interest in and handling of the history of affairs at the Council of Trent.[24] We have seen that in mid 1612 James, through his Venetian ambassador, offered English sanctuary to Sarpi, so that the King was obviously being well posted on the Friar's activities. Late in 1613 George Carleton, the Ambassador's cousin, sent Sarpi a copy of his *Consensus Ecclesiae Catholicae contra Tridentinos*, and in the following year Dudley Carleton was able to write to an English correspondent that the Servite had now determined upon the form of his *Historia*. In 1615–1616 de Dominis was in Venice and, presumably, in some degree of contact with Sarpi and Micanzio. Since he did not leave Venice until late in September 1616 and since Wotton could write to James at the end of July 1616 that the manuscript was completed and that he had seen it, it is possible (though not certain) that de Dominis saw it at that time. It seems most unlikely that de Dominis brought a copy of the manuscript to England; otherwise why would Archbishop Abbott, in whose house he was staying, have needed in mid 1618 to send Nathanael Brent (at the King's command) to Venice to transcribe and send back a copy? One of Abbott's letters to Brent, the final one, moreover, indicates that he and "the Old Man" (de Dominis) talked about Sarpi's *other* works in manuscript. If de Dominis ever had a copy of the *Historia*, his failure to produce it at the first opportunity was as egregious a blunder as his decision to return to Rome. But he *could* be serviceable in the business. As an Italian and a Venetian (of sorts), as a learned ecclesiastic, and as a distinguished ex-Catholic whose sympathies were in 1618 apparently as "Protestant"—at least anti-Roman—as those of the historian himself, de Dominis must have seemed to Abbot and King James exactly the right figure to act as editor for the volume. And now, in September 1618, two years after "Spalato's" French leave from Venice, Abbott had all the canzoni in hand. That, I think, was most likely the moment when de Dominis first saw a copy of the *Historia*. Whether the decisions to print the book without waiting for the outcome of the Synod of Dort[25] and to add the abusive title and dedication and to risk revealing the author's identity under an anagram were left for de Dominis to make independently is anybody's guess. In any case, the book appeared as we have it early in 1619. And so far as Sarpi is concerned, it almost certainly did not appear "senza il consenso dell'Autore"[26] or without his "beneplacito."[27]

Once the book was in print, big as it was, it spread like wildfire. By the end of the seventeenth century, Englishmen (and other Europeans) could have seen it in no fewer than twenty-five different issues and in five languages. As early as 24 April 1619, Brent wrote to his old friend Carleton at The Hague that he had been employed to translate the work into English.[28] While he was engaged in this task, by early June 1619, copies of the original had made their way to Venice and to Rome (and elsewhere on the Continent) and were promptly placed on the *Index*.[29] Brent's translation, published by Barker and Bill, the King's printers, appeared in 1620 and had later editions in 1629, 1640, and 1676. The second edition contains an appendix of added materials, the contents of which are thus listed on the verso of the title page:

The Appendix of this Second Edition, conteining;

51

1 An Epistle of Gregory the First, Bishop of *Rome* to *Maurice* the Emperour.

2 A Passage of the History of *Fr. Guicciardine* Florentine, concerning Pope *Alex. 6.* left out of his third Booke in the printed Copies.

3 A second passage of the same Author, conteining a large discourse of the meanes, whereby the Popes of *Rome* atteined to their greatnesse, that they now enjoy, left out of the fourth Booke.

4 A third passage of the same Author, left out of his *10.* Booke.

5 Certaine passages out of the Letters of the Lords de *Lansac, Pibrac, Ferrier, &c.* taken foorth of the *Instructions*, and *Missives* of the Kings of *France*, and their Ambassadours sent to the Councell of *Trent*, Published in French. An. *1608.*

6 *Andr. Dudithius*, Bishop of *Quinquecclesiae* in *Hungary*, his Testimony of the Council of *Trent*, in his Epistle to *Maximilian 2.* Emperour.

7 An Epistle of Bishop *Jewell* unto Seignor *Scipio*, a Senatour of *Venice*, touching the causes moving the Church of *England* to refuse Communion with the Councell of *Trent*: now first published according to the Originall annexed.

8 Lastly, the foresaid Epistle of *Dudithius*, written by himselfe in Latine.

The reader will scarcely need special spectacles or tuning devices to perceive the anti-Romanist tendency of the intruded pieces. This lumber was carried on into the edition of 1640; and to that of 1676 there were also added "the Life of the Learned Author: and the History of the Inquisition" (title page). Each of the three parts had its own title page, the *Life* (Micanzio's) occupying pages i–cvi of the second numeration.

The Latin translation, bearing the imprint "Augustae Trinobantum" but without indication of printer, was also issued by John Bill in 1620. It was begun by Bedell's old friend Adam Newton, whose Latin was adequate to the task but whose Italian was less so. When Newton had finished the first two Books, de Dominis took over the translation of the next four; and the final two were rendered by Bedell himself.[30] The service that de Dominis thus performed in bringing the book into the ken of James (that learned king) and the rest of the learned world, though less than he claimed for himself in the Italian edition, was, in fact, substantial. For the translation into "the universal Language" proved very serviceable and was issued at least six times after the first edition: in Frankfurt (1621); in Geneva (1622); in Leyden (1622); again in 1622 without indication of place; and in Gorinchem, or Gorkum (1658)—this edition styling itself on the title page the "fifth and last," though it was followed by one at Amsterdam (1694) and one at Leipzig (1699).

The first German translation (Frankfurt, 1620) was apparently not reprinted in the seventeenth century, if ever.[31] But the two French translations were widely distributed. The first—that made by Giovanni Diodati, the Genevan-Italian Calvinist who had once at Wotton's urging visited Venice, incognito, to look into the possibilities of introducing the Reformed religion there and who was famous as the translator (1607) of the Bible into Italian —was published at Geneva in 1621. Thereafter appeared other editions or issues at Troyes (1627, 1635, 1650, 1655) and at Paris (1665), this last describing itself on the title page as the "fourth" edition. The second French translation, appearing late in the century and picking up when the Diodati had run its course, was the work of Amelot de la Houssaie, who also translated, interpreted, or defended other works by Sarpi. Of this translation the first edition was published at Amsterdam (or Paris) in 1683 in quarto and was followed by three others within the two decades left in the century: in 1686, 1693, 1699. A full decade elapsed before there appeared a second edition —at Geneva, naturally—of the original Italian text, said (but falsely) on its title page to be "riveduta e corretta dall'Autore." This was reprinted at Geneva (and perhaps elsewhere), sometimes with and sometimes without indication of place, in 1656 and 1660. With this supply available, a reasonably diligent and determined scholar could have laid hands upon a copy at any time during the last eighty years of the century.

"Vino vendibili suspensa hedera nihil opus," said Erasmus. Here was a merchandisable, heady wine: available, reputedly scandalous, forbidden by Holy Church. Chains couldn't have kept readers away. Unbound, the volume may have weighed in folio a mere four pounds; but its explosive potential was greater than that of all the gunpowder stored under Parliament in those touchy days of 1605.

There was power here to rock the world.

5 --- Exit the Fat Bishop

IN STEPPING AHEAD to 1619 we have attended to events out of proper chronological sequence. And now, while Sarpi and Fra Fulgenzio tend the shop in Venice, we must carry our disorderly conduct even further. This seems the proper place to finish our account of de Dominis.

Even while he was working on the Latin translation of Sarpi's *Historia del Concilio Tridentino* and getting into print the final installment of his own Latin *De Republica Ecclesiastica*, de Dominis was beginning to have second thoughts about the green pastures he had abandoned in order to come to England. After the first bloom of English enthusiasm and adulation had worn off under the attrition of the Archbishop's slowly revealed *vera imago*, he began to sense that he was not receiving all the attention and preferment he was convinced were his due. Perhaps he then recalled, a little wryly, the bitter taunts and prophetic utterances of a pamphlet issued close upon his exodus from Rome, *A Survey of the Apostasy of Marcus Antonius de Dominis, Sometyme Arch-bishop of Spalato. Drawne out of his owne Booke, and written in Latin, by Fidelis Annosus, Verementanus Druinus, Devine: and Translated into English by A. M.* ([St. Omer?], 1617). The book, obviously of Jesuit inspiration, tells de Dominis of the sympathy he may expect from those northern heretics to whom he has fled:

> You know not *(Antony)* and little do you imagine, what fierce and furious windes, I meane proud and peremptory sects rage in the Northern parts, which if you can assemble to a generall Councell, or keepe them where they are in peace, verily you shall be more omnipotent than *AEolus*. But afore-hand I tell you, they will not set a rush for you. Maydes and Boyes will laugh you to scorne, they will preferre their skil

55

of Scripture before yours, with sentences flowing thicke and threefold
from their tongues, & uttered with one breath, they will overload you.
If you dare but mutter against what they say, you shall be stiled *Papist*;
if you do not straight yield to beleeve them, they will take pitty of your
eyes, that having beene so many yeares togeather accustomed to Popish
darkenesse, cañot now behold the cleere shining light of the Gospel.
This is the *Calvinian* nature, which if you be ignorant of, you will learne
to your cost.[1]

The author of the pamphlet had not, of course, had opportunity to read
de Dominis's fulsomely flattering dedication of the *Historia del Concilio
Tridentino* to King James, but he chides the Archbishop for king-flattery
almost as if he had read it. "You may seem," he says, "to have coyned [this
doctrine] of purpose, that therby you might make your selfe a free passage
to the Court and Kitchin of the King of Great *Britany*" (p. 125). After
warning de Dominis not to be misled by the apparently enthusiastic reception he has had among heretics, the author says:

These are but conceits, prayses wherwith to make a vaine shew of triumph over us, and flatter you to your face, who behind your backe play
upon you with scoffes, loading you with the disgracefull titles you truly
deserve, and with some also which perchance you have not merited;
when not long ago at S. *Dunstans* you made a speach in the street, do
you not know, what the people then present uttered against you? They
called you great-bellied-Doctour, made fat under Antichrist; and some
there were also that sayd, that before you ranne away from the Pope, you
got your owne Neece with child, and that feare to be punished for it,
made you trudge away with your great load of flesh in such hast.[2]

The general message of the hortatory ending adds up to: Repent, and return
to your first faith—and Rome. Perhaps this, too, was playing at the back of
the Archbishop's memory when he began to brood on his great deservings
and small rewards.

Some of his discontent has been anticipatorily touched upon in the
earlier estimates of his character. But another document illustrative of his
grumbling greed will not be amiss here. A letter of 24 November 1621 from
Thomas Locke to Sir Dudley Carleton reads as follows:

The Bp: of Spalato sent to me againe to come to him, wch I would
have done wthout sending for, if I had knowne of his being in towne.
And though I told him that yo[r] Lp: intended to gratifie him according
to yo[r] promises, yet he grewe verie impatient; he said he perceived that
yo[r] Lp: went about to mocke him, but he would not be so served, the K

should knowe it, And had bin better peradventure to have given 1000^{li}. I desiered him to have a little patience, & not to Conceive such a thought, I told him that yor Lp: did thincke yo^u might expect so much at his hands, and that in this perticular you should be as thanckfull, in performing what you intended, as any other had bin, Then he said that Si^r Jo: Kidderminster had dealt better with him, And that he never borrowed nor a farthing of yor Lp:. I asked him whether there could be no other services but in borrowing of money, not that he had received (he replied) unlesse yo^u would yor words you had spoken to bring him hither, for wch yor Lp: received honor in that he was come into the land, yet that yo^u fayled in yor promise to help him to 200^{li} p[er] añu[m] from my Lo: of Cant. wch he did not now injoy accordinglie; I told him that peradventure my Lo: of Cant. did thincke him sufficientlie provided for otherwise, he said 300 nor 4 nor 500^{li} a yeare . . . were sufficient for him, he was a Prelate &c., And for the gratuitie that he was to receive of yor Lp: it was verie smal for he protested he gave a cleere 300^{li} that he might have had, wth a greate deale of such like.[3]

A small "deale of such like" would go far toward alienating those who really tried to help him, even if only to use him for their own larger purposes in waging a war against Rome. And his enemies were constantly on the alert to seize any opportunity to catch him off balance or to silence his blasts against the church he had abandoned with such an embarrassing fanfare. No love was lost between him and Gondomar, the Spanish ambassador in London—for obvious reasons. But de Dominis, given to jeering and bitter jests it will be recalled, went out of his way to exacerbate Gondomar's hostility. As seems to have been well known to everyone about the court and to the public at large, the Ambassador suffered from a painful and embarrassing fistula, which caused him to do much standing and which necessitated his use, even for normal sitting, of a "chair of ease."[4] Fuller, in his *Church-History* relates the cruel public jest by which de Dominis won the hatred of Gondomar and, it may be, sealed his own death warrant: "One of his *sarcasmes* he unhappily bestowed on Count *Gondomar*, the *Spanish* Ambassador, telling him, That *three turns at* Tiburne *was the onely way to cure his Fistula.*"[5]

While de Dominis was stirring up Spanish animosity and fretting over his life and hard times among the unappreciative English, two events happened in Italy which led him to believe that the complexion of affairs there might very drastically have changed. On 28 January 1621 died Pope Paul V, Sarpi's old and frustrated, unforgetting and unforgiving opponent—the pope, also, who had most reason to be offended with the Archbishop's conduct. In his stead there was elected on 9 February 1621, as Gregory XV, de Dominis's old Bolognese friend Alessandro Ludovisi, who had been promoted to the cardinalate in the year of the Archbishop's flight. Archbishop Abbott, who was in the best position on the English side to know the truth of the under-hand transactions and the sequence of overt actions (in some of which he himself was a principal actor), supplies a concise résumé:

> By meanes of a couple of Italians, the Spanish embassador did secretly worke with him to draw him away: hee promised him a pension of 12000 crownes a yeere, or the bishopricke of Salerna in the kingdome of Naples, besides acceptation from the bishop of Rome, and a remission for his departure from that sea. And accordingly, by the Spanish em-bassador resident at Rome, there was in shew a trafiking for these thinges. These baites did so farre catch this ungodly man, that hee gave his consent to bee gone; and upon the 16 of January last [that is, in 1622], wrote unto our kinge being then at Newmarket, to crave his leave to bee gone, under colour to seek reconcilement betweene the reformed and the Roman churches.
>
> The kinge marvelled at it, and upon good advise caused such ques-tions to bee at sundry times propounded unto him, as drawing from him answeres in writing, under his owne hand, to declare him to bee a meere worldly man, without conscience or religion. The Spanish embassador having gayned this upon him, and having made him odious both to God and man, to protestant and papist, did utterly desert him, professing openly, That hee did not care if the kinge heere did hang him. And when hee was told by one, That the kinge had great reason to take it ill at his hands, that hee had debauched and perverted one whom hee es-teemed so much, the answere of Gondomar was, That hee did looke for thankes at the kinges hands, for ridding and freeing him of so wicked and ungodly a person. These thinges being made knowne sundry waies unto Spalato, did so farre alter him, that hee would have bene glad to have bene stayed in this country, as at severall times hee expressed to the deane of Winchester and Dr. Goade; but wee did not thinke it fitt to continue such an apostata heere; and therefore, in the presence of twelve counsellors, bishops, and other learned men, hee was injoyned by such a day to depart the realme, and not to returne upon his perill.[6]

How early de Dominis's discontent with his status in England began to push him toward the return to Rome is not known. As early as 5 February 1620, however, something of his "poco gusto" with his hosts had begun to be understood in Rome, where it was rumored that he contemplated moving to France. A letter of that date from Pope Paul's Secretary of State to Mon-signor Bentivoglio, nuncio in France, discounts the probability.[7]

Meanwhile, in his pique, Gondomar was setting in motion a subtle scheme which was to undermine his jeerer, discredit him with King James, and lure him to his destruction.[8] According to Fuller, who is less full of particulars than we should like him to be,

> the Ambassadour writeth to His Catholick Majesty; He to his Holinesse, *Gregory* the fifteenth, that *Spalato* might be pardoned, and preferred in the *Church of Rome*, which was easily obtained. Letters are sent from *Rome* to Count *Gondomar*, written by the Cardinal *Millin*, to impart them to *Spalato*, informing him, that the POPE had forgiven, and forgotten all which he had done or written against the Catholick Religion; and, upon his return, would preferre him to the Bishoprick of *Salerno* in *Naples*, worth twelve thousand crowns by the year. A Cardinals Hat also should be bestowed upon him. And, if *Spalato*, with his hand subscribed to this Letter, would renounce and disclaim what formerly he had printed, an Apostolical *Breve*, with pardon, should solemnly be sent him to *Bruxels*. *Spalato* embraceth the motion, likes the pardon well, the preferment better, accepts both, recants his opinions largely, subscribes solemnly, and thanks his Holinesse affectionately for his favour. *Gondomar* carries his subscriptions to King JAMES, who is glad to behold the Hypocrite unmasked, appearing in his own colours; yet the discovery was concealed, and lay dormant some daies in the deck, which was in due time to be awakened.[9]

The "due time" was precipitated by de Dominis himself, who wrote to James from the Savoy on 16 January 1621 [= 1622], requesting permission to leave the realm. The old animosities, he said, were dead; the new pope was interested in de Dominis's wish to unify the fractured faith; his advancing years made the British climate hard for him to endure; and besides, he missed his old-home friends. He had finished what work he could do in England, and might now (recalling and extolling always James's virtues and generosity) better serve the cause of universal religious amity elsewhere.[10]

After five days of nervous waiting, de Dominis had an answer—of sorts. He was waited upon by the Bishops of London and Durham and the Dean of Westminster, who, at the King's command, examined him upon certain points of conduct and doctrine, found him wanting, got his signature to compromising positions, and reported to His Most Serene Majesty. According to a contemporary "official" account, one of the queries James instructed the examiners to pose was why de Dominis "should hold intelligence with the Popes, *Paulus quintus* and *Gregorius decimus quintus*, and never so much as make the least signification thereof unto his Majestie, whereas at the same time he imparted diligently all Letters that came unto him from

P. Paulo, and F. Fulgentio, and his other Friends in those parts." To this, when asked, de Dominis replied that he had not received letters directly from the popes, but only had heard rumors (from Gondomar?) of their attitude towards him.[11] A second interrogation produced still further questionable responses,[12] and was followed shortly, on 3 February, by a second letter from de Dominis, again asking James's leave to depart. This in turn brought on further questioning at Lambeth on 30 March by a commission of which the Archbishop of Canterbury was head, who,

> in the name of the rest, by HIS MAJESTIES speciall command, in a long Latine Speech, recapitulated the many misdemeanors of *Spalato,* principally insisting on his *changing of Religion,* as appeared by his purpose of returning to *Rome:* and that, contrary to the Laws of the Realm, he had held correspondency by Letters with the *Pope,* without the privity of the *King's Majesty.* To which Charge when *Spalato* had made, rather a shuffling Excuse, than a just Defence, the Archbishop in *His Majestie's* name commanded him to depart the Kingdome, at his own peril, within *twenty daies,* and never to return again. To this he promised obedience, *protesting he would ever justifie the Church of England for orthodox in fundamentals, even in the presence of the Pope, or whomsoever, though with the losse of his life.*[13]

Despite another change of mind and some last-minute attempts to obtain permission to remain in England,[14] de Dominis left within the appointed term; and Fuller, with less than his wonted charity, wrote in his *Church-History,* under the beginning of the year 1622, that "this year began happily, because with the end of that arrant *Apostata* in this Land, and his fair riddance out of the limits thereof."[15]

In Brussels de Dominis waited for several months for a papal brief that never arrived. Then, with a fatally misplaced trust in the friendship of Gregory XV, "formerly his Collegue, and chamberfellow,"[16] he proceeded without guarantees to Rome. He was not made Bishop of Salerno, nor was he given a red hat. Upon his agreeing to write recantations of his former anti-Roman works (the *Historia del Concilio Tridentino* excepted because the former Cardinal Ludovisi, now pope, knew that he was not the author of that work),[17] he was absolved of charges of heresy, readmitted to the Church, and, briefly, while the new pope lived, enjoyed a pension. His principal work after his return was *Sui Reditus ex Anglia Consilium* (Rome, 1623), as sharp and inconsiderate in its attack on the Anglican Church as had been his former *Consilium* against Rome. The *Sui Reditus Consilium* was answered, by royal command, in a well reasoned but bitterly railing work by Richard Crakanthorp, *Defensio Ecclesiae Anglicanae,* published posthumously in 1625.

On 8 July 1623 Pope Gregory XV died. The new pope, Urban VIII, elected on 6 August, promptly stopped payment of de Dominis's pension. The move struck the Prodigal Son in a tender spot. For this reason and, no doubt, from the frustration of his expectations, the former Archbishop overspoke himself, stubbornly refused to write further recantations, defended as unanswered (if not unanswerable by any save himself) some of the positions he had once held in his *De Republica Ecclesiastica,* and found himself suddenly under such suspicion as laid him fast by the heels in the prison of Sant' Angelo. Within a year he was dead ("under suspicious circumstances," Protestant writers have always said), and his decline and fall caused sufficiently noisy repercussions in England and elsewhere.[18] The story can best be told by excerpting some of these contemporary responses to it.

A letter to Sir Thomas Roe from Michael Branthwaite, an English agent at Venice, dated from Venice "this 6th of Maie stilo novo, 1624," offers the following remarks about de Dominis in Rome:

> After the archbishoppe of Spalato his retourne from Englande to Rome, and his peace made by the Spanish theare; I heare he was commaunded by the pope and inquisition to write and publishe a recantation of those bookes he put forthe at his first revolt, againste the authoritie of the churche of Rome; but more especiallie to cuer that greate wounde he had given the pope, by callinge him monstrous heade of the same. Which palinodia he was content to singe, but soe perfunctorilie, as upon perusal, it gave pregnant occasion of newe mistrust: insomuche that the pope and inquisition gave order to the cardinal Clesel (his auncient friend and acquaintance) to advertise him in some sharpe maner of this his faintnesse. Which the cardinal did, but in suche a manner, that the bushope answered him, (thinkeinge he had rather come as a friend to advise, then from authoritie to check) That he neither wold, nor colde, write anie more in that behalfe; addinge withall, That he neither had that meanes nor respect he looked for in that place [new setting, same old song]; with other circumstances of discontent. Which answer the cardinal (rather striving to gaine the creditt of a strict negotiator, then a mitigator of his friendes offence) did relate with such disadvantage to the bushoppe, that upon Thursdaye fortnight he was sente for by the pope and inquisition; and after some howers of examination, was committed prisoner to castel Sant Angelo; where it is thought he shall spende the reste of his daies in muche miserie, or shortlie be putt to deathe abroade with greate reproche: howsoever, I thinke the matter be not greate; for he that is of one religion in his youthe, and of another in his midle age, will be of none before he dies.[19]

"Committed prisoner to castel Sant' Angelo." A cold wind blows through those words, although de Dominis, never much of a realist perhaps, does not seem to have thought so. In a long letter in Italian, written to a kinsman in Venice and dated from his prison 18 May 1624, de Dominis protests his innocence and his puzzlement at the incarceration, being conscious, he says, of "not having given the least cause for it, *nec in opere, nec in verbo.*" He has no fear, being innocent; no harm will befall him. Those who are wiser than he are "holding" him here for the chastisement of his soul, "for some good end, and for his spiritual profit." He consoles himself during his "retention" by plucking flowers from "the most fair garden of the Sacred Scriptures." After all, he is not being kept on bread and water: he has all the comforts of home.[20]

While de Dominis was thus vaporing to himself in the Pope's guest rooms, the Inquisition was taking no holiday.

> The cardinal Scaglia, somtimes commissarie of the inquisition at Rome, havinge had authoritie to examine and searche the papers of the late imprisoned archbushoppe of Spalato, founde he hath plotted to transfer himselfe into Greece, to avoide the popes importunitie, who stil laboured him to write a recantation to those bookes he putt forthe (at his revoult) againste the authoritie of the churche of Rome: and it is thought, if not for that plot, he had beene at libertie before this. Howsoever, in this durance, they use him with faire termes, til they maie drawe somthinge from him to repaire the greate breache he hathe made in that church. I cannott learne he yett consentethe to write anie more; soe that it maie be (contrarie to all expectation) he will, in the ende, prove a martyre.[21]

A martyr, perhaps; but in whose martyrology?

Not everyone, it seems, agreed with de Dominis's appraisal of the elegance and ease of his accommodations. Bishop Hacket, writing long after "Spalato's" death, records a visit to the unfortunate Archbishop in his prison:

> *Sir Edward Sackville,* (who shortly succeeded his Brother *Richard* in the Earldom of *Dorset*) was at *Rome Ann.* 1624. and had Welcom given him with much Civility in the English College, so far that he presum'd to ask, rather out of curiosity than Love, to see this Prisoner *de Dominis.* Mr. *T. Fitz-herbert* the Rector did him the Observance to go with him to the Jayl. He found him shut up in a Ground-Chamber, narrow and dark; for it look't upon a great Wall which was as near unto it as the breadth of three spaces [*sic*: but what is meant?]. Some slight forms being pass'd over, which use to be in all Visits, says Sir *Edward, My Lord of* Spalato, *you have a dark Lodging: It was not so with you in*

62

England. *There you had at* Windsor *as goode a Prospect by Land, as was in all the Country: and at the* Savoy *you had the best Prospect upon the Water, that was in all the City. I have forgot those things,* says the Bishop; *here I can best Contemplate the Kingdom of Heav'n.* Sir *Edward* taking Mr. *Fitz-Herbert* aside into the next Room; *Sir,* says he, *tell me honestly, Do you think this man is employ'd in the Contemplation of Heav'n?* Says the Father Rector, *I think nothing less; for he was a Male-content Knave when he fled from us, a Railing Knave while he liv'd with you, and a Motley parti-colourd' Knave now he is come again.* This is the Relation which that Honourable Person made *Ann.* 1625. which I heard him utter in the hearing of no mean Ones.[22]

All these accounts are, to some extent, private. More clangorous, more public, more nearly official (or at least semiofficial) notices of the final scenes in the last years of de Dominis's life and death may be read in two contemporary pamphlets, both published in 1624, T. H.'s *Newes from Rome, Spalato's Doome* and the anonymous *A Relation Sent from Rome,*[23] "published by command" at the press of John Bill, "Printer to the Kings most Excellent Majestie." The *Newes from Rome* is the more comprehensive of the two, giving a running account of de Dominis's whole career. Neither has any good word to say for the Archbishop; both are sufficiently lurid. Since these two represent the staple of the English public's information concerning de Dominis, I propose to reproduce them rather fully.

By-passing the first three chapters of the *Newes from Rome,* the remaining four may be abridged as follows.

Chap. IV. Shewing how this *Dalmatian* Mountebancke, *M. Anthony,* came to be fully discovered by the practice of the *L. Gundamar,* Embassadour from the King of *Spaine.*

The substance of Gondomar's accusations to James against de Dominis (kettle versus pot) amounted to this, "that the *Popes Holinesse* had sentenced the Bishop for foure notorious and capitall Crimes, to wit, Incest, Simonie, Drunkennesse and Bloud-shed, *Grandia quidem peccata*" (p. 16). Then the charges are specified:

First, he accused him for having had three bastards with his sisters daughter: a businesse that might well make him (if any thing) irregular.

Secondly, hee charged him for Simoniacally attaining to, and leaving of his two Bishoprickes of *Segnia* and *Spalato.*

Thirdly, he urged against him, that the Religious men in *Segnia, Dalmatia,* and the Citie of *Venice,* had all written unto his *Holinesse,* that he was very scandalous, in regard of company keeping and usuall drunkennesse.

> Fourthly, he accused him for a most bloudie treacherie against the
> *Isocchi* [that is, Uskoks], many of whom the Venetians by his meanes
> slew. [P. 17]

These charges are then further particularized (pp. 17–22). The English,
not unnaturally, were slow to believe Gondomar's charges (pp. 21–22), taking them to be part of Romish trickery. So Gondomar set about in another
way to undermine Spalato: he pretended to have a letter from Rome promising de Dominis a cardinalship if he would return. Spalato, greedy gudgeon
that he was, swallowed this bait, and was persuaded to write a letter to the
Pope promising to return. This letter, coming into Gondomar's scheming
hands—hardly by accident—was betrayed to the English authorities (pp.
23–25).

> *Chap. V.* Shewing how that *Spalato* being discovered, he desired leave
> of his Majestie to returne into *Italy*, upon pretence to reforme and re-
> unite the Christian world.

King James, though aware of de Dominis's "levitie, was willing to be quit
and freed of him" (p. 26) and gave permission for his departure. The essence
of this has already been related.

> *Chap. VI.* Shewing what entertainment *Marcus Antonius de Dominis*,
> the nominall Bishop of *Spalato* found upon his late returne to *Rome*.

Far from receiving another archbishopric or a cardinalship, when he landed
in Italy, de Dominis was quickly subjected to a series of forced restraints (pp.
28–29), compelled to write a pamphlet attacking the Church of England
(pp. 30–31), and finally popped into Castel Sant' Angelo. The chapters ends
thus:

> Besides the *Penance* injoined him, of writing his said selfe-accusing-
> condemning booke, hee hath since endured many mortifying passions,
> flagellant diseases which terminated in a mortall incurable consumption,
> he having (as is supposed) of late breathed his last in the Castle of Saint
> Angelo, neere the Popes Palace of *S. Peters*, where he found the case
> strangely altered, in regard of what his friend L. *Gundamar*, promised
> him here in England. [P. 31]

> *Chap. VII.* Shewing the manner of the titular Arch-bishop of *Spalato*
> his commitment to the Castle of *S. Angelo* within the precincts of *Rome*,
> and the reasons of his said imprisonment.

Here the author observes of the Castel Sant' Angelo that "of those that are committed to this said Castle, few or none ever after see the sun-shine" (p. 32). He then describes one manner of execution (probably imaginary) followed in this prison—that of caging the prisoner in a box and then dropping the box through a trap door into a deep pit (p. 33).[24] This tidbit is followed by a notice that since Spalato's death, news has come from Rome of a further indignity visited upon him by the Pope, "*viz.* to frie in the *fire*, and to be *burnt* flesh and bones to cinders, in the sight of many thousands of people" (p. 34). There follow the "reasons" for this condemnation and suffering: (1) Spalato, after a period of imprisonment, had petitioned for leave to travel to Naples for his health's sake and had been refused—he was always a slow learner—whereupon, discontent (he was always discontent), he had "uttered words against the discipline of the Church of *Rome*" (pp. 34-35)—he was an inveterate utterer—and had been reported to the Pope. (2) Asked when he would write books countering those he had written against Rome while in England, he pleaded illness and the need to travel from Rome for his "health" (p. 35)—certainly no understatement. (3) A monk who had accompanied Spalato in England was bribed to spy upon him and reported that he still maintained certain unspecified Lutheran doctrines (p. 36). The same monk secured incriminating letters of heretical tendency written by de Dominis and reported (p. 36) that he had plotted to escape from Rome.[25]

At this point it becomes more profitable for us to follow the account in the well detailed "official" *Relation Sent from Rome.* This being exceedingly brief, can be transcribed in its entirety:

> The late Archbishop of *Spalato* being dead, his *Body* was put into a well pitched Coffin, and that into another greater than it; and so it was carried to be kept in the *Convent* of the *Holy Apostles*, and there committed to the charge of the Reverend Fathers of that place, untill such time as the Cause of the said Archbishop (still depending) should be determined by the *Sacred Congregation*; that according to their Sentence, whatsoever justice did require might bee done upon him.
>
> The *Sentence* being framed, and ready to bee put in execution, the said *Body* was first recognized, according to the Forme of Law; and was taken the twentieth of this present Moneth of December forth from the Convent where it was kept, and caried to the Church of *Minerva*, and there laid upon a Table in an eminent place, together with his *Picture*, and a little sacke full of *Bookes*, which he had printed: where it stood all the night.
>
> The next morning at the time appointed, the most Illustrious, and most Reverend Lords *Cardinalls* Supreme Inquisitors, with many others, (to the number of sixteene, or thereabout,) being met together, after they had delivered over a certaine *Millanois* (who under the feigned

name and habit of a *Greeke*, notwithstanding he had never beene made Priest, had presumed to celebrate Masse both in the Holy House of *Loretto*, and other where) unto the Secular Powers the 23. of this present Moneth aforesaid, to be first hanged and then afterwards burnt, was the *Sentence* of the said Archbishop read to this effect.

First of all, The Manner of his Escape and going into *England* was recompted; and what he had there done in preaching, and in printing; and how that upon better advice, and bethinking of himselfe, he preferred a *Supplication* unto our Lord the Pope, shewing, that hee would willingly returne againe into the bosome of the *Holy Church*, if hee might bee secured of his pardon; and also that he would abjure all and every heresie which he had heretofore maintained. He came to *Rome*, He did all accordingly, He obtained grace, and pardon of his Holinesse, and so continued there for a long time.

But because his *Conversion* was not sincere, and from his heart, but feigned only; He began at length in his familiar discourses, to breake forth into most heinous heresies, and would needs maintaine, that what hee had said before was true.

Thereupon hee was put into the *Holy Inquisition*; and in the *Processe* which was framed against him, we finde that he held the *Heresies* here under written.

1 *That the Councell of* Trent *had declared many things to be* de fide, *which were not.*

2 *That all the Sects of Heretickes might be reduced unto one Church, if the Church of* Rome *would remit some of those things, which in processe of time she had determined to be* de fide, *instancing in particular in the Article of* Transubstantiation.

3 *That there might be made an union between the Church of* Rome *and the* Protestant *Heretickes, they both agreeing in* articulis fundamentalibus.

4 *That it may well be questioned, of some Articles, and of many things defined in the Councell of* Trent *to be* de fide, *whether they were sufficiently discussed, and defined, yea or no.*

5 *That he who holdeth and beleeveth the* Fundamentall *Articles, although he doth not hold the Rest, is not therefore separated from the Church, but is united to it in the Faith. Because that only the* Fundamentall *and* Essential *Articles, are* necessary *to salvation. The rest are matters of* controversie.

6 *That what the Councell of* Trent *hath defined to be* de fide *in matter of Justification, of Predestination, of Grace, and of the Sacraments, that they conferre grace* ex opere operato, *belongeth not to the Faith.*

7 *That he was ready to maintaine, even with the losse of his life, that all men might abound in their owne sense (in other matters,) so that they did agree in* Essentialibus fidei.

8 *That the* Primacie *of the Pope of* Rome *is not* de jure divino, *or at least it may be disputed whether it be, or be not, untill such time as the question may be decided.*

9 *That the* Anathematismes *of the Councell of* Trent, *are no definitions of Articles of Faith.*

10 *That the Heretickes were not condemned in the Councell of* Trent *for any Heresies that they taught; but only because they taxed the Church of* Rome *of Heresie.*

11 *That to deny Transubstantiation, Purgatory, and worshipping of Images and Saints, is not to deny matters that belong to the substance of Faith. That therefore the* Protestants *have the* true *Church.*

12 *That the Church of* Rome, *and the Church of* England *are* one *and the* same *Church, both the one, and the other,* Catholike *and* Orthodox.

13 *That it is not* de fide, *that a Generall Councell, together with the Pope, is the Judge of controveries of the Faith.*

14 *That the bond of Matrimony solemnized and consummated, may be dissolved by the adulterie of either partie.*

15 *That the bond of Matrimonie may be dissolved as well for other causes, as for adulterie.*

16 *That the Secular Prince upon a reasonable cause may ordaine, that the bond of Matrimonie solemnized and consummated, may be dissolved.*

There were some other Articles besides, but they fall within the compasse of these.

After these false and hereticall Propositions were read; it was related how they that were of the kindred of the said Archbishop, (or whosoever else would pretend to bee willing to undertake the defence of his cause) were cited; And some of them made their apparance at the time appointed them; but when they saw the *Processe*, together with the Archbishops owne *Confessions*, they renounced him, and would doe nothing in his behalfe. Whereupon the most Illustrious and most Reverend Lords proceeded unto a definitive *Sentence*. Which was, to declare him unworthy of the favour of the Holy Sea Apostolike; to deprive him of all his honour, benefit, or dignitie; to confiscate his goods, and to give him over to the Secular Powers; as *De facto* they then gave him over, That *He* and his *Picture*, together with his *Bookes* he had written, should be burned.

This *Sentence* being read, the said *Coffin* there present, the *Picture*, and the *Bookes* were delivered over to my Lord the Governor of *Rome*, who desired, that the *Corps* might be reviewed, and recognized anew; which was done accordingly. And presently the said Governor gave order, that the *Corps* together with the other things should bee carried into *Campo di Fiori*, to bee there burned.

But because they found no man that was willing of himselfe to carry him to the said place; therefore the Serjeants tooke up certaine Porters, whom they bound and constrained to goe along with them, and to take up the said *Corps, Picture*, and *Bookes*, which being caried into *Campo di Fiori*, were there instantly burned.

And because the said Archbishop, towards the end of his life, made shew as if he had beene penitent for the heresies which hee had held *de novo*, after his former abjuration, and asking pardon for them, he had the favour done him to be made partaker of the most holy Sacraments. But notwithstanding because hee had relapsed, He was therefore given over to the Secular Power. Which was all that occurred in this action.

Inscriptio.
Marcus Antonius de Dominis
Late
Archbishop of Spalato.

Most impiously bent his stile against the Church of God which had extraordinarily well deserved of him.

Having wounded and stabd her through, he so left her without cure, and wretchedly betooke himselfe to the English altars.

That thence the swine might the more securely gruntle against the Pope and Catholikes.

Returning home againe, but no convert; his apostaticke spirit he forsooke not.

He died
(and the voice of a pentinent man I would he had not uttered)
Impenitent.[26]

A letter of 21 December 1624 from the papal secretariat to Monsignor Sacchetti, nuncio in Spain, confirms this account without going into the particulars. I translate from a copy of the letter:

Marco Antonio de Dominis, formerly Archbishop of Spalato, known, unhappily, for his impious writings and for his books filled with falsehood, with which at the same time he made known and obscured his name, returned under the Pontificate of Gregory XV (of blessed memory) to the bosom of the Apostolic Roman Church, renouncing his pestiferous opinions in conformity with the sacred Canons. But because long-followed habit often binds spirits inextricably in chains, it was not long before he disclosed himself no less a heretic than was at first declared. Whence, interrogated by the Inquisition and imprisoned, while his trial was pending he fell sick and came to the end of his days, as I informed your Lordship at the time in another letter of mine. But although *in extremis* he reasserted his detestation of his double apostasy and his rebellion against Catholic doctrines, nevertheless the Sacred Congregation of the Holy Office, having found him clearly lapsed into Heretical perversities, sentenced him as such and declared his memory execrable; and this morning his body was consigned to the Secular Court, for example to the Guilty, releasing it to the deserved punishments.[27]

In the end no friendly voice, either Protestant or Catholic, would speak for the Archbishop.

"De mortuis nil nisi bonum" says the old adage, although in de Dominis's case no one seems to have heeded it. After his death the most savage and systematic attack (of many) upon him came from Richard Crakanthorp, whose *Defensio Ecclesiae Anglicanae* (1625) was commissioned to answer the Archbishop's *Sui Reditus Consilium*.[28] In the controversial manner of the time, this was a point-by-point rejoinder to the criticisms and fault-finding of de Dominis; and, its bitterness and name-calling aside, it was considered an excellent, if arbitrarily limited, defense of Anglican doctrine.[29] But others abounded who held him in low (or in no) esteem and found harsh epithets to bestow upon him. To Thomas Scott (who also held no brief for Gondomar), he was "that arch-hypocrite *Spalato*";[30] to Francis Osborne, he was a double paradigm for hypocrisy and atheism: "He may be suspected of *Hypocrisie*, if not of *Atheism*, that too suddenly leaps out of one Opinion into another," begins Osborne's "A Discourse in Vindication of Martin Luther,"

> as appeared in the Bishop of *Spalatto,* who in my days left *Italy* for fear of *Paul the fifth,* his enemy, and reconcil'd himself to the *Church of England*; but the old Pope being dead, and his *Kinsman* in the *Chair,* he resumes his former Errors, and goes to *Rome,* in hope of Preferment, where contrary to promise, he dies miserably. When Falshood is fallen-out with for any other respect, than Love of Truth, it inclines to Atheism, and is so far from mending the Condition of the Convert, that it renders it worse.[31]

These and other unadmirable facets of his personality were duly noted and execrated by Thomas Jackson, by Arthur Wilson, by Robert Johnston, and by others previously cited.[32] But by far the most interesting English treatment accorded him after his demise came from the pen of one of the Jacobean dramatists.

This play, Thomas Middleton's *A Game at Chesse* (1625), one of the most scandalously successful of its time, established an unprecedented nineday "run" on the London stage before being closed down by the authorities. Under the guise of a chess game, and with characters named for the pieces, it is basically a satire on the negotiations for the Spanish marriage and the conflict of religious interests involved.[33] It is also something more. Its connection with Sarpi is remote or nonexistent; but it offers incidental exposition of Jesuit "policy" (which Sarpi was forever equating with Spanish policy) and of the personal conflict between Gondomar (the Black Knight) and de Dominis (the Fat Bishop), here ultimately aligned with the Black House (Spain, Catholics). Eventually, of course, the White House (England, Protestants) triumphs, defeating the Jesuit-Catholic machinations in both the main and the secondary plot (the attempted seduction of the White Queen's Pawn).

As for the Jesuits, the principal point is quickly set. The speaker of the Prologue, Ignatius [Loyola] is made to say, "I would doo anye thing to rule alone,/Tis rare to have the world reignd in by one";[34] and the sentiment is repeated by the Black Queen's Pawn in a reference to the Jesuit "Father Generall" and "the Universall Monarchie, wch hee/And his Disciples principallie ayme at."[35] There is also, later on, a reference to the expulsion of the Jesuits from Venice and their burning of their papers—possibly an echo of some account, Sarpi's or another's, of the 1605–1607 quarrel.[36] More general references to them and their "mystery" permeate the play.

The Fat Bishop is first introduced at the beginning of Act II, scene ii; and the characterization is an unsparing reflection of the contemporary English estimate:

[*Fat Bishop.*] Pawne !
[*Fat Bishop's Pawn.*] I attend at youre greate holines service
F. B. For great I grant you, but for greatlie holie
  There the soyle alters, fatt Cathedrall Bodies
  Have verie often but leane litle soules
  Much like the Ladie in the lobsters head,
  A great deale of Shell and Garbidge of all colours,
  But the pure part that should take wings, and mount
  Is at last Gaspe, as if a man should gape
  And from this huge Bulke lett forth a Butterflye,
  Like those big-bellyed Mountaynes wch the Poet
  Delivers, that are brought abed wth Mousflesh,

Are my Bookes printed, Pawne? my last Invectives
Agaynst the Blackhouse?
F. Bs. p. Readie for publication,
For I sawe perfect Bookes this morning (Sir)
F. B. Fetch mee a fewe wch I will instantlie
Distribute 'mongst the white house;
F. Bs. p. With all speede, Sir,   *Exits Bs. p.*
F. B. Tis a most lordlie life to rayle at ease,
Sitt, eate, and feede uppon the Fat of one kingdome,
And rayle uppon another wth the Juice on't,
I have writt this booke out of the strenght & marrowe,
Of 6 and 30 dishes at a meale,
But most on't out of Cullisse of Cock sparrowes
Twill stick and glut the faster to the Adversarie,
Twill slit the Throat of theire most Calvish Cause
And yet I eate but litle Butchers meate
In the Conception,
Of all things I commend the Wh. house best
For plentie and Varietie of Victualls,
When I was one of the black Side profest
My flesh fell halfe a Cubit, time to turne
When my owne Ribs revolted, but to saye true
I have no preferment yet, that's sutable
To the greatnes of my person and my parts,
I grant I live at ease, for I am made
The Mr: of the Beds, the long Acrë of Beds,
But there's no Marygolds that shutts and opens,
Flower-Gentles, Venus Bath, Apples of Love,
Pincks, Hiacinths, Honysuckles Daffadowndillies
There was a time I had more Drabs then Beds
Now I've more Beds then Drabs;
Yet there's no eminent Trader deales in Holesale
But shee and I have clapt a Bergayne up
Lett in at Watergate, for wch I have rackt
My Tennants pursestrings that they have twangd agen;
Yonder Black Knight, the Fistula of Europe,   *Enter Bl. Kt.*
Whose disease once I undertooke to cure   *and Bl. Bp.*
Wth a high-holborne Halter, when hee last
Vouchsafte to peepe into my priviledged lodgings,
Hee sawe good Store of plate there, and rich hangings,
Hee knewe I brought none to the whitehouse wth mee,

I have not lost the use of my profession
Since I turned whitehouse Bishop. . . .   *Enter his pawne*
                                    (ll. 1–55)   *with Bookes!*

The entrance of the Black Knight (Gondomar) at this point gives the clue to his part in the undoing of this ecclesiastical Falstaff. The Black Knight's subsequent entrapping of the Fat Bishop, we are permitted to infer, will result from the double impulse of zeal for the Knight's (Catholic) cause and his stinging urge to personal revenge.

Bl. Kt. Looke more Bookes yet,
     Yond greasie turnecoate Gurmandizing Prelate
     Do's worke our house more mischeife by his Scripts
     His Fat and fulsome Volumes,
     Then the whole bodie of the adverse partie
Bl. B[ishop]. Oh twere a Mr: peice of Serpent Subteltie
     To fetch him a this side agen,
Bl. Kt. And then dam him
     Into the Bagg for ever, or expose him
     Agaynst the adverse party wch now hee feedes uppon
     And that would double dam him, my revenge
     Has prompted mee alreadie, Ile confound him
     A both sides for the phisick hee provided
     And the base Surgeon hee invented for mee;
     Hee told mee hee had found a present Cure for mee
     Wch I grew proud on, and observd him seriouslie,
     What thinke you twas, being Execution daye
     Hee showde the hangman to mee out at Windowe
     The common hangman;
Bl. B. Oh Insufferable!

                                    (ll. 56–77)

We need not follow the whole working out of Gondomar's scheme. At the beginning of Act III de Dominis is further characterized, with special stress upon his inordinate ambition: the letter with which the Black Knight tempts him hints broadly at the prospect of *Sede Vacante* (III, i, 39)—and the Fat Bishop thinks he may be ample to fill *that* "Chayre of Ease" (III, i, 49). Later scenes emphasize his ingratitude and hypocrisy (IV, iv, 88–89) and his covetousness (IV, iv, 116–19). When the play ends and all the vicious characters are popped into "the Bagg," the Fat Bishop is still vociferating his claims to preeminence—

Crowde in all you can

72

> The Bishop will be still uppermost Man
> Maugrë King, Queene, or polititian.

(V, iii, 235-37)

As we remarked when he made his entrance, Marco Antonio de Dominis was not a lovable man. He was proud, haughty, carnal, ambitious, devious, learned—and not a little stupid. But that he was a hypocrite or a dissolute sensualist are pretty strong assessments and hard to prove. For all his shiftings in the externals of faith,[37] he was consistent in emphasizing the essentials of Christianity, not details of dogma; and I believe that he really thought he might be able to reunite the divided churches and restore religious peace to the Western world.[38] But, in the end, his character was too weak for the accomplishment of his goals. As one of his English critics wrote, "De Dominis his Cake was Dough."[39]

Perhaps he deserved a better exit line.

6 --- Some Originals and Some Englishings

AFTER THE NOISE of battle had died down in Venice with the lifting of the interdict, Sarpi's life was not permitted to lapse back into that studious disengagement from worldly entanglements which had been his before he became a world celebrity. He continued to reside in his humble convent quarters, but he also continued to act as Consultore to the state and to enjoy an ever-growing ascendancy over the minds of the most influential group among the Senate, *i giovani*, whom we might think of in modern parlance as "the Young Turks." Despite the added precautions taken on his behalf by the government, there were further plots, fortunately abortive, against his life. Since he had refused to heed his citation to Rome and since he remained under personal excommunication, there were those religious (not necessarily pious) who would have considered it meritorious to ease the papacy of the embarrassment it had to bear through his mere continued activity.

It was in this period, too, principally, that he began and vigorously pursued that amazing exchange of letters with illustrious foreigners, both orthodox and heretical, which, edited still only in part, remain so enigmatic a key to his mind and spirit. Yet these constitute but a small fraction of the enormous outpouring from his pen during the years between 1607 and 1623.

The time has come for us to look at this production and to view it, if we can, as it would have been viewed by Englishmen of the seventeenth century.

Of primary concern from this point of view are those Sarpian works which achieved translation into English during the century. Almost no other measure is so accurate a gauge of a foreign writer's popularity or the chances of dissemination for a particular book. And in seventeenth-century England no Italian writer was more often translated than was Paolo Sarpi. Leaving aside his works written and published during the interdict, and the *Historia del Concilio Tridentino*, what were his *other* works which found an English garb?

It is seldom easy, and frequently impossible, to state precisely when a book of Sarpi's was written or even when and where it was published. Apparently the earliest that we need to be concerned with here is his *Historia particolare delle cose passate tra'l Sommo Pontefice Paolo V. e la Serenissima Repubblica di Venetia gl'anni MDCV. MDCVI. MDCVII*, written in the period 1607–1608, but not published until 1624. Two editions of that year carry the place designations of Geneva and Mirandola in their imprints; and another, reading Lione, was probably printed in Venice and in 1625 rather than in 1624 as the imprint shows. It might be noted, in passing, that Sarpi finished the writing of this account in the year of Alberico Gentili's death at Oxford. The work was quickly translated into English by Christopher Potter (the "grave" Potter), who was elected Provost of Queen's College, Oxford, in 1626. In that same year Potter's translation was published in London by John Bill, a name we have become accustomed to seeing in connection with English-printed books having anything to do with Sarpi or de Dominis. Bill's title page reads: *The History of the Quarrels of Pope Paul V. with the State of Venice. In seven Books. Faithfully translated out of the Italian, and compared with the French Copie.* It is a substantial volume of 435 quarto pages.

In the epistle "To the Reader," the translator (who signs the "Epistle Dedicatorie" with only the initials "C. P.") expresses his opinion of Sarpi in some strongly admiring lines:

> The Author of this Excellent *Historie* was the same wise and worthy *Frier*, who of late with so great judgement and fidelitie hath revealed unto the World that piece of the *Mystery* of *Iniquity*, those *Arcana Imperii Pontificii*, in the *History* of the *Trent Councell*, which shall bee a lasting Monument of his memorie, and Fame to all Posterity. His owne Countrey-men knew well how to value and reward his Vertues, judging him a Person capable to assist in their Highest *Counsels* of *State*: But at *Rome* his goodnesse easily merited the extreme hatred of the *Courtiers* (though hee lived and died in the outward Comunion of that *Church*,) so farre, that they sentenced and martyred him in his Picture (being defeated in their reall attempt upon his Person) as a *Mezzo Lutherano*, an *Heretique*, such as are, in their account, all those that cannot beleeve that thirteenth Article of the *Roman Creede, Subesse Romano Pontifici &c. est de necessitate salutis*.[1]

"This Excellent *Historie*," it will be recalled, was the work which Sarpi wrote at the request of de Thou.[2] In addition to Potter's English version, there were contemporary translations in French and in Latin,[3] the latter being the work of Sarpi's old friend William Bedell, who the next year was to be appointed Provost of Trinity College, Dublin. Bedell's translation, dedicated to King Charles I, is, like the original, divided into seven Books.[4] At the end are printed some "Regulae Jesuitarum" that were said to have been found in their college at Padua when they were expelled from the Republic in 1606 and, following these, some Latin poems, the most interesting of which was written by Giovanni Marsilio, Sarpi's old associate in the time of the interdict. It is entitled "In Meretricem insignem" (= Rome) and concerns the attempted assassination of Father Paul. I quote only the last four lines:

> Haeccine Relligio est? Qui scribunt vera, necantur?
> Estqúe sacra infandi dextra ministra mali?
> Heu! Heu! Qui *Christi* caulas tam immanè cruentant
> Non sunt Pastores: credimus esse Lupos.[5]

A work of Potter's own serves to identify him as the translator of Sarpi's *Historia particolare.* This is ponderously entitled *A Sermon Preached at the Consecration of the right Reverend Father in God Barnaby Potter D.D. and L. Bishop of Carlisle, at Ely House in Holbourne March 15. 1628. By Christopher Potter D.D. Provost of Queenes Colledge in Oxford. Hereunto is added an Advertisement touching the History of the Quarrels of Pope Paul 5 with the Venetians; Penned in Italian by F. Paul, and done into English by the former Author* (London, 1629). The consecration sermon—Barnaby was Christopher's uncle—of no particular interest except that it is strongly anti-Catholic, is contained in pages 1–84. Then follows (pp. 85–127) Sarpi's piece, headed (by Potter) "An Advertisement to the Reader, touching the History of the Quarrels of Pope Paul 5. with the State of Venice." Potter's reason for presenting this new statement supplementary to his translation of 1626 is explained in "The Translator to the Reader":

> In a more perfect Copie of that *Historie* pretended to bee printed at *Lions*, but indeed at *Venice*, MDCXXIV (which I have lately seene by the courtesie of my worthy and learned friend M. *W. Boswell,*) there is annexed at the end, by the same judicious *Author* of the *Historie*, (and wanting in that Copy of *Geneva*, which before I followed,) a particular and memorable Information touching some essentiall circumstances in the Accommodation of that great Difference. Which because it is the life of the whole *History*, and serves much to cleare the *Venetian* cause from the forgeries of the *Court of Rome*, (which was the Authors maine

intention,) I have thought meet here to communicate it with the Reader, done out of Italian into English with fidelity: as followeth.[6]

A manuscript in the British Museum, Sir Edward Dering's journals, 1670–1673, contains as its third item (folios 17–19) a highly compact Latin epitome in seven "books," Book by Book, of the *Historia particolare*.[7] This is entitled "Litis Pontificiae cum Rep: Veneta ex Italico Patris Pauli compendium Latinum." Sir Edward was the son of Sir Edward Dering, Bart. (1598–1644), who also had some interest in the great Venetian dispute. The item is instructive in showing how late an interest in Venetian government lingered on in England.

Somewhere around 1609 Sarpi wrote (but did not then publish) his *Trattato delle materie beneficiarie*. The title of the first edition was *Historia del P. Paolo sopra li benefici ecclesiastici*, the imprint reading "In Colonia Alpina [= Geneva], P. Albertino, 1675." An edition of the *Trattato* in the Marciana (Venice) bears the name "Lione" in the imprint but lacks indication of printer or year—which suggests surreptitious printing in Venice. Another edition, dated 1676 and allegedly printed in Mirandola, was also probably printed in Venice.[8] This is the work which Professor Getto calls "perhaps the most significant of this group of writings which precede the *History of the Council of Trent*" and "the most memorable among Sarpi's lesser writings."[9] The existence of four independent translations into English would seem to bear out these judgments. But the only one of these with which we are immediately concerned is that by William Denton, published in 1680. As Denton is to receive fuller discussion later in this chapter, we may postpone our remarks on his translation of the *Trattato*.[10]

A work of curiously anomalous status is *The Free [True] Schoole of Warre*, published in 1625 by John Bill.[11] The "Epistle to the Reader" (sigs. Aiii–Aiv verso) is signed "W. B.," generally assumed to be William Bedell, who significantly says, "I present him unto thy view with his owne lineaments and parts, in his *Entire*; only I have apparreled him in *English Clothes*."[12] Yet Bedell, in a letter to his "very loving freend Mr Dr [Samuel] Warde Master of Sydney College in Cambridge," 28 April 1628, quite clearly indicates that *he* is responsible for the Latin version only: "I have begun to translate into Latin a litle Tract of Padre Paolo, set forth in Italian, and Englished also, as I thinck, by Dr Brent of Merton College, touching the question whether Catholicks may beare armes under the States. Wherein sundry tricks of the Papacy are discovered."[13] He adds in a postscript that the volume he refers to is "not above 4 sheetes of paper in the Italian." Now Nathanael Brent, who had already translated *The History of the Council of Trent* and who was indeed then Warden of Merton College, Oxford, would have been a most likely translator of this further piece of Sarpiana;

but why, if he were the translator (and the "I" of the prefatory epistle), should he have used the initials "W. B."? I have no answer for this tangled question.

Nor have I seen a copy of those "4 sheetes of paper in the Italian." But there is no question that Bedell had. For in another letter to Dr. Ward, 7 May 1628, he sends his completed translation and adds some interesting information:

> Salutem in Christo Jesu.
>
> Good Mr Doctor: I send you here the Tract that I mentioned in my last which I have since coming from London (where I got the Italian copy) put into Latin. The English Translator in sundry things understood not the Author, especially towards the latter end. I do thinck it a treatise very worthy to see the light, whereby sundry mysteries of the Papacy are discovered. What Title to put in the first leafe I doubt: what thinck you of *Quaestio Quodlibetica. An liceat* ec. For the name of Quodlibet seemes to be from thence because in them Schoole men followed not the order of the Sentences but disputed de quovis proposito. (The Italian Copy is the same in the first leafe which I have set in the Latin: only in this Order. Tractatus An liceat ec.) Whether it might not be fitt to ad the authors name at least thus, *Authore R.P.P.S.V. recens ex Italica conversa?* For dedication I would make none, not set to my name. But the print and the volume I would wish the same with the History of the Interdict.[14] If Mr Buck will print it, the sooner the better. If not; I desire to receive the Copy at my coming to you. . . .[15]

As it turned out, Master Buck (Thomas Buck, Cambridge printer) could and did arrange to print the pamphlet in the font and type desired by the translator. But in the end it was decided not to name the author, however veiledly; and the *Quaestio Quodlibetica*, with its subtitle *An liceat stipendia sub Principe religione discrepante merere*, appeared at Cambridge in 1630 without preface, dedication, or any names at all—including that of the printer. If Bedell was right in suspecting Brent to be the translator of the English version, his second letter raises a puzzling question: Brent's Italian was adequate to see him through eight Books of the *History of the Council of Trent*; why was his comprehension of the tongue graveled by "4 sheetes" of the *Quaestio Quodlibetica*? I have no answer to that question either.

That Sarpi's interest in the problem posed by the title-page question may have been brought to the surface by one of his distinguished visitors is hinted in Fra Fulgenzio's *Vita*. When the Prince of Condé, visiting Italy in 1622, asked Sarpi various probing questions (such as whether he had written the *Historia del Concilio Tridentino*),[16] among them was "whether it be lawfull to make use of the service in armes of those that differ from us in religion."[17]

This is clearly simply the question of the pamphlet with its shirt drawn on backward.

A longer and more important work deals with the origin and practices of the Inquisition within the Venetian state. From the oldest manuscript—in the hand of Sarpi's emanuensis, Marco Fanzano, and containing alterations by Sarpi himself—we learn that the work dates from 1613.[18] Prepared as a *consulto* or review of Venetian legislation and practice, it came to be used also as a guideline or *regula* for the state inquisitors.[19] In its printed forms it appeared under two rather disparate titles: *Historia della Sacra Inquisitione. Composta gia dal R.P. Paolo Servita: ed hora la prima volta posta in luce. Opera pia, dotta, e curiosa: a' Consiglieri, Casuisti, e Politici molto necessaria. In Serravalle, appresso Fabio Albicocco. MDCXXXVIII*. It seems unlikely that the imprint is more than a cover for a Venetian printing. The alternate form of title reflects a little more accurately the content and purpose of the volume: *Discorso dell'origine, forma, leggi, ed uso dell'Ufficio dell' Inquisitione nella citta, e dominio di Venetia. del P. Paolo dell'Ordine de' servi, Teologo della Serenissima Republica. M.DC.XXXIIX.*[20] Though lacking indication of place or printer, this is identical with editions later reprinted by the (or *a*) Venetian printer Roberto Meietti.[21]

The first (and only) English translation, appearing almost on the heels of the original publication, shows by the phrasing of its title and the beginning of "The Printer to the Reader" (sig. A3) that it was made from the so-called Albicocco printing: *The History of the Inquisition: Composed by the Reverend Father Paul Servita, who was also the Compiler of the Councell of Trent. A Pious, Learned, and Curious Worke, necessary for Councellors, Casuists, and Politicians. Translated out of the Italian Copy by Robert Gentilis* (London, 1639). The Robert Gentilis (or Gentili) who made the translation was the gifted son of the famed Alberico Gentili. Among his half-dozen or so translations from several languages are Englishings of Bacon's *Historia ventorum* and of two works by the popular Count Virgilio Malvezzi. A little misleadingly, Gentili translates not only the text of the *Historia* but also, word for word, "The Printer to the Reader":

> The hidden Treasure never availed any, as Solomon the wise said. This present Booke, like to a great Treasure was always much Esteemed by the best Politicians, but it lay hidden because it went not abroad, but in a Manuscript, and came onely to the hands of the Governours of the Venetian State, and of some few forraigne Princes, who by especiall favour were made partakers of it. Now a liberall hand hath communicated it to the world, that every good Statesman may participate of it. Receive it with a cheerefull Countenance, and beleeve it will not a little profit thee and others. Farewell.[22]

The English printer (J. Okes or Humphrey Mosley) thus appears to be saying something which, perhaps true in the first instance, was more logically
spoken by the Italian printer. Gentili's translation was reprinted—but without his name—in 1655 and again in 1676 (with the translator's name) together with the fourth edition of Brent's translation of *The History of the
Council of Trent.* Spaced at these intervals, Sarpi's *History of the Inquisition*
became, next to the Tridentine *History* itself, the most continuously acces-
sible of his works in seventeenth-century England.[23]

A work even more difficult to pin down precisely is the *Discorso sopra
le ragioni della risolutione fatta in Val Telina contra la tirannide de'Grisoni,
& Heretici* (Venice? 1624?). Here the date of composition, place of publication, and date of publication—even the authorship—are all uncertain. Presumably, however, the work was composed after 1620 and, since it was of
topical interest, not too many years earlier than its English translation. This,
published without the translator's name, was entitled *A Discourse upon the
Reasons of the Resolution taken in the Valteline against the tyranny of the
Grisons and Heretiques. To the most Mighty Catholique King of Spaine,
D. Phillip the Third. Written in Italian by the Author of The Councell of
Trent. and Faithfully translated into English. With the Translators Epistle
to the Commons House of Parliament.* The translation was entered in the
Stationers' Register under date "28° Junii 1628" to William Lee and appeared
in that year with an imprint reading "London, Printed for William Lee, at
the Turkes head in Fleetstreet, next to the Miter and Phoenix. 1628."[24] The
first 29 pages of this 101-page quarto are taken up with an address "To the
Knights, Barons and Burgesses of the House of Commons, assembled in
Parliament" and is signed at the end "Philo-Britannicos." In the course of
his address the unnamed translator refers to the author as "an Authour of
great worth, and greater works."[25]

The identity of Philo-Britannicos is disclosed elsewhere. In the same
British Museum volume of miscellaneous tracts containing *A Discourse upon
the Reasons* there is bound in *The Cruell subtilty of Ambitoin* [sic], *Discovered in a Discourse concerning the King of Spaines Surprizing the Valteline. Written in Italian by the Author of the Historie of the Counsell of
Trent. Translated by the Renowned Sir Thomas Roe Knight, Many times
Embassadour in Forraine parts, with his Epistle to the House of Commons
in Parliament. Shewing the onely way in Policie to counterplot the designes
of Promoting Unjust Interests of State.*[26] Like *A Discourse* it bears the imprint "London, Printed for William Lee, at the Turks Head in Fleetstreet
next to the Miter and Phoenix. 1650." And except for the title-page changes
it is an exact reissue of the 1628 volume: same distribution of pages, same
ornaments, same decorative capitals, and so forth. Now, William Lee, according to Henry R. Plomer, was doing business at the Turk's Head in

Fleetstreet from 1627 to 1665.[27] It is difficult, therefore, to understand the logic of the compilers of the *Short Title Catalogue* when they remark concerning the 1628 volume (*STC* 21757ᵃ): "From its identity with the ed. dated 1650 it is probable that both were issued at the latter date." To my way of thinking, nothing is more probable than that this is improbable. The work was topically relevant in 1628; Roe, the translator, died in 1644; the work was entered to Lee in the Stationers' Register, 1628, and it is Lee's name which appears on both title pages. A simple, and more likely, solution would seem to be that in 1650 Lee had a new title page printed to aid him in disposing of unsold sheets remaining from the 1628 printing.

In *The Negotiations of Sir Thomas Roe* (London, 1740) are two interesting letters to Roe from Michael Branthwaite, both of which in part concern Sarpi. In the letter dated from Venice "this 20/30 of December, 1623," we read:

> The laste weeke procʳᵉ [procuratore] Soranzo and his collegue Renier Zen, late ambassadors with his holines, entred into the colledge (accompanied with, at the leaste, 200 *purpurati*) to give up an accompt of theire ambassage; concerninge which there is nothinge more as yett broken forthe into publique knowledge, then that they have given his holines contente in all demaundes, that of fra. Paolo onlie excepted; who hathe this longe time beene excommunicate, and not longe since *in effigie* burned at Rome for an heretique. His holines wolde have his bodie taken up, and throwne to the dogges (which by this time, I thinke, they will scarce eate); and under fearfull threatninge, wills them not to proceed in making anie monimente for him, that had beene suche an enemie to the Roman churche, especiallie in writinge that councell, or rather, I maie call it, anti-council of Trent, whereof nowe his is declared author after his deathe. And this is all I can afforde your lordship, for the presente, of this place. [P. 209]

The second letter, again from "Venice this 4/14 of March, 1624," continues the observation about Sarpi's monument in Venice:

> The monimente (whereof I have made mention in some of my former lines) which this Republick had given order sholde be erected in memorie of the deceased fra. Paolo (as my selfe hathe beene an eye-wittnesse) was almost broughte to perfection; but nowe of late, upon newe revewe, I finde it at a full stoppe: whereby I perceive there to be some freshe threatninges from Rome; or they are contente to let his memorie die with himselfe: which I thinke it will hardlie doe, havinge lefte moniments behinde him *aere perenniora*, which even time, the devowrer of all thinges, will not easelie obliterate. [P. 232]

Two other post-interdict writings of Sarpi, both mentioned in the catalogue of his writings with which the *Vita* of Micanzio ends, are the *De Iure
Asylorum* and his addition to and continuation of Minuccio Minucci's *Historia degli Uscochi*. Minucci's book, which brings the history of the Uskoks
down to 1602, was published within the succeeding two years. Sarpi's *Aggionta* continues it to 1613, his *Supplimento,* to 1615. The first edition of
these Sarpian contributions to Minucci's *Historia,* appearing without date
or place of publication, is assigned by Cozzi to 1617 or early 1618.[28] The
English translation which Sir Henry Wotton proposed to make (or have
made) of these works, if ever completed, cannot now be traced.[29] Nor was
there an English translation of the *De Iure Asylorum,* though the work was
sometimes cited by seventeenth-century Englishmen. Like the *Historia
dell'Inquisitione,* the *Su le immunità delle chiese,* of which the *De Iure
Asylorum* is a modified version, was originally a *consulto* and was presented
to the Senate 16 May 1620.[30] The *De Iure Asylorum* was first printed by the
Elzeviers in 1622 at Leyden.[31] Other than the *Historia del Concilio Tridentino,* these were the only ones of Sarpi's post-interdict works to be printed
during his lifetime.

As the last item in his list of Sarpi's writings, Micanzio notes the
"Manuscritti—Epistolae ad D. D. Gillotum, Leschasserium, & alios." Among
those miscellanous discreetly unnamed "alios" was Jerôme Groslot de l'Isle,
the recipient of a number of Sarpian letters collected and edited in 1673 by
Jean Albert Portner, though the editorship is also sometimes attributed to
Gregorio Leti.[32] The collection contains 123 letters, principally addressed to
Groslot; a few at the end are addressed to others, including Jacques Gillot.
The dedication, signed simply "L'Editore," is followed by fourteen pages of
remarks from "Lo Stampatore al Lettore," which is in turn followed by a
lengthy "Tavola" summarizing the principal contents of each letter. Then
comes a brief "Catalogo dell'Opere del Padre Paolo uscite alla Luce," containing nine titles—among them those we have been discussing—with the
omission, of course, of the *Delle Materie beneficiarie,* not printed until 1675.
At the end of the volume, following the text of the letters, the editor quotes
two Latin epigrams of Sarpi's composition. I mention these details only because the English translator, although he introduces a long and informed
statement of his own, translates this front matter and reproduces (without
translating) the epigrams. The English reader, in a word, was not to be de-
prived of anything in the transfer of languages. The only substitution he
allows himself is that of an English dedicatee: Daniel Finch, Earl of Not-
tingham, for August, Duke of Brunswick-Lüneburg.

The English translation, which appeared just twenty years after the publication of the original, was the work of Edward Brown, Rector of Sundridge
in Kent.[33] Brown's choice of a patron to whom to dedicate his work was in

some part a payment of a debt: through the Earl's recommendation Brown had accompanied Sir John Finch, the Earl's uncle, as Chaplain when Sir John had gone as ambassador to Constantinople (1672). He was especially indebted to Sir John, he says, for some recommendations as to his reading:

> Another Book he commanded me to read over and consider, which is this, which I now present to your Lordship's View in our own Language; a Book that his Excellence had a very great Value for, as he was a great Admirer of all Father *Paul's* Works, from that convincing Strength of Reason, that curious way of arguing, and all the other Vertues and Ornaments which have so mightily indeared this wise and good *Venetian* to all considering and impartial Christians, that know what *Peace* and *Truth* truly are.[34]

Brown's own principal addition to the work, his "Preface of the English Translator" (pp. ix–lxi), besides containing an animated comparison between Sarpi's *History of the Council of Trent* and Cardinal Pallavicino's (pp. xxxii ff.)—which Brown calls "the Spight-History to that of the Father's"—also contains the translator's estimate of the Venetian friar:

> These *Letters* of this wise and excellent Person, which you have read, or are going to read, have been highly valued by many great Men that have read the Italian Edition of them; they have displeased some, (and who they are, you will soon find out, if you do not know already) but they are Men whom we Englishmen above any other Nation in *Europe* are the least bound to gratify. . . .
>
> . . . I doubt not but abundance of brave English Souls will be highly satisfied with the Freedom and Ingenuity, the Wisdom and Truth, the Judgment and Sincerity of this great and noble-spirited Man, that as he received much Advantage from Englishmen, so has return'd it to them by the Copies of his *History of the Council of* Trent, and that of the *Venetian Controversy with the Pope*, sent first hither to be published, before any other part of the World. And the Hopes of benefitting my Country, added to the Pleasure I took in translating these *Letters*, made me quite forget the Labour and Toil of my part in them.
>
> . . . In all these *Letters* and the Freedom that is used in them, there is not a Syllable that touches the Secrets of the Republick. The Father was a down-right honest, as well as a wise and learned Man; and he was no freer of his Thoughts, then what consisted with his Place and Dignity. As for his Freedom about things of Religion, we will talk of that by and by, when we come to see what his Enemies say of him, out of Envy and Partiality. But for other things, there is as little offensive in them, I should think, as can well be, considering those times, the De-

signs that were then on foot, the Persons who carried them on, the worthy Gentleman that he corresponded with, the manner he did it in, and his own searching inquisitive Temper, and his great Wishes for the Peace of the World, and the Happiness of all Nations.[35]

At the end of the prefatory matter Brown has placed an "Advertisement" which probably reflects an arrangement with Richard Chiswell, his enterprising publisher, in whose list of current publications (at the end of the *Letters*) there was already entered Brent's fourth edition of *The History of the Council of Trent*:

> The Second Volume will consist of the *Life of Father Paul*, written by Father *Fulgentio*, with Notes upon many Passages of it; and a *Treatise of the Interdict*, written by Father *Paul*, and the other Divines of *Venice*, in the time of the Controversy between Pope *Paul* V, and the most serene Republick of *Venice*, never published in English before: Together with the Answer of *John Marsilio*, Father *Paul*, and Father *Fulgentio*, to the Sentence of *Excommunication, Citation* and *Admonition*, issued out against them.[36]

But this "Second Volume," alas, never saw the light of day; and the translations mentioned in the advertisement, if ever completed, cannot now be traced.

Two other works call for notice but not discussion here. The first, an excerpt from Brent's translation of *The Historie of the Councel of Trent*, was published in 1673 as *The Papacy of Paul the Fourth*. It will be examined at a later point in this study.[37] The second, published first in 1689 as *The Opinion of Padre Paolo, of the Order of the Servites . . . given to the Lords the Inquisitors of State. In what manner the Republick of Venice ought to govern themselves . . . to have perpetual dominion. Delivered . . . in the Year 1615.* No name of translator appears, but from the reprint of 1693, with a new title, *Advice given to the Republick of Venice*, we learn that he was "Dr. [William] Aglionby." The original was of spurious attribution, and some (but not all) copies so indicate, for example, *Opinione falsamente ascrita al padre Paolo Servita, come debba governarsi internamente et esternamente la Republica Venetiana, per havere il perpetuo dominio* (Venice, 1685). Its presence in English translation simply illustrates once again the attractive power of Sarpi's name throughout the seventeenth century.

7 --- Trio

THE "PERSON OF QUALITY," John Saint Amand, who in 1651 published the English translation of Fra Fulgenzio's *Vita del Padre Paolo*, did not wholly satisfy everyone with his performance. His translation was, however, under a separate title page, reprinted in the 1676 edition of *The History of the Councell of Trent*, where it stands as the first of the three items constituting that folio. And for the English reader of the second half of the century it was virtually the sole source of biographical information concerning Sarpi.

One of those expressing dissatisfaction with it was Edward Brown, to whose translation of the *Letters* we must now briefly return. "Father *Paul* hath had much wrong done him," says Brown,

> in the English Translations of some of his Works; and it was an unlucky thing that that worthy Gentleman who took so much Pains in translating his Life (written very curiously by Father *Fulgentio*) above forty Years ago, should do it so obscurely and roughly, and unintelligibly, by a too near pursuance of the literal Sense, (as he himself confesseth in his *Preface* to the *Reader*) and that, besides this, he followed some very ill Copy of it, which might be that of *Leyden*, in 1646. and was not so diligent and attentive to Father *Fulgentio*'s way of writing as he ought to have been. Upon the Request and Complaints of divers great Men of this Church about this Matter, I have tried to make a new Translation of it, which shall be carefully examined by a MS Copy of that Life, which Sir *Roger Twisden* procured from *Venice*, by the means of his Brother, that was intimately acquainted there with Father *Fulgentio*, and had it transcribed many Years before ever it was printed, and is now in the Possession of his Son Sir *William Twisden*, who is an Honour to Gentility and Learning, as his excellent Father was before him,

and his Children like to be after him; and I hope they will be, upon the Remembrance of the fair Example of Vertue, Goodness, and Love of good Books, which their Family have set before them. Which Life of this wise and religious Father *Paul*, with some other things of his, will make up the Second Volume, which will quickly follow the Publication of these *Letters*, and give a great deal of Light to many Particulars in them, which I left without any Note or Intimation, because they appear so plain in the Account of the Father's Life.[1]

The passage is valuable not only for its revelation of Brown's intentions but also—and at this juncture, chiefly—for calling attention to Sir Roger Twysden's (1597–1672) very lively interest in Paolo Sarpi and his works. An eminent descendant of an established Kentish family, strong-principled in politics, a learned and able historian and antiquary, Sir Roger is one of the most captivating figures of his era. By marriage he was related to the Finches and the Yelvertons; Sir Henry Vane (the elder) was a first cousin, Sir Edward Dering (the elder), a second cousin. Before matriculating in Emmanuel College, Cambridge, he was educated (a few years ahead of John Milton) under the elder Alexander Gill at St. Paul's School. Much of his career was politically disturbed, though towards the end of his life he had some years of quiet retirement and study. None of his published works is directly concerned with Sarpi; but his library and the books he owned and annotated tell another story.[2]

One of Twysden's few publications gives some very slight indication of his interest in Sarpi's works. A copy of his *An Historical Vindication of the Church of England in Point of Schism, as it stands separated from the Roman and was reformed I. Elizabeth* (London, 1657) in the British Museum is an exceptionally tall large-paper copy with Twysden's own very extensive manuscript additions and changes.[3] Both the text and the manuscript additions exhibit a substantial learning, with much citation of authorities. Among the many are Sarpi and Bellarmine—Sarpi being cited repeatedly for the *Historia del Concilio Tridentino*[4] and Bellarmine for his *Risposta ad Apologia del Padre Paolo*,[5] the first certainly and the second presumably in Twysden's library. The painstaking care and fullness of the revisions are highly characteristic of the author.

Another book which we know to have been in Sir Roger's possession is *A Full and Satisfactorie Answer to the late unadvised Bull, thundred by Pope Paul the Fift, against the renowned State of Venice* (1606), a translation of Sarpi's *Considerationi sopra le censure*. A copy preserved in the British Museum has on its title page the ownership designation "Roger Twysden 1627."[6] It has no manuscript notes but is much (and very neatly) underscored throughout.

A further trace of Twysden's interest in Sarpi is provided by the catalogue of an early nineteenth-century book auction: *A Catalogue of the Duplicates and a considerable Portion of the Library of Sir John Sebright, Bart. . . . Also the very curious collection of Manuscripts . . . collected by Sir Roger Twysden and Mr. E[dward] Lhwyd . . . which will be sold by Auction by Leigh and S. Sotheby . . . on Monday, April 6, 1807, and Six following days (Sunday excepted).*[7] The manuscripts were sold on the seventh day of the sale (pp. 44–52). It is not always clear which were Twysden's and which Lhuyd's, though the several Italian items probably belonged to the former and the Welsh items certainly to the latter, a prominent Celtic scholar. There cannot be much doubt about item 1213: "Discorsi di F. Pad. Paulo, sopra la Materia dell'Inquisitione, in propria manu. Pat. Pauli et absque dubio genuinum, in papyro Folio." There is also much Sarpiana among the *printed* books, though these may have belonged to Sebright. One item among them is a 1619 *Historia del Concilio Tridentino*, which Seccombe says the British Museum acquired at this sale.[8] In any case, the Museum does have such a volume.[9]

And a fascinating volume it is. Like *A Full and Satisfactorie Answer*, it carries the title-page legend "Roger Twysden 1627," and it has throughout copious notes in Twysden's neat and legible hand. The book has obviously been minutely and intelligently perused; the marginal annotations exhibit great learning. Beneath the pseudonym on the title page Twysden has written: "Paolo Sarpio Veneto. Cuius Nomen in Libris edit. Venet. 1606. sic scriptum reperitur. Padre Maestro Paulo da Venetia, del ordine de Servi. Nat. Venet. 1552. 14° die Augusti. Obiit Venet. 1623 Ianuarii. AEtat. 71." On the blank flyleaf facing the title page he has written:

> Editio prima, Authoritate Regiâ publicata, reliquie omnibus anteponenda. Licet insunt hâc nonnulla Errata, quae in Genevensi, An-o 1629 editâ, corriguntur: quam ideo meliorem esse Frater meo [viz. Georgio Twysden][10] affirmavit P. Fulgentio. An. 1632. Addebatque P. Paulo fuisse in mente Res gestas Pontificum ad nostra tempora, continuasse. Atque eundem Paulum fuisse authorem huius Historia mihi saepe affermavit Nat. Brent Legum Doctor & eques auratus; Leg[atus]-que Venetiis jussu Regis ab Archiepiscopo Cantuariensi missum, ut exemplar transcriberet & in Angliam mitteret. Quod fecit, ab ipso Authore exemplaris ei copiâ factâ: non tamen ante plenam Inquisitionem ab ipso *Paulo* factam, qualis erat iste Brentius, cuius Fidei committeret; quem etiam Phrasis & Modus loquendi Authorem fuisse prodeunt. Verum hic apponam Curiae Romanae de hac Historia judicium. vid[elicet]. *La narratione e vera, ma le conseguenze sono cattive.* Hoc communicatum D. Cordes Parisiensi, ab Episcopo quodam Romae

agente cum primum edita fuit, & qui hanc esse Curiae opinionem probè
novit, mihi inde rescriptum erat Literis Dat. Paris. 27. Apr. Stylo novo
1632. Roger Twysden.
    Idem affirmavit Mons. de Puys. Nota, ambo erant Romani Catholici,
virique doctissimi.

[Here a line is drawn across the page and the entry continues.]

Author huius Libri videtur esse R.P. Paulus Venetus, cui Sarpio Cogno-
men Gentile fuit. Haec Gul. Bedellus, Epistolâ Dedicatoria Historiae
Interdicti Veneti, ad Carolum Regem. Elogium Authoris lege lib. 13,
Thuani Hist. Tom. 5. Nec non eâdem Epistolâ Bedelli, qui P. Paulum
familiariter Venetiis cognovit. Reipublicae erat Theologus & magni inter
Venetos nominis: Qui eam non solum viventem, sed etiam post mortem
prosequuti sunt. Reipublicae causam contra Interdictum Paul 5. 1606.
optimè & tamen modestè defendebat, cuius Interdicti particularem Historiam (editam tamen non ante Authoris mortem) conscripsit, ex Italica
per Gul. Bedellum in Latinam conversam.

The marginal notes are varied in nature. Twysden has supplied running
dates for each page (top). Sometimes he comments on the text; sometimes
—very often in the earlier Books—he corrects it; sometimes he supplies additional references. The notes are predominantly in Latin, though many are in
Italian and a smaller number in English. Occasionally Twysden will supply
cross references to the text of the Geneva (1629) edition.[11] He has also, for
easy reference, meticulously numbered the paragraphs in each Book. One of
his added references (on p. 212) cites Sarpi's own "Trattato dell' Interdetto,
edit. Venet. 1606." And at the end of Book II, where the date of the death of
the French King is given as the twenty-first of the month, Twysden's marginal note reads: "deve stare 31 come dall' Istoria vera di F. Paolo."
    "As in the true text"—? A puzzling phrase, but as nothing compared
with the puzzlement Twysden has provided us elsewhere. For in the Folger
Library there is a splendid large-paper copy of the *Historia del Concilio
Tridentino*, elaborately interleaved (as are others of Twysden's books) with
blank pages of heavy paper at the front and at the end of the volume, as well
as between the individual Books.[12] Although none of these pages has been
written upon, they seem to be there for the purpose of extensive annotation
or commentary. Had Twysden in mind the preparation of his own critical
edition of the *Historia*? Perhaps, as other facts about the volume seem to
indicate.
    To begin with, this volume, like the British Museum copy, has on its
title page Twysden's signature and the date 1627. It has also, differently
placed, *all the Latin statements transcribed above*. No comment of any sort,

no underlining, no mark appears in the Epistle by de Dominis; but beginning with the first page of text and extending to the last, Sarpi's *Historia* is variously marked and most copiously annotated in Twysden's tiny and well-controlled hand. Variations of ink and slight variations of script suggest that the entries were made over some considerable but indeterminate period of time.

The procedure has been most systematic and workmanlike. At the inner margins of each opening (top) the number of the Book has been written in; at the top outer margins of each page the year treated of on that page of the narrative has been written in. Every paragraph has been numbered, beginning anew with each Book. The underlining, in a faded red throughout, has been neatly controlled by a ruler. Faint but clearly visible penciled guidelines reflect the care with which the marginal entries have been written, and a specially devised set of interlinear symbols within the text identifies the appropriate marginal note. Occasionally, when Sarpi has enumerated a series of events or articles or points of argument, Twysden has supplied interlinear numerals to facilitate reference. And the very frequent marginal cross references by paragraph or by supplied numeral and page show that this was not wasted effort: Twysden was thoroughly familiar with the text of the *Historia*.

Not all the annotations in the Folger copy are identical with those in the British Museum copy, though many are. More accurately, the two sets might be described as partly repetitious, partly complementary. I would hazard the guess that the Folger copy was intended as the master copy and that the process of transfer (and incidental augmentation) was never completed. An enormous expenditure of effort has gone into both copies.

With respect specifically to the Folger volume, the cross references loom large in the total of annotations. There are occasional corrections of statements in the text, and there are many additional references, especially ones appertaining to English affairs. There is very little citation of Biblical texts, but much of the Fathers, councils, and miscellaneous writers on ecclesiastical matters. One needs to remember that Twysden was a historian, not a theologian. There is perhaps a slight slacking off of annotation, barely noticeable, in the Eighth Book. As in the British Museum copy, there are entries in both Latin and Italian, but here there are no English entries. And in the Index, the "Tavola delle cose più memorabili nella presente historia," there are literally hundreds of supplementary entries. The volume was clearly intended to be put to intensive use.

Though Twysden mentions many writers and works, it does not follow, of course, that every book cited in these marginal annotations was in Twysden's own library. But given his known interest in all that concerned Sarpi and considering his repeated references to Sarpi's *Trattato dell' Interdetto*[13] and to both the Italian second edition (Geneva, 1629)[14] of the *Historia del*

Concilio Tridentino and the London (1620) Latin version,[15] it may perhaps be legitimate to assume that he did own copies of these works. From the frequency of the references, I would guess also that he owned a copy of Fra Fulgenzio Micanzio's *Confirmatione delle Considerationi del P.M. Paulo di Venetia . . . contra Gio. Ant. Bovio* (Venetia, 1606),[16] as well as, possibly, de Dominis's *De Republica Ecclesiastica.*[17]

Nothing short of a complete reproduction could do justice to these rich and varied marginalia. By way of wholly inadequate illustration, I transcribe a single entry of medium length, chosen almost at random, and concerning the year 1562.[18] It annotates the opening statement of paragraph 40 (as numbered by Twysden): "Non é da tralasciare il parer di Paolo Giovio Vescovo di Nocera, che in sostanza disse," and so forth.

> *Hic* non est Paulus Jovius Historiarum Scriptor qui obiit Florentiae 1552. teste Thuano, et aliis. Sed alius eiusdem nominis et loci episcopus, de quo in Cathalogo eorum qui huic concilio affuere, sic legitur, *Paulus Iovius, Comensis, electus eps Nucerie̅,* inter episcopos Pii quarti: cum alter Jovius a Xlemente VII° creatus erat. vide Thuan. lib. xi. in fine. atque hic promotus erat ad episcopatum a Pio 4° 29 Novembr. An° 1560 Vide Catalogum eorum qui huic concilio interfuerunt edit. Lovanii 1567. in fol.

The trimness of the hand can be envisaged if it is recognized that this entire entry covers a marginal space measuring approximately 2¼ by 2¼ inches— and without crowding the edges!

A less intent student of Sarpi's works, but one who nevertheless was reasonably familiar (and a little light-fingered) with them, was the well-known James Howell (1594?–1666). A graduate of Jesus College, Oxford, supervisor of a glass manufactory, traveler, linguist, secretary, government agent, epistoler, hack writer, jailbird, historiographer royal (after 1661), hob-nobber with the literary elite, bachelor, and begging *bon vivant*, Howell was just about all things to all men. Always seeking favor and place and seldom securing more than a temporary relief from his chronic indigence, Howell somehow managed to scrape a living from his constant writing—and is said to have been the first "man of letters" (witness the *Epistolae!*) to have done so. How he made literary capital of Sarpi will appear from the following notes.

Howell's first major publication, Δενδρολογια. *Dodona's Grove, or, The Vocall Forrest* (1640) is not directly concerned with Sarpi, but it is full of suggestive associations with Sarpi-connected persons and places. *Dodona's Grove* is one of the more attractive of Howell's rather ponderous allegories.

The talking trees of the "Vocall Forrest" represent various European powers, kingdoms, cities. In the conduct of Howell's rather heavy political satire, they share attention with snapshots of eminent individuals, one of whom is a certain Mordogan, better known to de Dominis as Gondomar.[19] At one point there is included an account of Prince Charles and Buckingham's visit to Spain.[20] And in a section entitled "A Character of Adriana" the reader is presented a sketch of the Venetian Republic, full of often repeated observations, Howell's own and those of others.[21] The *Historia del Concilio Tridentino* is not mentioned nor, so far as I can see, drawn upon. But Howell makes one observation upon the theory of history which would have set well with any of Sarpi's admirers: the "prime vertue of story is verity."[22]

Howell cannot be given much credit for another work, published a few years later, which sometimes goes under his name. This is *St. Pauls Late Progress upon Earth, about a Divorce 'twixt Christ and the Church of Rome, by reason of her dissolutenes and excesses . . . Rendred out of Italian into English* (London, 1644). The Italian from which it is "Rendred" with reasonable faithfulness to the spirit is Ferrante Pallavicino's *Il divortio celeste, cagionato dalle dissolutezze della Sposa Romana, et consecrato alla simplicità de' scropolosi Christiani* (Villafranca, 1666)—or of any readers who are of "sano intendimento." Briefly, the argument of it is this: Christ, in heaven, seeing the dissoluteness of his "Spouse" (the Roman Church), wishes to divorce Rome as an adulteress. God the Father sends St. Paul to look over the evidence on earth. He visits Italy, returns to heaven to report universal wickedness there, and the divorce is granted. In the original and in the translation, the work is a continued attack upon Urban VIII. In Howell's rendering (not so arranged in Pallavicino), Sections 7–10, dealing with St. Paul's visit to Venice, show the author's familiarity with at least the fairly recent history of Venice and reflect points at issue in the famous quarrel with Pope Paul V. Pallavicino does not mention Sarpi, but the content of these sections is strongly reminiscent of the Servite's writings on the jurisdictional dispute. And his sympathies, like Sarpi's, are wholly with the Serenissima. It may be, then, that Howell was here getting a taste, slightly diluted, from Paolo Sarpi's cask. We shall have occasion, shortly, to return to *St. Pauls Late Progress*.

The most widely known of Howell's literary productions has no immediate connection with Sarpi, Micanzio, or de Dominis. Nevertheless, it has a place in this account. I refer, of course, to his *Epistolae Ho-Elianae. Familiar Letters Domestic and Forren* (London, 1645). These famous letters, it has long been recognized, are not to be depended upon for matters of fact. They are, indeed, in some degree fictional. But they are still highly valuable for matters of opinion and for reflection of interests of the time in which they were written. They show much interest in the affairs of Gondomar;[23] they satirically notice Pope Urban VIII;[24] they reflect their author's knowledge of Italy and his taste for Italian literature; and, in Section I, the "Italian" section, they contain bits that the frugal Howell repeats in *S.P.Q.V.* —to which we now turn.

S.P.Q.V. A Survay of the Signorie of Venice, of Her admired policy, and method of Government, &c. With a Cohortation to all Christian Princes to resent her dangerous Condition at Present (London, 1651). Such is the title of the work in which Howell's submerged interest in Sarpi first comes incontestably to the surface. *S.P.Q.V.* is a handsome small folio, with a double engraved frontispiece and a title page in black and red, which prominently displays a cut of the winged Lion of St. Mark. But more than pretty pictures engages our attention here.

Shortly after his graduation from Jesus College, Howell had been employed as steward in the glassware house in Broad Street, and in this capacity was sent abroad in 1616 (when he was twenty-two) to study techniques, to buy material, and to hire professional workmen. Naturally, he visited Venice, the center then, as now, of fine work in glass. He does not say so, but he could at this time have caught a glimpse of the famous Venetian friar; he could in any case hardly have missed hearing much about him.

The *Survay* is little more than launched before Howell introduces, casually, the name of Father Paul. Discussing the relations of church and state, and allowing full admiration for the adroit management of the Serenissima in this regard, he says:

> She hath allso two very eminent men, the one a sound Divine [Fra Fulgenzio?], the other a learned Casuist, that have a pension from the Republic, who are allwayes ready in case She have any contestation with *Rome*, to defend and vindicat Her by public writing, and to satisfy the world of her proceeding, as *Paolo Servita* did.[25]

This is followed at an interval of a page or so by a piece of incidental but wholly typical praise of Venetian government:

> But if ever any hath brought humane government and policy to a *science* which consists of certitudes, the Venetian Republic is She, who is as dextrous in *ruling* men as in *rowing* of a gallie or gondola, otherwise She could never have lasted so long, and kept in such an exact obedience 3. millions of men, for therabouts by frequent censes that have bin made is the number of her subjects.[26]

We need not enter systematically into an analysis of Howell's combined history and encomium, one prominent member of a rather numerous group of admiring accounts. But his version of the familiar story is more dependent upon Sarpi than Howell keeps us advised. He does not, I think, draw upon

Sarpi's *History of the Inquisition* when he records an attempt (in 1567) to introduce the Roman Inquisition into Venice.[27] Nor, apparently, does he draw upon Sarpi's account of the expulsion of the Jesuits when he treats that topic.[28] But sandwiched in between these two are some strange goings-on.

In the normal course of his chronological narrative, Howell comes (p. 135) to the dogeships of Marino Grimani—whom he calls Marini Grimarci—and of his successor, Leonardo Donato. Naturally, he relates here (though in summary fashion) the causes, beginning, progress, and conclusion of the scandalous dispute between Venice and Pope Paul V.[29] And when he reaches the end and translates Donato's declaration of the removal of the Venetian censures and the lifting of the interdict, he adds:

> The Duke having publish'd this Declaration, the Senat was not a little perplext with a doubt of no mean consequence, which was, that the Pope for his part having made no mention at all concerning books and writings publish'd in the behalf of the sayed Decrees, nor of the Authors of the sayed books, which were two very important points, and which did threaten a breach of the whole reconcilement; the State doubting that the Pope by this silence and Omission had an intent to proceed afterwards against the Authors of the sayed books, by the ordinary way of Ecclesiastical Justice, and thinking it dishonorable to abandon those that had done them so good and faithfull service, after mature consultation, the Senat made a very notable and honorable Decree, that the Signory should protect them against all dangers, and assign them a perpetual Pension.[30]

Why the reticence about mentioning Sarpi's name? The answer is probably tied up in the contents of the immediately succeeding twenty-odd pages of Howell's book.

Here, having now told the story of the interdict briefly, Howell calls a full halt and prepares to deliver

A particular Narratif of the notable Contestation 'twixt *Paulus Quintus*, and the Republic of *Venice*, 1606. &c.,

which begins thus: "Now, in regard that ev'ry Corner of Christendome did ring aloud and sounds yet to this day of that high Contestation 'twixt Pope *Paulus Quintus* and the Republic, I shall spend a little more oil and labour to acquaint the judicious Reader with the circumstances thereof."[31] What follows is nothing more nor less than a skillful summary of Sarpi's *Historia particolare*—made, however, with an eye on Potter's translation and not requiring too much expenditure of his own "oil and labour." It takes Howell five full pages to get around to mentioning Sarpi, and then without the faintest suggestion that it is the Servite friar whom he is adapting: "The Senat with much maturity ponder'd these *Breves*, and therupon sent to confer with their learnedst Counsellors in the Civill Lawes, amongst whom they admitted *Paul* of *Venice*, of the Order of the *Servites*, an eminent Divine and Canonist, with other *Padovan* Doctors, to consult what answer they should return the Pope."[32]

Howell's method of using Sarpi in this surreptitious manner, unlike that of Peter Heylyn and some other nontattling borrowers who copied out whole blocks of contiguous matter, was instead to abstract and paraphrase. A detailed and thoroughgoing comparison of his text with its original would cost more "oil and labour," and would take up more space, than it would be worth; his *method* can be illustrated by the comparison of two brief but representative passages. Upon the opening of the two Papal *breves* (or injunctions) at the succession of Leonardo Donato following the death of Grimani, which required the Venetians to revoke their laws to which the Pope objected, the Senate deliberated:

> To this the Senat answer'd 28. of *Jan. Anno* 1606. as followeth: "That with grief and amazement they understood by his Holines Letters, that he dislik'd the Laws of the Venetian Republic, prosperously observ'd for so many Ages, and never tax'd by any of his Predecessors, the revokement wherof wold not only shake, but utterly overthrow the very fundamentalls of the State; that he interpreted those Laws to be prejudiciall to the Sea Apostolic, and the Authority thereof, blaming those who had made them as infringers of the Churches Liberty, notwithstanding that they were known to be persons of singular piety, and to have done good service to the Sea of *Rome*, and were now doubtlesse in heaven; that the Senat according to his Holines advertisement had narrowly examin'd both the New and the Old Laws, and could find nothing in them but what might be decreed by a Soveraign Prince, concluding, that the Venetians did not think they had incurr'd any censures, and that therefore his Holines so repleat with Religion and Piety, would not without pondering well the cause, continue his menaces."[33]

The original in Sarpi, spread over several pages instead of being compressed into a single paragraph, but showing in phraseology and sequence where Howell's eyes had dwelt, reads as follows:

> But for that time the *Senate* understanding the judgement of the *Doctors*, made answer the 28. of *January*, in these words for substance; That with much griefe and wonder they understood by the Letters of his *Holinesse*, that the *Lawes* of their *State* observed carefully through so many ages, and never questioned by any of his Predecessors, (the re-

voking whereof would subvert the Foundations of their *Common-wealth*) were reprehended as contrary to the authority of the *See Apos-tolique*; and that they which made them (Persons of great pietie, merit-ing well of the *See Apostolique*, who are now in Heaven) were noted for violators of *Ecclesiasticall* Libertie: That according to the admonition of his *Holinesse*, they had examined, and caused to examine their Lawes old and new, but had found nothing which might not well be ordained by the authoritie of a Soveraigne *Prince*, or which might justly offend the *Popes* authority. . . . That for these reasons the *Senate* could not perswade themselves that they had incurred any Censures . . . much lesse yet could they beleeve that his *Holinesse* (full of Piety and Religion) would persist without knowledge of the cause in his Comminations.[34]

Towards the end of his book, when he is collecting statements from various writers on Venice, Howell cites the *Interdicti Veneti Histor.* Lib. I (omitting Sarpi's name): "The Republic of *Venice* excludes all Ecclesias-tiques from the participation of her goverment [*sic*], and only She neither gives or takes any pensions from the Court of *Rome*."[35] And, curiously, for all his dependence upon Sarpi and his occasional naming of him, when Howell towards the end of his book draws up a list "Of the famous and re-nowned men which *Venice* hath produced," he fails to mention Sarpi![36]

Two further remarks and we may leave *S.P.Q.V.* By shifting the order of Pallavicino's satire and beginning St. Paul's earthly visit at Venice, Howell manages to incorporate into *S.P.Q.V.* almost the entire text of his *St. Pauls Late Progress.* And when he has completed his account of Venice, he offers the reader a reflection upon his own method and ideal of writing "history" —a sentiment which he shared with his model, Sarpi: "Thus have we drawn at length the History of *Venice* in the smallest thread we could and freest from thrumbs, the Author being a profess'd enemy to superfluities, and im-material circumstances."[37]

A considerably later work of Howell's, his *Proedria Basilike: A Dis-course Concerning the Precedency of Kings . . . Whereunto is also adjoynd a distinct Treatise of Ambassadors, &c.* (London, 1664),[38] is the only other of his works in which I detect a sizable and unmistakable Sarpian element. At the outset Howell gives a list of "The Civilians, Antiquaries, and His-torians, both *Latin, English, British, Italians, Spanish*, and *French*, that were consulted, and Cited in the Compilement of this Work." Twenty-one names represent the English; thirty, all the other tongues mentioned. Below the list he adds the following remark: "Besides these Authors, many Ancient Rec-ords and Manuscripts have bin consulted; and the perusing of old Parch-ment-Records is a hard and harsh Work; it may be said to be like the peeling of old Walnuts."[39] But the list does not name Sarpi.

After the preliminaries, the body of the work is divided into four main sections: (1) "The King of Great Britain" (pp. 8–98); (2) "The King of France" (pp. 99–136); (3) "The King of Spain" (pp. 137–76); (4) "Of Ambassadors" (pp. 210–14). In the final section Howell's ninth "decade" (pp. 210–14) concerns "the wise Compliances, and Witty facetious Sayings and Carriage of divers Ambassadors." Among these (recalling other works by Howell) are numerous sayings (pp. 211–13) of Gondomar.

But the principal piece of Sarpian interest is contained in that part of the volume which deals with the King of France. Here, in a discourse forming part of the Tenth "decade," Howell gets down to "Examples and Historical Authority":

> Now, touching the point of Precedence, the notablest Contests that France hath had, have been with *Spain* in the *Council* of *Trent*, which lasted so many long years by intermissions: the relations whereof lie scatterd up and down in divers Histories, but we shall endeavour to give here a distinct and uninterrupted Narration thereof, but first we will speak of a signal Contest in *Venice*.[40]

I pass by this Venetian episode (pp. 119–22) to come directly to a special section—set apart, as was the "Interdict" portion of *S.P.Q.V.*—which he entitles "*Of the Council of* Trent" (pp. 122–32) and which he terminates with the following statement: "Thus you have a kinde of Epitome of the great *Council* of *Trent*, specially of the celebrous Contests, Intrigues, Competitions and Artifices twixt *France* and *Spain* in point of Prerogative of Place, and Priority of Session" (p. 132). This "Epitome," however, is not drawn from "divers Histories" "scatterd up and down," but comes straight from Sarpi's account, as may be seen in the correspondence of language, of fact, and of sequence in the following representative passages.

A

Howell: Upon the 21 of May [1563], at the General Congregation, the intention of the *Spaniards* appeerd more cleer: The Count of *Luna* after the foresaid solemn *Entry* absconded himself for 40 days, without appeering openly in any *Ceremony* or publik *Act*; and so being puzzled what cours to take in this busines, Somtimes he resolvd to enter the Assembly in the midst of the Emperours Ambassadors, and after they were sate to stand by them while his Commission was verified, and then retire to his House. But thinking this Cours not generous enough for his Masters honor, He prayed the *French* Ambassadors not to be there that day; which being denied him, the Spanish Bishops proposd that *Secular* Ambassadors shold be prayed not to enter the General Congregations, but only the day of their *Reception*, and that They wold be contented to assist the Ceremony at the *Session* only; alledging, that it was practisd so in other General Councils. But all the Ambassadors did mainly oppose this.[41]

Sarpi-Brent (1620 ed.): In the Congregation of the 21. of May the Count of *Luna* was received, forty daies after his arrivall, in regard of the difficulties for precedence with the French Ambassadors. In the mean while, many consultations were held to compose them; but the French would by no meanes yeeld that hee should have any place but below, and after them. Whereupon he thought to stand on his feet in the midst of the place amongst the Emperors Ambassadours (who had order from their Master to accompany him) and to stand by them untill he had finished his oration, and then to returne presently to his house. But this seemed dishonourable for the King. Therefore he laboured to perswade the French not to enter the Congregation that day; whereunto they not consenting, he thought to force them to it, by making some Spanish Prelat demaund, that Secular Ambassadours might not assist in the Congregations, because they were never admitted in the ancient Councells.[42]

B

Howell: The day of the *Session* being come, which was 29 *June*, being St. *Peters* day, after that the Bishop of *Valdasto* in *Savoy* had begun to sing the Mass of the *Holy Spirit*, ther was suddenly a chair of Black Velvet brought from the Sacristía or Vestry, which was plac'd twixt the last Cardinal and the first Patriark, wherin the Count of *Luna* sate; The Cardinal of *Lorain*, together with the *French* Ambassadors, made a great noise, and did rise up with an intention to depart, when they understood that the *Pax* and the *Censer* should be presented at the same time: But for fear to trouble the solemnity of the act, they were contented to protest only against it, and to declare that the *Right* of the King of *France* did not consist in an *Equality*, but in *Precedence*.[43]

Sarpi-Brent (1620 ed.): *Morone*, according to the Popes commaund, concealed the order, neither did the Frenchmen know of it at all. On Saint *Peters* day, the 29. of June, the Cardinals, Ambassadours, and Fathers being assembled in the Chappell of the Cathedrall Church, and the *Masse* being begun, which the Bishop of *Asti*, the Duke of *Savoy* his Ambassadour, did celebrate, on a sudden a murrey velvet chaire came out of the Vestry, and was placed between the last Cardinall, and the first Patriarke: and by and by the Count of *Luna*, the Spanish Ambassadour, came in, and sat upon it; whereat the Prelats kept a great murmuring. *Loraine* complained to the Legate of this sudden Act, concealed from him. The French Ambassadours sent the Master of the ceremonies to make the same complaint; telling them of the ceremonies of the *Incense* and the *Pax*. The Legats answered there would be two *Censers* and two *Paxes*; wherewith the French were not satisfied, and said plainly, that they would be maintained, not in paritie, but in precedence.[44]

These instances will suffice to illustrate Howell's use of Sarpi; but the whole eleven pages of his account would show similar correspondence. Since Howell sometimes gives a statement or a speech in Latin, he may perhaps also have considered the Latin translation of Sarpi.

A strongly anti-Catholic writer with a lively interest in Sarpi was William Denton, M.D. (1605–1691), the Oxford-educated physician to Charles I and, after the Restoration, the Physician in Ordinary to the royal household. His witty and pleasant conversation is said to have made him a favorite among the women of Charles's court; but his writings are all serious, strictly religio-political.

The first of them in point of time is entitled *Horae Subsecivae: or, a Treatise Shewing the Original Grounds, Reasons, and Provocations necessitating our Sanguinary Laws against Papists* (London, 1664). This is described on the title page as being "By D. W. Esq." The general thesis of the pamphlet, expressed in the running title is "Death inflicted on Roman Catholicks, Not for Religion, but for Treason." Nowhere in the eighty-four pages of text is Sarpi mentioned; but a comparison of texts and a paralleling with later products of Denton's pen show that he is indebted to Sarpi for his account of the quarrel between Pope Paul V and Venice,[45] "the wisest Republick in the world," and for a series of remarks on the expulsion of the Jesuits from Venetian territory.[46] A single brief passage will serve to illustrate Denton's utter dependence:

> Wherefore 14. *Junii* 1606. they did decree, That that [*sic*] the *Congregation* of *Jesuites*, having been received at *Venice* from their first beginning, and there ever since favoured, they on the contrary returning nothing but *Ingratitude* towards the *Republick*, and shewing themselves still inclinable to do all sorts of evil offices to the *State*; in which disposition they yet continued by insupportable Enterprizes, and insolent Calumnies, seeking all occasions to offend them. For these causes they should never be admitted or received in any place of the *State*, nor this Decree revoked, unless the whole Process against them were first read in full *Senate*, (*which consists of* 180 *Senators*) should give suffrage for their *Revocation*. And this was one certain Argument of their enormous

and evident crimes, that there was not any one person of so great a number, who spake any thing in favour of them: and in the *Scruteny* made
by secret voices, all were found unanimous to decree their perpetual
banishment.[47]

As may be seen, this differs hardly a word from its original in Sarpi:

> All was proposed in *Senate*, who deliberated hereupon the fourteenth
> of *June*, and made the Decree which followeth; That the Congregation
> of *Jesuites* having beene received at *Venice* from their first beginning,
> and there ever since favoured, they on the contrary returning nothing
> but ingratitude towards the *Republique*, and shewing themselves still in-
> clined to doe all sorts of evill Offices to that *State*: in which disposition
> they yet continued by insupportable enterprises, and insolent calumnies,
> seeking all occasions to offend them: For these causes, they should never
> be admitted or received in any place of the *State*, nor this Decree re-
> voked, unlesse the whole Processe against them were first read in full
> *Senate*, (which consists of no lesse than 180. Senators,) whereof five
> parts (the whole being composed of six) should give suffrage for their
> revocation. And this may be one certain argument of their enormous
> and evident crimes, that there was not any one Person (of so great a
> number) who spake any thing in favour of them: and in the Scrutiny
> made by secret voices, all were found unanimous to decree their per-
> petuall banishment.[48]

A decade or so later Denton has become a little more explicit about his
sources—though not much. In *The Burnt Child dreads the Fire: or an
Examination of the Merits of the Papists, Relating to England, mostly from
their own Pens* (London, 1675), with respect to papal worship of images, he
can call one of his witnesses *almost* by name, even though the evidence is
only hearsay:

> Take but the judgment of one of your own Church, even of that
> incomperable Servite, who lived and died in the same Communion: At
> the end of the Confession of his Faith, (whereof he hath made 54
> Articles, much more Orthodox than those of *Trent*,) concludes thus:
> *viz. Quemadmodum credimus de ceremoniis sacramentorum quod
> nomini fas sit eas immutare, sic etiam credimus de lege dei, nulli mor-
> talium hic licere quidquam Innovare, detrahere aut adjicere; quia scrip-
> tum est,* Deut. 4. 2. *Ne addite ad verbum illud quod praecipio vobis*
> neque detrahite *de eo.*
>
> *Homini itaque Christiano fas non est detruncare Decalogum, quod
> tamen fecit Pontifex Romanus, cum propter commodum suum expunxit
> praeceptum de non faciendis Imaginibus ne plebs persentisceret imagines
> eius atque Idola a Deo esse prohibita,* f. 255.[49]

One other passage is given a half-hearted identification:

> As much as they are troubled with Compulsion, when it is used against themselves, yet they can glory in it when they use it against others; Witness *Peter Damesius* the French Kings Ambassador to the Council of *Trent*, who in his solemn Oration to that Synod, vapoured, that the Kings of *France* had never suffered any Sect in any part of *France*, nor any but Catholicks; yea, have procured the conversion of Strangers, Idolaters and Hereticks, and have constrained them with pious Arms to profess the true and sound Religion, (*rectius Heresie.*) He shewed how *Childibert* compelled the *Visigothes* (who were *Arrians*) to joyn themselves to the Catholick Church; and how *Charles* the Great made Wars 30 Years with the *Saxons* to reduce them to Christian Religion. *Cons. Tr.* 186.[50]

The appended reference is perfectly adequate for identification of Denton's source. It simply doesn't tell the reader that the last two-thirds of the passage, beginning with the phrase "the Kings of *France*" and excluding the parenthetic "*rectius Heresie*," are drawn verbatim from the Brent translation. We should be grateful, I suppose, for even so much acknowledgment.

There is no problem of underrecognition for Sarpi in the next of Denton's performances, his translation, *A Treatise of Matters Beneficiary*.[51] The small folio (of only eighty-four pages) is dedicated "To the King's most excellent Majesty," and most of the dedicatory epistle is taken up with eulogy of Sarpi. It shows Denton in some characteristic phrasings and attitudes. I transcribe about four-fifths of it.

> May it please your Majesty,
>
> To give me leave most humbly to offer unto Your Majesties perusal, a small Posthumous work of a poor *Theatine* of the *Order* of *Servi* newly taught *English*, who Lived and Dyed in the *Communion* of the *Church* of *Rome*, yet happily as worthily *Great*, as that or any other Age, either before or since hath produced. *Great*, for universal Learning, for wisdom in Councils, for discerning right reason from Sophistical-Schoolquirks, for faithfully recording *Antient Monuments* and *customs* of the *Church*, so that every one that reads them may safely swear, not only to the truth, but to the Impartiality of them, being written without respect to this or that *Church* in particular, but to *Holy Church* in general. *Great*, for soundness of Judgment, for admirable dexterity in summing up intricate, wrangling and prevaricating disputes, into short perspicuous and pithy Results: *Great* also, for Holyness of Life and Conversation, contentedness and moderation of desires, not seeking high things for himself (thereby imitating Christ himself, who when the

Multitude would have taken him by force to make him a King, with-drew himself into a Mountain alone) never altering his Habit, Condition, or Cell, though esteemed the very Oracle of *Venice*; who stoutly, yet with great Modesty and Reverence towards his *Holy Father* the *Pope*, defended the just Rights of that *Wise Republick*, against his *Holiness* and all his *Conclave*, to his eternal Honour, confounding all the wits (which were not few) of that Age by the effort of invincible reason, fairly appealing to the Judgment of all the world by his Pen, and at the end and close of the Accommodation, refusing to give Rome itself the satisfaction, though but of words, and esteemed as insignificant the *Popes Breve* offered for taking away his Censures and his *Instrument* of *Absolution*, and the *Instrument* for the *delivery* of the *Prisoners*, and the *decree* of the *Senate* for the *Restitution* of the *Religious*, &c. All wyles and tricks of the *Court* of *Rome* granted (Covertly and with design to Cajole) unto the *Cardinal* of *Joyeuse*, which they did not dare to divulge in formal Copies, but only dispersed under-hand some Abridgements of them to Amuse, and cheat the World. He so confounded the *Jesuits* that that State so Solemnly Banished them their Dominions, that they were never to be re-admitted, nor the Decree revoked, unless the whole Process against them were first read in full Senate, whereof five parts of six should give Suffrage for their Revocation: And who, though by the Constitution of that Republick, as an Eccelesiastick could not formally sit in their Council, yet that State had that Esteem for him, that they so far dispensed, as that he was permitted to sit therein behind a Curtain, that he might be Master of all their Debates and Advisoes, and in due time and place give his own. I might add much more concerning the *Articles* of his *Faith*, whereof there are 54 at the end of his *History* of the *Inquisition*, Published in *Latin* by *Andreas Colvius*, Printed at *Roterdam* 1651, where he is Stiled *Splendor & Ornamentum Orbis*, the *Glory* and *Ornament* of the *World*, but I forbear, lest under pretence of an *Epistle Dedicatory*, I should seem to write an *Epitaph*. If I have too far transgress'd already, I can only plead for my excuse, that he being rested from his Labours, it is but just, that his good works should follow him, and his praises celebrated.[52]

There follows this laudatory epistle an announcement of "The Printer to the Reader" (p. [v]) in which the printer explains why he has printed so brief a treatise in such a large format. He has done so, he says, in order "that it may suit and be Bound with the Authors other small works, lately Printed with his History of the *Council* of *Trent*, to which ere-long I hope more may be added."

Other works of Denton's show a continued regard for and draft upon

Sarpi—his *Jus Caesaris*, for instance.[53] Here, although he had translated *A Treatise of Matters Beneficiary* in the preceding year, he is so laughably confused and unintelligible in his reference to Sarpi on benefices (p. 87) that it is difficult to tell which work of Sarpi's is referred to. What is one to make of an entry that reads "*Hist. Coun: Fr. Petro Soave Polano. Trattato delle Beneficiare*"? But another passage in this work, concerning the origin and operation of the Inquisition, is easier going. Most of the information and part of the wording are drawn from Sarpi:

> Into the Kingdom of *Naples* it was not brought, there being little correspondence between the *Popes*, and the *Kings* thereof. In the Year 1484. the *King* of *Spain* admitted it into his Dominions; yet so cautionate and jealous was he, as he reserved himself to be *Lord paramount* thereof, of choosing the *Inquisitor General*, who the *Pope* confirms: And for the rest, the *Court of Rome* was not admitted to intermeddle any farther; so that though the King seemed willing to gratifie the *See Apostolick*, yet did he reserve the Supremacy of Power, over all Causes and Persons Ecclesiastical, to himself; and so doth the *State of Venice*, by their *Coadjutors* and *Inspectors* of the *Tribunals Inquisitory*. In which Republick, the Inquisition doth not depend on the *Court of Rome*, but properly belongs to the Republick Independent, set up and constituted by the same, and established by contract and agreement with *Pope Nicholas the Fourth, prout* in his *Bull* of 28. *Aug.* 1289. wherein is inserted the very determination of the greater Council made the *fourth* of the same Month. And therefore, as they ought, are to be governed by their own Customs and Ordinances, without being obliged to receive Orders from the *Pope*: And indeed before the admittance of the *Inquisition* there was in effect the same Office, though meerly Secular, to which *Noblemen* were raised, to enquire after *Hereticks*; and this the Republick made good afterwards against the See-Apostolick, in the Years 1289. 1301. 1605. 1606. and 1607. upon Disputes, maintaining their Civil Authority *in Ecclesiasticis* to be their undoubted Right, and cannot be taken away by any *Bull* or *Decree*, made in any manner, by any *Pope* to whom soever. *Hist. Inquisit.*[54]

An appendix to *Jus Caesaris*, entitled "Unreasonableness of some Popish Doctrines," cites "Padre Paolo. Hist. of the Inquisition, *Sparsim*" on one of Sarpi's favorite themes, papal juggling with suppression of books favorable to secular authority as against ecclesiastical.[55] And in the same appendix Denton makes a remark that shows him to have been alert to other activities and interests of Sarpi:

> During the Quarrels between Pope *Paul* the Fifth, and the State of *Venice*, there wanted not *Writers* that reckoned up the intollerable *oppres-*

sion of *Princes*, by *Popes*, who both in times past and present, make lamentable and continual complaints of them. A Catalogue of which Books may be seen at the end of the Memoirs of *Philip de Canay*, and also in *Goldastus*.[56]

"Frier Paolo" is presently cited again, this time, fittingly, to controvert an argument of Bellarmine's.[57] A final item in Denton's *Jus Caesaris*—though separately paged—is entitled "An Apology for the Liberty of the Press." And this also calls upon Sarpi for expert testimony: "It hath been long since observed by the judicious and worthy *Servite Padre Paolo*, to be plain by all Histories, that Ecclesiastical Jurisdiction and Liberty hath occasioned all the Disputes and differences which have happened between his *Holiness* and other *Princes* in these latter Ages (p. 4)." This carries no identification as to specific work, but derives from "The Exposition of the nine and twentieth Chapter" of *The History of the Inquisition*.

Still another work of Denton's, *Jus Regiminis: being a Justification of Defensive Arms* (London, 1689), without naming a specific work, instances Sarpi as an advocate of "lawful resistance of unlawful Force": "*Padre Paolo*, eminent for his great Learning, Judgment and Faithfulness in all his Writings" (p. 74). Within this volume a final work (without separate title page, though paginated and signatured separately) is "Some Remarks Recommended unto Ecclesiasticks of all Perswasions." It, too (p. 38), recalls "Padre Paolo" on abuses within the Church—presumably in reference to the *Historia del Concilio Tridentino*.

In sum, Denton seems to have been thoroughly acquainted with several works of Paolo Sarpi—*The History of the Quarrels of Pope Paul V. with the State of Venice, The History of the Council of Trent, The History of the Inquisition*, and *A Treatise of Matters Beneficiary*, which he translated. Such familiarity with the historical writings of Sarpi entitles Denton to be heard respectfully when he offers his praise of "that incomperable Servite."

8 --- Plutarch — Somewhat Diminished

IN THE SAME YEAR that Edward Brown was finding Fra Fulgenzio's *Vita* of Sarpi mismanaged in its English version and was planning, as we have seen,[1] to make his own more satisfactory rendering, a book was published by another clergyman who had found the *Life* quite useful and much to his taste. The book was a posthumous publication, its author having died almost a quarter of a century earlier. That author was John Hacket (1592–1670), identified on the title page of his book as "Late Lord Bishop of Lichfield and Coventry." His book was called, in its full dress, *Scrinia Reserata: A Memorial Offer'd to the Great Deservings of John Williams, D.D. Who some time held the Places of L^D Keeper of the Great Seal of England, L^D Bishop of Lincoln, and L^D Archbishop of York. Containing a Series of the Most Remarkable Occurrences and Transactions of his Life, in Relation both to Church and State* . . . (In the Savoy, 1693). A remarkable book and not the least "Remarkable Occurrence" in the history of Sarpi's fortunes in seventeenth-century England.

As a Bishop, the author, not unnaturally, was a strong royalist. He was also a loyal (not to say ardent) advocate of Williams's policies and actions— so that the biography tends a bit toward the hagiographic. Hacket quotes classic and modern authors freely, disgresses often, and is somewhat longer-winded than is necessary. But in the process he does record many events and names of interest. His narrative, because of Williams's immediate connection with de Dominis, provides much information and comment on the doings of that unhappy man. He is a frequent quoter of Spenser,[2] Bacon,[3] and Jonson;[4] and he refers to *"Sir Roger Twisden,* a noble Scholler."[5] Although he does not quote directly from Sarpi at any point,[6] he quite obviously (and *almost* self-admittedly) has taken Micanzio's *Life* of Sarpi as his great model —but with some disparity of scale: Micanzio's *Vita* is a duodecimo of 300 pages; Hacket's *Scrinia Reserata* is a folio in two separately paged parts of 228 and 230 pages!

For one who sees parallels from beginning to end in the lives of his two heroes, Hacket is not always alert to his opportunities. In fact, he misses one at the very outset. Speaking of the young Williams's prodigious memory, he says, "I think *bôna fide*, there was no man born more like to *Eumnestes* in our Divine Poet Mr. *Spencer's* Description, Recording all Things which this World doth *weld*, laying them up in his Immortal Scrine, where they for ever Incorrupted dwelt."[7] The Spenser reference is apt, and perhaps suggested to Hacket the title for his biography; but he can hardly have failed to see—even if he failed to remember—Fra Fulgenzio's emphasis on precisely this gift in the young Sarpi.[8]

He has not proceeded far beyond this point, however, before he lays his cards on the table. Williams, says his biographer, was of an equable disposition and nonpartisan turn of mind.

> Therefore how many Slanders must they put up quietly, who were of Mr. *Williams* his Equanimity, sociable with them that were in point-blank Contradiction in some Quarrels of Polemical Divinity, nay as ready to prefer the one side as the other, how sure is this to be called by our *Furioso's* lukewarm and undigested Christianity? I have seen the Life of the Renowned Frier *Padre Paulo* of *Venice*, written in *Italian* by his *Confrere Fulgentio*, and Translated tersely and faithfully into *English* by that Gentleman of great and elegant Parts Mr. *John Saintamand*, sometimes Secretary to the Heroical Prelate, of whom I write, when he was Lord-Keeper: Out of that Piece I shall observe many Things, as I can overtake them in fitness of Time; this comes to me now under my Hand, that *Fulgentio* cannot deny, that Father *Paul* was Libel'd for a stupid insensible Man, quite careless of Religion, because when two perhaps were divided which was the Truth, he made a good Construction of them both.[9]

Hacket then proceeds to relate how the good Williams, refusing to take sides in a current "vehement" dispute between a faction supporting Augustine on the efficacy of Grace and another attacking him, was for his moderation looked upon by both sides as guilty of "Sluggishness, Craftiness, Neutrality and the like; as if in points unfundamental and unresolv'd, every man must be a *Guelph* or a *Gibelline*."[10]

Concerning Williams's range of interest and abilities—especially his study of the law—which made possible the focusing within a single individual of the highest achievements in politics and divinity (or, with Sarpi, of divinity and politics), Hacket remarks:

> It were a Tyranny, more then barbarous, to confine a Wit, that hath a Plummet to sound the depth of every Well that the Arts have digged; or to clip his Wings, that he may not fly into every Bush as freely as the Fowls of the Air. *Padre Paulo* the Frier, the brightest Star in the Hemisphere of *Italy*, was second to none in Divinity while he liv'd; equal with the best Doctors in *Rome* or *Siena* in explicating Canon or Civil Laws; and above all the Practisers of Padua, or in the World, in understanding the *Aesculapian* Art, says *Fulgentius*.[11]

For our purposes there is no need to follow the chronology of Williams's career, but a few facts and dates may prove useful. He was a descendant of an ancient Welsh family, was educated at St. John's College, Cambridge (B.A. 1601, M.A. 1605). His promotion in the church was rapid and smooth, many plums falling into his hands through royal or other powerful favor. Of the three high positions held by him and mentioned in Hacket's title page, he became Lord Keeper after the fall of Bacon (1621), Bishop of Lincoln in the same year (3 August), and was translated to the archbishopric of York 4 December 1640 and enthroned 27 June 1642. His political career, inextricably intertangled with his ecclesiastical, was much more stormy; and after various fines and imprisonments, some lapses from the path of strict moral integrity, and the failure of the royal cause, Williams died in 1650. The very next year saw the publication of St. Amand's translation of Micanzio's *Vita* and Hacket's undertaking of his biography of the late "L^D Archbishop of York." At the moment our concern is with Williams's accession to the Lord Keepership.

Although Hacket recognizes Williams's unlikely preparation for the Lord Keepership when he came to it—no ecclesiastic had held the post for well over half a century—he can still write:

> Neither King *James*, King *Charles*, nor any Parliament, which gave due Hearing to the frowardness of the same Complaints, did ever appoint that any of his Orders should be retexed: Which is not a Pillar of Honour, but a Pyramid. *Fulgentius* hath Recorded the like upon the Wonder of his Age, Father *Paul* of *Venice*, that being Provincial of his Order, and hearing many Causes, none of the Judgments that he gave (which were innumerable), were ever Repealed upon Instance made to higher Judgment. Neither do I find that any of his Fraternity did maunder, that the Frier was a Stripling but 28 years old,[12] and therefore but a Novice to make a Provincial, who is a Judge and a Ruler over his Fellows. He had better luck in that then our Dean,[13] who was 39

years old when he atchieved this great Honour, yet some (it is presumed they were nettled with Emulation) utterly disliked his Age, that it was not wrinkled with Gravity.[14]

On one moderately substantial point Hacket is sadly confused: he does not really know the identity of Sarpi's biographer. Observing that the offenses of de Dominis against the "Court of Rome" were very serious indeed, even more serious than those of that "Fulgentio," who only a little earlier had been entrapped into a fateful return to Rome, he marvels at the addlement of wit that could permit the Archbishop to stick *his* neck into such an obvious noose.

> How durst this bold Bayard look the Court of *Rome* in the Face upon any Terms, whose Writings were more copious against the Amplitude of the Papacy, than ever came out of the Press? An *Italian* never forgives an Injury. But Indignities written, and with the Pen of a Diamond, against the Sublimity Pontifical, are more unpardonable with them, than Blasphemies against Christ. Had Cardinal Mellino, his Confident, been elected Pope, the Pope would have forgotten all that the Cardinal had promised him. What had *Fulgentio* the Servite done, to be compared with his *Scopuli*, and such jerking Books? He had maintained the Venetian just Laws against *Paul* the Fifth's Abrogations; yet ever abode in the Bosom of the Roman Church. He had wrote the Life of Frier *Paul*, whom they hated, to the full pitch of his Praise. But what were these Toys to the Ecclesiastical Republick of *Antonius de Dominis*? Yet after twelve years that *Fulgentio* had provok'd them, he having obtained safe Conduct to go to *Rome*, under the Fisher's Ring, and *Berlingerius Gessius*, the Apostolical Nuntio at *Venice*, pawn'd his Faith to the poor Man for his Incolumity; yet he was cited before the Inquisition, Condemn'd, and Burnt in *Campo di Flora*: And his Ashes were scarce cold, when this daring Wretch came wittingly into the Den of the Lion.[15]

He is, of course, confusing Fulgenzio Manfredi and Fulgenzio Micanzio—it has happened before. The former was the unhappy victim of curial duplicity; the latter was the author of the *Life of Father Paul* and Sarpi's successor as Consultore to the Venetian State. He outlived Sarpi by many years (d. 1654).

We do not meet with another parallel drawn from the Servite Fulgentio until we come to the second part of Hacket's volume. But there the process of seeing double is renewed and, if anything, intensified. Concerning the court spies that were set to watch upon Bishop Williams's actions and words, Hacket says,

> But the Bishop would take no knowledge, that such a Snare was laid; esteeming of it as Physicians do of *Cancer Occultus,* that it is more safe to let it alone, than to go about to cure it: nor was it easie for him to keep in his Freedom: Which yet many times had subtlety mixt with it; such as *Fulgentius* says was in *Padre Paulo,* That he would seem open in his Talk, out of an admirable Dexterity to make others speak freely.[16]

And when Williams, under the machinations of Buckingham and others, had fallen into disfavor with Charles, he refused to believe that the King was really against him—a natural sentiment, perhaps, in one who had enjoyed so much favor under the King's father. The dying James had received his last Communion at the hands of Williams: "Yet still the Bishop would not think his Case was in that extremity, that the Kings Anger was in it: For as it is spoken of *Padre-Paulo,* in his Life, That he was less sensible of Fear than ordinarily men use to be; so this man would affright himself with nothing, least of all, with that which was close and uncertain."[17]

Not all the suggestions of parallels come to Hacket from his basic model: he can see Williams alongside a hero in *The Faerie Queene* or exemplifying a Baconian principle. When the Bishop is being snapped at on all sides and has "no Favour, but Innocency to bear him out," Hacket is reminded of Spenser: "*Honour is least where Odds appear the most,* says our great Poet *Spencer, Lib.* 2. *Cant.* 8." And "when the Brunt was over" and the Bishop might have had revenge but refused to take it, his faithful Boswell is reminded of Bacon: "And my L. *Bacon* tells us well what a Gallantry it is; *For in taking Revenge a man is but even with his Enemies; in passing them over he is superior.*"[18] But Hacket could have found a parallel even for this in Fra Fulgenzio's *Life,* where he writes concerning Sarpi's forgiving spirit towards his attackers: "As a Philosopher . . . he had eradicated out of his soule all spirit of revenge (which is a kinde of savage Justice, but deeply inserted into humane nature)"[19]—phrasing which itself recalls the opening of Bacon's essay.[20]

During the time that he was Dean of Westminster some thirty-six "frivolous" articles of discontent were pressed against him by some of the "Prebendaries of the later Instalment" (p. 91). These the Bishop (or, rather, Dean) was able triumphantly to shake off; and his situation at that moment sends Hacket scurrying to Fra Fulgenzio for a parallel:

> But because there is nothing new under the Sun, I will pluck for a parallel to this in the Life of *Padre Paolo: Soto* and *Archangelo* his profest Enemies, objected against him to Cardinal *Severino* the Grand Inquisitor: First, *That sometime he kept Company with Hereticks.* 2. *That he wore a Cap upon his head.* 3. *That he wore Slippers after the French fashion.* 4. *That he did not recite* Salve Regina *at the end of the*

Mass. Flea-bites, like the former, of which you can see no mark in an hour.[21]

Again, when the Bishop was attacked for his position concerning a trivial matter of ceremony, his biographer saw a parallel to Sarpi: "It was a Task most laudably perform'd by *Whitgift, Bridges, Hooker, Morton, Burgess*, to maintain the use of innocent Ceremonies, with whom Bishop *Williams* did ever jump; and, as *Fulgentius* says in P. *Paulo's Life*, would defend and observe all Ordinances, the least considerable, and no whit essential."[22]

Once the Bishop was attacked in a "libel," which, instead of ignoring, he chose to answer—even though a number of cogent reasons should have cautioned him to silence:

> The Bishop had more reason to take that course, because the Rulers of the time frowned on him; and he that Answers a Calumny keeps it alive, he that will not, starves it: . . . 'Tis much he did not listen to this, and if it were but for another reason, that he thought Learning did surfeit of too many Books, and that the most of our late Authors were more troublesome than profitable: To which Sir H. Wootton's Motto comes near, *That the Itch of Writing makes a Scabby Church.* And what else made so great a Wit as Fryer *Paul* profess, (it is in his Life) *That he would never write any thing with intention to print it, unless Necessity constrain'd him?*[23]

The Bishop of Lincoln, fallen into the toils of his enemies by means of intercepted letters and alleged conspiracy against his superiors, reminds Hacket of Sarpi and of that "troublesome persecution" brought upon him by the ambition and unprincipled intriguing of Gabriele Collisoni:

> What a Spider's Thread is here to pull a Man into the *Star-Chamber* by it? So *Fulgentius* tells us of *Padre Paulo*, that he wrote a Letter in Cypher to *Gabriel Collison*, touching at the Court of *Rome*, as if some came to Dignities by evil Services; which *Collison* revealed to St. *Severino*, Cardinal, and Head of the Office of Inquisition, for which *Paul* was trounced with continual disturbance. And our Inquisitor St. *Severo*, did not make use of the like, or rather less opportunity.[24]

Passing over Hacket's bitter, railing attack on Milton, "that black-mouth'd *Zoilus*," that "petty School-boy Scribler" who dared say nasty things about the *Eikon Basilike*, and "durst graple . . . with the Prince of the learned men of his Age, *Salmasius*"—and many other interesting matters—we come to what is probably the strangest moment in this strangest of Plutarchian exercises: the death of the Hero. When Hacket comes to relate the death of *his* hero, he cannot resist seeing in it parallel circumstances to the death of Fra Fulgenzio's:

He is gone before me, whom I desir'd not to outlive: A Squinancy, whereof he dyed, was the Death of the only Pope that was born in *England, Hadrian* the Fourth: But the whole Conflux of the Disease that took him away, was in all circumstances the same with *Padre-Paulo's* the Servite, as the Author of his Life sets it down, that his Feet could receive no warmth, (the same Symptom that laid hold of this Prelate) and that a Catarrh destroyed him. There are many Diseases dangerous and mortal; this is often cured by the launce of a sorry Chyrurgion, of whom there was none in that place.[25]

"In all circumstances the same"! Was the good Bishop remembering the lament of David: "Saul and Jonathan were lovely and pleasant in their lives, and in their death they were not divided"?

Bishop Hacket's own *Life* was written by a fellow clergyman, Thomas Plume, and published in 1675 as *An Account of the Life and Death of the Right Reverend Father in God, John Hacket, late Lord Bishop of Lichfield and Coventry*.[26] It is a far less compelling and singular account than Hacket's *Scrinia Reserata*, but it provides information on a point or two of interest to this study of Sarpi, and it introduces us to the owner of one of the most important private libraries in the England of the late-seventeenth century.

With respect to Hacket's royalism, Plume says what we might have guessed for ourselves from reading the *Scrinia Reserata*, that

to the memory of King James no man living bore greater respect than our Bishop did for his great wisdom, learning, pacific disposition and affection to the Church, to which he thought he might be styled a bene-factor equal to Constantine the great. His life he long intended to write, and to that purpose the Keeper [Williams] conferred upon him Mr. Camden's MS. Notes of that King's reign till his own death, 1623; and his dear friend and fellow servant, Mr. John St. Amand [translator, it will be recalled, of Micanzio's *Vita del Padre Paolo*], communicated to him many choice letters and secrets of State of his own collection, who in like manner designed the same thing, to whom the Bishop recommended the perfecting thereof.[27]

Plume also notices a quality in Hacket which the Bishop had himself emphasized in his characterizations of Archbishop Williams and Sarpi—his tendency to seek a moderate position:

In the Quinquarticular Controversy[28] he was ever very moderate, but being bred under Bishop Davenant, and Dr. Ward, in Cambridge, was addicted to their Sentiments. Bishop Usher would say, Davenant understood those Controversies better than ever any man did since S. Austin; but he used to say, he was sure he had three excellent men of his mind in this controversy. 1. Padre Paulo, whose Letter is extant to Henisius, 1604. 2. Thomas Aquinas. 3. S. Austin.[29]

From the collocation of names in the last sentence, it would appear that Father Paul was thought of as traveling in very select company. For his presence on the shelves and for some of the company he kept there, we turn now to the catalogue of the library of the Reverend Thomas Plume, D.D. (1630–1704).[30] Plume's library is preserved virtually as the Doctor left it and contains, I estimate, approximately six thousand titles.

The Sarpi entries in the *Catalogue* (listed under Paolo, *Servita*: p. 129) are the following:

> An apology, or appologeticall answere made . . . unto . . . Cardinall Bellarmine. *4to.* 1607. *STC* 21757.
> — The free schoole of warre. *4to.* 1625. *STC* 21758.
> — Historiae Concilii Tridentini libri octo. *fol. Augustae Trinobantum* [London]. 1620. [*STC* 21764.]
> — The historie of the Councel of Trent. fol. 1640. *STC* 21763.
> — The history of the quarrels of Pope Paul V, with the State of Venice. *4to.* 1626. *STC* 21766.
> — Interdicti Veneti historia. *4to. Cantabrigiae,* 1626. *STC* 21767.
> — Quaestio quodlibetica. *4to. Cantabrigiae,* 1630. *STC* 21768.

Also present are Fulgenzio Micanzio's *The Life of the Most Learned Father Paul* (1651) and six works from the pen of Marco Antonio de Dominis: *De pace religionis . . . epistola* (1666), *De Republica Ecclesiastica libri x* (1617–1622), *A Manifestation of the Motives* (1616), *Papatus Romanus* (1617), *The Rockes of Christian Shipwracke* (1618), and *A Sermon Preached . . . in the Mercers Chappell* (1617). If he had read them all, the Reverend Thomas Plume would have felt quite at home in the terrain we have thus far traversed. And probably his interest would not have flagged in what is to follow.

9 --- A Parcel of Parsons (and Some of Their Friends): Pre-Restoration

INASMUCH AS SARPI was identified with Venetian defiance of the interdict and was known as anti-Curialist, Englishmen tended, not altogether logically, to consider him also anti-Catholic, or quasi-Protestant. And since everything he wrote was of politico-religious concern, it is not at all surprising to find his works most commonly read, cited, and discussed by clergymen. References to "Father Paul" abound on all sides, but particularly in sermons and in treatises on ecclesiastical matters. It is, of course, not always feasible or sensible to distinguish between secular and ecclesiastical performances; but it will be convenient in this chapter to examine in a group some selected writings of a score or more clerics.

As good a starting point as any is a work written by George Carleton, D.D., Bishop of Chichester and cousin of Dudley Carleton. We have already met him—in Venice, where in 1613 he had sent to Sarpi a copy of his *Consensus Ecclesiae Catholicae contra Tridentinos*, the book which his cousin Dudley, the English ambassador, thought responsible for determining the form of Sarpi's *Historia del Concilio Tridentino*.[1] We renew our acquaintance with him now for the purpose of looking at a copy of one of his books which does not contain even a mention Sarpi, but which has, nevertheless, a considerable Sarpian interest. This is his *Directions to know the True Church* (London, 1615), printed (like his *Consensus*) by John Bill, King's printer; and the copy of it with which we are concerned is preserved in the British Museum.[2] This little volume contains manuscript notes in at least two hands, one that of an eighteenth-century owner who has supplied full and occasionally vitriolic remarks. The argument of the work is that the English Church is the *true* Catholic Church, keeping old ideals and traditions which Rome itself observed before the corruptions of the Council of Trent.

Under the date on the title page the eighteenth-century owner, realizing the affinity of arguments, has written: "Before the Printing of Fra P. Paolo Sarpi's Histy of the Trent-Council." On pages 75 to 77 (of Carleton's text) we read: "This Councill of *Trent*, (to give you some taste of it) was neither generall, nor free, nor lawfull . . . [Yet] This is that Councill that hath changed the faith of the Church, that was held from the Apostles to that time unchanged." Opposite the passage on page 75, in the margin, the same eighteenth-century owner has written: "See Fra Paolo's truest History of it in Italian but translated into Latin, & French (by the late Elegant Dr Courayer with excellent notes) & English."

At the end, for the purpose of exposing their ridiculousness, Carleton cites certain decrees and opinions of the Council of Trent, bringing in the doctrine that "the revelation of God made to the Church . . . is divided* into two partie-rules, Scripture, and Traditions."[3] The annotator of the manuscript has supplied the asterisk and explains in the margin: "By 40 or 50 ignorant Italian Bishops of Dioceses of 2 or 3 Parishes each, & 2 or 3 Lords Cardinals, & a hundred Lawyers all of them sworn slaves to the Prince-Bp of modern Rome." Carleton's final statement (p. 111) reads: "And therefore if they will seeke a true Church, they must seek such a Church which holdeth still the same rule of faith with the true Church of Christ, which was before the Trent Council, and must stand till the end of the world." To this the annotator supplies the remark—drawn from Sarpi's own text[4]—"Pope Paul 4th called these Trentines to Cardinal Bellay sessanta Vescovi di manco habili et quaranta Dottori de meno sufficienti, that is, 60 Bishops of the Less Learned, and 40 Doctors of Lesser abilities."

Another document of which the interest is basically its manuscript annotations, but unfortunately a volume lacking any indication of provenance, is a copy of the first Latin translation of the *Historia del Concilio Tridentino* preserved in the Bodleian Library.[5] In this, as in the Twysden copies, we see the results of intensive study and of painstaking annotations. These latter, however, do not consist of commentary. They are, instead, restricted to underscoring and the supplying of page equivalents for the English edition—which a comparison shows to have been that of 1620. Hundreds of lines are underscored throughout all eight Books, fewer, possibly, in the last two Books than elsewhere, though even they have clearly been read with the utmost care. A few symbols also appear in the margins, and occasionally a page will lack underscorings but nevertheless will carry a reference to the corresponding page in the English text. Presumably the volume was given this elaborate preparation for the purpose of convenient duple reference in some work of religious controversy or discussion. What that work may have been, if it was indeed written, I have so far been unable to discover.

The principal Anglican controverter of de Dominis's *Consilium reditus*, as we have seen, was the learned Richard Crakanthorp. But de Dominis was not the only Romanist with whom he crossed swords—or pens. Another of his victims was the celebrated Neapolitan canonist Dr. Marta, who in Sarpi's later days was a professor at Padua and a malcontented informer in the pay of James I. Crakanthorp's blast was contained in a fat quarto of over eight hundred pages in three parts entitled *The Defence of Constantine*.[6] The *Defence* is an attack on the alleged "Donation of Constantine" and an overwhelming refutation of the arguments in favor of it presented by Steuchus, the Vatican Librarian; by Gretzer, the German Jesuit; and by Dr. Marta. Much of the book is, in fact, a point-by-point refutation and demolishing of Marta. Throughout, Crakanthorp accuses (and convicts) Marta of looseheaded logic, of falsifying sources, of deliberate fabrications in his dogged attempts to support the indefensible papal claims to temporal authority. Sarpi is not quoted or mentioned; but the attitude assumed by Crakanthorp is implicit or explicit in almost everything written by the Servite friar.

The second part of Crakanthorp's volume, the "Treatise of the Popes Temporall Monarchy," continues the general theme of papal usurpations and continues to cite the "wrong-headed" arguments of Marta, but thereafter drops him. Interestingly, at one stage in the development of his thesis (that is, that the Pope's claim to temporal authority is false and unfounded), Crakanthorp adduces as evidence the Venetian quarrel with Pope Paul V and ends by quoting Sarpi:

> *Anto. Quirinus*[7] in defence of the Venetian State, writes thus; *Christ did not diminish the rights of Empires, Cities, and Princes, but he confirmed the same, yea he would not in any sort meddle in* that, *quod res mundanas & temporales spectet*, with temporall causes. Againe,[8] *It is most evident, that the Venetian Common-wealth is as a* free Prince, *qui à nemine pendet ex natura sui principatus*, which by the very nature of Principalitie, depends on none: Againe,[9] *This Venetian Common-wealth doth professe Dominium suum à solo Deo habere, quod ipsis est ius fundamentale*, that it hath their dominion from God only, and this is the very fundamentall law of their State; and to this subscribed *Antonius Rebetti, Michael Angelus*, and many others both Divines and Lawyers.[10]

Frier Paul[11] in the same quarrel writes in this manner, *The Venetian State potestatem sibi à Deo datam*, exerciseth that power which is given unto them by God, *even from the beginning of their State unto this time*: And what power that is, he declares, calling it *antiquam & absolutam veri sui Imperii libertatem*, the ancient and absolute, (and therefore not depending on the Pope) libertie of their true Empire.[12]

From the casual manner in which three separate works (two of them Sarpi's) on the Venetian quarrel are thrown into this juxtaposition, it is clear that Crakanthorp was no stranger to the literature of that controversy.

Two slight works printed in 1623, the year of Sarpi's death, continue the Anglican "true Church" vein of Carleton's *Directions*. Both use Sarpi only minimally but give evidence that their authors had been reading *The Historie of the Councel of Trent*. The first of these, by Robert Abbot, "Preacher of Gods Word at Cranebrooke in Kent," is entitled *A Hand of Fellowship, to helpe keepe out Sinne and Antichrist. In certaine Sermons preached upon severall occasions* (London, 1623). In the first sermon—rather longer than could have been conveniently delivered in a preaching "hour"—which is called "Davids Desires" and contrasts Anglican and Catholic religions, we read this odious-invidious comparison:

> If wee should hold a Councell, wee need none of the trickes of the Councell of *Trent*. We need not either propound our Canons in such ambiguous termes, as will admit of divers constructions, like the ancient Oracles of *Apollo*; neither need wee to create either Archbishops or Bishops to fill up the number (that our voyce may be the more full) who have neither Church nor Dioceses. Wee need no bloudie Inquisition to clap the title and punishment of an Heretike upon everie one who doth smell either by conversation or conference of a religion opposite to us.[13]

In the margin, opposite this passage, may be read: "*Upsalensis* and *Armachanus* were created Arch-bishops (as we reade) in the Councell of *Trent*, who yet were Nullatenenses." The reference is undoubtedly to Brent-Sarpi.[14] It is a mere chance that in the margin of the next page one should find a reference to the *Profectionis consilium* of that other highly questionable Archbishop, M. A. de Dominis.

The second work, by Richard Bernard, called *Looke beyond Luther*,[15] is an Anglican attempt to show the "catholicity" and antiquity of the Church of England. In the supplementary part—the "Authors farther helpe to stay the honest-hearted Protestant from Apostacie" (running head)—we read:

> Secondly, if any impious opinions could be found among us, it must be considered, whether they be broched by private persons, or tenents

held by the Church in her publike Records: If the former, then are they not the Churches; if the Church should hold any such, how can they prove, that she maintaineth them obstinately?[16] For obstinacy is not to be imputed unto us, till all lawfull, good, and sufficient meanes have been used to convince our judgement, and the same also by such, as have lawfull and full authority to judge and determine thereof. But hitherto this hath not been done, neither can it be, but by a lawfull and free general Councell, which the Conventicle of Trent was not: till then we are not to be condemned of obstinacy, and so as yet no Heretikes.

At this point the marginal reading runs, not very helpfully, "See the Historie of the Councell of Trent." The advice is good, but we should appreciate some details of "farther helpe to stay" our honest Protestant hearts "from Apostacie"—or, at least, uncertainty.

A small quarto by Anthony Wotton (1561?–1626), a divine of Puritan leanings, *Runne from Rome. Or, a Treatise shewing the necessitie of Separating from the Church of Rome . . .* (London, 1624), poses a minor problem. The work is mainly an anti-Bellarminist tract (one of a great many), but it also looks beyond Bellarmine to the great source of Counter Reformation doctrine. The Epistle, "To the Christian Reader,"[17] informs that reader of the author's intention to "dispute against the doctrine of faith delivered in the said Councell [of Trent]." To put that council in an unfavorable light at the outset, he quotes the following:

> *Andreas Dudithius* Bishop of Quinquecclesiae [Funfkirchen, Petschen in Hungary], and Embassadour in the Council of Trent for Maximilan the second Emperour: in an Epistle [of 1567] to the said Emperour, (wherein he delivereth his judgement about granting the Cup to the Laitie, and the marriage of Priests,) writes thus of the Councell of Trent.

> What good could be done in that Councell where voyces were taken by number, not by weight? If argument, if reason might have prevailed, if we had had some and those not many to take part with us, though we should have bin but a few: yet had we overthrowne the great forces of our adversaries: but when all stood upon number, wherein we were much inferiour, we could not get the better, though our cause were the better. The Pope was able to set an hundreth of his against every one of ours: and if an hundreth were not sufficient, he could upon a sudaine have created a thousand to succour them that were readie to faint and perish. Therefore we might see every day hungrie and needie Bishops, and these for the most part beardlesse Younkers, and wastfully ryotous,

come in flocks to Trent, hired to give their voices according to the Popes humour, unlearned indeed and foolish, but of good use to him for their audaciousnesse and impudence. When these fellowes were joyned to the Popes old flatterers, then iniquitie got the upper hand and triumphed: neither could any thing be decreed but according to their liking, who thought it the highest point of religion to defend the power and royot of the Pope. There was in the Councell a grave and learned man who could not endure this indignitie: but the Councell by terrour threatning and bayting him as one that was no good Catholike, drew him to yeeld to that which he did no way like of. In a word, things are brought to that passe by their dishonesty who came thither prepared and made for the nonce, that it seemed to be a Councell not of Bishops, but of puppies [puppets?]: not of men, but of images, who (as it is reported of *Daedalus* Statues) were moved not by their owne but by other mens nerves, and muscles. These hireling Bishops most of them were like Country Bagpipes, which must have breath blowne into them before they can sound. The holy Ghost had nothing to doe with that Coventicle, all things were argued by human pollicy, which was wholly employed in maintaining the immoderate, & indeed most shamelesse Lordship and Domination of the Pope. From thence were answers looked and wayted for, as it were from the Oracles of *Delphos* or *Dodona*: from thence the holy Ghost, who (as they brag) is President of their Councell, was sent shut up in the Carriers budgets and packes, who (a thing worthy to be laught at) when the waters were up as it falls out many times, was faine to stay till they were downe againe before he could repaire to the Councell. By this is came to passe that the Spirit was not carried upon the waters as in *Genesis*, but along besides the waters. O monstrous and incredible madnes! Nothing that the Bishops as it were the Bodie of the Church resolved of, could be of any force, unlesse it came first from the Pope as the head of the bodie.[18]

Now, the original from which this is translated is in a Latin work of Dudith's which had not, so far as I can discover, previously been translated into English.[19] The quoted part of the letter (from the Apologia—or Excusatio—to the Emperor for Dudith's giving up his bishopric of Five Churches and taking a wife) is an excerpt beginning "quid enim profici potuit in eo concilio" and ending "o portentosam . . . nisi Papa autor fieret." It is precisely this excerpt which is printed in 1620 in the Newton–de Dominis–Bedell Latin translation of Sarpi's *Historia del Concilio Tridentino*. An English version (though differently worded) appears in the *second* (1629) edition of Brent's translation, but is not in the first edition. Unless Wotton was copying some earlier but unrecorded translation, the chances are very strong that he was using the addition to the Latin of Sarpi's *Historia*, rather than the original text of Dudith. The matter is certainly of no great moment, but a slight touch of piquancy is added to the situation by the fact that later in the century the Bishop of Worcester, William Lloyd, in his *Papists no Catholicks: and Popery no Christianity* (London, 1679),[20] copies out and quotes *in extenso*[21] this same block of Dudith's letter, not from Brent but from Wotton. It is a patent case of the High Church plowing with Low Church's heifer.

A more interesting work from almost any point of view is *A Manuduction, or Introduction unto Divinitie: containing a Confutation of Papists by Papists, throughout the important Articles of our Religion; their testimonies taken either out of the Indices Expurgatorii, or out of the Fathers, and ancient Records; but especially the Manuscripts* (Oxford, 1625). This was the work of Thomas James (1573?–1629), first Librarian of the Bodleian. It is not a large book,[22] but it makes large use throughout of de Dominis and Sarpi and has interesting comments on both men. De Dominis is cited primarily because he is considered a "Papist," but perhaps also because of the recency and scandal of his demise.[23]

In his comment on the twenty-second Article, speaking of indulgences, James remarks:

> First, for the originall of them, we subscribe to the *Councell* of *Trent*: *It is certaine, and cannot be concealed, that in no Christian Nation of the Easterne Church, either in ancient or moderne time, there ever was any use of Indulgences of any kind whatsoever. . . . Afterwards, from the Councell of Vienna, the abuses began, which did increase very much, untill the time of Leo the tenth.*[24]

The marginal reference opposite the italicized statements reads: "P. 822. *Hist. Conc. Trid.*"—which might seem to refer to either the Italian or the Latin text. The passage comes, however, straight from Brent's translation. A few pages farther along, James says concerning the abuse of pardons: "If wee cast our eyes upon the History of the Councell of *Trent*, we shall see many horrible abuses of Pardons."[25] And sure enough, when we cast our eyes upon the place suggested in James's reference, we find the case to be as he has said. In speaking of "Reliques and Pilgrimages" (p. 71), James mentions the "dis-sainting" of Becket as a "traytor" and marginally refers to "*Hist. Conc. Trid.* p. 87." Later, touching the nonpreaching of Romanist bishops, James remarks (p. 103): "If you cannot, nor will not learne so much of me, yet learne it of your owne *deere Councell* of *Trent*."[26] In each instance the reference is accurate and is to the text of Brent's translation.

At the end James offers "certaine needfull Advertisements to the Christian Reader" regarding the authors he has principally used, whether of printed or of manuscript books, and whether "purged" or unpurged. Of these last he says:

> I have singled out but three amongst the rest: the first is *Geo. Wicelius*; the second, the *Author of the Councell of Trent*;[27] the third and last is, *Ant. de Dominis*, all which I alleage the more willingly, because all these three were either peace-makers, or reformers of those Additaments, or superadditaments, that time or ignorance, or that evill one hath brought in step by step into the Church of Rome.[28]

He then proceeds, in the following pages, to say something a little more particular about each of these principals. The remarks on Sarpi read thus:

> I will onely touch upon the Author of the Historie of the Councell of Trent, whom (because *Ant. de Dominis*, whom I cannot call *Ant. de Domino*, because he served more Masters, called *Pietro Soare* [sic] I will also call him by that name, doth so farre shew to every one-eyed Reader, that the Councell of Trent, though it were called against, and condemned *Martin Luther*, and his Religion; yet if the Councell had been free, and their voyces decisive without the Pope (though the Italian Bishops were three to one in number) and there had beene no foule play in calculating the voyces, still I say, leaving the clokebag behind, the Councell of Trent might have turned *Lutheran*.[29]

A small work by Alexander Cooke, *The Abatement of Popish Braggs*,[30] still in the controversial mode but cast in a different literary form, also makes some use of *The Historie of the Councel of Trent*. This is a wooden and tedious dialogue between a "Protestant" and a "Papist." One brief quotation is enough—perhaps more than enough—to demonstrate its qualities:

> [*Prot.*] In the Scripture we read expresly, That our Saviour Christ did but *offer himselfe once*: And yet you say. That in precise manner hee offered himselfe twice. Once at his last Supper; and againe upon the Crosse.
>
> *Pa.* Some of us say so indeed: But there was a hot contention about it in the Councell at *Trent*: a good sort maintaining resolutely, That he did not offer himselfe at the last Supper: Of which number that famous *Mussus* was one, who was Preacher at twelve yeeres old, with whom all *Italy* was in admiration. But say on.[31]

A marginal note opposite the reference to the Council of Trent (p. 41) directs the reader to "The History of the Council of *Trent* in English, p. 545

& 555. & 574." The author's further citing of the decrees of the council depends upon the same source. Sarpi's work was, in fact, one of the major arsenals for all those intent upon belittling or confuting the positions held by the "Papalins." But this was a function which his *History of the Council of Trent* shared with his *History of the Interdict (Historia particolare)*: it has been apparent in English writings already considered, and it appears again in *A Treatise of the Holy Catholike Faith and Church* (London, 1627), by Thomas Jackson, Dean of Peterborough. The Dean's *Treatise* is another defense of the Anglican faith as against the Roman, and it is especially argued against Bellarmine. "It is an idle and frivolous distinction," he says.

> which some Canonists have framed to solve the truth of this Popes [Innocent III's] sentence. *Aliud est de re, actione aut contractu iudicare, & aliud iudicare de peccato: It is one thing to determine of the action or cõtract, another to determine or judge of the sin committed.* For as Father[32] *Paul* excellently observes, *quod inseparabile est distinguunt: they put a diversity without a differēce.*[33]

To judge from the language, Jackson had been working from Bedell's Latin *Interdicti Veneti historia*. But whether from the Latin or from the original Italian *Historia particolare*, the facts and the sentiments of the ensuing pages surely go back, ultimately, to Sarpi's account. The following is a fair specimen of the Dean's satiric turn of expression:

> Againe, all of them [that is, the canonists, supporters of the Pope] agree in this, that the Pope hath a supreame independent power to make co-active Ecclesiasticke Lawes for the welfare of the Church; & in as much as all temporall power is subordinate to the power spiritual, which, as his subjects say, is originally and plenarie in himselfe; hee may by vertue of his supreame spirituall power, disanull all such Lawes as any temporall State or Kingdom shall make, if these to his Holinesse unerring spirit, shall seeme contrary to the Lawes of God, or to the Lawes Ecclesiasticke, made by himselfe, or by his predecessors. Now in case any Temporall Princes or States, shall, after some monitions, refuse to repeale such Lawes as they have enacted, but hee dislikes; they stand obnoxious *ipso facto* to the sentence of excommunication.
>
> The exercise of this terrible power hath beene within these 400 yeeres, frequent in many Kingdomes, and famous of late against the *Venetians*. That ancient and renowned State for wisedome and gravity, and of all States professing Romish faith, alwaies most venerable for devotion, had made such a Lawe, as the Law of Mortmaine here in England, for repressing the excesse of *Levies* portion, which was become like a huge deformed wen in a faire and comely body: and being ad-

monished by the Pope to repeale this Law, and another edict necessary
for the preservation of peace; whereby the unruly Cleargie within their
territories were *subjected* to the censure of the State; because the *Venetians* would not obey his monitions, and betray their ancient liberties,
the Duke and Senate were excommunicated by his Holinesse. I do not
well remember, whether that State had made a decree,[34] that no provision should be carried out of their territories to *Ancona*: but put the
case, they had made such a Law, in as much as *Ancona* is a Citie which
belongs to *Peters* patrimony, a seigniorie or Lordship of the Church of
Rome, this Law must be controleable by the Pope, because it is prejudiciall to the Church. And the temporall Soveraignty of *Venice*, must
submit themselves unto the spirituall Jurisdiction of the Romish Church,
or feele the stroke of Peters sword.[35]

Two works by Henry Burton, "Rector of little Saint Matthewes in
Friday-street London," who may have been of kin to Robert Burton,[36]
though vexingly indefinite in their references, also exhibit familiarity with
Sarpi's Tridentine *History*. These are his *A Censure of Simonie* (London,
1624) and his *Truth's Triumph over Trent: or, the Great Gulfe betweene
Sion and Babylon* . . . (London, 1629). The former work cites *The History
of the Council of Trent* only twice; but between the lines one may read
more of Sarpi's account than the marginal allegations admit. Those marginal
records are pretty barren, "Hist. Concil. Trident." being the total legend
opposite a passage reading "so it hath beene the custome of the *Court of
Rome*, that Simonie should goe under the name of *Subsidiary or Eleemosynary pension*, either for the Popes Courtiers, or Cofers; But farre be it from
the Court of England."[37] The second Spartan reference at least adds an indication of the Book. At the beginning of Chapter XVI, "Of the cutting off,
or curing of Simonie," Burton supplies the note *"Hist. Concil. Trid. 1. 6."*
to identify his source for the passage reading "although, when the Article
of Simonie (among other enormities) came to bee considered of in the Councell of *Trent*, for reformation, it was cautelously *proposed, that the abuse
occurring in the collation of Benefices should not be mentioned, as being an
infirmitie, not to be cured with any remedie, but death.*"[38]

Other unmarked and unidentifiable passages, such as the following,
suggest a thorough conversancy with Sarpi:

> We must put a great difference betweene the now Church of *Rome*,
> and that which it hath beene formerly, and that even within these three
> or foure hundred yeeres. For in former times, as that Church hatched &
> fostered many enormities, both of Doctrine and Manners, which by degrees crept in, till Antichrist should come to his full stature; men might
> speake and write freely of the abuses of it. But now, within lesse then

these hundred yeeres, since the Councell of *Trent*, this Church is growne
to that superciliousnesse and height of pride, that no man may once
mention the least speck or blemish of that foolish Virgin, or rather,
filthy Whoore; nay those that have alreadie in their writings left any record or Monuments of *Romes* sin, and in especial, of this of Simonie, it
must passe through the fire of their *Index Expurgatorius*.[39]

The voice is Jacob's voice, but the hands (language) are the hands of Esau.

Burton's later book, *Truth's Triumph over Trent*, which draws also
upon Chemnitz's *Examen*, cites the *"Hist. Concil. Trid."* rather more frequently.[40] His main argument concerns the differences of the Anglican and
Romanist positions regarding *justification*; and his principal attack is leveled
against the pro-Tridentine positions—however discordant among themselves
—of Vega and Soto.[41] Advocates of Tridentine positions (or participants at
the Council) are referred to throughout as "Pontificians"—and in no friendly
voice. The most interesting of the references to Sarpi occurs in "The Preface
to the Reader":

Nor was it for nothing, that the Councell of Trent so improved all their
skill and strength, to oppose and oppresse the true Catholicke doctrine
of Justification, as whereby the Papall magnificence and the gaine of the
Romish Craftsmen for their *Diana*, was endangered. So that this their
Abortive was a hatching for seven moneths; so long was this Babylonish
Ramme, wherewith they would force heaven gates, a hammering in the
Trent-forge: so as the History noteth,[42] that the most expert in the
Church affirmed, That if all the Councels, assembled from the Apostles
times to that, were summed up together, they could not make up so
many Articles as the Trent-Fathers had amassed together, in this one
sixt Session of that Synod, the best part whereof also they were beholden
to *Aristotle* for. And no marvaile they were so puzzled, for they were
to encounter sundry difficulties: as first, the evidence of Scriptures: secondly, the concent of ancient Fathers; thirdly, the powerfull preaching
and writings of *Luther*. fourthly, the dissent of their Schoolemen; and
fiftly, the division of the Councell it selfe, some being Thomists, some
Scotists, some Dominicans, some Franciscans. To satisfie and reconcile
all which, was more than an Herculean labour. But what could be difficult to the Papall Omnipotencie, who could send his holy Ghost post
from Rome to Trent in a Cloake-bagge, which loosed all knots, and
decided all doubts?[43]

As a starting point for this chapter, we chose the worthy Dr. George
Carleton, "inspirer" of Sarpi. We may let it come to rest in a further observation or two concerning a work by "worthy" Dr. Thomas Fuller, his valu-

able *Church-History of Britain*,[44] which we have already drawn upon in connection with de Dominis. This is a thick small folio, divided into eleven Books, followed by separate histories of Cambridge University and of Waltham-Abbey in Essex, where Fuller was (in 1655) curate. *The Historie of the Councel of Trent* is mentioned only twice, but the work contains a good deal of Fuller's incidental anti-Italian spirit, part of which found vent upon de Dominis, to whose "defence" from this felonious assault Peter Heylyn came charging.[45]

In Book V, Section ii, paragraph 7, concerning Henry VIII's marriage case at Rome, Fuller, without quoting from Sarpi, refers us marginally to "Hist. of Councel of *Trent*, p. 69"—an exact reference to Brent's (1620) translation. But it is also an exact reference for the second (1629) edition of the Brent-Sarpi, and there is reason to believe that it is this edition which we are asked to consult. For in Book IX, Section i, paragraph 42 (p. 70), Fuller summarizes Bishop Jewell's answer to Scipio's letter concerning the English absence from Trent and says (in the margin): "See it at large at the end of the History of the Councell of Trent." This letter of Jewell's does not appear in the 1620 edition; but in that of 1629, we may find it in our choice of English (pp. 842–62) or Latin (pp. 863–81). We could hardly ask for better service unless we were to expect the Doctor to advise us to consult the work in either the Bodleian or in Sion College, London. It was, in fact, already on the shelves in both when Fuller was writing.[46]

References to Sarpi's *History of the Council of Trent* crop out in some unexpected places—and (surely one of the unlikeliest) in another work of Fuller's, his *The Historie of the Holie Warre*. An account of the First Crusade, celebrated in the poetry of Tasso's *Gerusalemme Liberata* and here in Fuller's prose, does not simply cry out for references to the Council of Trent, but Fuller manages to work in two.[47] In the language of the time, Sarpi's *History* had become an ubiquitarian classic.

10---A Parcel of Parsons (and Some of Their Friends): Post-Restoration

ONE OF THE GENTLEST spirits ever to inhabit a human frame dwelt in that of the long-lived Izaak Walton (1593–1683). The author of the beloved *Compleat Angler* was not a clergyman himself, but few clergymen can ever have had a more sincere admirer. His *Lives* of Donne, Wotton, Hooker, Herbert, and Sanderson have become classics of our literature. And two of them, those of Wotton (1651) and of Bishop Robert Sanderson (1678), have a place in our account of Sarpi.

The "Life of Wotton"[1] contains, naturally, some notices of Wotton's Italian interests. Walton mentions, among other things, that Alberico Gentili, then Professor of Civil Law at Oxford, was one of Wotton's admirers.[2] When Walton has shipped Wotton off to "fruitful Italy, that darling of Nature, and cherisher of all arts" (p. 261), he has, eventually, to get around to Father Paul. After giving a brief account of events leading up to the interdict, Walton continues:

> Matters thus heightened, the State advised with Father Paul, a holy and learned Friar,—the author of the *History of the Council of Trent*—whose advice was, "Neither to provoke the Pope, nor lose their own right": he declaring publicly in print, in the name of the State, That the Pope was trusted to keep two keys, one of Prudence and the other of Power: and that, if they were not both used together, Power alone is not effectual in an excommunication.[3]

In the event, however, it seems that the Pope was in no mood to listen to such a reasonable voice:

In this condition—which lasted almost two years—the Pope grew still higher, and the Venetians more and more resolved and careless; still acquainting King James with their proceedings, which was done by the help of Sir Henry Wotton, Mr. Bedel, and Padre Paulo, whom the Venetians did then call to be one of their consulters of State, and with his pen to defend their just cause; which was by him so performed, that the Pope saw plainly he had weakened his power by exceeding it, and offered the Venetians absolution upon very easy terms.[4]

An entry in Wotton's will, dated 1 October 1637, tantalizes the curiosity: "To the above-named Dr. Bargrave, Dean of Canterbury [and formerly Chaplain to Wotton in Italy in succession to Bedell, now married to Wotton's niece], I leave all my Italian Books not disposed in this Will." It would be worth a pretty penny to know which works of Sarpi's were among them.

Only one passage in the "Life of Sanderson" bears upon Sarpi; but since in it Sanderson draws a parallel between himself and Sarpi, it is a pity that Hacket could not find in the Lord Keeper–Archbishop Williams the quality which would have permitted him to make one more comparison:

> And at this happy time [Walton speaking] of my enjoying his company and this discourse, he expressed a sorrow by saying to me, "Oh that I had gone Chaplain to that excellently accomplished gentleman, your friend, Sir Henry Wotton! which was once intended, when he went Ambassador to the State of Venice: for by that employment I had been forced into a necessity of conversing, not with him only, but with several men of several nations; and might thereby have kept myself from my unmanly bashfulness, which has proved very troublesome, and not less inconvenient to me; and which I now fear has become so habitual as never to leave me: and besides by that means I might also have known, or at least had the satisfaction of seeing, one of the late miracles of mankind for general learning, prudence, and modesty, Sir Henry Wotton's dear friend, Padre Paulo, who, the author of his Life says, was born with a bashfulness as invincible as I have found my own to be: a man whose fame must never die, till virtue and learning shall become so useless as not to be regarded."[5]

A work of a temper much different from that of the gentle Izaak Walton's is the posthumously published *The History of Romish Treasons*,[6] by Henry Foulis (1638–1669). This is a thick folio consisting of a 39–page Preface (dated "Novemb. 10. 1666") and 726 pages of text. It is a remarkably learned work, considering that it came from the pen of one still under thirty. In it Foulis shows himself about equally unfavorable in his views of

Presbyterians and of Romanists. Part of this temper shows through in an amusing and early reference to Pope Urban VIII:

> In the compiling of this History (such as it is) I have not dealt with the *Romanists* as the Hot-headed *Puritans* us'd to do, whose strength of Arguments lye chiefly in canting, misapplying Scripture, confidence and railing; and if they can but make a noise with the *Whore of Babylon, Antichrist*, the *Beasts Horns, &c.* they suppose the Pope is confuted sure enough, at least the good Wives and Children are frighted out of their little wits, and take him to be the strangest Monster in the World, with so many Heads and Horns; insomuch, that Pope Urban VIII did not amiss, when he desired some *English* Gentlemen to do him onely one courtesie, *viz.* to assure their Country-men, that he was a man as much as themselves.[7]

The first of the many references to and quotations from Sarpi comes quite early in the text and is, appropriately, drawn from his account of the Jesuits: "And this knack of credulity, was lately indeavoured by the *Jesuites* to be an Article: the famous and judicious Father *Paul* assuring us, that the third of their *Rules* found at *Padoa* 1606 was, that[8]—*Men must believe the Hierarchical Church, although it tell us, that that is black which our eye judgeth to be white.*"[9] Some early references to anti-Venetian pamphlets (pp. 56, 61, 69), in addition to his later section on the interdict,[10] give evidence that he had read both sides of the argument. But only one of the early references is of immediate relevance to Sarpi:

> And the *Carmelite* Fryar, *Giovanni Antonio Bovio*, findes fault with Father *Paul* the *Venetian* (famed for his learning, judgement, moderation and integrity) that amongst the Offices belonging to the Pope, he doth not set down,[11] *his translating of Empires, setting up and pulling down of Kings, since he hath such authority.* An Article, that I dare say *Bovio* never learned from the Virgin *Mary*, whom they brag to be the Patroness and Foundress of their Order.[12]

Fra Fulgenzio's *Life of Father Paul*—in the English version— is quoted various times,[13] dispersedly through the volume. The first of several paragraphs which are heavily documented with exact page references from *The Historie of the Councel of Trent* comes on the heels of the first reference to Fra Fulgenzio's *Life*. Besides epitomizing Sarpi's general attitude toward the council, the paragraph is noteworthy also for recording that "unlucky proverb" about the cloak-bag sent from Rome:

> And for confirmation of this [that is, Roman chicanery and deviousness], we need go no farther than their Council of *Trent*, it being a long

time before the Popes would be perswaded to call it; and when 'twas held, 'twas carried on with so much cunning and jugling, even to the trouble and grief of many *Roman* Catholick Divines there, that the *Legates* would permit nothing to be concluded upon, but according as they received directions and orders by Letters from the Pope; which occasioned the unlucky Proverb, That *the Council of* Trent *was guided by the Holy Ghost, sent to them from* Rome *in a* Cloak-bag. Insomuch that several of the Divines there did divers times publickly complain, that it was not a free one:[14] and both the Emperour,[15] and the King of *France*[16] call'd it a *Convention*.[17]

A briefer passage, important for the respectful terms in which it characterizes Sarpi, makes use of his *History of the Council of Trent* to describe the bull of Pope Paul III leveled against Henry VIII: "And what a notable thing it was, Father *Paul*, (one of the most judicious Fryars that ever set Pen to Paper) shall tell you.—*A terrible thundering Bull, such as never was used by his Predecessors, nor imitated by his Successors.*"[18]

For the entry under the year 1561 several consecutive paragraphs with multiple citations of *The Historie of the Councel of Trent* demonstrate the attention with which Foulis combed Sarpi's text. No other seventeenth-century work which I have examined shows a more concentrated draft upon that text.

> That which they call the *General Council of Trent* now sitting, the Queen [Elizabeth] is desired to send some thither: but this she thought would be to little purpose, seeing the designe of that *Convention* (as the Emperour and the *French* King[19] call'd it) was more of Interest then real honesty: Besides, it had now continued about XV years, and so improbable to alter any thing upon her desire. Nor was the Council it self free, as appears by the several complaints[20] put in there against such forcible abuses; some things, as the Institution of Bishops,[21] not being permitted to be discussed, the Pope fearing to be the looser: Nor was the *Secretary*[22] just in taking and setting down the suffrages; whereby he returned the Votes as he pleas'd. Nor would they allow any thing to be concluded on, but as they received Instructions[23] from the Pope; which occasioned the Proverb, That *the Holy Ghost was sent from* Rome *to* Trent *in a cloak bag*.
>
> Besides, Ambrose Coligna, a *Dominican*, publickly[24] preach'd against the *Protestants*, affirming that Faith and safe-conduct is not to be kept with them. And when some of the Reformed Divines went thither, the Legat[25] brake off the Debates, not letting the Council proceed; and suspended the Council for two years, pretending fear of Wars: against which action the *Spanish* Bishops protested.[26] And when the Legats

party fears to be out-voted, then do they send to the Pope to make more Bishops, and convey them to *Trent*:[27] which Legats undertook not onely to direct, but command the whole Council; which spoil'd its Freedom.

To these may be added the tricks used to carry on their designes, and prevent a baffle, either by new making of Bishops, the better to out-vote, or suspending of all from acting or voting; or by removing them to other places, so to divide the Council; as when they were adjourn'd to *Bologna*,[28] whither those that depended on the Pope went, the rest refusing, staid still at *Trent*, not submitting to this removal or division.

And little might here be expected but partiality, seeing the *Italians* were almost three to one of the number there; all the Subscribers amounting to no more then 255, of which 187 were *Italians*; so that bating the interested *Italians*, there remains but a poor Catalogue of Bishops, in respect of the great number that are in the Christian World; yet must this be look'd upon as one of the most famous General Councils in the whole World: yet the *Romanists* cannot agree about its Juris-diction or Authority; for though the *French*[29] hold the Council to be above the Pope, yet his Holiness looks upon himself as no wise bound[30] to observe the Canons of *Trent*.

In short, should the English Clergy have appear'd in this Council, they must either have been there as Free-men, frankly to Dispute and Debate as others did: But thus they could not, having been before con-demn'd as Hereticks by Julius III. And at *Trent* here they were so Zealous, as to Excommunicate the Archbishop and Elector of *Colen*[31] for Heresie. If they could not appear as Free-men, then they must under the capacity of *Offenders*, as it were to receive sentence of condemnation: but to this they thought they had no reason to submit themselves; and we need not doubt how things would have gone with them.[32]

Such wholesale and unmixed dependence upon Sarpi's *History of the Council of Trent* exemplifies very well the status of "authority" which that work had attained in Protestant England. By the time Foulis was writing, Pallavicino's *Istoria* and other Catholic accounts were available (as well as some others that were distinctly Protestant); but it was overwhelmingly Sarpi's which held the field. Similarly, though there were numerous pro-Papal, anti-Venetian works dealing with the interdict—and Foulis was fa-miliar with some of them—it was Sarpi who was read, quoted, *and believed*. Any English account of that important moment in history is almost certain to be based upon Sarpi. And Foulis is no exception. The great piece of Sarpiana in his *The History of Romish Treasons* comes in a twenty-page stretch of Book IX, Chapter One, entitled "*The Quarrels betwixt Pope* Paul *the Fifth, and the* Venetians," pages 619–39. The entire account is based upon Sarpi; and pages 635–38 are devoted to a sketch of his life and an estimate of his character—based on Fra Fulgenzio's *Life*, with which Foulis has already shown himself familiar. In transcribing the three and one-half folio pages of this final part of the Chapter, I make no apology for including so long a passage; for, in its way, it constitutes a fitting supplement to the account in Chapter One of this study and to the casually selected bits from Fulgenzio's *Life* in Hacket's *Scrinia Reserata*.

And it may be, upon this Rumour [that is, that Cardinal de Joyeuse, in secretly making the sign of the Cross under his hood, had tricked the Venetians into submitting to absolution], or some such idle Report, some Historians do say, that they indeed did receive Absolution. But in this History I find most reason to reply upon the Credit of Father *Paul*. One of the most famous Pen-Champions that the *Venetians* imploy'd in this Quarrel, was the said learned and judicious Fryer, of the Order of the *Servi* commonly known by the name of Father *Paul*, of whom a word or two by the by.

He was born at *Venice* M.D.LII. He naturally addicted himself to his book, whereby when young, he gain'd great Reputation, so that *William* the famous Duke of *Mantova* intertain'd him as his Chaplain, in the year M.D.LXXIX. he was created *Provincial* of his Order, which he executed without partiality: he went and lived some time at *Rome*, where he got acquainted with the best, his parts making him known, to Pope and Cardinals as well as others. Being return'd to *Venice* he followed his studies close, and in all manner of learning was so excellent, that all Strangers that went to *Venice* desired his acquaintance, upon which he was foolishly accused by the Court of *Rome* as a Companykeeper with Hereticks.

At this time, the Order of the *Servi* was in some trouble, by reason of their Protector, Cardinal *San Severina*, who against all right or reason, was resolved to make one *Gabriel Collison* General of the *Order*, being thereto perswaded by his Briberies: the whole *Order* opposed this, and herein Father *Paul* was a little engaged, but carried himself with great discretion and moderation. But at last *Gabriel* was made *General*, and a seeming peace was made.

When the late Quarrel began between the Pope and the *Venetians*, they chose Father *Paul*, to be one of their chief Assistants, who by his solid reasons staggerd the Papal Pretensions: which so concern'd the Pope, that he would have had the *Father* brib'd from his Duty to the Common-wealth; but this failing, other designs were set on foot. *Gaspar Schoppius*, a man well known for his railing and pernicious principles of

Government, freely told Father *Paul*, that the Pope had long Hands, and might reach him, but wisht rather to have him alive at *Rome*, and the Father was by several great Personages informed, that Plots were laid against his Life: but he trusting to his Innocency neglected his Security.

But this confidence might have cost him his Life, for one Evening in the Street at *Venice*, he was assaulted, received two wounds in his Neck and one in his Face, entring at his right ear and passing through the Jaw bone, and out again betwixt his Nose and his Cheek, and the *Stelletto* was left sticking in, the Villain not having strength enough to pull it out.

The number of these *Assassins* were five, who having a *Gondola* ready, got presently to the House of the Pope's *Nuncio*, then resident in *Venice*; thence in a flat Boat, with Ten Oars and well armed. prepared for the purpose, they departed that night, towards *Ravenna*. Being now in the Papal Territories, they were secure, and vapour'd of the Fact, and were nobly received at every place; at last they got to *Rome*, where they were well also entertain'd, with assignation of Entertainment. And here they staid some time, till the world cryed shame, that such abominable Villains should be sheltred and entertain'd from Justice, by his Holiness: upon which the Pope, was forced for his Honour sake, to order their departure out of the City; yet they had some allowance granted them, but so small, in respect of those Glories they expected, that they became mal-content, so that at last every one of them came to an evil end.

But to return to Father *Paul*, he was had home to his Monastery, the most famous Physicians and Chyrurgions in those parts imploy'd about him, so that after some time he perfectly recovered, to the joy of the whole Senat, who by publick *Proclamations* took order for his future Security, assigning him a Guard, increase of Stipend, with a House at St. *Marks* at the publicke Charge. But the Father desired to be excused from all such state, cost, and trouble, resolved to continue in his Monastery amongst his Brethren of the *Order*. The Senate perceiving this to be his earnest desire, gratified him, but caused some building to be added to his Chamber, from whence by a little Gallery, he might have the Commodity to take Boat the better to avoid Treachery, in his returns sometimes by night, from the publick Service.

Seeing the Senat had thus carefully provided for his security, so that there was danger to use any more force, some other designs were set on foot, 1609. *Fra Antonio da viterbo* who served as an *Amanuensis* to the Father, was solicited, to make him away with a Razor, which he might conveniently do, considering his intimacy, and the great trust the Father put in him, or if not this, to poyson him. *Antonio* refused to act this wickedness himself, especially to such a good Friend and Patron, but would afford his Assistance if others would be the Actors. So at last it was concluded, that he should take the Print in Wax of his Keys, which he should deliver to another Fryar *Giovar* [*sic*] *Francisco*, whom Fryar *Bernardo* (the Favourite of Cardinal *Borghese*, Nephew to the Pope) had imploy'd about this thing; by which means having Counterfeit Keys, they might send in some Ruffians or *Bravo's* to murther the Father.

But some Letters of this Plot, by chance being taken, there was enough discovered, to have *Francisco* and *Antonio* seised on. *Francisco* was condemn'd to be hang'd, but had his pardon by a full discovery of the whole design, and delivering unto them all the Letters concerning this black Plot; what great Personages were in this action, is not known; the Councel of *Venice* thinking it best to conceal them, for the Honour of Religion.

To tell all the Attempts against him would be tedious, these are enough; and against him it was that the Court of *Rome* bent all their spight, he being an Enemy to the prop of all their Greatness, *viz.* their Usurpations and Authority over Temporal Princes; and his Reasons obtain'd him the greater ill-will from that Bishop, because they seem'd to be favour'd by other Potentates: The Pope fearing that in time other Territories might follow the Example of the Venetians. And when his *Coercive* Authority is once despised, he will remain but a weak Governor within the narrow Limits of his Churches Patrimony; which may render him incapable of preferring his Favourites abroad; and the Glory of his idle and wasting Courtiers, will be eaten up, by the more thrifty Citizens. Thus their Charity to themselves, made them the more violent against the Fryar *Paul* though he acted nothing, but what became the duty of a good Subject to his Prince and Country.

The Father hoped, that the malice of his Enemies would vanish by degrees: and when Pope *Paul* V. dyed, he expected all heart-burning to cease, but here he found himself mistaken, and the Quarrel and Enmity intail'd as it were upon the Pontifick Chair. For Gregory XV. succeeding, 1621, bare the same ill-will, looking upon the Father as the chief-Counsellor, nay and Incendiary too of the *Venetians*, insomuch that he told their Ambassador, that, *there would never be a peace between the Republick and the See Apostolick, but such an one as Father* Paul *should* approve of.

The Father informed of this, was grieved beyond measure, that he should be held a *Beautefeu*, and so rather than any difference should arise about him, resolved peaceably to retire himself from his own Country. To live amongst the *Protestants*, might expose himself to Calumnies; to dwell where the Ecclesiasticks might over-power him, or where the

134

Temporality would not trouble it self in his Protection, was to expose his Life to Poyson and Stellettoes again. Upon this difficulty he determin'd to reside at *Constantinople*, or some of the Eastern Countryes.[33] And for this Peregrination he began to make Preparations, take advice, get safe-conducts, &c. But being informed that the Pope releas'd much of his displeasure towards him, he was the less careful in hastning.

And now he began to be ancient and feeble, and dyed in his Manastery at *Venice*, with great Tranquility and Settlement of mind, 1623. in the LXXI. year of his Age.

The Father was little, humble, grave, but withal chearful; of his dyet very sparing, insomuch, that every day with him, was almost a Fast: he was merciful and good to his greatest Enemies, begging Pardon for those, who designed his death.

His Learning got him renown every where, being good for the *Oriental* Languages, besides *Greek, Latin,* and other *Europaean;* was famous for his skill in *Mathematicks, Physick, Anatomy, Chymistry, Astranomy:* in all which he was a dayly Practitioner and Discoverer of many Excellent Rarities: Insomuch that the chiefest Artists, thought themselves happy in his advice and acquaintance. And make honourable mention of him.[34]

For Politicks, he was held not only the greatest, but the most honest Statesman in his time, admirable vers'd in the *Laws,* knowing in all Histories, and his skill in *Geography* made the world his own. Divinity was his calling, and what an excellent man he was at his Pen, may appear by his divers writings, many of which are not yet publish'd, but some remain as Rarities lockt up in the Cabinets of Princes, whilst others lurk as Secrets in the Archives of the wise *Venetian* Councel. But a Specimen of his great Abilities, may be gather'd from his *History of the Council of Trent.* where he was pleas'd to vail himself under the Title of

Pietro Soave Polana.

Which by an Anagrammatism, makes the Fathers name, Sirname, and Country, thus

Paolo Sarpio, Veneto.

his Fathers name being *Francisco di Pietro Sarpio.*

There is also abroad of his *A History of the Inquisition*; a *History of the Quarrels between Pope Paul* V. *and the Venetians,* and several other things in justification of his Country in those Troubles, which with his other writings (and Commendations of him) have faln under the lash of their *Index Expurgatorius.*[35]

The Court of *Rome,* whilst he lived carryed the greatest bitterness against him, dayly writing Lybels and Invectives against him, stufft up with Lyes and Forgeries, insomuch that *Bellarmine*, (though his Pen was ingaged against the Father in the Venetian Quarrel) told the Pope that such notorious Falsities and Calumnies would bring more Scandal than Credit to his Cause.

Amongst the rest of his Enemies was *Maffeo Barbarini* Nuncio in *France* at the time of the Quarrel, and afterwards Pope *Urban* VIII. who in his Aiery and Romantick humour rais'd and invented many unworthy Stories of the Father, far unbefitting a Person of his Place and Dignity.

Nay so implacable were the *Roman* Favourites, that their Slaunders and Malice followed him to his Grave, publishing impudent and fabulous Stories concerning his death, of his dying Howling, of strange Apparitions of Black Dogs, of Terrible Noises heard in his Cell and Chambers, and several such like lying Forgeries, as those idle people used to invent upon *Luther, Calvin*, and others who will not truckle to the Usurpations of the *Roman* Court. But the people of *Venice*, who knew him better, accounted him a Saint, hanging up their *Votive Tablets* at his Sepulchre,[36] till the Senate, to satisfie Pope Urban VIII. forbad such Ceremonies to be used to his Monument. And so much by the bie, of the Learned and Judicious Father *Paolo Sarpi*.[37]

A figure much more resoundingly famous than Foulis was Edward Stillingfleet (1635–1699), the learned, pious, liberal-minded Bishop of Worcester. The latitude of his mind, however large, constricted a bit at the thought of Rome; and two at least of his numerous expressions of distaste for the papacy fall under our purview here.

In *A Discourse Concerning the Idolatry Practised in the Church of Rome* (1671), which went through four editions in five years, Sarpi's *History of the Council of Trent* is both quoted and cited.[38] The longest of the quotations is brought on by the discussion of a question much canvassed at Trent: Does the sinfulness of the officiating priest or the sinfulness and unpreparedness of the communicant render the Sacrament ineffective?

This will appear more plain by the account given of it in the *History* of that *Council*. "After, they treated of condemning those, who deny *Sacraments* do confer grace to him that putteth not a bar, or do not confess,[39] that *Grace* is contained in the Sacraments, and conferred, not by vertue of faith, but *ex opere operato*; but coming to expound how it is contained, and their causality, every one did agree that grace is gained by all those actions that excite devotion, which proceedeth not from the force of the work it self, but from the vertue of devotion, which is in the worker, and these are said in the Schools to cause grace *ex opere operantis*. There are other actions which cause grace, not by the devotion of him that worketh, or him that receiveth the work, but by vertue of the work it self; such are the Christian *Sacraments*, by which grace is received, so that there be no bar of mortal sin to exclude it, though there be not any devotion: So by the work of Baptism, grace is given to the Infant, whose mind is not moved towards it, and to one born a Fool, because there is no impediment of sin. The *Sacrament* of *Chrism* doth the like, and that of *extream Unction*, though the sick man hath lost his memory. But he that hath mortal sin, and doth persevere actually or habitually, cannot receive grace by reason of that contrariety; not because the *Sacrament* hath not vertue to produce it *ex opere operato,* but because the receiver is not capable, being possessed with a contrary quality."[40]

Stillingfleet refuses to believe that there was any real unanimity among the Catholics at the Council of Trent. Maybe Catholics, he speculates, really do believe "that the *Pope* and *Council* can put an end to all Controversies among them, when they please"; but he observes that they haven't done so. And he wonders "what made them so extreamly cautious in the *Council of Trent*, of meddling with any thing that was *in Controversie among themselves?*"[41] He has some unflattering theories; but, in any case,

> they could not agree, so much as about the Title of the *Council*, many of the Bishops were for[42] adding to the Title of *the most holy Council*, [*Representing the Church Universal*][43] which was eagerly opposed by the *Italians*, and with much ado avoided by the *Legats*, being no small controversie about words, but of very great consequence, about the *power* and *authority* of *Pope* and *Council*, if they had been suffered to go on with it. But the *Pope* hearing of this dispute, at the beginning, sent word to the Legats,[44] *not to broach any new difficulties in matter of faith; nor to determine any of the things controversed among Catholicks, and to proceed slowly in the Reformation.* Excellent instructions, for the advancement of *Peace* and *Holiness*! Whoever will for that end peruse that incomparable history of the *Council*, will find how high the *Controversies* among themselves were, between *Bishops* and *Regulars* about priviledges; between the *Dominicans* and *Franciscans*, in many weighty points; between the *Italian Bishops* and others, about *Residence*, and the extent of *Episcopal power*; between the *Divines*, in most of the matters of doctrine; as might easily be shewed at large, if I loved the pains of transcribing; but I had rather referr the Reader, to that excellent history it self.[45]

A sentiment I share with Brother Stillingfleet; but it must not deter me from transcribing yet further samples of his excellent observations.

The second of the Bishop's works which we are concerned with is called *The Council of Trent Examin'd and Disprov'd by Catholick Tradition* (London, 1688). This is a skilled controversialist's attempt to prove from the ancient practices of the church and from the Fathers and other writers acceptable to Catholics, as well as from the text of the Tridentine canons, that for certain doctrines essential in Christian faith, no such tradition as that claimed by the Council of Trent had existed before the meetings of that council. It was as if the council had declared, "Look, we have just coined an old Chinese proverb"; and the Bishop's hackles rose at that. "I intend," he says, *"to go through the most material Points . . . and to prove from the most Authentick Testimonies, that there was no* true Catholick Tradition *for any of them. And if I can make good what I have undertaken, I shall make the* Council *of* Trent *it* Self *the great Instance against the* Infallibility *of* Tradition."[46] The "most material Points," as reflected in the six divisions of the table of Contents, are these:

1. Point examined about *Traditions being a Rule of Faith equal with Scriptures.*
2. *About the Canon of Scripture defined by the Council of Trent.*
3. *About the free use of the Scripture in the vulgar Language prohibited by the Council of* Trent.
4. *About the Merit of Good Works.*
5. *Of the number of Sacraments.*
6. *Of Auricular Confession.*

Stillingfleet is one of the few English writers to make any use of Cardinal Pallavicino's *History* of the Council of Trent. And it is to be noticed that he does so *in order to confute Catholic arguments*, so that proponents of Tridentine positions may be condemned by their own "most allowed" writers:

> By the *Postulata* it appears, that a *Catholick Tradition* is such as must be known by the sound Members of the Church, and especially the Divines in it. But it appears by the most allowed Histories of that Council, this Rule of Faith was not received there. For Cardinal *Pallavicini* tells us that it was warmly debated and canvassed by the Bishops themselves. [He then cites Pallavicino's *"Hist. Concil.* Trident. *l.* 6, c. 14, n. 3." concerning differences of opinion about Tradition aired by the Bishops of Fano, of Bitonto, and of "Chioza."] . . . We are extremely beholden to Cardinal *Pallavicini* for his Information in these matters which are past over too jejunely by *F. Paul.*[47]

With respect to the Tridentine Canon of the Scripture (Point 2), both Sarpi and Pallavicino are cited: "We are to observe," says Stillingfleet, with regard to the council's pronouncing canonical "the Books of *Tobias, Judith, Wisdom of* Solomon, *Ecclesiasticus, Maccabees* and *Baruch*,"

> that these Books were not so received by all even in the Council of *Trent.* For what is received by virtue of a *Catholick Tradition*, must be universally received by the members of it. But that so it was not appears by the account given by both the Historians. *F. Paul* saith, *that in the Congregation*[48] there were two different Opinions of those who were for a particular Catalogue; one was to distinguish the Books into three parts, the other to make all the Books of equal authority; and that this latter was carried by the greater number.[49]

He then cites Pallavicino on this point[50] and, elsewhere, on others.[51] The use of Pallavicino as an "approved" writer is, of course, legitimate. The application of such a term to Sarpi undoubtedly caused some lifting of Catholic eyebrows. To cite him as a Catholic author in arguing against Catholics was a little like eating one's cake and having it too. But the practice was widespread among Protestants, who liked to look upon the Venetian rebel as one of "theirs"—at least in spirit.

In an earlier chapter[52] we had occasion to notice the peculiarity of Bishop William Lloyd's quotation of part of Dudith's letter, derived at second hand from *The History of the Council of Trent* by way of Anthony Wotton's *Runne from Rome.* A smaller work of Bishop Lloyd's, *The Difference between the Church and Court of Rome*,[53] gives firmer evidence that he was really familiar with Sarpi's work and indicates the kind of distinction that Englishmen frequently made:

> I know men are apt to believe that which they vehemently wish, and very wise and sober men were induced to think heretofore a closure with the Church of *Rome* no impossible matter; but the case is quite altered since the time of the Council of *Trent*, which has establisht every thing that ought to be remov'd; and shew'd the world how vain their hopes were from Synods, and universal Councils; how formidable the very approaches to Reformation were to those Fathers abundantly appears from that History of *Padre Paolo*; and this is acknowledged abundantly by my Author.[54]

A work of quite different order and extent, published in the following year, *The Morning-Exercise against Popery*,[55] exhibits the familiar anti-Catholic bias expressed "vehemently" by "zealous" Protestants outside the

Anglican fold. Joseph Glanvill, who found dissenters more willing to write a whole "Horseload of Books" against the Anglicans than really to write effectively against the Romanists, had at least to make exception for Baxter, Pool, and Owen, adding: "And there are some Sermons of the *Presbyterians* extant, *Morning Lectures* against *Popery*: These are the most, the chief of their Performances I ever heard of."[56] The *Morning-Exercise* consists of twenty-five sermons preached from the Southwark pulpit of Nathanael Vincent (1639?–1697), a dissenting minister of Cornish descent, and edited by him. The preachers are not identified, but they were drawn from Vincent's "Fathers and Brethren" and delivered their sentiments at his invitation. It is not clear whether he himself contributed any of the sermons; but he signs "The Epistle to the Reader" and ends it by congratulating himself "that ever such a Project against *Popery* came into my mind."[57]

At least half a dozen of these sermons show direct acquaintance with one or another of Sarpi's works, so that the volume provides us another measuring-stick for the dissemination of those works among the English clergy of the time. The preacher of Sermon II, "Christ, and not the Pope, Universal Head of the Church," certainly has the Venetians (and probably Sarpi) in mind when he says that cities and kingdoms "are not to be Unchurched, or Interdicted Gods worship" because of erring magistrates—though the Pope has laid "such inhumane and unchristian kind of Discipline" upon the Venetians and others.[58]

Sermon III, "Kings and Emperours, not rightful Subjects to the Pope," shows by several references that the preacher has been examining both *The History of the Quarrels* and *The History of the Council of Trent*. The quarrel of the Venetians and Pope Paul V is instanced to support the contention that clerics are subject to due secular authority—"as to their perpetual honour, and to the good example of all Christendom, the Illustrious Republick of *Venice* made both the proud Pope *Paul* the Fifth, and the stubborn Clergy of their State to learn and acknowledg."[59] A few pages along in his text, the preacher, citing Becket's refusal to acknowledge Henry II's authority over clerics, even though they might be guilty of crimes, adds (in a marginal note): "And of later years, the like bred a quarrel betwixt the Serene Republick of *Venice*, and *Paul* the fifth."[60] Neither of these allusions to the interdict would of itself constitute firm evidence that the sermoner was using Sarpi. But in a third allusion to the Venetians he leaves us in no doubt:

All this I have said is evident from an undeniable instance of *Paul 5th.* who better informed, or bolder resolv'd, told the *Venetians, He would not endure them to judg Ecclesiastical Persons who are not Subjects unto Princes, and whom they cannot chastise though they be Rebellious.* By this[61] Princes may see how little Power that Indulgent Father the Pope would leave in their hands, who in Criminal cases of highest nature will so boldly deny them all power to judg Ecclesiasticks.[62]

The direct citing and quoting of *The History of the Quarrels* in this instance permits us to assume a little more confidently that it was also drawn upon in the earlier instances.

In any case, the preacher's familiarity with Sarpi is not limited to his account of the interdict. For in the same sermon he touches upon the "generosity" of popes who "give" what is not theirs to give. In the order of things, he says, princes grant privileges and exemptions to the clergy—not vice versa; and this order exists until the Prince sees cause for recalling his own grant,

> which future cause may (by conjecture from what hath already been acted in our view) soonest arise from an usurping Ingratitude (the hereditary infirmity of the Papal See) which never giveth to any, what it can by fraud or force keep to it self: as the Grave and Impartial Author of the Council of Trent well observeth,[63] on the Pompatick and Ridiculous Act of *Paul* the Fourth; giving the Kingly Title over *Ireland* to Queen *Mary*, who had derived it from her Father, and her Brother, and had assumed it to her self at her first coming to the Crown.[64]

The sermon does not end without some still further discussion[65]—again not necessarily, but presumptively, from Sarpi—of the famous Venetian quarrel.

Sermon XIX, "Of Indulgences," cites *The History of the Council of Trent* thrice.[66] The preacher is more than a little amused at the ridiculous inconsistency of Cardinal Morone, who "as chief President,[67] granted to every one that was present in the Session, or had assisted in the Council, a plenary Indulgence; when they had but then decreed, that the sole dispensing of them belongs to the Pope."[68] It is not amusement, however, but disgust, which leads him to point out that whatever the papacy and its supporters may claim, the chief aim of indulgences is to gain MONEY—an abuse. Julius II, he says, gave funds gained from indulgences to his relatives and followers; "and the Indulgences of *Saxony*,[69] he gave unto his Sister *Magdalene*, wife unto *Franceschetto Cibo* Bastard Son of Innocent the 8th"[70] (Brent's language).

Sermon XXII, "The Right of every Believer to the blessed Cup in the Lord's Supper," and Sermon XXIII, "The Popish Masse no proper Gospel Sacrifice," both cite (the second *quotes*) the *History of the Council of Trent* at various points from a Latin translation.[71] And the final Sermon (XXV), "The Visibility of the true Church," is of double Sarpian interest in that it makes use of both the *History of the Council of Trent* and *The History of the Quarrels*.[72] From the latter the preacher selects and sends winging in the direction of Baronio a shaft which the Cardinal richly deserved for the unfeeling cruelty of his remark respecting the Venetians:[73] "Our Lord did not bid *Peter* feed his Sheep with Iron and Steel, or his Lambs with twisted Wire; though *Baronius* said, Peter's Ministery hath two parts. *To feed, and to kill. Hist. of the Quarrels of Venice*, p. 65."

In contrast (but not very sharp contrast) to the collected dissent of *The Morning-Exercise* may be named the "orthodox" *Works of the Most Reverend Father in God, John Bramhall D.D. Late Lord Archbishop of Ardmagh, Primate and Metropolitane of all Ireland. Collected into One Volume. In Four Tomes* . . . (Dublin, 1676). There is in the *Works* much citation-quotation of Sarpi and of *The History of the Council of Trent*, principally in Tome I, and especially in Bramhall's *A Just Vindication of the Church of England from the Unjust Aspersion of Criminal Schism*, together with his replies to various controversial attacks on that work. It is here, incidentally, that he refers to Urban VIII as "the wisest Pope you have had of late, who by his moderation and Courtesie cooled much of that *Heat*, which the violence of his Predecessors had raised against the *Court* of *Rome*."[74]

The first Sarpi reference in the *Just Vindication* concerns Henry VIII's persecution of Protestants:

> After this the Pope himself, (though he was not well pleased to lose so sweet a morsel as *England* was) so well approved of *Henry* the Eighth's rigorous proceedings against the Protestants, that he proposed him to the Emperor as a pattern for his imitation. Insomuch, as some strangers in those dayes coming into *England*, have admired to see one suffer for denying the Pope's Supremacy, and another for being a Protestant at the same time.[75]

This is documented, marginally, by *"Hist. Conc. Trid., L.* 1 *p.* 78. Ed. 1658" —which means, presumably, the Latin edition of Gorinchem.

In praising the English laws respecting mortmain, Bramhall indicates that other places and times have had similar restraints upon the clergy's insatiable greed:

> He might have remembered, that the troubles between the Pope and the *Venetians*, did spring partly from such a Law.
>
> Briefly, with a little search he might have found like Laws in *Germany, Poland, France, Spain, Italy, Sicily*; And if he will trust *Padre Paolo*, in the Papacy itself.[76] The Prince cannot wrong his Subject that is an Owner and Possessor of Lands or Hereditaments in a well ordered State, Then why should it be in the power of a Subject that is an Owner, to wrong his Prince and his Country? But by such alien-

ations of Lands to the Church in an excessive and unproportionable measure, the Prince loseth his Right, that is, both his Tribute, and his Military Service, and Fines upon change of Tenants. The Commonwealth loseth its supportation and due protection. Therefore they were called the Laws of *Mortmain,* because the Lands so alienated to the Church were put into a dead hand, from whence they never returned: And so in time the whole Signory should be Churches, as it is elegantly expressed[77] by the *Venetian* Orator to *Paul* the Fifth, *Nè fortunis omnibus exuantur, nè quicquid sub Coelo* Veneto *homines arant, serunt, aedificant, omnia veluti quodam Oceano Ecclesiae absorbeantur, nihilque sibi religioni fiat unde Rempublicam, patriam, tecta, templa, aras, focos, sepulcra majorum defendere possint; Lest the Citizens should be turned out of their estates, lest all which men plow, sow, build under the* Venetian *Heaven should be swallowed up into the Ocean of the Church; and nothing be left wherewith to defend the Commonwealth, their Country, their Houses, their Temples, their Altars, their Fires, and the sepulchers of their ancestors.*[78]

After citing Chemnitz's *Examen* and referring his readers to "*Chaucer* in sundry places" on Church greed, Bramhall returns to Sarpi and the need for eternal vigilance against a grasping, aggressive Rome: "We read that *Charles* the Fifth[79] renewed an edict of his predecessors at *Madrid,* That *Bulls and Missives sent from* Rome *should be visited, to see that they contained nothing in them prejudicial to the Crown or Church of* Spain."[80] He then proceeds to give an excellent summary of the contended points between the Venetians and the Pope, drawing his information (as we have come to expect) from Sarpi's *Historia particolare,* which is repeatedly cited in the margins.[81]

No more than his other orthodox (and dissenting) brethren can the Archbishop refrain from observing that at the Council of Trent "the Fathers were noted to be guided by the Spirit, sent from *Rome* in a Male,[82] where divers not onely new Bishops, but new Bishopricks, were created, during the sitting of the Convent, to make the *Papalins* able to over-vote the *Tramontains.*"[83] Indeed, his resistance is rather lower than theirs; for this Holy-Ghost-in-a-satchel figure was emphatically a favorite of his, occurring not only here but elsewhere.[84] Other references to Sarpi's *History of the Council of Trent* are fairly frequent in the *Works* but need no further special attention.[85]

An "English" deacon with the unexpected name of Hippolite du Chastel de Luzancy provides us some Oxford *Reflexions on the Council of Trent,*

143

which are not altogether without Sarpian interest.[86] He describes his work as "a Treatise against the Council of Trent, that is, against a Conventicle of this last age, wherein the ancient Faith was opprest by the establishment of modern errors, and Religion by the interests of a politic faction."[87] This bespeaks an attitude consistent with that held by Sarpi. But then the Deacon opens "The Preface" by assuring us that he will *not* draw upon the historians of the Council:

> The occasion of these ensuing discourses which are here made public, was a Treatise entitl'd, *Considerations upon the Council of Trent.* Its author has manag'd his subject with so much dexterity, that I could not but judg it agreeable to that love all Christians ought to have for truth, and to my own duty in particular to dispel the mist he has attempted to cast before men's eyes.
>
> To perform this with solidity, I thought it not so proper to rely upon any particular historian of that Council, there being but four who have treated of it, whose testimonies are not free from exception. *Soavius* [that is, Sarpi] is suspected by the Romanists, (as *Palaviciny* by the Protestants) tho with less justice. *Scipio Henricus* [Errico] is more addicted to his Society then to his Church, and is more intent to defend the Jesuits, then to justifie the proceedings of the Bishops. And for *Aquilius* his survey *De tribus Historicis,* it is rather a pamphlet injurious to the Church of *Rome* it self for its want of sense and learning, than a just censure. But it appeared much more easie and useful, to give a true character of the Council drawn out of its own acts, and shew much essential defects in it, that all the artifice of its defenders can never satisfie a rational and impartial enquirer.[88]

On the next leaf de Luzancy issues a further disclaimer of reliance upon "suspect" authority:

> In these discourses I avoid the citing of any authors, but such as for their learning and piety are venerable in the Church of *Rome;* a design which no judicious persons can ever disapprove, since it hapens but too often that we combat men, whose sentiments their own communion disowns; and after a long and tedious disputation we receive no other answer, but that the Church of *Rome* is not bound to make good all the assertions of her privat followers.[89]

Nevertheless, he does cite Cardinal Pallavicini;[90] and after quoting an unfavorable comment on the Council of Trent, he makes the following bow in the direction of Sarpi: "Nor are the Authors of these last words either Protestants or Heretics. Neither is it that famous *Venetian,* whom they call *Atheist,* because he brought out of darkness, those artifices the Popes made

144

use of, to betray the cause of God."[91] Further, he presently refers to "Il. Concil. de Trent. P. 408" as the source of a wry comment quoted as emanating from Pope Paul IV: "And he said of them to Cardinal *Bellay, It had bin a great weakness in his Predecessours, their having sent to the Mountains of* Trent *three-Score Bishops of the less learned,* Sessanta Vescovi de manco *habili, & forty very ordinary Divines, &* quaranta dottori de meno sufficienti."[92] So difficult was it in the seventeenth century to write about either Venetian liberty or the Council of Trent and leave Sarpi out of the picture— even when one set one's mind to the deliberate exclusion.

A book published by Archbishop John Tillotson after the author's death was *A Treatise of the Pope's Supremacy* (London, 1680), written by Isaac Barrow (1630–1677). This employs much citation of the ancient Fathers, Latin and Greek, to indicate the erroneousness of modern (that is, Tridentine) papal claims—to supremacy of Rome over other sees, to ecclesiastical over secular authority, to the Pope's infallibility, and so forth. Considering the similarity of positions, the work contains surprisingly few citations of Sarpi. The following is typical in tone and application:

> Some points are so tough and so touchy, that no-body dare meddle with them, fearing that their resolution will fail of successe, and submission. Hence even the anathematizing Definers of *Trent* (the boldest undertakers to decide Controversies that ever were) did wave this Point; the Legates of the Pope being injoined, *to advertise, That they should not for any cause whatever come to dispute about the Pope's Authority.*[93]

The History of the Council of Trent is cited three further times, each time with a specific page reference.[94]

A work by William Sherlock (1641–1707), Dean of St. Paul's, may be included here as part of the pro-Anglican attack upon Bellarmine (and other Romanists) and as yet another instance of the effort to use "Catholic" authors to demolish, or at least to discredit, Catholic arguments. The work in question is entitled *A Brief Discourse Concerning the Notes of the Church. With some Reflections on Cardinal Bellarmin's Notes* (London, 1687). In the "Thirteenth Note"—"the Confession of Adversaries"—Sherlock cites Sarpi to this effect:[95]

> Cardinal *Mattheo Langi*, Archbishop of *Salzburg* told every one that the Reformation of the Mass was honest, the Liberty of Meats convenient, and a just Demand to be discharged of so many Commandments of Men; but that a poor Monk should reform all was intolerable. The Doctrine was not so obnoxious as to offend the most moderate and considering Men of the Roman Church; many of them have upon occasion frankly declared on our side.[96]

145

It is that "poor Monk" Luther who is responsible also for Sherlock's other recourse to *The History of the Council of Trent*, a passage in "The Fourteenth Note," which concerns "the unhappy end of the Church's Enemies." Luther's death occurring not long after the opening of the Council of Trent, some of the Romanists were inclined to view his demise as an instance of God's vengeance against a heretic. But Sherlock, following Sarpi, reads it differently:

> Hear therefore what many Learned Men of the Church of *Rome* say, who cannot be suspected of any partiality in Favour of him. *The Fathers in Trent*, (saith Father *Paul*) *and the Court of* Rome, *conceived great hope, seeing that so potent an Instrument, to contradict the Doctrines and Rites of the Church of Rome, was dead, &c. and the rather because that Death was divulged throughout* Italy, *with many prodigious and fabulous Circumstances, which were ascribed to Miracle, and the Vengeance of God, tho there were but the usual accidents, which do ordinarily happen in the Deaths of Men of sixty three Years of Age.*[97] So that in Father *Paul*'s judgment, there was nothing in his Death, but what was common.[98]

Throughout the *Brief Discourse* Bellarmine's fifteen "notes" by which the true Church can be recognized are, of course, all made to witness for the Anglican rather than the Roman faith.

Equally hostile to Catholic policy and doctrine is a contemporary work by the politician Slingsby Bethel (1617–1697), *The Interest of the Princes and States of Europe*.[99] The book is a survey—a little out of date, as the author admits[100]—of the governments, economics, and religions of the states of Europe, in which the author "hath throughout, with all Integrity, endeavoured nothing but the Truth in matter of Fact."[101] He is something of a realist, opposes that wicked usurper Oliver Cromwell, and argues, generally, that liberty of conscience in religion is beneficial to any kingdom. Nevertheless, his anti-Catholic bias appears on all sides.

In the long section on "The Interest of England" one paragraph shows most of these positions and exhibits in addition the customary veneration of seventeenth-century Englishmen for the wisdom of the Venetian government:

> And even the wisest Popish States acknowledge the reason of this principle, Sir *Walter Rawleigh* affirming that the *Venetians*, as not holding it safe to have any in their Councils, who have Foreign dependance by Oath, Homage, natural Obligation, Pension, or Reward, when their Senate is Assembled, cause Proclamation (before shutting of the doors) to be made, for all Priests to depart, and he who in this Common-wealth, is called the Divine of the State (an Ecclesiastical Person, to be advised

146

with in matters of Religion) is commonly chosen such a one, as is reputed the least Bigot in that Religion, as in the memory of some living, *Padri Pauli*, and after him *Fulgentio*, both successively performed that Office, and were esteemed Favourers of the Reformation, and Correspondents with *Diodati* of *Geneva*: and if Papists dare not trust their own Clergy in their Counsels, upon the account of their Foreign dependance, Protestants upon the same account, have no cause to trust Popish Subjects in their Countries, longer, than until they that are now living, die away, and that they can breed their Children to the Protestant Religion.[102]

A few other writers of the late seventeenth century may be glanced at and dismissed more summarily. The Anglican counterpart to the Presbyterians' *Morning-Exercise* was a volume edited by Archbishop Thomas Tenison, *Popery not Founded on Scripture*.[103] The work is in two parts, continuously (but erroneously) paged. Only the Introduction (pp. 5–16) is by Tenison; the sixteen other "severall Tracts" are the work of fourteen other Doctors of the Anglican Church, eight of the tracts being in two parts. All the principal doctrines of Catholic (that is, Tridentine) faith are examined and scripturally "confuted." The entire collection is a sort of concerted attack, principally, upon Bellarmine.

In Part I of "The Sacrifice of the Mass," by Dr. Richard Kidder (1633–1703), Bishop of Bath and Wells, it is argued that even some Catholics themselves admit they cannot support their doctrine concerning *this* Sacrament from Scripture:

> This was frankly acknowledged by *Georgius di Ataide*, a Divine of the Kingdom of *Portugal*, in the Council of *Trent*,[104] who was against those who went about to prove the Sacrifice of Mass from the Scriptures, and *sought to find in the Scriptures that which is not there, giving occasion to the Adversaries to calumniate the Truth, while they see it grounded upon such an unstable Sand.* He added, *as to the Fact of* Melchisedic; *that Christ was a Priest of that Order, as he was the only Begotten, Eternal, without Predecessor, Father, Mother, or Genealogy. And that this is proved too plainly by the Epistle to the* Hebrews, *where* St. Paul, *discoursing at large of this place, doth handle the Eternity and Singularity of this Priesthood, and maketh no mention of the Bread and Wine. He repeated the Doctrine of St.* Austin, *that when there is a fit place for any thing to be spoken, and it is not spoken,* an Argument may be drawn from the Authority negatively.[105]

Part I of another tract, "Celibacy of Priests, and Vows of Continence," by Dr. William Payne (1650–1703) draws from *The History of the Council of Trent* the opinion of "Rodolpho Pio di Carpio" (margin) concerning the "inconvenience" of a married clergy:

> And therefore an Italian Cardinal in the Council of *Trent*, where the Marriage of Priests was greatly prest to be granted by many Catholick Princes, wisely told the Council, *this Inconvenience would follow from it, that having House, Wife and Children, they will not depend on the Pope but on their Prince, and their Love to their Children will make them yeild to any prejudice of the Church, and they will seek to make the Benefices hereditary, and so in a short time the Authority of Apostolick See will be confined within* Rome.[106]

One of the Archbishop's own small productions, *A Discourse Concerning a Guide in Matters of Faith*,[107] is of interest for its reference to the Council of Trent as "the Pretended Council of Trent" (p. 16) and for its one reference to *The History of the Council of Trent*:

> God hath not set up any one Person in the Catholick Church in the Quality of an unerring Guide in the Christian Faith. The Bishops of *Rome* who pretend to this Prerogative, do but pretend: It is a tender point; and the *Pope's Legates*, in the *Council* of *Trent*,[108] were enjoyned to give forth this Advertisement, that the Fathers, upon no account whatsoever, should touch it, or dispute about it. They who examine it, will soon reject it as false and useless.[109]

One could hardly have expected Canterbury and Rome to see eye to eye on *that* topic.

Two works by David Abercromby, M.D. (d. 1701–2?), are of some slight Sarpian interest. One, his *Academia Scientiarum* (London, 1687), with text in Latin and English, is of small value except as indicating what were "the Arts and Sciences" in 1687 and who were regarded as "authorities" in each. In the Appendix, however, among the "new Discoveries in Anatomy," he does include *"the Circulation of the Bloud, by Dr.* Harvey, *though some, upon no very good grounds, ascribe it to* Paulus Venetus [that is, Sarpi]."[110] The other, his *A Moral Discourse of the Power of Interest* (London, 1690), dedicated to the admired Robert Boyle, is a strongly antipapal examination of business and personal ethics: usury, simony, and wire-pulling chicanery in religion. It reduces to the simple thesis that everything can be bought for gold. The Roman Church's mad scramble after money, he thinks, and her opposition to any reform that would put down money-getting practices, were the real reasons for her opposition to reform in the Council of Trent:

148

No wonder then if the Council of *Trent* did so much oppose a thorough Reformation; for it being made up of Rich Cardinals, Bishops, Generals of the Regular Orders, and of Clergymen of all sorts, they foresaw their Fate, if they discouraged the Abuses slipt into the Church of *Rome*: Yet the Popes were so afraid, that some knowing, and well-meaning Men among them, should endeavour the new modelling of their Church into a better frame, that they suffered nothing to be done in the Council but by and with the Consent of their own Legates, *proponentibus legatis*; which gave occasion to some to say, that the Holy Ghost was sent every week from the then Pope to the Council in a Cloakbag, because of the Pope's sending his weekly Instructions to the Fathers, with express Orders to act according to the secret Resolutions of his Privy-Council.[111]

Abercromby does not name Sarpi as his source, but the traces seem fairly clear.

In *The Genuine Remains* of Thomas Barlow (1607–1691),[112] Librarian of the Bodleian (1642–1660) and Bishop of Lincoln (from 1675), occur several uses of or references to Sarpi and *The History of the Council of Trent*. Many of the separate "remains" are in the form of letters written by the Bishop to satisfy enquiries directed to him by sundry individuals. The longest single piece (pp. 1–121) is "Αυτοσχεδιασματα, or Directions to a young Divine for his Study of Divinity, and choice of Books, &c."[113] In the recommending of books, under the heading "*Historici Eccles.*," after listing a number of general surveys and earlier books, Barlow says:

> Two Historians more I would commend (for understanding the state of Religion since *Luther*) both persons of great Moderation and Fidelity (tho of different Religions), and writ what they might and did know.
> 1. *John Sleidani Comment. de Statu Religionis ab* 1517 *ad* 1556.
> 2. *Thuani Historia ab Anno* 1543. *ad Annum* 1607.
> 3. Add to these Father *Paul*'s History of the Council of *Trent*: all excellent persons; *Cedro digna locuti*.[114]

A vastly learned and expert controversialist himself, one of the most informed men of his time in questions at issue between Protestants and Romanists, Bishop Barlow lists as the first writer under his heading "Writers of Controversies," "1. Dr. *Crakanthorp contra Archiep. Spalatensem, Quarto. Lond.* 1625. No book I have yet seen has so rational and short account of almost all Popish Controversies."[115]

There are other parts of the *The Genuine Remains* in which *The History of the Council of Trent* is quoted or cited variously in support of a variety of arguments.[116] But perhaps the most interesting reference to Sarpi is to his *Historia particolare.* In "A *Letter* to the *Earl* of *Anglesey,* of the *Council* of *Trent* not being *receiv'd* in *France,*" part of the Bishop's answer— the first citation, in fact—is drawn from Sarpi:

> I say then,
>
> 1. That *Father Paul* of *Venice* (that great *Scholar* and *Statesman*) who had intimate familiarity with the most eminent *French* Statesmen and Scholars, (both at *Venice* and *Paris;*) *Father Paul,* I say, tells us in Print;[117] *That the* Trent *Council was not receiv'd in* France in the Year 1616.[118]

At the end of the discussion, Barlow again cites Sarpi. A certain monk, Johannes Cabassutius, having asserted in his *Notitia Conciliorum* that the Council *was* received in France in 1615, Barlow remarks: "But *Father Paul* of *Venice* (a far more credible Author) says it was not received *Anno* 1616. and so it could not be received *Anno* 1615."[119] So much for Cabassutius.

A final work to be noticed here is *The Council of Trent No Free Assembly,*[120] edited by Michael Geddes, whose only original contribution to the volume is "An Introductory Discourse of Councils," pages 1–82. The letters here translated—those of Vargas and others at Trent—all tend to support the views expressed by Sarpi in his *History of the Council of Trent.* Sarpi is, in fact, several times mentioned in Geddes's "Discourse," as is also Pallavicino, the latter with just a sniff of suspicion: "If *Pallavicino* may be believed . . ." (p. 73). Pallavicino is named as the only writer giving an account of Vargas's alleged turning to Pope as against Council.[121] "Which instance of *Vargas* having changed his Measures, whatever the former may be, we have great reason to believe is false, notwithstanding Father Paul agrees with *Pallavicino* as to the main of it."[122]

Most importantly, in trying to explain how these vital letters have come into his hands and why they have escaped publication before this moment, Geddes can only assume that they must have been given originally under condition that they not be published during the lifetime of the individuals involved. Geddes got them, he says, from Dr. Stillingfleet, Bishop of Worcester, who had received them from the "Right Honourable *Sir William Trumbull,*" grandson of James I's Envoy to Brussels.[123] He then goes on to say that this former Envoy

> was a most zealous Protestant, which he has derived to all that have descended from him; and he came into England from his Foreign Employment, about the time that Father *Paul*'s History of the Council of *Trent* was first printed in *London.* That was the most proper time for publishing these Letters, and must have [would have] established the Credit of the Celebrated History, beyond all attempts to detract from it.[124]

But by the time Geddes was writing, the "Credit of the Celebrated History," so far as England was concerned, had long been firmly established.

Interesting and important as are some of the works examined in these two related chapters for establishing a view of Sarpi's general reception among the English clergy, they are still but second growth and underbrush. We now come to another part of the forest.

11 --- Heavier Timber

MANY—PERHAPS MOST—modern English readers when they see the name Sarpi (or Father Paul) associate it with that of Milton. And with reason. Two sturdier opponents of shams and subterfuges, two more ardent advocates of liberty, both intellectual and political, would be hard to find in the seventeenth century. Nor does Milton hide his Sarpi under a bushel.

The English poet's impassioned plea "for the Liberty of unlicenc'd Printing" in his *Areopagitica* (1644) will come first to mind. There, as preface to the scathing satire of his "lordly Imprimatur[s]," "complementing and ducking each to other with their shav'n reverences" in "the Piatza of one Title page," he acknowledges the source of his historical review: "And that the primitive Councels and Bishops were wont only to declare what Books were not commendable, passing no furder, but leaving it to each ones conscience to read or to lay by, till after the year 800. is observ'd already by *Padre Paolo* the great unmasker of the *Trentine* Councel."[1] The language indicates that Milton is here *probably* referring to that digressory "discourse of the author, cōcerning the prohibition of bookes" (margin) in *The Historie of the Councel of Trent*, but not necessarily.[2] Sarpi has an even longer and more "Miltonic" discussion of the same topic in "The Exposition of the nine and twentieth Chapter" of his *The History of the Inquisition*, which supplies much of the same data that is reported in the *Areopagitica*.[3] Milton's apt description of Sarpi as "the great unmasker of the *Trentine* Councel" is matched (perhaps outdone) by that which Milton's and Sarpi's friend Wotton supplied for the "Oxford" portrait: *Concilii Tridentini Eviscerator*.[4]

Milton has, scattered through his prose, a dozen or more references to Sarpi, mainly to *The History of the Council of Trent*. Not to "run into a paroxysm of citations again" (as Milton himself phrases it), I shall call attention to but two of these, both from *Of Reformation touching Church Dis-*

153

cipline in England. The interest of the first lies chiefly in Milton's recognition of the role Sarpi played in the events of the interdict.

> You know Sir what was the judgement of *Padre Paolo* the great Venetian Antagonist of the *Pope*, for it is extant in the hands of many men, whereby he declares his feare, that when the Hierarchy of *England* shall light into the hands of busie and audacious men, or shall meet with Princes tractable to the Prelacy, then much mischiefe is like to ensue.[5]

The second passage occurs slightly later in the second Book of the tract. Speaking of gradual papal encroachment upon and usurpation of secular rights and authority as seen in the long history of conflict between church and state, Milton asks, "Why may not wee as well, having been forewarn'd at home by our renowned *Chaucer*, and from abroad by the great and learned *Padre Paolo*, from the like beginnings, as we see they are, feare the like events?"[6]

Hanford describes Milton as "a persistent and enthusiastic book collector," and every evidence confirms the description.[7] So far as is known, Milton left no catalogue of his library. But even lacking the bona-fide confirmation of any list in a will or other document from Milton's hand which might be accepted in a court of law, one may, nevertheless, be permitted in his case some speculation which falls just short of certainty. Milton's *Commonplace Book* enables us to follow at least some of his reading for a period of thirty years or more, between the early thirties and the early sixties of the century.[8] His common practice of giving exact page references for quotations or citations also enables us to identify precisely the editions of some of the works he read. It is also possible to establish, at least inferentially, something of the order in which or date on which the works were read. And this is what Ruth Mohl, in her edition of the *Commonplace Book*, attempts to do. Milton need not, of course, have *owned* all the books he cites; but after his university years, the probability that he did is greater than that he did not. The entries in the *Commonplace Book* demonstrate, minimally, that he had read the work of Sarpi closely and with interest. These entries Miss Mohl dates provisionally between 1641 and 1643, adding (verifiably), "Milton's thirteen references to the history of the Council of Trent are to the Italian edition of Paolo Sarpi, *Historia del Concilio Tridentino*, published in London in 1619."[9] It is certainly no surprise to find that Milton, Italophile as he was, should have chosen to read his Sarpi in that "strana favella" that he loved next to his own and Virgil's tongue.

There are in the British Museum two manuscripts almost coeval with Milton's reading of *The History of the Council of Trent*, both of which bear witness to the vogue of Sarpi in the England of Charles I. One of these, described as being Meric Casaubon's miscellaneous papers, contains on the recto and verso of folio 28 an Italian résumé of the chief arguments (contra Sarpi) in a book by Hernando Bastida supporting papal authority against the Venetians and all secular states.[10] On folios 59 and 60 it also contains a list, dated 1639 and headed "Catalogus librorum Gulielmi Somnerj," which is divided into classes. Under the heading of "hystory and Antiquity" is entered "Hist. of the councell of Trent. fo." (folio 59 verso)—probably Brent's translation. On the next page, another entry suggests, somewhat enigmatically, further Sarpiana: "The Venetian Controversy. 4."

The other manuscript, of less varied interest but more nearly akin to the entries in Milton's *Commonplace Book*, is described as "Historical Collections of the Earl of Derby."[11] The folios from 16 through 88 verso are headed "Collections out of the History of the Councell of Trent 1645" and consist of extracts with comments, Book by Book. The extracts considerably outweight the comments; and on folio 88 verso, after the extracts and observations, almost with an audible sigh of relief, the transcriber-commentator has written, "End of the last booke of the Councel of Trent." It is not given to everyone to relish *every* word on 825 folio pages of ecclesiastical history, even when the work is written by such a masterly politician as Paolo Sarpi.

A work written somewhat earlier, and left in manuscript at the death of its author, achieved a posthumous partial publication just about at this period. The *Historia rerum Britannicarum* of Robert Johnston (1567?–1639), a work in twenty-two Books, was not published in complete form until 1655, though the first three Books appeared in print at Amsterdam in 1642.[12] A respected history to which we have already referred in connection with de Dominis, Johnston's book, being in the "universal tongue," helped to spread the reputation of Sarpi not only in England but in the Protestant parts of the Continent as well. Book XII ends (1605) with a brief notice of the jurisdictional dispute between Venice and Paul V (p. 417). Book XIII (under the year 1606, pp. 428–29) continues the account of the Venetian quarrel, mentioning among the Venetian supporters "*Antonius Quirinus, Senator Venetus; Frater Paulus, Ordinis Servorum Monachus; Ioannes Marsilius, Neapolitanus*; & Theologus anonymus" (p. 428).

But for us the major entry is elsewhere: one of those lugubrious yearly summations of notable deaths. In Book XX, under the date 1623, Johnston lists the deaths of four famous writers: William Camden, John Owen (the epigrammatist), Paolo Sarpi, and Philip de Mornay. Sarpi's, the longest entry, I transcribe *in toto*:

Hoc quoquè Anno, *Paulus Venetus, Servitarum Ordinis Theologus*, non obiit, sed ad vitam evolavit aeternam; nulli inferior Iudicio, Ingenio; admirabili Facundiâ, literis reconditis, & exquisitis; non magis doctrinâ, quàm rerum usu Prudens; ut maiorem, nec divinarum, nec humanarum

155

rerum Scientiam, nec Integriorem, nec Sanctiorem vitam quisquam desideraret, qui in Scripta eius incidisset, ut mihi quidem videtur. Is tantis Virtutibus ornatus, liberâ, integrâquè mente, *publicam Venetorum Causam adversùs Pauli V. Pontificis maximi fulmina, libello edito defendit*; qui crudelissimis Edictis detonuit in eos, & *depravatam Romanae Ecclesiae disciplinam, Caerimoniarum Vanitatem, & Pontificis Auctoritatem, Ambitum, Potentiam*, eâdem libertate exagitavit. Posteà etiam, *Commentarium in Concilium Tridentinum scripsit.* Quae res gravissimam Pontificis Offensionem excitavit; & illi Perniciem penè creavit. Nam mox, *Sicarii in eius Caput subornati, Scloppeti ictu, in Claustro Servitarum vulnerarunt: & concensâ Naviculâ, ad hoc praeparatâ, per Canales aufugerunt.* Civitas, Casu inopinato consternata, decrevit, ut in Sicarios inquireretur; legibus ageretur; & pro Salute *Assertoris unici Dignitatis, Potentiaequè Venetorum*, in posterum excubaretur. Qui magnas à libertate Venetâ Insidias, suâ Prudentiâ depulit. Pro quibus Meritis, in Mortuum omnes Divini & humani honores congesti. Antè Tumulum, magnâ turbâ, multisquè precibus supplicatum est. *publicato Romae Epitaphio in laudem defuncti; & Venetae Plebis*, in Mortui, memoriam funebri Pietate; *Paulas Pontifex*, Diplomate suo, *Venetam Plebem* extemplò coërcuit, & *Defuncti Tumulum luminibus frequentari prohibuit*: dequè eâ re Senatum monuit; & clarè pronuntiavit, *Defunctum Sacris interdictum fuisse.* Resp: ut *Pontificem* placatum haberet, ac Armorum Necessitatem effugeret, *Plebis Superstitionem Edicto cohibuit.* Durabit diu atrox Memoria vulnerum, quibus *Romani Pontificis Amplitudinem, Religionis, Iurisque Pontificii Auctoritatem*, haec discordia afflixit. *Extabunt Pauli Monachi Volumina, ingenti Acerbitate scripta; & Acerbiora Lutheri, Calvini, & Reginaldi libris*; quos Contemptus Romanae Religionis, Caerimoniarumque, iniquiores fecit.[13]

One of the strangest, rarest, and most valuable of catalogues ever put out by a bookseller is *A Catalogue of the most vendible Books in England*, by William London of Newcastle.[14] London's *Catalogue* was published in parts in 1657, 1658, 1660. The books listed under the various headings are all in English or Latin, although they include many translations from French and Italian. Among the latter are "S[r] *N. Brent*. The History of the Councill of *Trent* ... Writ in *Italian* by *Polano*, now Englished. folio";[15] "The History of the inquisition in *Rome*; by Father *Pa. Servitta*, the Author of the Council of *Trent*. 8°";[16] and "D[r] *Potter*. The History of the quarrels of *Pope Paul* the 5. with the state of *Venice*, writ in *Italian*, by the Author of the counsell of *Trent*, now Englished. 4°."[17] Included also are Fra Fulgenzio's "The life of the most learned Father *Paul*, of the order of the Servy; Counseller of state to the most serene Republick of *Venice*, and Authour of the

History of the Counsell of *Trent*; Englished from the Italian by a person of quality. 8°."[18] as well as Guillaume Ranchin's "A review of the counsell of *Trent* . . . translated from French to English. folio."[19] With the special canniness which booksellers seem often to develop, London perceived that for seventeenth-century Englishmen any title page bearing the name of Father Paul or mentioning the Council of Trent was indeed "most vendible" ware.

Peter Heylyn (1600–1662) was an Oxford scholar of some distinction, a controversialist whose writing activities and acerbic temper (when he had his pen in hand) earned him many enemies.[20] He was accused by those enemies of leaning towards Catholicism, perhaps because of his support of Laud. He became one of the chaplains in ordinary to King Charles I in 1630, but he never attained any very high preferment and led a disturbed life. Contentious and ambitious by nature, he managed to live in constant strife with his fellow clergymen, especially those of puritan (or Presbyterian) persuasion. It remains an astounding fact that he produced so much—and so much that was learnedly exact—after he had become virtually blind (1651). Following his attack on Fuller (in *Examen Historicum*, 1659), Fuller answered him gently and pleasantly and made further efforts to mollify him, so that they ended by becoming friends—one of the few agreeable notes in Heylyn's career.

No one would ever accuse Heylyn of writing an elegant English. But he was enormously learned, and he knew how to conduct an argument in a clear and orderly (though often overlengthy) manner. Humor and lightness of touch he had not, or only in spare supply; though he could on occasion deliver a pungent *sarcasmus* or a piece of cutting repartee. Perhaps he learned something of his ordonnance from Sarpi, with whose works he was early and late demonstrably familiar.

The first of Heylyn's books to show his acquaintance with Sarpi was his *Microcosmus* (Oxford, 1621, 1625).[21] In his introductory discourse, "The Generall Praecognita of Historie," where he lists the "best writers of ecclesiasticall historie," he does not mention Sarpi; nor does he mention him in the section on Germany when he describes the city of Trent, writing merely: ". . . *Trent* on the river Adesis, in which the Councell was held by Pope *Paul* the third, it beganne in the year 1546, against the doctrines of *Luther* and *Calvin*."[22] But in the second and subsequent editions, with the erroneous date corrected, this statement was supplemented by the following (from Sarpi):

> This Councell continued, sometimes assembled, sometimes dissolved, for the space of 18 yeares; and before the first meeting here, had at diverse other places bin intimated and dashed; furthered by some,

and hindred by others for 22 yeares together. The effects of this Councell I cannot better describe, then in the words of the history hereof,
which are these: *This Councell desired and procured by godly men, to
re-unite the Church, which began to be divided; hath so established the
schisme, and made the parties so obstinate, that the discords are irrecon-
cileable*:[23] and being managed by Princes for reformation of Ecclesiasticall Discipline, hath caused the greatest deformation that ever was
since Christianitie did beginne: and hoped for by the Bishops to re-
gaine the Episcopall authority, for the most part usurped by the Pope;
hath made them loose it altogether, bringing them into greater servitude;
on the contrary feared and avoided by the See of *Rome*, as a potent
meanes to moderate the exorbitant power thereof, mounted from small
beginnings, by diverse degrees, to an unlimited excesse; it hath so established and confirmed the same over that part which remaineth subject
unto it, that it never was so great nor so soundly rooted. So farre the
words of the History.[24]

The next of Heylyn's books to make some limited use of Sarpi is his
Theologia Veterum, published long after he had escaped this period of his
callow youth.[25] The work is an extended serious exposition of and commentary upon the Apostles' Creed, in three Books, folio, of over five hundred
pages. In this rather unpromising context Heylyn allows himself an unexpected literary allusiveness, ranging through Christian and pagan authors
and quoting Ovid—generally in Sandys's translation—with surprising frequency.[26] Of peripheral interest for our topic are his comment on the
Crakanthorp answer to de Dominis,[27] his reference to Chemnitz as "*Chemni-
tius* that learned and laborious Canvasser of the Councel of Trent,"[28] and
his characterization of Andreas Vega as "one of the great sticklers in the
Council of *Trent*."[29]

The History of the Council of Trent is quoted on but three occasions,
though its presence is felt in other parts of the text. In the first instance, it is
called upon to confirm a difference of opinions about the conduct of Henry
VIII:

> For when the Princes of those times applauded the piety and cour-
> age of King *Henry* the Eighth, in that without any alteration in *Religion*
> he had suppressed the Popes Authority in all his Dominions: The *Papal*
> faction thought the censure to be very unjust, *Primo & praecipuo Ro-
> manensium fidei Articulo, de Pontificis Primatu immutato*, considering
> that the first and chiefest *Article* of the *Faith*, that of the *Popes Su-
> premacy*, was so changed and abrogated.[30]

The second is less concerned with control of the population explosion than
with the control of political loyalties: "It pleased the *Popes*, for politick and

worldly ends, to *restrain the Clergy* of that *Church* from marriage, because that having Wives and Children, they would be more obnoxious [that is, susceptible] to their *natural Princes*, and not depend so much as now, on the See of *Rome*."[31] On the next page of his text Heylyn says that the taking away of the cup from the lay communicant is "sacrilegiously robbing him of the one half of his *birth-right*" and commends certain churches where the communion is preserved for him in both kinds: " ... so tenaciously adhered unto by the *Bohemians* (where the *Hussites* had their first original) that in small time they got the names of Calistini,[32] and *Sub utráques*, from their participating of the *Cup*, and communicating under both kindes, when none else durst do it."[33]

Heylyn's next Sarpi-connected publication was his *Ecclesia Vindicata: or, the Church of England Justified* ... (London, 1657). The book is in two Parts, the second (and longer) carrying as its own running head *The History of Episcopacie*. Only the first Part contains references to Sarpi; and again, as in the *Theologia Veterum*, there are three specific references to his works. Heylyn repeats, perhaps from himself, the Latin "Article of Faith" mentioned above in connection with Henry VIII: *"Primo & praecipuo Romanensium fidei articulo de Pontificis primatu immutato*, as my Author hath it."[34] And Henry is still in his mind (as in this passage) when he later elaborates:

> And when K. Henry the 8. following these examples, had banished the Popes authority out of his Dominions, Religion still remaining here as before it did . . . that Act of his was much commended by most knowing men, in that without more alteration in the face of the Church *Romanae sedis exuisset obsequium* (saith the Author of the *Tridentine* History) he had freed himself and all his subjects from so great a Vassallage.[35]

On the same page, commenting on how near the Venetians had been to a similar rupture with Roman Catholicism, he continues to cite Sarpi but changes documents: "How neer the Signeury of *Venice* was to have done the like, *anno* 1608. the History of the *Interdict*, or of the Quarrels betwixt that State and Pope *Paul* the 5. doth most plainly shew."[36]

About a score of years after Heylyn's death there was published ΚΕΙΜΗΛΙΑ 'ΕΚΚΛΗΣΙΑΣΤΙΚΑ. *The Historical and Miscellaneous Tracts of the Reverend and Learned Peter Heylyn, D.D. Now Collected into one Volume . . . And an Account of the Life of the Author: Never before Published* (London, 1681). The volume is a stately folio having a fine engraved portrait of Heylyn as frontispiece. It contains the *Life* and five of Heylyn's works, the third of which (pp. 499–[640]), originally published in 1660, is entitled *Historia Quinqu-Articularis: or, A Declaration of the Judgment of the Western Churches, and more particularly of the Church of England; in the Five Controverted Points, Reproached in these Last times by the name of Arminianism* .... The preface, "To the Reader," is dated 26 December 1659; a "Postscript to the Reader" is dated 29 December 1659. That Heylyn composed the long and intricately argued work, even with generous aid from Sarpi, between those two dates is quite improbable—especially so when one recalls that by that time his eyes were virtually useless to him and that, like his great contemporary Milton, he had to depend upon the services of an inept amanuensis.

The *Historia Quinqu-Articularis* is divided into twenty-two chapters, and Heylyn tips his hand at the very beginning: *"In the pursuance of this work,"* he says, *"I have exemplified so much of the Debates and Artifices in the Council of* Trent, *as concerns these points."*[37] The five controverted points are then particularly paraded (pp. 518–19):

a) "Of Divine Predestination"
b) "Of the Merit and Efficacy of Christs Death"
c) "Of Mans Will in the state of depraved Nature"
d) "Of Conversion, and the manner of it"
e) "Of falling after Grace received."[38]

After discussing the previous history of these points in Chapter I, Heylyn opens his second chapter, "Of the Debates amongst the Divines in the Council of *Trent,* touching *Predestinations,* and *Original* Sin," with an explicit avowal of his reliance upon Sarpi:

> In such conditions stood affairs in reference to the Doctrines of *Predestination, Grace, Free will, &c.* at the first sitting down of the Council of *Trent,* in which, those points became the subject of many sad[39] and serious Debates amongst the Prelates and Divines, then and there assembled, which being so necessary to the understanding of the Questions which we have before us: I shall not think my time ill spent in laying down the sum and abstract of the same, as I find it digested to my hand by Padre Paulo, the diligent and laborious Author of the *Tridentine History*; only I shall invert his Method, by giving precedency to the Disputes concerning *Predestination,* before the Debates and Agitations, which hapned in canvasing the Articles touching the Freedom of mans Will, though those about Free-will do first occur in the course and method of that Council: It being determined by the Council, as that Author hath it, to draw some Articles from the Writings of the *Protestants,* concerning the Doctrine of *Predestination*: It appeared that in the Books of *Luther,* in the *Augustan Confession,* and in the *Apologies* and *Colloquies,* there was nothing found that deserved Censure; But much

they found among the Writings of the *Zwinglians*, out of which they drew these following Articles; *Viz.*

[*]1. For *Predestination* and *Reprobation*; that man doth nothing, but all is in the will of God.

2. The *Predestinated* cannot be *condemned*, nor the *Reprobate* *saved*.

3. The *Elect* and *Predestinated* only are truly *justified*.

4. The Justified are bound by Faith to believe, they are in the number of the *Predestinated*.

5. The Justified cannot fall from Grace.

6. Those that are called, and are not in the number of the *predestinated* do never receive Grace.

7. The Justified is bound to believe by Faith, that he ought to persevere in Justice until the end.

8. The Justified is bound to believe for certain, that in case he fall from Grace, he shall receive it again.

In the examining of the first of these Articles, the Opinions were diverse. The most esteemed Divines amongst them thought it to be Catholick, the contrary Heretical, because the good School-Writers (St. *Thomas, Scotus,* and the rest) do so think, that is, that God before the Creation, out of the Mass of mankind, hath elected by his only and meer mercy, some for Glory, for whom he hath prepared effectually the means to obtain it, which is called, to *predestinate.* That their number is certain and determined, neither can there be any added. The others not *predestinated* cannot complain, for that God hath prepared for them sufficient assistance for this, though indeed none but the Elect shall be saved. For the most principal reason they alledged, that S. *Paul* to the *Romans* having made *Jacob* a pattern of the *predestinated,* and *Esau* of the *Reprobate,* he produceth the Decree of God pronounced before they were born, not for their Works, but for his own good pleasure. To this they joyned the example of the same Apostle: That as the Potter of the same lump of Clay, maketh one Vessel to honour, another to dishonour; so God of the same Mass of men, chooseth and leaveth whom he listeth: for proof whereof S. *Paul* bringeth the place where God saith to *Moses, I will shew mercy on whom I will shew mercy, and I will shew pity on whom I will shew pity.* And the same Apostle concludeth: *It is not of him that willeth, or of him that runneth, but of God who sheweth mercy*; adding after, that God *sheweth mercy on whom he will, and hardneth whom he will.* They said further, That for this cause the Council of the Divine Predestination and Reprobation is called by the same Apostle, the height and depth of Wisdom unsearchable and incomprehensible. They added places of the other Epistles, where he saith,

We have nothing but what we have received from God, that *we are not able of our selves, so much as to think well*: and where, in giving the cause, why some have revolted from the Faith, and some stand firm, he said, it was because *the Foundation of God standeth sure, and hath this seal; the Lord knoweth who are his.* They added divers passages of the Gospel of S. *John*, and infinite Authorities of S. *Augustine*, because the Saint wrote nothing in his old Age but in favour of this Doctrine.[*]140

All the portion of the foregoing quotation between asterisks (which I have supplied) is copied verbatim from Sarpi-Brent, and is to be found on pages 197 and 198 of the 1620 edition. Some of the matter preceding the first asterisk is also paraphrased from the same source. The next seven paragraphs of Heylyn's text are likewise copied (with no marginal indication of source) from successive paragraphs in Sarpi-Brent. The two final paragraphs (p. 513) of Heylyn's chapter slip into the discussion of the council's conclusions about original sin and carry marginal references to "*Hist. of the Council*, fol. 175" and "*Idem*. fol. 181." The first of these two final paragraphs, aside from the transitional first sentence (six lines), derives word for word from Sarpi-Brent (p. 165); the second paragraph—in the substance of the first half and in the *ipsissima verba* of the second half—derives from page 173. It does not, however, quite faithfully represent the text in *The Historie of the Councel of Trent*; for where Sarpi lists five of the "Anathematisms" pronounced by the Tridentine Fathers, Heylyn records only the first three. The entire chapter, then, should be credited to Sarpi rather than to Heylyn. And much the same thing may be said for Chapter III.

Heylyn moves on, in "his" Chapter III, to a discussion of "The like Debates about Free-will, with the Conclusions of the Council, in the Five Controverted Points." Like the preceding chapter, this is divided into ten numbered sections, each generally containing a single paragraph, although the first and tenth sections have internal numbered subdivisions. Here again Heylyn copies Sarpi-Brent slavishly but not with care or great acuteness. The first section, which I copy out in full, begins the only slightly modified lifting from Sarpi-Brent (1620 ed., p. 194). Thereafter, in sections II-VII (pp. 514–16) Heylyn simply transcribes from the successive paragraphs on pages 195–97 of *The Historie of the Councel of Trent*. Here, then, is Section I:

These Differences and Debates concerning Predestination, the possibility of falling away from the Faith of Christ, and the nature of Original sin: being thus passed over; I shall look back on those Debates which were had amongst the Fathers and Divines in the Council of Trent, about the nature of Free-will, and the power thereof. In order whereunto these Articles were collected out of the Writings of the *Lutherans*, to be discussed and censured as they found cause for it. Now the Articles were these that follow, *viz.*

1. God is the total cause of our works good and evil, and the Adultry of *David*, the cruelty of *Manlius*, and the Treason of *Judas*, are the works of God as well as the Vocation of *Saul*.

2. No man hath power to think well or ill, but all cometh from absolute necessity, and in us is no Free-will, and to affirm it is a meer fiction.

3. Free-will since the sin of *Adam* is lost, a thing only titular, and when one doth what is in his power, he sinneth mortally: yea, it is a thing fained, and a Title without reality.

4. Free-will is only in doing ill, and hath no power to do good.

5. Free-will moved by God, doth by no means co-operate, and followeth as an Instrument without life, or an unreasonable Creature.

6. That God correcteth those only whom he will, though they will not spurn against it.[41]

That this contains the barest minimum of transitional "filler" and that it cost Heylyn no organizing or constructive thought can readily be shown by comparing it with the corresponding passage in Sarpi-Brent:

Therefore Prelates and Divines were deputed to collect Articles, out of the works of the Lutherans, that they might be censured.

The Articles were, 1. God is the total cause of our works, good and evil: and the adultery of *David*, the cruelty of *Manlius*, and the Treason of Judas, are works of God, as well as the vocation of *Saul*. 2. No man hath power to think well or ill, but all cometh from absolute necessity, and in us is no Free-will, and to affirm it, is a meer fiction. 3. Free-will, since the sin of *Adam*, is lost, and a thing only titular, and when one doeth what is in his power, he sinneth mortally; yea, it is a thing feigned and a title without reality. 4. Free-will is only in doing ill, and hath no power to do good. 5. Free-will moved by God, doth by no means cooperate, and followeth as an instrument without life, or as an unreasonable creature. 6. That God converteth those only whom he will, though they will not, and spurn against it.[42]

The transcription of the sixth article, presumably by an amanuensis but allowed to stand in the final printing, shows the kind of disastrous inexactness of which Heylyn's book is occasionally guilty. At the end of Section VII (p. 516) Heylyn reaches a point in Sarpi-Brent (p. 197, middle) where the discussion veers to predestination—and the next and succeeding paragraphs (pp. 197–200) supply Heylyn with the content of his Chapter II, discussed above. It should be noted, incidentally, that whereas I have quoted Sarpi-

Brent in the edition of 1620, the page references in Heylyn indicate that he was using the third (1640) edition.

Sections VIII and IX of Chapter III, a little less literally, also draw upon Sarpi-Brent. Here, however, the drafts are duly acknowledged by correct marginal page references to the 1640 edition of *The Historie of the Councel of Trent.* Chapter IV likewise begins with a backward-looking glance at points already discussed in Sarpi's *History*, but then quickly moves on to the use of other sources.

So far as I can determine, no further use is made of Sarpi-Brent until Chapter XIII, "The Doctrine of the Church of *England,* concerning the certainty or uncertainty of Perseverance." The first four sections of the chapter again quote heavily from Sarpi's *History*—again, however, with proper marginal identification (pp. 573–74). Unfortunately, the amanuensis or the printer or the proofreader or some other wandering-witted contributor to the vagaries of this *Quinquarticular* history has permitted (p. 573) "Levipandus" to stand for Seripandus and "Calarinus" for Catarinus. At this late date one reads uncorroborated Heylyn at his peril.

It may certainly be doubted that Heylyn intended to deceive his readers as to the source of the work before them; but judged by modern standards, that work is inadequately, and certainly misleadingly, documented. In making use of a book so widely known as Sarpi's *History*, Heylyn perhaps felt that he had sufficiently set his readers on guard when he named Sarpi at the outset and then scattered throughout a few marginal references to the *History*. Nevertheless, a modern reader would never guess from Heylyn's references the extent of his indebtedness to his source. And in an age of savage controversy, when many of those whom he had antagonized would gladly have nailed his hide to the door of his Lacy's Court retreat at Abingdon, the fact that none of his contemporaries challenged him for being here what he himself described as a petty "compiler" must mean that they recognized his heavy indebtedness to Sarpi no more than modern writers have done—or cared no more.[43]

Luke de Beaulieu (d. 1723) was a French Protestant, educated at Saumur, who fled to England about 1667 for religious reasons; became an English citizen; attended Oxford University (Christ Church); took various degrees, and orders in the Church; and became mildly notorious through his association with various characters less mildly notorious in their time. He was also the author of several devotional works, including the popular *Claustrum Animae* (1677; 4th ed., 1699).[44]

Our concern with him is limited to one book, his *The Holy Inquisition, wherein is Represented what is the Religion of the Church of Rome: and how they are dealt with that Dissent from It* (London, 1681). There is throughout the book much incidental respectful citing of Sarpi (*History of the Inquisition*) and very important dependence on him in Chapter XIV, Section ii, pages 213–22, where Beaulieu deals with the *Index librorum prohibitorum*—that is to say, where he is following closely the text (as he admits) of Sarpi's Chapter 29.

Understandably, Beaulieu can see little good in the Inquisition and small hope for those who fall into its trammels. Once a man is cited to the Inquisition, he is sure to be

> laid up for a good while, except God in mercy release him. Indeed *Padre Paolo* makes mention of some who by the interposition of the Republick of *Venice*, or of some Princes have been set at liberty. . . . But these cases be rare, and generally when a man goes in he may bid adieu to the world; he must meddle no more with the concerns of it, no friends must visit or comfort him, nay, they may not mediate for him, where the Pope is supreme, as appears by a Bull of *Pius* V. cited by *Padre Paolo*; so that he is left to the mercy of them that think themselves obliged to have no mercy on him.[45]

The long arm of the Inquisition reaches everywhere in Catholic lands, and its tender mercies are such as Beaulieu feels little inclination to trust. No safe-conduct guards against it:

> But for all *Padre Paolo's* moderation, and his blaming the exorbitancies of that [Roman] Court, I doubt not but at *Venice* it self *Lutherans* or *Calvinists* would be as hardly dealt with, as any where else, and that their [that is, the Venetians'] mixt Inquisition half Ecclesiastical and half Secular would be near as severe to real Hereticks, though likely Roman Catholicks be not so much endangered and oppressed by it, as in other places. I am sure that with publick allowance the most bloudy Directories of the Inquisition, and the cruellest Books against Hereticks are printed at *Venice*.[46]

Chapter XII, "Of the Condemnation of Hereticks that are to be burnt," provides the author an opportunity to exercise some righteous indignation against the hypocritical formula of hand-washing by which the ecclesiastical Inquisitors, in handing over the condemned heretic to the secular power for the infliction of punishment, close their document with a plea that blood and life be spared. This he sees as the hollowest mockery, more horrible even than the horrible punishment itself:

> And Canonists are very prolix in proving that Hereticks are to be punished with death, and not only with death, but with fire, which is the most cruel, and not only to be burnt, but to be burnt alive.

> *Padre Paolo* tells us whence proceeds this custom of interceding for
> the condemned Hereticks, when they are going to be burnt. Mean while
> it may be observed how much their kindnesses & good words to Here-
> ticks are to be trusted, who constantly pray that they may not lose
> bloud or life, when they are going to murther them with the greatest
> barbarity.[47]

And the iniquity is not confined to the end of the process. The alleged
ruthless ambition and insatiable greed of the popes is subserved by this supple
instrument:

> Several Authors have observed with *Padre Paolo*, who gives many in-
> stances of it, in the first Chapter of his *History of the Inquisition*, that
> the Pope makes a gin of the notions and definitions of Heresie, and
> makes his Laws and Declarations about it serve the end of his ambitions
> and covetousness; giving the name of Hereticks, not where it is really
> due, but where he is displeased, desirous to conquer, or to ruin his
> enemies.[48]

By one of those inexplicable lapses incident to all who write books, in
Chapter XIII, Section iv, "Of the Authorities and Authors used in this book,"
Beaulieu fails to mention Sarpi. The omission surely does not arise out of
any intention to mislead the reader or to neglect Sarpi, whose name is prominently scattered throughout the book—as *Padre Paolo*, of course. In any case,
the omission does not curtail Beaulieu's draft upon Sarpi:

> The Civil Magistrates, as we see, are made Officers of the Holy
> Tribunal; even in *Venice, Padre Paolo* tells us, *c. 6.* the Inquisition
> would [that is, would like to] oblige the Assistants, who represent the
> State, to swear secrecy to them, making it a great Case of Conscience to
> reveal any of their proceedings without their leave, and backing it with
> this Maxim, *Che cause di fede [d]evono restarappo* [sic] *i Giudici della
> fede.* "That matters that concern the Faith must remain with the Judges
> of the Faith."[49]

This secretiveness, this pervasive and insidious interpenetration of all
reaches of society, frightens and horrifies Beaulieu—as well it might. The
power of the Inquisitors, who can influence all confessors and, through them,
all the people, is such "that where the Inquisition prevails, the Popes Edicts
are of more force than any Civil Laws or Evangelical Precepts. *Padre Paolo*,
chap. 26. [of the *History of the Inquisition*] gives an instance of it very
observable."[50] So strong does he feel this wicked power of the Inquisition to
be that he is sent scurrying off to another work of Sarpi's for further confirmation of his estimate: "*Paul* IV. would freely own, that it was *praecipuum*

nervum & arcanum pontificatus, the strongest nerve and deepest mystery of the Papacy. *Padre Paolo, Hist. Con. Trid.* l. 5."[51]

It is consideration of the extension of this awesome power in one of its manifold ramifications that leads Beaulieu to his most extensive draft upon Sarpi. The portion of his book in question is Chapter XIV, Section ii, "*Of the prohibiting of Books, and the* Indices expurgatorii," especially pages 213–22, which often mention (and virtually reproduce) much of Sarpi's *History of the Inquisition* in the part that deals with the *Index.* "Among the many priviledges of the Inquisitors," he says, "it is none of the least, that the Censure of Books belongs to them" (p. 213), for by this means they keep the people in ignorance and publish only "such Books as tend to establish the Roman Faith, and their own Authority"[52]—one of Sarpi's insistent charges. The officers of the Inquisition, being very numerous and not otherwise occupied, make it both dangerous and difficult

> to print or import any Books, that should savour of what they call Heresie, or maintain the just rights of Temporal Princes against the Spiritual Monarch.
>
> For this last, saith the Judicious *Padre Paolo, When a Potentate hath not the favour of him that commands in Ecclesiastical causes, Religion is made a pretext to oppress him.* Of which he gives instances *Chap.* 1. and amongst them, that when the Pope was fallen out with the *Venetians,* any Books that came out in Favour of the Republick, were forbidden by the Papal Inquisitions, under colour of Heresie.[53]

Then Beaulieu comes to the core of the matter and to passages which must also have fallen under Milton's eyes:

> Relating to this I shall transcribe out of the last mentioned Author [Padre Paolo] part of *Chap.* 29. *The matter of Books seems to be a thing of small moment, because it treats of words; but through these words come opinions into the world, which cause partialities, Seditions, and finally Wars; they are words, it is true, but such, as in consequence draw after them Hosts of armed men.*—"By forbidding Books which at *Rome* are not liked of, although they be good and godly, because they maintain Temporal Power, great wrong is done to Sovereign Princes, to such specially as would rule with the Arts of Peace, who use Books as a chief Instrument to cause people to believe as a firm truth, that the Prince is Ordained by God, and Ruleth with Divine Authority, and the Subject consequently in Conscience is bound to obey him, and not doing it offendeth God, because that the Prince, by the Law of God, is above every person that is within his Dominions, and may lay burthens on mens Estates, as publick necessities require. Where these things, which

are most true, are believed, a State may easily be governed: but where
contrary opinions are held, great disorders must needs happen. But as
there was always in Gods Church, those who made use of Religion for
worldly ends, so the number of them is more full. These under a spiritual pretence, but with an ambitious end, and desire of wordly wealth,
would free themselves of the obedience due unto the Prince, and take
away the love and reverence due to him by the people, to draw it to
themselves. To bring it to pass, they have newly invented a Doctrine,
which talks of nothing but Ecclesiastical greatness, liberty, immunity,
and jurisdiction. This doctrine was unheard of, until about the year
1300. Neither is there any Book concerning it, before this time, then did
they begin to write of it scatteringly in some Books, but there were not
above two Books which treated of nothing else but this, until the year
1400. and three until the year 1500. After this time the number en-
creased a little, but it was tolerable. After the year 1560. this Doctrine
began to encrease in such manner, that they gave over writing, as they
had used before, of the Mysteries of the Most Holy Trinity, of the In-
carnation of Christ, of the Creation of the World, and other Mysteries
of the belief, and there is nothing Printed in *Italy*, but Books in diminution of Secular Authority, and exaltation of the Ecclesiastical; and such
Books are not printed by small numbers but by thousands: Those people
which have learning, can read nothing else; the Confessors likewise
know none other Doctrine, neither need they any other Learning to be
approved of. Whence comes in a perverse opinion universally, that
Princes and Magistrates are human Inventions, yea, and Tyrannical,
that they ought only by compulsion to be obeyed; that the disobeying of
Laws, and defrauding the publick Revenues doth not bind unto sin, but
only unto punishment. And contrariwise, that every beck of Ecclesiastical persons, ought to be taken for a divine Precept, and binds the
Conscience; and this Doctrine is perhaps the cause of all the incon-
veniences which are felt in this Age."[54]

This is Beaulieu's main unbroken transcription from *The History of the
Inquisition*, but his account runs on in the same tenor for some pages, and
he continues to dip into Sarpi's arguments—always to the general effect that
the *Indices* and other Inquisitorial instruments have but a single purpose,
the enchancing of papal authority and prestige. On the very heels of the
foregoing long passage, Beaulieu adds: "Our Author [still Sarpi] adds, 'That
as they condemn and persecute Books that come out in the behalf of Kingly
power, so they geld the Books of ancient Authors, by new Printing them,
and taking out of them all that which might serve for Temporal Authority.' "[55] The same oppression, he says, is laid on books that concern not

government but religion. Nothing that runs counter to Rome can be printed; and even the Bible, "as a dangerous Book, that favours Hereticks, is streightly forbidden the People."[56] By the various *Indices*, put into the hands of confessors, not only do they

> keep from the people all instructive good Books: but they so mangle and alter those Books which they cannot keep out of their hands, *that at present, in reading of a Book, a man can no more find what the Authors meaning was, but only what is the meaning of the Court of* Rome, *who hath altered every thing*, as famous *Padre Paolo* complains and shews at large.[57]

And, as a final illustration of the contempt "that greatness hath for minors," he snatches one more snippet from the gospel according to the Venetian St. Paul: "*Padre Paulo* observes, that they not only take away what they like not, but that they also add what makes for their purpose."[58]

"As famous *Padre Paolo* . . . observes." What other Italian could have commanded in seventeenth-century England the trust and respectful admiration implied in that simple expression?

Among the many Englishmen who read and expressed opinions about Sarpi's historical writings in the seventeenth century, Degory Wheare (1573–1647) is one who is entitled to very special attention. He was the first professor of modern history in Oxford University, and his *The Method and Order of Reading Both Civil and Ecclesiastical Histories* was (and is) a quite exceptional work.[59] It began as a Latin dissertation in 1623, *De ratione et methodo legendi Historias*; was expanded and published in 1662; and underwent various transformations before being translated into English and further altered and enlarged. According to William Prideaux Courtney, "it was in use as a text-book at Cambridge until the beginning of the eighteenth century."[60]

In the part of Wheare's book which has to do with "The Method and Order of Reading Church Histories," Section XLV (pp. 292–96) mostly concerns Sarpi's *History of the Council of Trent* The appraisals of Sarpi and of history which are encountered there are in part quoted from others, but they are opinions to which Wheare can subscribe. Consequently, they may stand as something like an "official," or at least professional, judgment. I transcribe the entire passage:

> To this Century [that is, the sixteenth] belongs the History of the Council of *Trent*, which Council was summon'd in the year 1542. began in the year 1545. continued to the year 1563. the History of which

Council, written by *Pietro Soave Polano*, a *Venetian*, of the Order of the *Servi, a Man of admired Learning; of an exquisite Judgment; of an Indefatigable Industry; and of a modesty and integrity that is scarce to be equall'd; is in truth of more value than any Gold, I think I may say then any Jewels, and like to out-live the most lasting Monuments.* Which commendation is given deservedly to this Historian, by that worthy and learned Person,[61] who faithfully translated this History into *English* (who also was the first person who brought this pretious Jewell into these Western parts, and to the great good of the Church first published it) and in the preliminary Epistle has thus represented the Author's Character, and that not without good cause; for he having had a Learned Intercourse with him, and for some time conversed familiarly with him, knew him throughly. Yea the work it self confirms the truth of all this, which was extracted out of the *Memoires* and commentaries of Ambassadours; out of the Letters of Princes and Commonwealths, and from the Writings of the Prelates, Divines, and the very *Legates*, who were present in the Council; which Writings had till then been carefully kept, and out of them this History was extracted with so much labour, accuracy, study and fidelity (as the said most learned and famous Knight has there observed) that it may equal the best of all the Ancient or Modern Histories of that Nature. Neither are you, my Hearers, to conceive that this is the testimony of one single Person, concerning either the Work or the Authour: Be pleased then to accept a second and like testimony concerning both, from the *Latin* Translatour[62] also, a person of the same degree with the former, and for his great Ingenuity and Erudition of a flourishing Name. Who writes thus of that Authour. *Nor doth he stand in any need of my Commendation, his whole Work speaking him a person of an happy Ingenuity, and of a great and right judgment, liberally endowed with all sorts of Learning, and abundantly adorn'd both with Divine and Humane Knowledge, and that as well Moral as Political or Civil, whereby he has attain'd a high degree, both of Probity and Sweetness of Mind.* And of the Work it self he speaks thus. *As to what concerns the structure of this History, whether you consider the things themselves, or his Language: and in the things, if you observe the order of times, the Counsels, the things done, the events; and in the management of affairs, if you desire not onely what was done or said, should be discoursed, but also in what manner; and that when the event is told, at the same time all the causes should be unfolded, and all the accidents which sprung from wisedom or folly: all these, and a multitude of other such like things, which the great Masters of History require in a good Historian, he has performed so fully and exactly, that in forming the History of one Council, he hath represented all the Per-*

170

fections of History; and, upon this account, deserves to be numbered amongst the most noble Historians.[63]

To balance this ecstatic Newton-Wheare encomium, it may be fitting to record here another voice from later in the century. In a notable piece that precipitated a famous literary quarrel in England, Sir William Temple expressed a view which may be described as the finicality of the aristocratic amateur. Temple's "An Essay upon the Ancient and Modern Learning" appeared in 1692 in the second part of his *Miscelanea*; and in the due course of considering the "moderns," he comes upon Sarpi:

> Upon the subject of eloquence, they will have it, that Padre Paolo's Council of Trent, and Comines' Memoirs, are equal to Herodotus and Livy, and so would Strada be too, if he were but impartial. This is very wonderful, if it be not a jest; for Padre Paolo, he must be allowed for the greatest genius of his age, and perhaps of all the moderns, as appears in his other writings, as well as the Council of Trent; which is, indeed, no history of any great actions, but only an account of a long and artificial negotiation, between the court and prelates of Rome and those of other Christian princes: so that I do not see, how it can properly be stiled an history, the subject whereof are great actions and revolutions; and, by all the ancient critics upon history, the first part of the excellence of an historian is the choice of a noble and great subject, that may be worth his pains.[64]

Between the view that takes *The History of the Council of Trent* as the epitome of perfection in historical writing and the other view, just expressed, which questions whether it even deserves to be called "history" at all, there must be some safety island for the innocent bystander who looks upon it as a middling fair account of one of the most tremendous moments in the history of the modern world. The Council of Trent has occasioned more "revolutions" than Sir William seems to have thought.

One of the great practicing historians of his time, a younger contemporary of Sir William Temple's, was Gilbert Burnet (1643–1715), Bishop of Salisbury. I have not examined all the writings of this prolific divine, but it is perfectly clear from a sampling of them that Burnet knew and greatly admired Sarpi's *History of the Council of Trent*. A small pamphlet by him, *The Infallibility of the Church of Rome Examined and confuted. In a Letter to a Roman Priest* (London, 1680), does not name Sarpi, but does name Pallavicino in such a way as to imply a reference to Sarpi. Discussing the unrepresentative voting limitations of the alleged ecumenical council, Burnet says:

> How shall I be assured a Council thus constituted is infallible, espe-
> cially if I see or be told by the Historians of both sides, that all things
> are managed in the Council by factious Parties and intrigues? each Party
> studying to wait opportunities when they may carry a Vote, and bring-
> ing all of their faction to the Council. This was plainly the case at
> *Trent*, as even *Pallavicini* represents it. And you will hardly prevail on
> any who has considered a little what the direction of the Holy Ghost is,
> to make him believe that in a packt Meeting, where all is full of cun-
> ning and design, the Holy Ghost must be ever ready to direct them when
> they go to the Vote, and that this shall only be when the Bishops are in
> their Formalities at a Session, and not in a Congregation, which is the
> Council resolved in a Grand Committee.[65]

Similarly, when he speaks of the division of opinions which lay behind Tridentine "infallibility," he again makes no mention of Sarpi. But the content
of his statement, if not the precise language, is straight out of *The History
of the Council of Trent*:

> And we know that at *Trent*, when the Divines differed in many Points
> of Religion, the great business was to find a temper, and to contrive the
> Decree in such general terms, as might displease neither Party. And
> thence it was that two of the Divines that were in the Council, and dis-
> puted in the Points defined, but differed in their Opinions, after the
> Council had passed the Decree, did publish Treatises for their Opinions,
> both of them pretending the Council decreed of his side: And though
> this was done before the dissolution of the Council, yet the Council took
> no notice of it. By which it seems they designed their Decrees should be
> Oracles, as well for their misterious Ambiguity, as for their Authority.[66]

In others of his works the Bishop leaves no room for doubt. His important *The History of the Reformation of the Church of England* (1679) relies
upon Sarpi for matters of fact whenever it discusses the Council of Trent
and in various other ways pays the author's respects to Sarpi.[67] Attention to
the Venetian historian begins at once, in the Preface to the first volume,
where Burnet observes that whereas other countries have impartial historians
of their Reformation, England as yet lacks hers:

> The Changes that were made in Religion in the last Century have
> produc'd such effects every where, that it is no wonder if all persons
> desire to see a clear account of the several steps in which they advanced,
> of the Counsels that directed them, and the Motives both Religious and
> Political that enclined men of all conditions to concur in them. *Germany*
> produced a *Sleidan*, *France* a *Thuanus*, and *Italy* a *Frier Paul*, who have
> given the World as full satisfaction in what was done beyond Sea as

they could desire. And though the two last lived and died in the Communion of the Church of *Rome*, yet they have delivered things to Posterity, with so much Candour and Evenness, that their Authority is disputed by none but those of their own Party.[68]

The History of the Council of Trent is cited (marginally) later in the volume.[69]

What is perhaps the most significant of his statements about Sarpi in *The History of the Reformation* occurs in the second volume, when Burnet has come down in his account to the year 1552:

> And being to have no other occasion to say any thing more of this Council, I shall only add, that there had been a great expectation over Christendome of some considerable event of a General Council for many years. The Bishops and Princes had much desired it, hoping it might have brought the differences among Divines to a happy composure; and have setled a Reformation of those abuses, which had been long complained of, and were still kept up by the Court of *Rome*, for the ends of that Principality that they had assumed as Sacred Kings. The Popes for the same reasons were very apprehensive of it, fearing that it might have lessened their Prerogatives; and by cutting off abuses, that brought in a great Revenue to them, have abridged their Profits. But it was, by the cunning of the Legates, the dissensions of Princes, the great number of poor *Italian* Bishops, and the ignorance of the greatest part of the other, so managed, that in stead of composing differences in Religion, things were so nicely defined, that they were made irreconcilable. All those abuses, for which there had been nothing but practise, and that much questioned before, were now, by the Proviso's, and Reservations, excepted for the Priviledges of the *Roman* See, made warrantable. So that it had in all Particulars an Issue quite contrary to what the several Parties concerned had expected from it, and has put the World ever since out of the humour of desiring any more General Councils, as they are accustomed to call them. The History of that Council was writ with as much Life, and Beauty, and Authority, as had been ever seen in any humane Writing, by Frier *Paul* of *Venice*, within half an Age of the time in which it was ended; when the thing was yet fresh in Mens Memories, and many were alive who had been present: and there was not one in that Age that engaged to write against it. But about forty years after, when Father *Paul*, and all his friends who knew from what Vouchers he writ, were dead; *Pallavicini*, a Jesuit, who was made a Cardinal, for this service, undertook to answer him, by another History of that Council, which, in many matters of Fact, contradicted Father *Paul*; upon the credit (as he tells us) of some Journals and Memorials of

such as were present, which he perused, and cites upon all occasions. We see that *Rome* hath been in all Ages so good at forging those things which might be of use to its Interests, that we know not how to trust that Shop of false Wares in any one thing that comes out of it. And therefore it is not easie to be assured of the truth and genuineness of any of the Materials, out of which the Jesuite composed his Work. But as for the main Thread of the Story, both his and Father *Pauls* Accounts do so agree, that whosoever compares them, will clearly see, that all things were managed by Intrigues and secret Practises; so that it will not be easie for a Man of common sense, after he has read over *Pallavicini*'s History to fancy that there was any extraordinary influence of the Holy Ghost hovering over and directing their Councils.[70]

In his third volume Burnet takes occasion once more to praise Sarpi's Tridentine *History*. This time he does so by comparing its virtues with those of another conciliar history which he admires, L'Enfant's *History of the Council of Constance*:

> We have the celebrated History of the Council of *Trent*, first published here at *London*, written with a true sublimity of Judgment, and an Unbyassed Sincerity; which has received a great Confirmation, even from Cardinal *Palavicini*'s Attempt to destroy its Credit; and a much greater of late from that Curious Discovery of *Vargas*'s Letters.[71] But how well, and how justly soever the History that *P. Paulo* gave the World of that Council is esteemed, I am not afraid to compare the late History of the Council of *Constance*, even to that admired Work; so far at least as that if it will not be allowed to be quite equal to it, yet it may be well reckoned among the best of all that have written after that Noble Pattern, which the Famous *Venetian* Fryer has given to all the Writers of Ecclesiastical History.[72]

Burnet's *The Life of William Bedell, D.D., Bishop of Kilmore in Ireland* (London, 1685) contains, as might be expected from its partially Venetian setting, a good deal of attention to Sarpi. And that attention begins early in the book—almost apologetically: "I need not say much of a thing so well known as were the quarrels of Pope *Paul* the V. and that Republick; especially since the History of them is written so particularly by him that knew the matter best, *P. Paulo*."[73] However little the Bishop thinks it necessary to say, there follows a two-page summary (pp. 5–6) of the dispute, abstracted from Sarpi's *History of the Quarrels*, to which Burnet adds: "*P. Paulo* was then the Divine of the State, a man equally eminent for vast learning and a most consummated prudence; and was at once one of the greatest Divines, and of the wisest Men of his Age,"[74] and so forth—a passage later picked up and quoted by Thomas Pope Blount in his *Censura celebriorum authorum* (London, 1690).[75] The first twenty-odd pages of the *Life* are, in fact, principally interesting for their concern with Sarpi and with de Dominis rather than with Bedell himself. They reveal, incidentally, Burnet's preoccupation with the theory of Sarpi's crypto-Protestantism.

When the situation at Venice seemed propitious for a full break with Rome and an embracing of the reformed faith, says Burnet, the English Ambassador (Wotton) failed to present the King's book to the Senate. Meanwhile, the dispute ended, and this priceless opportunity was lost.

> It may be easily imagined what a Wound was this to his Chaplain [Bedell], but much more to those who were more immediately concerned in that matter; I mean *P. Paulo* with the Seven Divines, and many others, who were weary of the corruptions of their Worship, and were groaning for a Reformation. But now the reconcilement with *Rome* was concluded: the Senate carried the matter with all the dignity and Majesty that became that most serene Republic, as to all civil things: for they would not ask Absolution; but the Nuncio, to save the Popes credit, came into the Senate-House, before the Duke was come, and crossed his Cushion, and absolved him. Yet upon this they would not suffer any signs of joy to be made; nor would they recal the Jesuites. But in all these things greater regard was had to the dignity of their State, than to the interest of Religion; so that *P. Paulo* was out of all hopes of bringing things ever back to so promising a conjuncture; upon which he wisht he could have left *Venice* and come over to *England* with Mr. *Bedell*: but he was so much esteemed by the Senate for his great Wisdom, that he was consulted by them as an Oracle, and trusted with their most important Secrets: so that he saw it was impossible for him to obtain his *Congè*; and therefore he made a shift to comply as he could with the established way of their Worship; but he had in many things particular methods, by which he in a great measure rather quieted than satisfied his Conscience. In saying of Mass, he past over many parts of the Canon, and in particular those Prayers, in which that Sacrifice was offered up to the honour of Saints: He never prayed to Saints, nor joyned in those parts of the Offices that went against his Conscience; and in private Confessions and Discourses, he took people off from those abuses, and gave them right Notions of the purity of the Christian Religion; so he hoped he was sowing Seeds that might be fruitful in another Age: and thus he believed he might live innocent in a Church that he thought so defiled. And when one prest him hard in this matter, and objected that he still held communion with an Idolatrous Church, and gave it credit by adhering outwardly to it, by which means others that

175

depended much on his example would be likewise encouraged to continue in it: All the answer he made to this was, That God had not given
him the Spirit of *Luther*. He expressed great tenderness and concern for
Bedell, when he parted with him; and said that both he and many others
would have gone over with him, if it had been in their power: but that
he might never be forgot by him, he gave him his Picture, with an
Hebrew Bible without Points, and a little Hebrew Psalter, in which he
writ some Sentences expressing his esteem and friendship for him; and
with these [*]he gave him the unvaluable Manuscript of the History of
the Council of *Trent*, together with the History of the Interdict and of
the Inquisition; the first of these will ever be reckoned the chief pattern
after which all, that intend to succeed well in writing *History*, must
copy.[*][76] But among other Papers that *P. Paulo* gave him, some that
were of great importance are lost: for in a Letter of Mr *Bedells* to Dr.
Ward, he mentions a Collection of Letters that were sent him Weekly
from *Rome* during the contests between the *Jesuites* and *Dominicans*,
concerning the efficacy of Grace; of which *P. Paulo* gave him the Originals; and in his Letter to Dr. *Ward* he mentions his having sent them
to him. These, very probably, contained a more particular relation of
that matter than the World has yet seen, since they were writ to so curious and so inquisitive a Man; but it seems he did not allow *Bedell* to
print them, and so I am afraid they are now irrecoverably lost.[77]

At the end of the *Life* and preceding *The Copies of Certaine Letters*
there occurs "*An Advertisement concerning a Character given by Sir* Henry
Wotton *of F*. Paul *the Author of the History of the Council of* Trent." This,
one of the most important statements made by any Englishman actually
acquainted with Sarpi in person, is too long to be reproduced here and too
significant to be abridged. I have reluctantly resorted to the expedient of
placing it in an Appendix.[78]

Burnet, whose travels took him to Italy in 1685, found the memory of
Sarpi somewhat faded in the Venice of that period. In the *Letters* relating
his travels, the third letter, dated from Florence, 5 November 1685, contains
remarks on his visit to Venice, among others this:[79]

> I went to the Convent of the *Servi*, but I found Father *Paul* was not in
> such consideration there, as he is elsewhere. I asked for his Tomb, but
> they made no account of him, and seemed not to know where it was. It
> is true, the Person to whom I was recommended was not in *Venice*, so
> perhaps they refined too much in this Matter. I had great Discourses
> with some at *Venice* concerning the Memorials out of which Father *Paul*
> drew his History, which are no doubt all preserved with great Care in
> their Archives; and since the Transactions of the Council of *Trent*, as

they are of great Importance, so they are now become much controverted, by the different Relations that Father *Paul* and Cardinal *Pallavicini* have given the World of that Matter. The only way to put an
End to all Disputes in Matter of Fact, is to print the Originals themselves. A Person of great Credit at *Venice* promised me to do his utmost
to get that Proposition set on foot, tho' the great Exactness that the
Government there hath always affected, as to the Matter of their Archives, is held so sacred, that this made him apprehend they would not
give way to any such Search.

Burnet should have known, of course, that in a decadent Venice, thoroughly
cowed by the Church, no straight answer was to be expected concerning the
bones or reputation of the erstwhile chief antipapal gadfly.

One of the works, it will be recalled, which had prompted (or shamed)
Bishop Burnet into the writing of his own *History of the Reformation* had
been that of John Sleidan (or Philippson), published at Strassburg in 1555,
in Latin. An English version of this notable history was published in England some eight years after the Bishop's *History* as *The General History of
the Reformation of the Church, from the Errors and Corruptions of the
Church of Rome: begun in Germany by Martin Luther, with the Progress
thereof in all Parts of Christendom, from the Year 1517, to the Year 1556.
Written in Latin by John Sleidan, L.L.D. and faithfully Englished. To
which is Added, A Continuation to the End of the Council of Trent, in the
Year 1562. By Edmund Bohun, Esq.* (London, 1689). Bohun, the translator-
continuator, we have met before as the translator-enlarger of Wheare's
Methodus.[80] The separate title page for his continuation of Sleidan reads:
*A Continuation of the History of the Reformation to the End of the Council
of Trent, in the Year 1563. Collected and written by E. B. Esq.* (London,
1689). This part of the volume is separately paged and has its own index.
Detached from the Sleidan, it could thus pass as an independent production.

Bohun's volume represents an oddity in that it is, so to speak, both the
father of Sarpi's work (in that Sarpi begins his *Historia* by acknowledging
his dependence upon Sleidan) and the son of the *History of the Council of
Trent*, insofar as Bohun draws largely upon that *History* for his narration
of the events of 1562–1563, especially in his account of the last session of the
Council of Trent. The specific page references supplied by Bohun indicate
that he used the 1676 edition of Brent's translation.

Borrowings from Sarpi and allusions to him are scattered throughout,
and the whole temper of Bohun's writing reflects the potent influence of the
great Venetian. A selection of a few of the more original passages will give

the reader a fair notion of Bohun's dependence and method of proceeding. At the end of his account of the Conference of Poissy (pp. 58–61), for instance, Bohun says that the Queen of France sent to Philip II to "excuse" the Conference "Jacques de Monbron, a Person of good Birth and Repute" and in the margin he says: "In the History of the Council of *Trent*, call'd Jaques de Montbrun." On the next page (p. 62), in his account of Paul Vergerius's opposition to the papal bull intimating the reopening of the Council of Trent, Bohun's choice of details and phrase indicates that he is following *The History of the Council of Trent* (ed. 1676), pages 408–9.

Under the year 1562, beginning his account of the resummoned council, Bohun writes:

> The History of this Council is so well described by *Petro Soave Polano*, a Venetian, which is in English, that I need the less insist upon it; but I shall however remark some few things from *Thuanus* [that is, Jacques de Thou] and others, for the Enlarging or Confirming the Credit of that History, which is much cryed down by the Roman Catholicks; as certainly they have good Reason to be offended with that Author, who with so much Truth and Impartiality has discovered the Artifices of that Assembly, for the keeping up the Grandeur of the *Court of Rome*, and the Suppression and Baffling that Reformation, which the most Learned of the Church of *Rome* then so much desired and panted after.[81]

Bohun's narrative (pp. 62–64) of the reception of the Pope's legates sent variously to one power and another to invite them to the reopened council follows in its order (and sometimes in its phrasing) the Brent-Sarpi account in *The History of the Council of Trent*, Book V, pages 412–13.

In his version of the second session of the renewed council, held on 26 February 1562 and dealing with the censuring of books and the issuing of a safe-conduct for all who were to come to the council, Bohun falls back upon Sarpi's account:

> Seventeen Bishop were by Name appointed to bring in a Catalogue of such Books as were intended or thought fit to be Prohibited. *Polano* observes, that they carried this so high as to *deprive Men of that Knowledge which was necessary to defend them from the Usurpations of the Court of* Rome, *by which means its Authority was maintained and made Great. For the Books were Prohibited and Condemned, in which the Authority of Princes and Temporal Magistrates is defended from the Usurpations of the Clergy; and of Councils and Bishops from the Usurpations of the Court of* Rome, *in which their Hypocrisies or Tyrannies are manifested, by which the People, under the pretence of Religion are*

deceived. In summ, a better Mystery was never found out than to use Religion to make Men insensible.[82]

The extent to which Bohun was adapting and transcribing his source appears from a comparison with the corresponding passage from the end of Sarpi's digression on the censuring of books (pp. 441–43):

> But it is a thing considerable above all, that under colour of faith and Religion, Books are prohibited and condemned, with the same severity, in which the authority of Princes and Temporal Magistrates is defended from the usurpations of the Clergy; and of Councils and Bishops, from the usurpations of the Court of *Rome*; in which hypocrisies and tyrannies are manifested, by which the people, under pretence of Religion, are deceived. In sum, a better mystery was never found, than to use Religion to make men insensible.[83]

The French ambassadors, on their arrival, wrote to the French Resident in Rome to announce their coming and to ask that he suggest to the Pope that the latter order his legates to proceed with caution and to allow such liberty of speech and decision as would prevent their falling "under the old Reproach of having *the Holy Ghost sent them from* Rome *in a Portmanteau.*"[84] Slightly lower on the same page Bohun says, "The Twentieth of *May* the *French* Ambassadors were admitted in a Congregation, where they made an unacceptable Oration, an abstract of which is in *Polano*"—as, in fact, it is (on pp. 475–76). A few pages further along, in relating the election of Maximilian as King of the Romans at the Diet of Frankfurt, Bohun uses the date eighth of September and indicates that the "Diet ended about the end of *December.*" Marginally, he comments on the date thus: "Polano in his History of the Council of *Trent*, saith the Election was made the 24th of *November*. So that the first date seems to be the day of the opening of the Diet."[85]

The French ambassadors, after some delay, laid before the council the items they had been instructed to require. This was on 4 January 1563, and Bohun says of them: ". . . as may be seen at large in *Polano* his History, p. 609. I shall not here trouble the Reader with them."[86] And neither shall I; for they are long and they are indeed, as reported, listed out in Sarpi's *History*.[87] Similarly, the bitter oration of the French ambassador de Ferrier is mentioned on page 95 of the *Continuation*; Bohun adds, "*Polano* in his History of the Council of *Trent*, has the sum of this Oration" and gives a marginal reference to page 721 (of the 1676 ed.)—where it can be found.

Other pieces of information and the sequence of some events, as well as bits of phrasing here and there, Bohun undoubtedly picked up from Sarpi—who, along with de Thou, seems to have been his principal source. The final summary, itself borrowed from Sarpi, intimates that much of the preceding account is to be credited to him.[88]

> Thus ended the Council of *Trent*, which was desired and procured by *Godly men* to reunite the Church which began to be *divided, but hath so established the Schism, and made the parties so obstinate, that the discords are become irreconcileable. And being intended by Princes for the reformation of the Ecclesiastical Discipline, hath caused the greatest corruption and deformation that ever was since Christianity began: The Bishops hoped to regain the Episcopal Authority, usurped for the most part by the Pope; and it hath made them lose it altogether, bringing them into greater servitude. On the contrary it was feared and avoided by the* See *of* Rome *as a potent means to moderate their exorbitant power, which from small beginnings mounted by divers degrees to an unlimited excess; and it hath so established and confirm'd the same over that part which remains subject unto it; that it was never so great, nor so soundly rooted.* Thus far *Polano*.[89]

As another specimen of the manner in which Bohun manages his quotations from Sarpi, I subjoin the corresponding passage from *The History of the Council of Trent*—drawn not from the end of that work but from the very beginning:

> 3. For this Council desired and procured by godly men, to reunite the Church, which began to be divided, hath so established the Schism, and made the parties so obstinate, that the discords are become irreconcileable: and being managed by Princes for reformation of Ecclesiastical discipline, hath caused the greatest deformation that ever was since Christianity did begin: and hoped for by the Bishops to regain the Episcopal authority, usurped for the most part by the Pope, hath made them lose it altogether, bringing them into greater servitude: on the contrary, feared and avoided by the Sea of *Rome*, as a potent means, to moderate the exorbitant power, mounted from small beginnings by divers degrees unto an unlimited excess, it hath so established and confirmed the same, over that part which remaineth subject unto it, that it was never so great nor so soundly rooted.[90]

Whatever were Bohun's other sources, it appears that in Sarpi was his beginning and his ending.

12 --- Through A Glass Darkly

A WRITER'S WORKS become known abroad through varied means. If he writes in a language having a general currency, they may simply be transported physically to their new home and there be read in their original form. This happened in the early part of the seventeenth century (and to a limited extent) with the works of Sarpi in England. Many surviving book lists or catalogues of libraries, public and private, indicate that at least some Englishmen owned and read the *Historia del Concilio Tridentino* and other Sarpian works in Italian. Or, again, a writer's works, wholly or in part, may be translated into Latin or into the native tongue—as we have seen happen in England to Sarpi's principal writings. Or (and commonly, as was the case with Sarpi) his works may be so extensively quoted, copied, adapted, alluded to, controverted, or explicated as to become almost part of the literature of the alien land. These are the more or less routine ways in which an author's ideas are spread and his reputation grows beyond the limits of his native land. They are his overt witnesses to posterity.

But there are also certain other less direct, often undeclared and unrecognized, ways in which his ideas or his very words may be transmitted. For one reason or another his name may be suppressed and his merited praise unnoted; or in contrary fashion, and generally with intent to profit or to scandalize, his name may be attached to a work which he did not write. If he is deemed a figure of sufficient stature, biographical sketches will appear in international reference works. And it may also happen that his work will be picked up and incorporated, verbatim or modified, in other foreign works which do not have any obvious immediate relation to his own but which, translated in their turn and credited to their "authors," thus help to disseminate his ideas without necessarily helping to augment his reputation. To some such performances as these, as they relate to Sarpi, we must now turn our attention.

181

King James I, of all British monarchs the one most afflicted with that form of the King's evil known as *cacoethes scribendi*, would probably never win many laurels for his modesty or for promoting the merits and reputations of others. He was, nevertheless, by his Venetian ambassadors and agents kept fully aware of the activities of Paolo Sarpi in his defense of Venetian liberty, in his countering of Bellarmine, and in his devastating revelation of the papal juggling behind the scenes at the Council of Trent. He kept a watchful eye on the events of 1606–1607 in the Serenissima; and indubitably it was by his collusion and under his authority that *The History of the Council of Trent* was smuggled piecemeal into his kingdom, dedicated to himself, and published by Bill, printer to the Crown.

Yet for all this, in his printed works James publicly refers to Sarpi but once—in his *Triplici Nodo, Triplex Cuneus. Or an Apologie for the Oath of Allegiance* (1607). Here, in answering the two briefs of Pope Paul V urging English Catholics not to take the oath and in confuting Bellarmine's Epistle to G. Blackwell, Archpriest, the King takes occasion, in passing, to refer to Paolo Sarpi: "How those untoward contradictions shall be made to agree, I must send the Cardinall to *Venice*, to *Padre Paulo*, who in his Apologie against the Cardinals oppositions, hath handled them very learnedly."[1] It is hardly a trumpet blast from the housetop.

Equally buried and obscure, though similarly routine and casual in its praise of Sarpi, is a remark of Francis Osborne's. In the Epistle to his "Historical Memoires on the Reigns of Q. Elisabeth, and King James," Osborne finds cause to praise epistles as sources of historical information. "Epistles," he says,

> being the *quintessence* of the *Writers judgement*, as they are undoubtedly the *Elixir* of his *Rhetorick*. And he that desires a more exemplary manifestation of this infallible (though for ought I ever observed, seldom practised) *Truth*, may find it in that *learned Italian's History of the Council of Trent*; a Piece that challenges all the *veneration* our partial *Modern Readers* do or can offer at the *Shrines* of *Antiquity*; a folly sure not so conversant in the world before *Printing*, otherwise the most part of *New Books* from time to time had still been buried in their Swadling-clouts for want of *Transcription*.[2]

Sometimes, as with Sir Thomas Pope Blount's *Essays*, coming so late in a century that had lived on familiar terms with Sarpi's reputation even when not with his works, a general or ambiguous reference may be reasonably assumed to point in Sarpi's direction even when there is no quotation from him or mention of his name. In Essay II, "The great Mischief and Prejudice of Learning," for instance, when he argues that statesmen ought

182

not to meddle in church affairs nor churchmen in state affairs, Blount thus comments on the policy of the Venetian Republic:

> Upon these therefore, and such like Considerations, the Wise *Venetians* have so slight an Opinion of the *Politicks* of their Church Men that whenever any thing that is of a considerable Nature, occurs to be debated in the *Senate*, before any suffrage passeth, they cause Proclamation to be made, for all *Priests* to depart: And the proper Officer, with a loud and audible Voice, pronounceth these Words, *Fuora I Preti, Out Priests*. And it is further Remarkable, That he who in this Common-Wealth is call'd the *Divine of the State* (an Ecclesiastical Person to be advis'd with in Matters of Religion) is commonly chosen such a One, as is reputed the least addicted to *Bigottry*.[3]

The last sentence here perhaps points directly to the reputation of Paolo Sarpi, and would most likely have been taken by the seventeenth-century reader so to do—though there is no earthly way to prove this. Similiarly, two references to the Council of Trent in the volume are not so worded as to enable one to determine whether Blount is referring to Sarpi's *History* or to another source.[4] Here again, however, the presumption heavily favors Sarpi. And instances of this ambiguous sort of reference or allusion in seventeenth-century English writing could be multiplied by the score.

With another work, also published late in the century, the case is on a different footing. In the six-volume Venetian edition of the works of Sarpi, allegedly published between 1673 and 1685, the several items carry their own separately dated title pages and attribution to the press of Roberto Meietti, the original publisher of many of Sarpi's works appearing in his own lifetime. Within the volume, also, some of the items are separately paginated, so that it is difficult to determine whether the discrete copies to be found in some libraries represent separate issues or merely detached copies from the composite set. Whatever the truth in this regard may be, one work—*Opinione falsamente ascrita al padre Paolo Servita, come debba governarsi internamente et esternamente la Republica Venetiana, per havere il perpetuo dominio*—both constitutes the final (separately paged) item in Volume Six of the "Meietti" collection and exists as a separate volume.[5] To complicate matters still further, at the end of the *Opinione*—clearly described on the title page as "*falsamente ascrita al padre Paolo*"—there is appended (pp. 109-16) by the publisher or editor an "Avviso che serve di giunta" in which it is patently assumed that Sarpi *was* the author of the piece:

> Quest'opra del Padre Maestro Frá Paolo Sarpi Servita Consultore della Serenissima Republica di Venezia, che fú data á Padri del Governo, affinchi servisse per regola nelle loro azioni per adempire il de-

siderio che havevano di far perpetuare la loro carissima Patria, é stata in fine con destrezza levata da un recondito Gabinetto per darla in luce.

L'opra é ripiena di avvisi sí eccellenti, che chi la legge non puó, che confessare che l'Autore é stato uno de'primi huomini del secolo; e che puó pareggiare il Boccalini. Chi esaminerá á pieno il governo di quella Serenissima Republica, vedrá, che quello Stato há fatto stima grande di quei avvisi, giá che si veggono tutti posti in opra, e che servono di regola esatta ne'maneggi. Má adesso le cose sono talmente cambiati di faccia, come prevedeva lo stesso Padre Paolo, che secondo il tempo oprano que'saggi, e prudentissimi Signori.[6]

There is no certainty as to the date of original composition of the *Opinione*; its alleged date of publication is 1685. For us, its interest is two-fold: its being a scandalous underhanded attack upon Venetian policy, attributed to Sarpi, and its being translated (by William Aglionby) into English—*The Opinion of Padre Paolo, of the Order of the Servites . . . given to the Lords the Inquisitors of State. In what manner the Republick of Venice ought to govern themselves . . . to have perpetual dominion. Delivered . . . in the year 1615* (London, 1689). Another edition of the translation appeared in 1693.

Zera Fink, in his *The Classical Republicans*, has assessed this performance with great justice. After commenting on the harm done to Venetian reputation by the infamous *Squitinio della libertà Veneta* (1612)—probably the work of the Marquis of Bedmar, Antonio de la Cueva— Professor Fink turns his attention to the *Opinione* and its English version:

> This work purported to be the secret instructions drawn up by Sarpi at the order of the Senate for the future guidance of the republic. It is Machiavellian in character in the sensational sense of the word. That Sarpi wrote it is highly questionable; it is quite likely that it is a spurious work designed to blacken both Sarpi's reputation and that of the republic, and as such is to be considered as arising out of the same campaign as that which produced the *Squittinio*. In any case, it contains much that could not but injure the traditional view of the republic. Not only are many of the purported maxims unscrupulous in their advice, but the extended criticisms of the defects of the constitution ill accorded with the conception of Venice as a masterpiece of politics. This work was not published in an English version until 1689; it is clear, however, that it circulated before that time in manuscript both on the Continent and in England.[7]

It is unfortunate, no doubt, that so scurrilous a work should be associated with the name of so noble a figure and so patriotic a Venetian. But that it was attributed to Sarpi is evidence that the perpetrators and purveyors of the work considered his name a sufficient magnet to attract readers. Any modern advertising agent would understand the motivation.

When after the restoration of the Stuarts the English began to have some shaky apprehensions that Catholicism might again find its way into the realm, there arose a lively debate over the question of the restitution of ecclesiastical lands and other properties which had been impropriated to the state and thence had devolved into private hands. One of the prime documents in this debated point, issued in semianonymity, was *The Papacy of Paul the Fourth. Or, the Restitution of Abby Lands and Impropriations, an indispensable condition of Reconciliation to the Infallible See*, &c. (London, 1673). As we shall see, the text of this small quarto of thirty-five pages contains matter of more than common interest to the history of Sarpi's fortunes in England.

The "Epistle Dedicatory," directed to Viscount Mountague, is signed (sig. A3) by the publisher, "I. S."; the "Epistle to the Reader" (sigs. A4, recto and verso) is signed by an otherwise unidentified "E. A." And nothing is said on the title page concerning authorship of the work. But following the excellent advice of Osborne to scrutinize epistles, I extract from the one to the reader the following revelatory remarks:

> And that thou mayst not have the least suspition concerning the truth of the following *Narrative*, I assure thee, I have most faithfully taken it from Father *Paul*, a person of unquestioned integrity, and that lived and died in the Communion of the *Romane* Church: As thou mayst be satisfied by comparing it with his relation of the Government of Pope *Paul* the Fourth, in his exact *History of the Councell of Trent*. For which, as the Christian Church is highly obliged to him upon many *other* accounts, so particularly for the *Life* of this Zealous *Pope*, in which his extraordinary kindness for the two things is more especially remarkable because they seem to stand in no small need of so Great an Authority to recommend them, viz. *Perjury* and *Inquisition*. Besides that, we may learn from this *Pope*, how exceedingly convenient *Infallibility* is for the Catholick Church; when we see that it may sometimes fall out, that a *Pope* may be but little better than a madman: In which case *Infallibility* must need be a very great Security to the Catholick Faith.[8]

The indebtedness to Sarpi is here clearly enough acknowledged, though the acknowledgment is so placed that readers less curious than Francis Osborne might easily overlook it. What is not clear, even here, is whether "E. A." has made an independent rendering of the Italian or has borrowed his translation as well as his matter. Turning to the relevant section in Brent-Sarpi, we quickly perceive that this tract is simply a selection from Brent and that, with some omissions, it reproduces the exact language of his translation.[9] A comparison of two brief passages will suffice to illustrate E. A.'s method of proceeding:

> In the Year of our Lord One thousand five hundred fifty and five *Marcellus Cervinus* [Cardinal of Santa Croce] was created Pope, and retained his Name; but, having sate no more than twenty two daies, died: The Cardinals being assembled again in the *Conclave*, he of *Ausburg*, assisted by *Morone*, made great instance, that among the Capitulations which the Cardinals were to swear to, one should be, that the future Pope should, by Counsel of the Colledg, call another Synod within two years, to finish the Reformation begun, to determine the Controversies of Religion that remained, and to find a means to cause the Councel of *Trent* to be received in *Germany*.[10]

The statements "In the Year of our Lord . . . died" summarize matters treated by Brent on pages 389–91 of the *Historie*; "The Cardinals being assembled . . . *Germany*," except for spellings and punctuation, exactly reproduces a continuous segment of page 391 in Brent.

The second passage, forming part of Sarpi's "character" of Paul IV, runs thus:[11]

> *Paul* the Fourth was naturally of a lofty mind and courage, and trusted much in his knowledg and good fortune, which did accompany him in all his actions: whereunto the power and fortune of the *Papacy* being added, he thought every thing was easy. But two humours did flote in him by turns; one, which by custom to make use of Religion in all his attempts, did induce him to employ his *Spiritual* Authority. The other was put into him by *Charles Caraffa* his Nephew, who, being valiant, and exercised in War, made Cardinal of a Souldier, did retain his martial Spirits, and perswaded him to use his temporal power, saying that the one without the other is despised, but being joyned, are instruments of great matters.[12]

Here again, with the exceptions noted above, the transcription is total.

Nor, in this dispute, was the influence of Sarpi restricted to this single substantial piece. Two other performances, at least, likewise draw upon him. The first of these, by Nathaniel Johnston (1627–1705)—who in the preceding year had published the long and remarkably Baconian *The Excellency of Monarchical Government* (London, 1686)—was entitled *The Assurance of Abby and Other Church-Lands in England to the Possessors . . .* (London, 1687).[13] In his long discussion of the problem Johnston twice calls in the aid

186

Through a Glass Darkly

of *The History of the Council of Trent*, each time employing multiple citations. The first instance occurs in the fifth of his ten "Sections," or chapters, and concerns alienation of Roman Catholic Church lands in other countries besides England.

> In the Year, 1563.[14] *Pius 4th.* being Pope, and *Charles* the 9th. King of *France.* The Queen Regent of *France* sent Letters to *Rome*, and *Trent*, in the end of *May*, that "consultation had been had how to pay the Debts of the Crown, that a Decree had passed for Alienating to the value of 100000 Crowns of Ecclesiastical Immoveable Goods, and it was confirmed by the Kings Edict and Sentence of the Parliament. The French Ambassador was Ordered to move his Holiness to give his consent, alledging the exhausture of the Exchequer by the late War, that he designed to put his affairs in Order, that he might begin, as his purpose ever was since the making of the peace, to reunite all in the Kingdom to the Catholic Religion; and that he might be abler to force whosoever should oppose him, he meant to impose a Subsidy, and cause the Clergy to contribute their parts to it also; whereto the Church was so much more bound than others, by how much their interests were more in question. That all being considered, nothing was found to be more easie than to supply the necessity with the Alienation of some few Ecclesiastical Revenues, whereto he desired the consent of his Holiness.
>
> The Pope answered, that the demand was painted forth with a fair pretence of defending the Church, but it was the only way to ruin it; for the avoiding whereof his securest way was not to consent to it; and he was of opinion,[15] that the French would not proceed to the execution of it without him, and he thought without his consent none would adventure Mony upon them, because a time might come, that the Ecclesiastics would resume their Rents, and not restore the price; and he proposed the business to the Consistory, and resolved not to consent, but by divers excuses to shew, it was impossible to obtain that demand at his hands.
>
> The French[16] having considered the Popes Answer, resolved to Treat no more with the Pope for his favor in the Alienation, but to execute the Kings Edict approved in Parliament without any consent of his Holiness. This being suddenly performed, few Buyers could be found, which was a hindrance to the King, and no favor to the Clergy; for the Sale was made at low Rates, so that there was but Two Millions, and a half of Franks raised, small in regard of the things Alienated, being but Twelve for a Hundred, whereas it had been a small price, if they had given a Hundred for Four. Amongst the things sold, the Jurisdiction which the Archbishop of *Lyons* held until that time over the City, was

187

sold at the outcry for 30000 Franks, but the Bishop complained so much, that in supplement of the price, he had given unto him 400 Crowns yearly."[17]

Here and there Johnston has omitted a phrase or sentence present in his source or has modified Sarpi's language through summarizing paraphrase; but in the main the foregoing composite passage is faithful to Brent's text. And the same may be said for his return to Sarpi in Section IX: "The Exceptions against this Assurance of Abby-Lands to the Possessors, that it was not confirmed by Pope *Paul* the 4*th* fully Answered."[18] It is of some interest that immediately following his "Thus far *Soave*," Johnston should (pp. 173–74) quote Cardinal Pallavicino's *History* and should then proceed to show (to his own satisfaction) how "*Soave's*" assertions cannot be correct in this matter.

A much smaller work, a pamphlet of eight double-columned pages, lacking title page, publisher's name, and date (1688?), appears to be an answer (or appendix) to Johnston's book. This is the work of John Willes and, in lieu of a title page, bears the heading, "Abby and other Church-Lands, not yet assured to such Possessors as are Roman Catholicks; Dedicated to the Nobility and Gentry of that Religion." In this brief *opusculum* Sarpi's *History* is quoted or cited no fewer than four times, the references being to the second edition (1629) of Brent's translation.[19] Willes is not a careful writer. In his very first citation of Sarpi (p. 3, col. 2)—a bit of the *History* also quoted by Johnston[20]—he refers to Pope Paul IV as "Pope *Julius* the Fourth[!], (the very Person that is pretended to have confirm'd these Alienations)."

Regardless of such muddle-headedness, however, and regardless of the point of view maintained (which I have not attempted to record), all these works—even the slender last one—exhibit the great Venetian friar as an authority readily available to post-Restoration Englishmen, and as one who could be drawn upon to illumine domestic problems of a political and economic as well of an ecclesiastical nature.

The second half of the seventeenth century witnessed importations from France other than that of the exiled British royal house. French manners, French taste, French literature, all began to exercise an ascendency which all but replaced the long-standing influence of the Italians. Alongside this rising strain, however, admiration for the "model" government and "policy" of the Venetian Republic continued. In 1677, for Englishmen who followed the latest wares of the booksellers, the two phenomena were felicitously united in the performance of one man, Abraham-Nicholas Amelot de la Houssaie.

Amelot (1634–1706), sometime secretary to the French embassy at Venice, was an effective and controversial publicist, a prolific translator and commentator. Among his translations from several languages are versions of Machiavelli's *Prince*, of Tacitus, of Baltasar Gracián's *Courtier's Handbook*, and, as *Examen de la liberté originaire de Venise*, of the *Squitinio de la libertà veneta*.[21] More importantly for our present concern, he also figures as translator, adapter, and advocate of Paolo Sarpi. After the translation of the *Historia del Concilio Tridentino* made by Giovanni Diodati in 1620, his was the next to appear in French.[22] First published under the pseudonym of "le sieur de la Mothe-Josseval," equipped with "Remarques Historiques, Politiques, & Morales," and several times reprinted, this performance would have had among the cultivated and fashionable almost as much currency in England as in France. The long Preface, a vigorous defense of Sarpi's *History* against the attacks of Pallavicino and others (mostly Jesuits), also had the fortune to be translated into Latin and thus achieved further circulation.[23]

Even earlier, in 1682, Amelot translated from the Italian of Minuccio Minucci, Archbishop of Zara, and of Paolo Sarpi the *Historia degli Uscochi*.[24] To the original *History* of Minucci, which carried the account down to 1602, Sarpi had added a *Continuazione*, bringing the story forward to 1616, and then a *Supplimento*, or political commentary on the two earlier parts. Of the 385 pages of small octavo text in Amelot's translation, Minucci's account occupies pages 1–138; Sarpi's continuation, pages 139–256; and the supplement, pages 257–385. In the Preface, Amelot gives his reasons for translating the *History*, explaining at the end "qu'elle fait partie des Oeuvres de *Frà-Paolo*, que je me suis proposé de donner toutes en nôtre Langue."[25] He did not quite achieve this ambitious undertaking, but he had already published another book, ostensibly his own work, which had the effect of laying before the eyes of his fellow countrymen another installment of Sarpiana. And as this was almost immediately translated into English, it becomes of interest to us at this point.

This work, Amelot's *Histoire du gouvernement de Venise*, was published at Amsterdam in 1676 and at Paris in the following year, in which latter year it was also published in English translation as *The History of the Government of Venice . . . Written in the year 1675, by the Sieur Amelot de la Houssaie, Secretary to the French Ambassador at Venice.*[26] The Third Part of the volume (pp. 227–87) is itself divided into three parts: "The Holy Office of the Inquisition of Venice" (pp. 227–53: pages badly misnumbered); "A Discourse containing the Chief Causes of the decay of the Venetian Common-Wealth" (pp. 253–66); and "The Manners and general Maxims of the Venetians" (pp. 267–87). Of these, the first division is almost entirely composed of a combination of information drawn from several of Sarpi's writings, especially his *History of the Inquisition*. In the third division, some of the "maxims" perhaps reflect the pseudo-Sarpian *Opinione*, discussed above. Concerning the content and method, particularly of the first division, here is Amelot's own statement:

> Such is the coherence and connexion betwixt the *Inquisition*, and *Government* of *Venice*, that one is not well comprehended without the other: wherefore I have made an abridgement of the Treatise of *Fra. Paolo* about the *Inquisition*, in which we may see the Measures the *Senat* took with the Court of *Rome*, and the Ecclesiasticks. But because my design is to give you an extract, not a translation of those passages, it cannot be thought strange that I have not followed the order of the Original, nor pinned my self up to the words of the Author, his sentiments being sufficient. And to give more light to the matter, in two or three places I have added something of his *History* of the *Council of Trent*, and of the Excommunication of the *Venetians*; a method which I suppose will not be displeasing to the Reader.[27]

One notes here Amelot's early interest in both the *Historia del Concilio Tridentino*, which he later translated, and the *Historia particolare*, the translation of which "en nôtre Langue" remained among his unachieved ambitions. As in Sarpi's original *History of the Inquisition* the longest section —"The Exposition of the nine and twentieth Chapter"[28]—is devoted to a discussion of the censuring of books, so in Amelot the longest section (pp. 244-53) of the first division is given to the same topic, Sarpi's account being followed with care as to substance.

For his services in making Sarpi's ideas known to the English of the later seventeenth century, Amelot de la Houssaie's name deserves to be remembered with those of Bedell and Brent, who performed similar services in the reign of James I.

A contemporary of Amelot's, the distinguished and erudite French Hebraist Richard Simon (1638-1712), also contributed his mite to maintaining and spreading the fame of Paolo Sarpi. A vigorously independent-minded pursuer of the truth wherever it led him, and practically the inventor of the "higher criticism" of Biblical texts, Father Simon's liberal views on the origin of the Old Testament writings and on some doctrines held by the Fathers earned him the antagonism of various powerful figures of the time (including Bossuet) and impeded the publication of his writings.

One of his works which earned him no favor with the ecclesiastical hierarchy was his *Histoire de l'origine et du progrès des revenus ecclesiastiques*, published under the pseudonym of Jérôme Acosta at Frankfort (Rotterdam?) in 1684 and quickly translated into English as *The History of*

*the Original and Progress of Ecclesiastical Revenues: wherein is handled
according to the Laws, both Ancient and Modern, whatsoever concerns matters Beneficial, the Regale, Investitures, Nominations, and other Rights
attributed to Princes. Written in French by a Learned Priest. And now done
into English* (London, 1685). The prefatory "To the Reader" in the English
version, presumably the work of the translator, begins thus: "It may seem
unnecessary to say more of this Treatise, than that it proceeds from the
famous Pen of Father *Simon*; who hath herein far outgon all who have
written on the same Subject, even the Learned Father *Paul*."[29] Father Simon, nevertheless, has clearly made use of Sarpi, as appears from the following references:

> There is mention made in the treatise of matters Beneficiary attrib-
> uted to *Father Paul*, of a form of a Contract called *Precaria*, which hath
> much enriched Monasteries. The Old *Cartularies*, are full of such kinds
> of Deeds, which consisted in a Donation made by private Persons, of
> their Estates to Churches, which they obtained back again from the same
> Churches, by Letters which they call'd *Precarias*, or *Precatorias* to be
> possessed by a kind of Copyhold, or Lease for Lives; for most part
> granted a Lease for five, six, and even for seven Lives, on condition of
> paying a yearly Revenue to the Monastery. People bestowed their Lands
> more willingly upon the Church, when they perceived that they still re-
> served the profits of them for many years.[30]
>
> The Popes are always on that lock with Princes, and what they can-
> not obtain at one time, they hope to obtain on another occasion. On this
> Maxim are founded all the *Concordats*, and other Accommodations
> which they have made with several Princes. And therefore the Argu-
> ments which[31] Father *Paul* draws from the nature of *Concordats*, to
> prove that Popes have not by right an absolute Power over the Revenues
> of the Church, are not altogether conclusive; because Popes will pretend
> that these *Concordats*, are only made by Provision, and for a time, till
> they be able to exercise their right in its full extent. That hath been a
> very advantageous Maxim to the Court of *Rome*, which hath obtained
> at one time, what was impossible to be obtained at another. They indeed
> propose matters according to the rigour, and their pretensions; but they
> suffer Princes to moderate them according to the Customs received in
> their Kingdoms. And that is the reason why several of the Popes Bulls
> are not received in *France*, and that they are not registered, till first they
> be examined, to see whether they contain any thing contrary to the Liber-
> ties of the *Gallican* Church[32]

About midway through his book Father Simon pauses for a summarizing backward glance and for a fleeting acknowledgment that Sarpi has already covered some of his ground for him:

> Thus far we have shewn the Original and Progress of Ecclesiastical Revenues, how they have been administered, and in what manner they have come into the Possession of Chapters and Monasteries. We have, besides, spoken of the power of Bishops and Princes, and of the Pope also, over such Revenues. It would be now time to shew more particularly, by what ways Popes have made themselves almost absolute Masters of the goods of the Church, and to observe the quarrels they have had with Princes upon that account. But since *Fra. Paolo* hath handled that in his History, and that it is sufficient to read the Decretals, to be informed in what manner their authority hath been by degrees established, I shall speak no more of that Subject. And it is for the same reason, that I have not said any thing neither of the Original of Tithes, because it hath been also well enough handled by *Fra. Paolo*.[33]

Any English reader who did not like or did not recognize the Simonized dilution was thus invited to take his Sarpi neat.

Much more significant than any of these somewhat oblique witnesses to the pervasiveness of Sarpi's ideas and reputation is the performance of yet another Frenchman. Pierre Jurieu (1637–1713) was a grandson of Pierre du Moulin, a French protestant theologian well known to Jacobean Englishmen, and a son of the protestant pastor at Mer (Orléans), to whose post he later succeeded. Educated at the protestant centers of Saumur and Sedan, he spent his long and tempestuous life in the exacerbations of religious controversy and the inanities of prophecies patched together out of his idiosyncratic reading of the Scriptures. His very numerous publications spared neither Catholic nor fellow protestant, and most of them have slipped into deserved oblivion. One, his *Traité de la Devotion* (Rouen, 1674), unmarred by the acrimony of others, had more than twenty editions in French and, translated into English (London, 1692), is said to have had an even larger number of editions across the Channel.

It is with another of his publications, however, that we are here concerned: his *Abregé de l'Histoire du Concile de Trente*, published at Geneva in 1682. A second edition was published at Amsterdam in the next year. Treading almost on the kibes of the Amsterdam edition came the English translation: *The History of the Council of Trent. In Eight Books. Whereunto is prefixt a Discourse containing Historical Reflexions on Councils, and particularly on the Conduct of the Council of Trent, proving that the Protestants are not oblig'd to submit thereto. Written in French by Peter Jurieu,*

Doctour and Professor of Divinity. And now done into English (London, 1684). As can be seen, nothing is here said which would identify the work as a simple abridgment and rearrangement of Sarpi's *History*; and unless the English reader were a devout follower of Osborne's advice about reading "epistles," he could come to the end of the 590 octavo pages of text without ever learning the true paternity of the book. Not that Jurieu had the least intention of deceiving or that he laid claim to any originality other than that of reordering Sarpi's original. He simply confined his explanations to the long (120 pp.) prefatory "Historical Reflections on Councils," to which we must now direct our attention.

In discussing (and condemning) ecclesiastical immunities of one kind or another, Jurieu gives (pp. lxx–lxxi) an abstract of the quarrel between Pope Paul V and the Venetians. This need not, of course, be derived from Sarpi's account, though it easily may be. The "Treatise of the Interdict of *Paul V*" by "The Divines of the Republick of Venice" is later quoted on the topic of "the Invalidity of Clandestine Marriages."[34] The "Historical Reflections" give passing attention to earlier councils but concentrate, as the title page promises, upon the Council of Trent, emphasizing its nonecumenical nature, its subservience to the Pope, its nonacceptance by even some of the Catholic states, its erroneous claims to infallibility. All he says tends to the justification of the Protestants for not accepting the decrees of the Council of Trent. He then finds that it is time to talk about Father Paul:

> It is manifest that the understanding of the Reasons we have produced, does wholly depend upon knowing the History of this Council. And consequently it is highly necessary for all such Protestants to be well instructed in this History as are desirous to be able to defend the refusal they make as Protestants to submit to the Council of *Trent*. The difficulty may be, to find a faithful Historian who may be credited in the matter. For it is certain that every one is not to be believed in it. We are told, that the Collections that the *Lutherans* may have made upon the conduct of the Council, can deserve but little Faith; that they were Parties; that Objects are strangely transformed by Passion; and that a relation by the Pen of an Author partial and byassed carries with it the tincture of his Passions. But it hath pleased God in his Providence to raise up even in the Church of *Rome*, a wise, a Moderate, a Judicious and sincere Man, one that in a word was the greatest Man of his Age, who hath carefully wrote this History. He has all the Perfections required to compleat an Historian. Of great Judgment, and Abilities, strong and clear Sense, perfectly instructed in Affairs, of a vast penetration, and one that wanted no kind of assistance needful to the compleating his Work. When this author began to appear in the World, the

memory of the Council of *Trent* was still fresh in Mens Minds: so that he may very well pass for a contemporary Author. He was a Neighbour to the place where the things he writes of had been transacted. He lived in a City full of Curious Persons, who had collected Memorials of what had passed in this great Affair: and was himself one that kept correspondence with all the Learned Men of *Europe*. Nay, he had great intimacy with Oliva Camillo,[35] who had been Secretary to the Cardinal of *Mantua* Legat and President of the Council in the last Convocation; and there is no doubt but he drew considerable advantages to his Work from such a Person, who had been an Eye-witness of all that had passed. Now since this Author was neither *Lutheran* nor Protestant, he is not in reason to be suspected of the Church of *Rome*: and as he was no servile Idolater of the *Roman* Court, he ought not to be suspected of the Protestants. There shines indeed throughout his whole Work an Air of sincerity and honesty, which happily united to his vast Abilities has made him pass as unquestionably the ablest of his Age in the Art of writing History.[36]

There follow twenty-odd pages of comparisons and of defense of Sarpi's *History* from the attacks of Pallavicino, Maimbourg, and others. The defense concludes with the following statement: "Let it be no more said, that Father *Paul*, under the name of a History of the Council of *Trent*, hath made a Satyr against the Court of *Rome*. For a hundred such Enemies as Father *Paul* can never prove so injurious to it, as the Illustrious Historian [Pallavicino] has who undertook its defence."[37]

Jurieu saves the most important part of his introductory remarks, as is proper, for the end. Here he explains what he has done by way of abridging and reordering Sarpi's materials. Though lengthy, the passages deserves reproduction in full. "But let it suffice," he says,

> to have spoken thus much of Father *Paul*'s Work, a word or two now of our own. In reading Father *Paul*'s History one may remark two things: The first, that it is filled with things absolutely necessary to be known of all men, but more particularly of the Protestants. The second thing is, that it is full of Theological Disputes and Reflections: which makes it indeed most useful for Divines; but less fit for others. There is scarce any, but a Profess'd Divine, who could have the patience to read a Folio Volume of seven or eight hundred Pages, of which two Thirds are most subtil and intricate School Disputes. Which having already been tedious to the Bishops who were of the Audience, it is not to be thought strange that they are now tiresom to the Readers. So that altho this Work be exquisite in its kind, yet it must needs be owned that it is useful but to a few.

The Original is in a Language that not many in this Country [France] understand. The Translation [Diodati's] that we have of it, is not new enough to satisfie such as can suffer nothing in our Language that has an air of Antiquity. Both the Translation and the Original are full of Graces that can never decay. And yet it is not to be denied but this Work hath lost some of its Beauties by changing Language. For these Reasons it falls out that this excellent Book is not so much read as it ought to be. It has been therefore conceived that the rendering this Work more Popular would be of great use to the World. And that is the design of the present Undertaking, there being nothing of importance forgotten here, yet Brevity is observed. And as for the Theological Disputes, you have here all that is Essential in them for the Knowledge of the Nature and State of the Controversies that were managed in the Council of *Trent*. You have the Principal Arguments made use of by the several Parties for maintaining their Opinions. But the tedious Discourses of the Divines and Prelates, which Father *Paul* reports at length, and with great exactness, are here omitted. This History will at least serve for these two ends: the one, to occasion that abundance of People will inform themselves in the Conduct of this Council, who had never done it, if they had no other means but that of Father *Paul*'s Voluminous Work. The other, to refresh the memory of those that have read that Work, and let them review in little what there they saw more at large.

In some places there is a diversity as to Order between this History and that of Father *Paul*; his being written in form of a Journal; which is the most proper indeed for exactness, but is not always so pleasing to the Reader. Great Affairs very rarely happen without interruption, several things intervene, and one and the same day may produce divers great Events. So that in observing the Order of Days, one is obliged to take the Reader from a subject of which he would fain see the Issue, and that makes him uneasie. In this History therefore the Connexion of things is observed; which in that of Father *Paul* are divided. And tho I have here observed the Order and Number of Books, yet there are many things in Father *Paul*'s History at the end of the Books, which are at the beginning here. Nay, there are some in a quite different Book; as the circumstances of the great Quarrel between the *French* and *Spaniards* for Precedence. They are dispersed in the three last Books of Father *Paul*; but are here brought all together in the beginning of the eighth Book. This hint was necessary, because such as may have the Curiosity to read any Translation at length, or to compare the two Histories, not finding their matter just where they looked for it, might question the fidelity of the Present Historian [Jurieu]. But I begin to perceive that the length of this Discourse, is a little contrary to the Design of this Work. For it being composed in favour of those who have little leisure or inclination for long Reading; it is to be feared they will complain, we have been somewhat too tedious in the Introduction.[38]

Jurieu's book is a genuine *abregé*, selecting from Sarpi the substance and not the phrasing. It represents, therefore, a substantial piece of rewriting, not of mere copying in a different order. The English translator, who follows his French text *au pied de la lettre*, seems not to have availed himself of the opportunity to crib from Brent when he renders the infrequent bits of Sarpian phrasing preserved by Jurieu. I do not find that the translation was ever republished.

English interest in Sarpi did not cease nor did his influence disappear with the ending of the seventeenth century and with the decline of the Venetian Republic. His *Treatise of Matters Beneficiary* received continuing attention on into the eighteenth century, as did his life. His *History of the Inquisition* was widely read throughout the seventeenth and eighteenth centuries. And his *History of the Council of Trent* remained, for Protestant readers, the standard account, making its way in a considerable number of copies into American colonial libraries. The early nineteenth century marked possibly the neap tide of his European reputation. In his own country, the Roman Church, predictably, has continued its bitter opposition to his memory almost into the present. But there are now signs, with a new critical edition of his works and with constantly renewed assessment of his literary and historical position, that our Venetian Phoenix is about to be reborn.

Epilogue - Reprise

A GARLAND OF SUPERLATIVES

ABOUT FEW MEN in the seventeenth century (or, for that matter, in any century) has there been such agreement in the chorus of admiration, such "Sweet concent of music's harmony." True, there were also some voices raised in violent denunciation—the voices of Curialists and Jesuits, chiefly, who saw no reason to love the man who relentlessly exposed their deviousness. But when all the babble of the contemporary contentions had died away and the age had reached a more mature and considered evaluation, the overwhelming impression remains that in Paolo Sarpi the world witnessed a singular and wondrous blend of piety, intellect, and integrity. Here are some of the voices that formed the chorus.

Il miracolo di questo secolo—Vincenzo Pinelli, as related by Fulgenzio Micanzio

The splendor and ornament not of Venice only, or Italy, but of the world—G. B. della Porta

Maestro Paulo . . . of great learning, piety, humility, discretion, and integrity of life . . . a miracle in all manner of knowledge divine and humane—William Bedell

The most deep and general scholar of the World—Sir Henry Wotton

A person truly of much Learning, of great judgment and integrity, and of most upright intention—M. A. de Dominis

The same wise and worthy *Frier*, who of late with so great iudgement and fidelitie hath revealed unto the World . . . those *Arcana Imperii Pontifici*, in the *History* of the *Trent Councell*—Christopher Potter

This wise and excellent Person. . . . The Freedom and Ingenuity, the Wisdom and Truth, the Judgment and Sincerity of this great and noble-spirited Man—Edward Brown

Splendor & Ornamentum Orbis, the *Glory* and *Ornament* of the *World* —William Denton, quoting Andreas Colvius

The judicious and worthy *Servite Padre Paolo* . . . eminent for his great Learning, Judgment and Faithfulness in all his Writings—William Denton

Padre Paulo the Frier, the brightest Star in the Hemisphere of *Italy*, was second to none in Divinity while he liv'd. . . . The Wonder of his Age, Father *Paul* of Venice—John Hacket

Father Paul, a holy and learned Friar. . . . One of the late miracles of mankind for general learning, prudence, and modesty, Sir Henry Wotton's dear friend, Padre Paulo—reported by Izaak Walton

One of the most judicious Fryars that ever set Pen to Paper. . . . One of the most famous Pen-Champions that the *Venetians* imploy'd . . . was the said learned and judicious Fryer . . . commonly known by the name of Father *Paul*. . . . The people of *Venice* . . . accounted him a Saint —Henry Foulis

The Grave and Impartial Author of the [History of the] Council of Trent—Anonymous, in Nathanael Vincent's *Morning-Exercise*

He who in this Common-wealth [of Venice], is called the Divine of the State . . . is commonly chosen such a one, as is reputed the least Bigot in that Religion, as in the memory of some living, *Padri Pauli*—Slingsby Bethel

Father Paul of *Venice* (that great *Scholar* and Statesman)—Bishop Thomas Barlow

Padre Paolo the great unmasker of the *Trentine* Councel. . . . *Padre Paolo* the great Venetian Antagonist of the *Pope*. . . . The great and learned *Padre Paolo*—John Milton

Concilii Tridentini Eviscerator—Sir Henry Wotton, on a portrait of Sarpi

Paulus Venetus, Servitarum Ordinis Theologus . . . nulli inferior Judicio, Ingenio; admirabili Facundiâ, literis reconditis, & exquisitis; non magis doctrinâ, quàm rerum usu Prudens; ut maiorem, nec divinarum, nec humanarum rerum Scientiam, nec Integriorem, nec Sanctiorem vitam quisquam desideraret—Robert Johnston

Padre Paulo, the diligent and laborious Author of the *Tridentine History*—Peter Heylyn

The Judicious *Padre Paolo*. . . . Famous *Padre Paolo*—Luke de Beaulieu

Pietro Soave Polano [that is, Sarpi] . . . *a Man of admired Learning; of an exquisite Judgment; of an Indefatigable Industry; and of a modesty and integrity that is scarce to be equall'd*—Degory Wheare, quoting Sir Nathanael Brent

A person of an happy Ingenuity, and of a great and right judgment, liberally endowed with all sorts of Learning, and abundantly adorn'd both with Divine and Humane Knowledge, and that as well Moral as Political or Civil, whereby he has attain'd a high degree, both of Probity and Sweetness of Mind—Degory Wheare, quoting Adam Newton

For Padre Paolo, he must be allowed for the greatest genius of his age, and perhaps of all the moderns—Sir William Temple (possibly ironic)

P. Paulo . . . a man equally eminent for vast learning and a most consummated prudence; and was at once one of the greatest Divines, and of the wisest Men of his Age—Gilbert Burnet; later repeated by Thomas Pope Blount

P. Paulo . . . was so much esteemed by the Senate for his great Wisdom, that he was consulted by them as an Oracle, and trusted with their most important Secrets—Gilbert Burnet

That Author, who with so much Truth and Impartiality has discovered the Artifices of [the Council of Trent]—Edmund Bohun

Father *Paul*, a person of unquestioned integrity—"E. A." (1673; unidentified)

A Wise, a Moderate, a Judicious and sincere Man [Sarpi], one that in a word was the greatest Man of his Age. . . . He has all the Perfections required to compleat an Historian. Of great Judgment, and Abilities, strong and clear Sense, perfectly instructed in Affairs, of a vast penetration, and one that wanted no kind of assistance needful to the compleating of his Work—Pierre Jurieu

Unquestionably the ablest of his Age in the Art of writing History—Pierre Jurieu

Modest, pious, learned, gifted to the point of genius, *impartial, sincere,* of incorruptible *integrity*—the attributes recur with convincing regularity. And they all add up to view of this remarkable man as the ornament and wonder of his age, the Phoenix of his beloved Serenissima.

Appendix

*An Advertisement concerning a Character
given by Sir* Henry Wotton *of F.* Paul
*the Author of the History of the
Council of* Trent*

Since there was so particular a mention made of Father *Paul* in the former
Life, I thought it would not be unacceptable to the Reader to see a Character
that was given of him by Sir *Henry Wotton,* in a Letter that he writ from
Venice to the Famous and Learned Dr. *Collings,* the Kings Professor of Divinity
in *Cambridge,* which is not printed in his *Remains:* And therefore I hoped it
would be received with the entertainment that is due to every thing that comes
from such a Hand, and is writ on such a Subject. And we may better depend
on Characters that are given in private Letters to Friends, than in more studied
Elogies, where the heat either of friendship or Eloquence is apt to carry a Man
too far; but Letters that pass among Friends, are colder and more careless things,
and therefore they ought to be the less suspected.

Sir,
        Though my Feet cannot perform that Counsel which I remember from
some Translation in *Siracides, Teras limen sensati viri;* yet I should at least have
often visited you with my poor Lines: But on the other side, while I durst not
trust mine own conceit in the power of my present infirmity, and therefore have
seldome written to any; I find my self in the mean time overcharged with divers
Letters from you of singular kindness, and one of them accompanied with a
dainty peaceful piece: which truly I had not seen before, so as besides the
weight of the Subject, it was welcome, even for the Grace of newness. Yet let
me tell you, I could not but somewhat wonder to find our Spiritual *Seneca* (you
know whom I mean) among these Reconcilers, having read a former Treatise
of his (if my memory fails me not) of a contrary complexion. Howsoever, let

---

* An excerpt from Gilbert Burnet's *The Life of William Bedell* (London,
1685), pp. 253–59.

him now have his due praise with the rest, for shewing his Christian Wisdom and Charity. But I fear, as it was antiently said of a *Roman* General, That *Bellum sese alit*, so it will prove, though in somewhat a different sense, likewise as true of this Church-warfare, That the very pleasure of contending will foment Contention till the end of all flesh. But let me leave that Sacred Business to our well-meaning Fathers.

And now, Sir, having a fit Messenger, and being not long after the time when love-tokens use to pass between Friends, let me be bold to send you for a New-Years-Gift, a certain Memorial not altogether unworthy of some entertainment under your Roof, namely a true Picture of *Padre Paulo* the *Servite*, which was first taken by a Painter, whom I sent unto him from my House, then neighbouring this Monastery. I have newly added thereunto a Title [margin: *Concil. Trident. eviscerator*] of mine own conception, and had sent the Frame withal if it were portable, which is but of plain Deal coloured black like the Habit of his Order. You have a luminous Parlor, which I have good cause to remember, not only by delicate Fare, and Freedome (the Prince of Dishes) but above all your own learned Discourse; for to dine with you is to dine with many good Authors. In that Room, I beseech you to allow it a favourable place for my sake.

And that you may have somewhat to tell of him more than a bare Image, if any shall ask, as in the Table of *Cebes*; I am desirous to characterize a little unto you such part of his Nature, Customes and Abilities, as I have had occasion to know by sight or enquiry. He was one of the humblest things that could be seen within the bounds of Humanity; the very Pattern of that Precept, *Quanto doctior, tanto submissior*; and enough alone to demonstrate that Knowledge well digested *non inflat*; excellent in Positive, excellent in Scholastic and Polemical Divinity; a rare Mathematician, even in the most abstruse parts thereof, as in Algebra and the Theoricks; and yet withal as expert in the History of Plants, as if he had never perused any book but Nature: Lastly, A great Canonist, which was the Title of his ordinary Service with the State: And certainly in the time of the Popes Interdict, they had their principal Light from him. When he was either reading or writing alone, his manner was to sit fenced with a Castle of Paper about his Chair, and over Head; for he was of our Lord of S. *Alban's* Opinion, That all Air is praedatory, and especially hurtful, when the Spirits are most imployed. You will find a Scar in his Face, that was from a *Roman* Assassinate that would have killed him, as he was turned to the Wall near his Covent; and if there were not a greater Providence about us, it might often have been easily done, especially upon such a weakly and wearish Body. He was of a quiet and settled temper, which made him prompt in his counsels, and answers, and the same in Consultations which *Themistocles* was in Action, as will appear unto you in a Passage between him and the Prince of *Conde*; The said Prince in a voluntary journey toward *Rome* came to *Venice*, where to give some vent to his own humours, he would often devest himself of his greatness, and after other less laudable curiosities, not long before his departure, a desire took him to visit the famous obscure Servite, to whose

Cloyster coming twice he was the first time denied to be within; at the second it was intimated, That by reason of his daily admission to their deliberatives in the place he could not receive the visit of so illustrious a personage, without leave from the Senate, which he would seek to procure. This set a great edge on the Prince, when he saw he should confer with one participant of more than Monkish Speculations: So after leave gotten, he came the third time, and there besides other voluntary discourse (which it were a tyranny over you to repeat) he assailed with a question, enough to have troubled any Man but himself, and him too, if a precedent accident had not eased him. The question was this: He desired to be told by him before his going away, who was the true unmasked Author of the late *Tridentine* History. You must know, that but newly advertisement was come from *Rome*, That the Archbishop of *Spalato* [M. A. de Dominis] being arrived from *England*, in an interview between him and the Cardinal *Ludovisio*, Nephew to Gregory XV. the said Cardinal after a complemental welcoming of him into the Lap of the Church, told him by order from the Pope, That his Holiness would expect from him some Recantation in Print, as an antidote against certain Books and Pamphlets, which he had published whilst he stood in revolt, namely his first *Manifesto: Item*, two Sermons preached at the *Italian* Church in *London*. Again, a little Treatise intituled, *Scogli*. And lastly, His great Volumes about Church Regiment and Controversies: These were all named; for as touching the *Tridentine* History, his Holiness, saith the Cardinal, will not press you to any disavowment thereof, though you have an Epistle before the Original Edition, because we know well enough that Fryer *Paulo* is the Father of that Brat. Upon this last Piece of the aforesaid Advertisement the good Father came fairly off; for on a sudden, laying all together, that to disavow the Work was an untruth, to affirme it a danger, and to say nothing, an Incivility; he took a middle Evasion, telling the Prince, That he understood he was going to *Rome*, where he might learn at ease who was the Author of that Work, as they were freshly intelligenced from thence. Thus without any mercy of your time, I have been led along from one thing to another, while I have taken pleasure to remember that Man whom God appointed and furnished for a proper Instrument to anatomize that Pack of reverend Cheaters. Among whom, I speak of the greater part, *Exceptis senioribus*, Religion was shuffled like a Pair of Cards, and the Dice so many Years were set upon us.

And so wishing you very heartily many good years, I will let you breath, till you have opened these inclosed.

Notes

CHAPTER 1

1. *La Vita del padre Paolo* was first printed in Leyden in 1646; it was translated into English in 1651 and into French in 1661 and was often republished.

2. Fulgenzio Micanzio, *La Vita del padre Paolo* (Leyden, 1646), p. 5.

3. Ibid., p. 6.

4. Fulgenzio Micanzio, *The Life of the Most Learned Father Paul, of the Order of the Servie. Councellour of State to the most Serene Republicke of Venice, and Authour of the History of the Counsell of Trent. Translated out of Italian by a person of Quality* (London, 1651), p. 4. The "person of Quality," we learn from John Hacket's *Scrinia Reserata* (London, 1693), p. 16, was "that Gentleman of great and elegant Parts Mr. *John* Saintamand." Saintamand (or Saint Amand) was "sometimes Secretary" to the Lord Keeper, John Williams.

5. Micanzio, *Life of Father Paul*, p. 7.

6. Ibid., p. 16.

7. Ibid., p. 17. I have corrected the misprinted Italian, as I shall do here-after, silently, when occasion arises.

8. John Milton, *Second Defence of the People of England*, in *Prose Selections*, ed. Merritt Y. Hughes (New York, 1947), pp. 339–40.

9. Micanzio, *Life of Father Paul*, p. 16. Again one is reminded of Milton's rigorous proposals in his tractate *Of Education*.

10. Ibid., sig. D5 verso (pagination confused).

11. Ibid., sig. E2.

12. This exaggeration began with Micanzio; but see also Aurelio Bianchi-Giovini, *Biografia di Frà Paolo Sarpi, teologo e consultore di Stato della Repubblica Veneta*, 2 vols. (Zurich, 1836), 1:57–86; Alexander Robertson, *Fra Paolo Sarpi, the Greatest of the Venetians* (London, 1911), pp. 60–107; Adelaide Rampolla Gambino, *Fra Paolo Sarpi. Studio storico e letterario* (Palmero, 1919), pp. 43–54. Calmer and more judicious appraisal, with further bibliographical indications, may be read in Giovanni Getto, *Paolo Sarpi*, 2d ed. (Florence, 1967), pp. 93–109; see also the general article by G. B. de Toni, "Fra Paolo Sarpi nelle scienze esatte e naturali," in *Paolo*

Sarpi e i suoi tempi: studi storici (Città di Castello, 1923), pp. 87–98.

13. Micanzio, *Life of Father Paul*, pp. 8–9. As to the number of theses defended, the Italian text reads (p. 12) 318, which Saint Amand reduces—possibly misreading the indistinct first digit—to 118.

14. Ibid., p. 15.

15. Ibid., p. 18.

16. Ibid., pp. 19–21.

17. Ibid., p. 19.

18. The Provincial is, in the various orders, the chief official or supervisory officer within his chapter's territory. He is given a term appointment and ranks next in authority under the Superior-General. See F. L. Cross, ed., *The Oxford Dictionary of the Christian Church* (London, 1957), p. 1118.

19. Micanzio, *Life of Father Paul*, p. 22.

20. Ibid., p. 25.

21. Ibid., p. 26.

22. Ibid., p. 27.

23. Ibid., pp. 29–32.

24. Ibid., p. 32.

25. Ibid., sig. D1 (pagination erratic).

26. Ibid., sig. D1 verso.

27. Ibid., sig. D2. I have not found the work by della Porta in which he speaks of Sarpi's "specular perspective"; but in his *Magiae Naturalis libri viginti* (ed. Frankfurt, 1591), "Prooemium," he speaks of *"R. M. Paulum Venetum ordinis Servorum . . . natum ad Encyclopediam: Non tantùm Venetae urbis, aut Italiae, sed orbis splendor, & ornamentum"* (pp. 288–89).

28. Micanzio, *Life of Father Paul*, sig. D2 recto and verso.

29. Ibid., sigs. D2 verso–D8 verso; quotation from D8 verso.

30. Ibid., sig. D8 verso.

31. Ibid., sig. E1 recto and verso.

32. Ibid., sigs. E2–E4; quotation from sig. E3 verso.

33. Ibid., sigs. E4 verso–E6.

34. On this occasion, says Fra Fulgenzio (sig. E5 verso), Sarpi reminded Santa Severina that in 1593, on "the vacancy of the Bishopricke of *Milopotamo*, his Lordship had begg'd it for him of his Holinesse"—without success, as it turned out.

35. Ibid., sigs. E8–F5 verso.

36. Ibid., sig. F6.

37. Ibid., sig. G2 verso. The Italian is badly garbled in the text.

38. Ibid., sig. G3.

39. That the new Pope had little affection for Venice, even before his election, may be seen in an often-recorded exchange between him and the Venetian ambassador to Rome, Leonardo Donata (or Donà), who was later Doge:

Borghese: "If I were Pope, I would place Venice under interdict and excommunication."

Donato: "And if I were Doge, I would trample your interdict and excommunication under foot."

Cf. Robertson, *Fra Paolo Sarpi*, p. 115. The precise language varies with the tellers of the tale.

CHAPTER 2

1. The phrase *Splendor & Ornamentum Orbis*, without reference to della Porta, is repeated in a Latin version of Sarpi's *History of the Inquisition* published in Rotterdam in 1651; see William Denton's translation of Sarpi, *A Treatise of Matters Beneficiary* (London, 1680), p. iv.

2. They are given fuller discussion

by several distinguished scholars in *La Civiltà veneziana nell'età barocca* (Florence, 1959): Ernesto Sestan, "La politica veneziana del Seicento," pp. 35–66; Luigi Salvatorelli, "Venezia, Paolo V e fra Paolo Sarpi," pp. 67–95; and Domenico Sella, "Il declino dell'emporio realtino," pp. 97–121. See also Federico Chabod, *La politica di Paolo Sarpi* (Venice and Rome, 1962; repr. 1968), pp. 43–103; Roberto Cessi, *Storia della Repubblica di Venezia*, rev. ed., 2 vols. (Milan and Messina, 1968), 2:158–64; and William J. Bouwsma, *Venice and the Defense of Republican Liberty* (Berkeley and Los Angeles, 1968), pp. 339–58. An older and more general sketch of Sarpi's role in the interdict is that of Laura M. Ragg, *Crises in Venetian History* (London, 1928), pp. 153–71.

3. For the Uskoks, in addition to Sarpi's own accounts supplementing Minuccio Minucci, see *La Repubblica di Venezia, la casa d'Austria e gli Uscocchi*, ed. Gaetano and Luisa Cozzi (Bari, 1965), "Nota storica," pp. 419–54; and Alberto Tenenti, *Venezia e i corsari* (Bari, 1961), pp. 13–28. Tenenti also has a chapter on the English trading and piratical incursions into the Mediterranean after Lepanto, pp. 78–114.

4. See Paolo Sarpi, *The History of the Quarrels of Pope Paul V. with the State of Venice*, trans. Christopher Potter (London, 1626), pp. 6–7.

5. Cf. Bianchi-Giovini, *Biografia di Frà Paolo Sarpi*, 1:229–32; Bouwsma, *Venice*, p. 349. Gregorio Leti, in a letter which he clumsily attributes to Traiano Boccalini in *La Bilancia politica di tutte le opere di Traiano Boccalini* (Castellana, 1678), pt. III, p. 89, has Boccalini writing to Sarpi and

saying, "[Il Papa] si trova talmente irritato, che havendogli l'altro giorno un Prelato di stima parlato con moderati concetti, à fine di divertirlo delle sue infantadi risolutioni contro la Republica, il Papa tutto sdegnato gli rispose, *questi vostri discorsi puzzano d'Heresia*, e pure non haveva altra passione, che verso il bene comune dello Stato, e della Chiesa."

6. In dating the sequence of events for 1600 to 1607, I generally follow the "Cronologia Veneziana del Seicento" of R. M. della Rocca and Maria Francesca Tiepolo in *La Civiltà Veneziana nell'età barocca*, cited above.

7. Actually, this was a 1536 modification of an even older law; see Sarpi, *Considerationi sopra le censure . . .* (Venice, 1606), p. 4a.

8. Paragraph adapted and condensed from Bianchi-Giovini, *Biografia di Frà Paolo Sarpi*, 1:233–35.

9. Della Rocca and Tiepolo, "Cronologia Veneziana," p. 264.

10. Cf. Bianchi-Giovini, *Biografia di Frà Paolo Sarpi*, 1:235.

11. Actually, Grimani had already died, on the twenty-third, and in those tricky moments the death had not been made public.

12. The sequence again is that in della Rocca and Tiepolo, "Cronologia Veneziana," p. 264. For Sarpi's peculiar role in Venetian policy at this juncture, see the acute observations of Raffaele Belvederi, *Guido Bentivoglio e la politica europea del suo tempo, 1607–1621* (Padua, 1962), pp. 28–29n, and the older essay on Sarpi by Francesco Fiorentino in *Scritti varii di letteratura, filosofia e critica* (Naples, 1876), esp. pp. 84–95.

13. The event was reported thus in a contemporary pamphlet: "The Pope

[was] like to a shrew, the more earnestly that hee was instanced, the more crossely hee gave his answeres; And in the end became so stately, as he would endure no more debatings or entreatings, but with a Papall sternnesse hee proceeded to the publishing of his Excommunication against this whole State, though in the same he made reservation of seven and twenty dayes for repentance." See *STC* 19482, *A Declaration of the Variance betweene the Pope, and the Segniory of Venice* (London, 1606), pp. 14–15. The same work (p. 15) speaks of "the raging passions of the Pope."

14. See Chabod, *La Politica di Paolo Sarpi*, p. 53.

15. Robertson, *Fra Paolo Sarpi*, pp. 141–42.

16. "La loro solita equivocatione," says Sarpi; see *Historia particolare delle cose passate tra'l Sommo Pontefice Paolo V. e la Serenissima Republica di Venetia gl'anni MDCV. MDCVI. MDCVII* (Lyons, 1624), Bk. II, p. 64.

17. In addition to Sarpi's own account of the expulsion of the Jesuits, *Historia particolare*, pp. 64–68, see also Bianchi-Giovini, *Biografia di Frà Paolo Sarpi*, 1:250–53; Alessandro Pascolato, *Fra Paolo Sarpi* (Milan, 1893), pp. 134–35; Robertson, *Fra Paolo Sarpi*, pp. 142–45. For a brief sketch of the Jesuits in Venice prior to the interdict, see Bouwsma, *Venice*, pp. 253–54.

18. For bibliographical accounts of these, see Francesco Scaduto, *Stato e Chiesa secondo Fra Paolo Sarpi* (Florence, 1885), pp. 153–260; Sarpi, *Istoria dell'Interdetto e altri scritti*, ed. M. D. Busnelli and Giovanni Gambarin, 3 vols. (Bari, 1940), 1:235–39, 3:267–70; and Bouwsma, *Venice*, pp. 344–403, esp. in the notes.

19. In one of the reported colloquies between Sarpi and Christoph von Dohna, 23 August 1608, Sarpi is recorded as having said, "Un uomo non può niente, senza l'occasione. Se l'occasione non si fosse offerta, io non avrei scritto niente. Spesso, mancando le occasioni, gli uomini non sono conosciuti." See Sarpi, *Lettere ai protestanti. Prima edizione critica a cura di Manlio Duilio Busnelli*, 2 vols. (Bari, 1931), 2:130. After that tremendous "occasione" Sarpi was no longer an unknown man.

20. The chronology of these works, together with that of certain other then unpublished consultations and opinions, may be consulted in Busnelli and Gambarin's *Istoria dell'Interdetto*, 2:275–87.

21. "Composto dalli sottoscritti theologi": Pietr'Antonio [Ribetti] Archidiacono, & Vicario General di Venetia; F. Paulo dell'Ord. de' Servi Theol. della Ser. Rep. di Venetia; F. Bernardo Giordano Minore Osservante Theologo; F. Michel'Agnolo [Bonicelli] Minore Osservante Theologo; F. Marc'Antonio Capello Minor Conventuale Theologo; F. Camillo Augustiniano Theologo; F. Fulgentio [Micanzio] dell'Ordine de' Servi theologo." The reading is that of the title page.

22. Translated into English by Bedell, and lent by him to Wotton, who was writing on the same subject, it was later (1626) published by Bedell; cf. Logan P. Smith, *The Life and Letters of Sir Henry Wotton*, 2 vols. (Oxford, 1907), 1:128–29.

23. I follow the account of the *Historia particolare* in Gambarin, *Istoria dell'Interdetto*, 1:245–255.

24. Possibly not; see above, chap. 3, p. 28. The full title of Querini's work is *Aviso delle ragioni della Serenissima*

Republica di Venetia, intorno alle difficoltà che le sono promosse dalla Santità di Papa Paolo V. Di Antonio Quirino senator venet:. Alla sua Patria e a tutto lo Stato della medesima Republica (Venice, 1606).

25. Cf. Bouwsma, *Venice*, p. 380.

26. See Baronius's *Paraenesis ad Rempublicam Venetam* (Rome, 1606). Baronius's known animosity to the Venetians was recognized even in England; cf. Leonel Sharpe, *A Looking-glasse for the Pope* (London, 1616), sig. e4, who remarks that Baronius urged Paul V to proceed against the Venetians. Sharpe also recalls and reports the scandalous scriptural perversion of Baronius's in the Consistory of 17 April 1606: "Baronius goeth farther, in the excommunication of the Venetians, to *Paul* the 5. there is a double ministery of *Peter*, to feede and to kill, for the Lord said to him feede my sheepe, and he heard a voice from heaven kill and eate" (p. 299). And Thomas Pope Blount, in his *Censura celebriorum authorum* (London, 1690), with unconscious irony places his account of Baronius (pp. 606–8) immediately before his account of Sarpi.

27. This often-related account is here abstracted from Bianchi-Giovini, *Biografia di Frà Paolo Sarpi*, 2:6–8.

28. Fra Fulgenzio records (*Vita*, p. 169) Sarpi's witty punning remark to his physician, Acquapendente, about his wound: "E pure il mondo vuole che sia data *Stilo Romanae Curiae*."

29. Bianchi-Giovini, *Biografia di Frà Paolo Sarpi*, 2:11. The original decree, passed in the Council of Ten on 10 October 1607, was published the next day throughout the territories of the state.

30. Not before 1606, however; Wotton's letters and dispatches for 1604–1605 are lost. See Smith, *Life and Letters*, 1:56.

31. The priest's name was Michiele Viti, as appears from the official proclamation, reprinted in Francesco Griselini, *Memorie anedote spettanti alla vita . . . [di] F. Paolo Servita*, 2d ed. (Lausanne, 1760), pp. 172–77. Earlier, as Wotton writes in a letter of 14 July 1606 directed to Robert Cecil, the Venetians had placed a similar *taglio* upon the head of a Paduan Jesuit, Padre Gagliardo, who had spoken against them at Mantua; see Smith, *Life and Letters*, 1:355.

32. E. S. Shuckburgh, ed., *Two Biographies of William Bedell, Bishop of Kilmore. With a Selection of His Letters and an Unpublished Treatise* (Cambridge [Eng.], 1902), pp. 236–37. In the same letter (pp. 234–35) Bedell speaks scathingly of the expulsed Jesuits.

33. There were, nevertheless, suspicions and charges from the nuncio or his spies that the English and Venetian "heretics" met, either at the "Ship of Gold" or elsewhere. See Smith, *Life and Letters*, 1:87n; Wotton himself, in a speech before the collegio on 15 October 1607 congratulating the Venetions on Sarpi's narrow escape, denied having had direct dealings with him (ibid., 1:406).

34. In a letter to Sir Robert Cecil, Earl of Salisbury and Secretary of State, June 22 1607, after the end of the quarrel, Wotton could write with some enthusiasm "that the light of God's truth increaseth here apace, through the grounds that have been laid by the public writings, and more by the private discourses of Maestro

Paulo and his assistants"; Smith, *Life and Letters*, 1:393.

35. Shuckburgh, *Two Biographies of William Bedell*, p. 231; my italics.

36. Printed in Bishop Gilbert Burnet's *The Life of William Bedell, D. D., Bishop of Kilmore in Ireland* (London, 1685), pp. 253–59—and elsewhere.

37. Smith, *Life and Letters*, 1:87.

38. Burnet, *Life of Bedell*, p. 8.

39. See Shuckburgh, *Two Biographies*, pp. 244, 247–50; Smith, *Life and Letters*, 1:87.

40. Smith, *Life and Letters*, 1:377, 387, 398–99.

41. Ibid., 1:399, 407. The second portrait, showing Sarpi's scarred face, is the one mentioned in the letter printed by Burnet. It is presently at Oxford. See the reproduction in Bouwsma, *Venice*, facing p. 527; also reproduced in Gaetano Cozzi, *Il Doge Nicolò Contarini* (Venice and Rome, 1958), facing p. 124, and in A. Lytton Sells, *The Paradise of Travellers* (Bloomington, Ind., 1964).

42. Pressmark 4051.b.38. M. A. Scott, *Elizabethan Translations from the Italian* (Boston and New York, 1916), p. 263, without paying proper attention to the second half of the title page she was transcribing, wrote, "I take this to be a translation of Father Paul's *Trattato dell'Interdetto di Venezia*. Venice. 1606. 4to." She apparently did not associate it with its real original, the *Considerationi sopra le censure*.

43. *A Declaration*, p. 27.

44. Ibid., pp. 28–29.

45. The author could wish, he says, "that the eyes and hearts of the renowned *Venetians*, may by the touch of Gods finger bee opened wider, to let in the Lord of glory, bringing in his traine his trueth and righteous-

nesse; and that their hands and puissance may bee so strengthened with an extraordinary addition of valour, as that they may from that nooke or corner of *Italy*, become as it were Gods harbengers to make way for him throughout that goodly countrey, to the suppression and demolishing of that so intolerable usurpation" (*A Declaration*, p. 52). Whoever wrote that was more than a *"mezzo Luterano."*

46. Sarpi, *An Apology, or, Apologiticall answere, made by Father Paule a Venetian, of the order of Servi, unto the Exceptions and objections of Cardinall Bellarmine, against certaine Treatises and Resolutions of John Gerson, concerning the force and validitie of Excommunication. First published in Italian, and now translated into English. Seene and allowed by publicke authoritie* (London, 1607).

47. *STC* 24719, entered to Cuthbert Burby, 10 December 1606. The separate parts are separately paged but the signatures are continuous.

48. Sarpi, *Concerning the Excommunication of the Venetians . . .* (London, 1607), sig. K1 verso.

49. Scott, *Elizabethan Translations from the Italian*, pp. 265–67, to her description of this volume adds particulars concerning the subsequent history of Sarpi's would-be assassins.

50. See, for instance, the *Raccolta degli scritti usciti in istampa, e scritti a mano, nella causa del P. Paolo V. co'signori venetiani* (Coire, Paulo Marcello, 1607). This contains nineteen separate pieces, each reprinting the original title page. Four of these are by Sarpi; another is the *Paraenesis* of Baronius. The Latin counterpart of this volume, though not comprised of exactly the same pieces, is entitled *Con-*

troversiae memorabilis inter *Paulum V. Pontificem Max. & Venetos* . . . *Acta et scripta varia* (In Villa Sanvincentiana, apud Paulum Marcellum, sumptibus Caldorianae Societatis, Anno 1607). There is a copy in the British Museum, pressmark 1008.a.12. Another collection (British Museum, pressmark 175.f.10), exclusively Romanist, consists of ten tracts emanating from Bologna, Milan, Ferrara, Rome, Mantua, and Recanati in the years 1606 and 1607. It likewise contains the *Paraenesis*. In the epistle to the Reader, Christopher Potter, translator of Sarpi's *The History of the Quarrels of Pope Paul V. with the State of Venice* (London, 1626), sig. A1 recto and verso, says that Melchior Goldast has collected, in Latin, all the Venetian tractates dealing with the quarrel. This I have not seen.

51. *Catalogus universalis* . . . (STC 14450). In abstracting the titles from his catalogue, I follow his own abbreviated and idiosyncratic forms of entry. Under "Fr. *Paolo* Venetiano" he lists *Dialogia alla Rep. di Vinetia* (Bologna, 1606)—which is not Sarpi's; *Apologia* (*Ven.*), three copies; *Considerationi sopra le Censure di P. Paolo 5to* (*Ven.*, 1606), Italian and Latin; and *Tr. de Interdicto.* Under "Paul. *Venetus*" he lists a different copy (with different pressmark) of the Latin *Considerationes.* Under "Rob. *Bellarminus*" he has entries of the *Risposta al Trattato de 7.* [misprinted as 17.] *Theologi Venetiani* (Romae 1606) and *Risposta ad uno libretto intitelato, Trattato sopra la validita delle Scommuniche di Gio. Gersone* (*In Rom.* 1606), two copies. Under "Caesar Baronius" he lists *Essortatione alla Rep. di Venezia* (*Rome* 1606) and (*Aug. Vind.* 1606),

Votum contra Remp. Venetam (1606), and *Sent. super excommunicat. Venetorū.* Under "Gio. Ant. *Bovio*" he lists *Risposta alle consideratione del Maestro Paolo* (*Romae* 1606). Under "Fr. *Fulgentius* Ord. Servorum" he enters the *Tr. de Interdicto Paulis 5ti* (*Ven.* 1606), copies in Italian and in Latin. With Quirini ("Ant. *Quirinus*"), he somewhat overdoes it, listing as separate works *Relatio rationum serenissimae Reip. Venetae oppositarum difficultatibus Pauli 5ti*, a *Dissertatio ad Remp. Venetam*, and the Italian *Aviso.* No doubt other titles connected with the dispute lie scattered throughout James's fine print, if one had the will to trace them out.

52. Thomas Coryat, *Coryat's Crudities Hastily gobled up in five Moneths travells in France, Savoy, Italy* . . . , 2 vols. (Glasgow, 1905), 1:379. The *Crudities* was entered in the Stationers' Register on 26 November 1610 and was first published in 1611.

53. Ibid., 1:380.

CHAPTER 3

1. Burnet, *Life of William Bedell*, pp. 256, 257.

2. The date is variously given as 1560 or (more commonly) 1566. But since de Dominis himself spoke in 1616 of "having seene almost threescore yeeres," I incline to the earlier date; cf. *A Manifestation of the Motives* . . . (London, 1616), p. 5.

3. Cf. the articles "Dominis, Marcantonio de," in the Firmin Didot *Nouvelle Biographie générale* (Paris, 1845–1846), vol. 14, and "De Dominis, Marc'Antonio," in *Enciclopedia Italiana* (Treccani), vol. 12 (with bibliography), by Eleanora Zuliani.

4. In fact, the designation is so usual that Peter Heylyn, in the first edition of his geographico-historical *Microcosmus, or A Little Description of the Great World* (Oxford, 1621), p. 203, when mentioning the chief cities of "Sclavonia," identifies Spalato only as "a sea towne standing East of *Sebenico*, the Bishop of which *M. Antonicus* [sic] *di Dominis* loathing the Romish superstition, came for refuge into *England* 1616."

5. See Tenenti, *Venezia e i corsari*, pp. 13–28. An amusing version of the Uskok threat appears in T. H.'s *Newes from Rome, Spalato's Doome* (London, 1624), Epistle, sig. A2 recto and verso: "The *Iscocchi* sent forth threats against their *quondam* Bishop, (I meane this same *Dalmatian* Bishop, *M. Anton. de Dominis*) that if they could lay hands on him, they would make a bag of his skin (as they are accustomed to make of swines skins for wine and oyle in those countries)."

6. Sarpi, letter to Simone Contarini, Venetian ambassador in Rome, dated 13 Dec. 1615; cf. Sarpi, *Lettere inedite di Fra Paolo Sarpi a Simone Contarini*, ed. C. Castellani (Venice, 1892), p. 62.

7. Castellani's suggestion, ibid., p. 62n, is that de Dominis at Querini's suggestion may have written the *Aviso* in Latin, and that when it was translated, the true paternity was obscured.

8. Smith, *Life and Letters*, 1:93.

9. Adolfo Albertazzi, *Romanzieri e romanzi del cinquecento e del seicento* (Bologna, 1891), p. 226.

10. Burnet, *Life of William Bedell*, p. 10.

11. News of this disaffection, probably discreetly disseminated by Bedell, must have reached England not much later than this. See John Chamberlain's letter to Dudley Carleton, 17 June 1612, concerning the arrival in England of some Carmelite friars defecting from Rome, in which he says that Bishop Lancelot Andrewes knew of their coming in advance and adds: "He told me likewise this other day of a certain Bishop [i.e., de Dominis] in the Venetian territorie, (but he had forgot his name) that is writing a worke against the Popes usurping jurisdiction." Letter printed in John Chamberlain, *The Letters of John Chamberlain*, ed. Norman Egbert McClure, 2 vols. (Philadelphia, 1939), 1:357.

12. For accounts of Dr. Marta see Smith, *Life and Letters, Henry Wotton*, 2:472–73; Cozzi, *Il Doge Nicolò Contarini*, pp. 131–32; Romolo Quazza, *La guerra per la successione di Mantova e del Monferrato* (Mantua, 1926), 2 vols., 1:415; Chamberlain, *Letters*, 1:333, 340. See also the Folger Library's Strozzi manuscript *Transcripts* (W.b. 132), esp. vols. 91, 129, 140 passim. One of Marta's ardently pro-papal works is answered, roundly, in Richard Crakanthorp's *The Defence of Constantine: with a Treatise of the Popes temporall Monarchie* (London, 1621).

13. See Folger Strozzi *Transcripts*, MS W.b.132, vol. 129.

14. *Calendar of State Papers, Domestic*, 1611–1618, p. 262.

15. Ibid., p. 273.

16. Account mostly based on Henry Newland, *The Life and Contemporaneous Church History of Antonio de Dominis* (Oxford and London, 1859), pp. 92–97.

17. Perhaps not so soon, but before the year was out. The title of the pamphlet in its English form, "Englished out of his Latine Copy," reads: *A*

Manifestation of the Motives, whereupon the most Reverend Father, Marcus Antonius De Dominis, Archbishop of Spalato (in the Territorie of Venice) undertooke his departure thence (London, 1616).

18. I by-pass here several brief but general accounts, such as those in the scandalous Arthur Wilson's *The History of Great Britain, being the Life and Reign of James the First* (London, 1653), p. 102, or the *Historia rerum Britannicarum* (Amsterdam, 1655) of Robert Johnston, "Scoto-Britanno," who speaks perceptively of the Archbishop of Canterbury's housing of de Dominis and *"ignorans se serpentem in sinu fovere"* (p. 515). De Dominis apparently remained with Abbott until the spring of 1619; see a letter of Abbott's to Nathanael Brent in Venice, 21 June 1618, and the note to it by Gaetano Cozzi, "Fra Paolo Sarpi, l'Anglicanesimo, e la *Historia del Concilio Tridentino,*" in *Rivista Storica Italiana,* vol. 68 (1956), fasc. iv, p. 604*n.*

19. Sir Thomas Roe, *The Negotiations of Sir Thomas Roe, in His Embassy to the Ottoman Porte, from the Year 1621 to 1628 Inclusive . . . Now first published from the Originals* (London, 1740), p. 102. The Archbishop's opinion of de Dominis is echoed by Bishop Burnet, *Life of Bedell,* p. 18: "He was an ambitious Man, and set too great a value on himself, and expressed it so indecently, that he sunk much in the estimation of the *English* Clergy, by whom he was at first received with all possible respect."

20. Thomas Fuller, *The Church-History of Britain; from the Birth of Jesus Christ untill the Year 1648* (London,

1655). The main entry on de Dominis occurs in Bk. X, Sect. vi, pp. 93–100.

21. The liberality of Fuller's account notwithstanding, he was attacked for some of his statements about de Dominis by the atrabiliar Peter Heylyn; see the latter's *Examen Historicum* (London, 1659), pp. 191–92.

22. A Latin version was also printed, in 1618, at Leeuwarden in the Netherlands: *Concio habita Italice a Reverendo Patre Marco Antonio de Dominis, Archiepiscopo Spalatensi primo die dominico Adventus Anno 1617. Londini in Mercatorum Capella, coram Italis ibi commorantibus, & aliis honorificiis in illa Synaxi & Comvent. . . .* (Leovardiae, 1618).

23. De Dominis, *A Sermon Preached,* p. 11.

24. Ibid., p. 15.

25. Ibid., pp. 61–62.

26. John Hacket, *Scrinia Reserata: A Memorial Offer'd to the Great Deservings of John Williams, D.D.* (In the Savoy, 1693), pp. 31–33; quotation from p. 33.

27. Had Archbishop Toby been reading *Volpone?*

28. Hacket, *Scrinia Reserata,* Pt. I, ¶ 109 (pagination defective).

29. Richard Crakanthorp, *Defensio Ecclesiae Anglicanae, contra M. Antonii De Dominis, D. Archiepiscopi Spalatensis iniurias* (London, 1625), p. 34.

30. Ibid., p. 37.

31. An amusing instance of the plot-and-counterplot atmosphere in which the events of de Dominis's life unrolled is recorded in Smith's *The Life and Letters of Sir Henry Wotton,* 1:64*n:* "On Aug. 26, 1617, the papal Nuncio [in Venice] wrote that he had had a visit from 'Giacomo Torre,' a native

of Navarre, who was living in the house of the English ambassador, and who had offered to go to England and set fire to the house of the Archbishop of Spalatro, and burn his books, and kill that famous convert to Protestantism. The Nuncio made the moral reply that it was not the way of Holy Church to murder heretics; and anyhow, as he wrote, he suspected that the proposal might be a stratagem planned by Wotton to get him to commit himself to the proposition."

32. De Dominis's *Papatus Romanus* was dedicated to James I and was published anonymously. It argues, in ten chapters, that *all* bishops are successors to the Apostles, not the Bishop of Rome only; that popes are usurpers of temporal power; that they are subject to conciliar decisions; that their power is verging to extinction.

33. The entire book is cast in the form of an address by the Church (as spouse of Christ) to her children, providing them with warnings against "the Rockes, which *Ambition* hath layd . . . and those which grew out of *Avarice*" (sig. b4 recto). Among the "rocks" of the first part of the book are the papacy, temporal power, excommunication; among those of the second part are the Mass, auricular confession, and purgatory. The tone throughout is distinctly antipapal, the argument largely against the idea that the Bishop of Rome should have any eminence or authority beyond those of any other bishop.

34. See John Harding, *A Recantation Sermon preached in the Gate-House at Westminster the 30. day of July 1620* (London, 1620), p. 4.

35. See the letter to Simone Contarini, 13 Dec. 1615, cited above, n.6

of chap. 3; and Boris Ulianich, ed., *Paolo Sarpi, Lettere ai Gallicani* (Wiesbaden, 1961), letter to Jacques Gillot, 17 Feb. 1607, p. 159.

CHAPTER 4

1. Horatio Brown, "Paolo Sarpi," a Taylorian Lecture, delivered 20 Nov. 1895, in *Studies in European Literature, being the Taylorian Lectures 1889–1899* (Oxford, 1900), pp. 227–28.

2. Cod. it., 5:25. The manuscript is basically in the hand of Sarpi's amanuensis, Fra Marco Fanzano, with corrections in Sarpi's own hand.

3. Others have said it. See, for instance, Giovanni Ponti, *Paolo Sarpi* (Torino, 1938), p. 64. Ponti believes that Sarpi lent his manuscript to de Dominis, who was about to leave for England, and that de Dominis either made a copy of it or had one made, unknown to Sarpi.

4. Until quite recently, this was the commonly accepted version; see Bianchi-Giovini, *Biografia di Frà Paolo Sarpi*, 2:307; Newland, *Life of de Dominis*, p. 109; Robertson, *Fra Paolo Sarpi*, pp. 238–39; M. A. Scott, *Elizabethan Translations from the Italian*, p. lviii; and Thomas Middleton, *A Game at Chess*, ed. R. C. Bald (Cambridge, [Engl.], 1929), p. 7n.

5. This was not true in Rome, however. There they knew that de Dominis was not the author. See above, chap. 5, p. 60. See also *The Letters of the Renowned Father Paul Counsellor of State to the most Serene Republick of Venice . . .*, trans. Edward Brown (London, 1963), Preface, p. xxx, speaking of Sarpi's reading about conciliar matters: *Here's a whole Knot of good Books, all together in this VIIIth Letter;*

and what he says further about such things, and declares that he had been imployed about the like, is a clear Instance of his own Pains in the History of the Council of Trent, *which set the World a wondring and guessing who could be the Author of that Book, as much as any Book that ever was printed; and made those that knew the Secret, laugh heartily at the* blind Archers *that shot their Conjectures so wide from the Mark; till the Spies of the Roman Court made such a Discovery, that it was shrewdly to be suspected that Father* Paul *was the Man that wrote it; and therefore when the Prince of* Conde *did so besiege the Father's Convent to get a Sight of him, and speak with him, which he could not do without leave from the Senate; and asked him amongst other intriguing Questions, Who was Author of the* History of the Council of Trent? *the Father (who was too wise for the Prince) told him only* that the Gentlemen of *Rome* could easily inform him of that Matter.

6. Sarpi, *Historie of the Councel of Trent . . .* , trans. Nathanael Brent (London, 1620), sig. ¶3; my italics.

7. Ibid., sig ¶[6] verso.

8. This has been the result, chiefly, of the excellent work of Frances Yates, "Paolo Sarpi's *History of the Council of Trent*," *Journal of the Warburg and Courtauld Institutes*, 7(1944):123–44, and of Cozzi, "Fra Paolo Sarpi," pp. 559–619. For what follows I am much indebted to both of them.

9. David Lloyd, *The Statesmen and Favourites of England* (London, 1665), p. 803.

10. Isaak Walton, *The Complete Angler & the Lives of Donne, Wotton,*

Hooker, Herbert & Sanderson, ed. Alfred W. Pollard (London, 1925), pp. 266–67.

11. For a full discussion of this fascinating—and puzzling—volume, see above, chap. 7, pp. 90–92.

12. Lewis Atterbury, ed., *Some Letters relating to the History of the Council of Trent* (London, 1705), sigs. A2 verso–A3 recto.

13. Ibid., p. 1.

14. Ibid., pp. 2–3.

15. Ibid., pp. 10–11. Fra Fulgenzio's part in "this Business" was, presumably (as with Wotton), to act as intermediary between Sarpi and Brent, for as continuing Consultore, Sarpi would still be technically inaccessible to an outsider.

16. See Cozzi, "Fra Paolo Sarpi," pp. 564–69, 573–78. Wotton, who replaced Carleton at Venice in the spring of 1616, wrote to James that the *Historia* was completed and that nothing was awaited except the decision of the author as to where to publish it. He had run through the manuscript, and he wrote (30 July 1616) very flatteringly that "it containeth many rare things never discovered [i.e., revealed] before, and surely will be of much benefit to the Christian Church, if it may be published both in Italian and Latin" (p. 579).

17. See *DNB*, s.v. "Brent, Sir Nathaniel."

18. According to Richard Crakanthorp, who loved de Dominis with something less than Christian charity, the Archbishop, out of his vanity, had overstated his claims for credit in the publishing of Sarpi's *Historia*: "Sed & in hoc quoque, tu vanus, quòd *Historiam illam tuâ operâ in lucem prodisse* ais. Debemus nos, debet &

Christianus omnis orbis tantum beneficium *Regi nostro serenissimo Regi Jacobo.*" See *Defensio Ecclesiae Anglicanae,* Chap. XX, p. 161.

19. The Italian original is printed in Bianchi-Giovini, *Biografia di Frà Paolo Sarpi,* 2:308.

20. Griselini, *Memorie anedote,* pp. 287–89, believes that the Atterbury letters are forgeries; Bianchi-Giovini, *Biografia di Frà Paolo Sarpi,* 2:308–9, accepts the letter.

21. Cozzi, "Fra Paolo Sarpi," p. 573. In what follows concerning the Carletons I accept the argument advanced by Professor Cozzi.

22. George Carleton, *Consensus Ecclesiae Catholicae contra Tridentinos* (London, John Bill, 1613).

23. Printed by Cozzi in the Appendix of his article, pp. 596–98.

24. Cozzi, "Fra Paolo Sarpi," p. 571.

25. This seems to have been the original plan. See Fra Fulgenzio's letter to Carleton, at The Hague, dated 7 June 1619, in Cozzi's article, "Fra Paolo Sarpi," p. 561.

26. Griselini, *Memorie anedote,* p. 289.

27. Bianchi-Giovini, *Biografia di Frà Paolo Sarpi,* 2:308 (in the letter discarded as spurious).

28. Cozzi, "Fra Paolo Sarpi," p. 561*n.*

29. By decree of 22 Nov. 1619; see *Index Librorum Prohibitorum* (Rome, 1841), p. 362. A later edition of the *Index* (Rome, 1948), p. 445, gives the date as 18 Nov. 1619.

30. Gilbert Burnet, *Life of William Bedell,* p. 22: "Sir *Adam Newton* translated the first two Books of the History of the Council of *Trent,* but was not master of the two Languages; so that the Archbishop of *Spalata* said

it was not the same Work; but he highly approved of the two last, that were translated by Mr. *Bedell.*" Burnet and I may be giving de Dominis too much credit here, for others say that Newton translated all but the final two Books. See M. A. Scott, *Elizabethan Translations from the Italian,* p. 514.

31. It is possible that there existed also a translation into Dutch, *Polani Historie des Consiliums van Trenten* ('s Gravenhage, 1621), 4to; see *Catalogus Bibliothecae instructissimae, Reverendi, Clarissimi, & Doctissimi Viri, D. Ludovici Gerardi à Renesse* (Dordrecht, 1672), Pars Prima, no. 67. This may, however, be simply a bookseller's way of treating a Latin title. I have not seen a copy, nor have I seen any other reference to such a publication.

CHAPTER 5

1. *A Survey of the Apostasy of Marcus Antonius de Dominis, Sometyme Archbishop of Spalato* ([St. Omer?], 1617), p. 117.

2. Ibid., p. 141.

3. *State Papers, Domestic, James I,* vol. 123, no. 123; quoted here from Middleton, *A Game at Chesse,* p. 144.

4. Depicted on the title page of Thomas Scott's political polemic *The Second Part of Vox Populi,* 2d ed. (Goricum, 1624); reproduced, facing p. 107, in R. C. Bald's edition of Middleton's *A Game at Chesse.*

5. Fuller, *Church-History of Britain,* Bk. X, Sect. vi, p. 95.

6. Letter to Sir Thomas Roe, dated from Lambeth, 20 Nov. 1622, in *The Negotiations of Sir Thomas Roe,* p. 102.

7. Strozzi Transcripts, Folger MS W.b. 132, vol. 98, *Lettere della Segreteria di Stato di Papa Paolo V à Monsr Bentivoglio Nuntio in Francia dall'Anno 1617 al 1620*. Another letter from the secretary to the nuncio, dated 10 Mar. 1620, concerns the censure of the *Historia del Concilio Tridentino* by the Sorbonne and instructs the nuncio to insist that the censure be given in general, all-inclusive terms—as do other letters in the volume.

8. Newland, *Life of de Dominis*, pp. 147–48, makes Gondomar the principal agent in the snaring of the Archbishop. But he had willing helpers; and Newland is not overstating the case too badly when he writes: "The deadly blow aimed at the Church of Rome by the Archbishop of Spalatro, the publicity of his secession, the abilities and learning by which he justified and distinguished his conduct, roused all the energies of the Vatican to destroy him by their power or ensnare him by their subtlety." The words would apply even better to Sarpi.

9. Fuller, *Church-History of Britain*, Bk. X, Sect. vi, p. 96.

10. Ibid.

11. Cf. Richard Neile, comp., *M. Ant. de Dominis Arch-Bishop of Spalato, his Shiftings in Religion. A Man for Many Masters* (London, 1624), pp. 7–8. Richard Neile, Bishop of Durham, was one of the examiners. A Latin version, also prepared by Neile, bears the title, *Alter Ecebolius M. Ant. de Dominis, Arch. Spalatensis* (London, John Bill, 1624).

12. Fuller, *Church-History of Britain*, Bk. X, Sect. vi, p. 97.

13. Ibid., p. 98.

14. Fuller, ibid., relates this fact in such a loose manner as to leave the reader with the impression that the change resulted from de Dominis's recalling the "late instance" of the unfortunate Minorite friar, Fra Fulgentius Manfredi (*not* Micanzio), a Venetian lured to Rome under a safe-conduct and put to death. But Fulgenzio's unhappy betrayal occurred much earlier, in August 1608; see Sarpi's prophetic letter, *Lettere ai protestanti. Prima edizione critica*, ed. Manlio Duilio Busnelli, 2 vols. (Bari, 1931), 1:43–44.

15. Fuller, *Church-History of Britain*, Bk. X, Sect. vi, p. 93.

16. Ibid., p. 99.

17. See Sarpi, *Letters*, trans. Brown, p. xxx; see also above, app., p. 203.

18. Compare this with Fuller, *Church-History*, Bk. X, Sect. vi, p. 99.

19. Roe, *The Negotiations of Sir Thomas Roe*, p. 237.

20. Ibid., enclosure in a letter from Branthwaite to Roe, 20 July 1624.

21. Ibid., p. 246.

22. Hacket, *Scrinia Reserata*, Pt. I, par. 112 (pagination disordered).

23. *A Relation Sent from Rome, of the Processe, Sentence, and Execution, done upon the Body, Picture, and Bookes, of Marcus Antonius de Dominis, Archbishop of Spalato after his Death*, small quarto (London, 1624).

24. Protestants were generally reluctant to believe that de Dominis died a natural death. The speculations rife as to the cause of his death are pretty well suggested in Fuller, *Church-History*, Bk. X, Sect. vi, p. 99: "As for his death . . . some say he was *stifled*, others *strangled*, others *stabb'd*, others *starv'd*, others *poyson'd*, others *smothered to death* [Query: How does this differ from being *stifled*?]; but my in-

telligence from his own Kinred at *Venice* informs me, that he died a *natural death. . . . Yea,* they say, *the Pope sent four of his sworn Physicians, to recognize his corps, who on their oath deposed, that no impression of violence was visible thereon."* The reader may judge for himself whether Fuller's last statement is meant to be ironic.

25. Perhaps so; recall the interest of Wotton in the interception of Jesuit correspondence, above, p. 22; and compare the unrelenting vigilance of the Curia in its attempt to secure letters of Sarpi, as indicated in the Strozzi Transcripts, Folger MS W.b. 132, vols. 91, 95.

26. This account, lacking the "Inscriptio," is substantially the same as that printed (from manuscript?) by David Dalrymple (Lord Hailes) in his *Memorials and Letters Relating to the History of Britain in the Reign of James the First* (Glasgow, 1762).

27. Original in Strozzi Transcripts, Folger MS W.b. 132, vol. 124.

28. Concerning this "command performance" and its method, see Peter Heylyn, *Theologia Veterum: or the Summe of Christian Theologie* (London, 1654), Preface, sig. B1 recto and verso.

29. In *The Genuine Remains of That Learned Prelate Dr. Thomas Barlow, late Lord Bishop of Lincoln* (London, 1693) is a set of "Directions to a young Divine for his Study of Divinity, and choice of Bookes, &c." Vastly learned and an expert controversialist himself, Barlow was one of the most knowledgeable men of his time in questions at issue between Protestants and Romanists. The first

writer he lists under the heading "Writers of Controversies" is "1. Dr. *Craķanthorp contra Archiep. Spalatensem, Quarto. Lond.* 1625. No Book I have yet seen has so rational and short account of almost all Popish Controversies" (p. 59).

30. Scott, *The Second Part of Vox Populi*, sig. B2 recto.

31. Francis Osborne, *The Works of Francis Osborn Esq. . . . The Seventh Edition* (London, 1673), pp. 402–3.

32. Thomas Jackson, *The Raging Tempest Stilled* (London, 1623), pp. 60–62; Wilson, *The History of Great Britain*, p. 102; Johnston, *Historia rerum Britannicarum.*

33. For a serious view of Gondomar's role in the diplomacy involved, see Garrett Mattingly, *Renaissance Diplomacy* (London, 1955), pp. 255–68.

34. Middleton, *A Game at Chesse*, Prologue, ll. 78–79.

35. Ibid., Act I, sc. i, ll. 57–58.

36. Ibid., ll. 255 ff.

37. Cf. the anonymous, but again apparently "official," publication *M. Ant. de Dñis, Arch-Bishop of Spalato, his Shiftings in Religion. A Man for many Masters.* In "The Printer to the Reader" (sig. A2) we read that the work was "collected by the Reverend Father in God, the Lord Bishop of Duresme (whom, together with some others, his Majestie used in this Service." The "collector" was Richard Neile.

38. De Dominis's irenicism has recently received attention in a lecture by Delio Cantimori; see "Avventuriero irenico," in *Prospettive di storia ereticale italiana del Cinquecento* (Bari, 1960), pp. 97–110.

39. Hacket, *Scrinia Reserata*, Pt. I, par. 110.

CHAPTER 6

1. Sarpi, *The History of the Quarrels*, sigs. ¶2– ¶¶.

2. See above, chap. 2, p. 17.

3. Sarpi, *Histoire des différens entre le pape Paul V et la république de Venise ès années 1605, 1606, et 1607. Traduite d'Italien en françois* (Paris, 1625). This is said to be the translation of Jean de Cordes. For some inexplicable reason Miss Scott, *Elizabethan Translations from the Italian*, p. 281, identifies "the French copie" as Diodati's translation of the *Historia del Concilio Tridentino*.

4. Sarpi, *Interdicti Veneti Historia de motu Italiae sub initia Pontificatus Pauli V Commentarius. Authore R.P. Paulo Sarpio Veneto. Recèns ex Italico conversus* (Cambridge, 1626).

5. Ibid., sig. Gg3.

6. Christopher Potter, *A Sermon Preached at the Consecration of the right Reverend Father in God Barnaby Potter* . . . (London, 1629), pp. 85–86.

7. Sir Edward Dering's journals, British Museum additional MS 22,467.

8. For the order of these editions and for later editions and translations, see Sarpi's *Scritti giurisdizionalistici*, ed. Giovanni Gambarin (Bari, 1958), pp. 307–11. Gambarin's is the standard modern one. A new English translation has recently been published by Peter Burke in the *Sarpi* (New York, 1967) volume of *The Great Histories* series, ed. H. R. Trevor-Roper.

9. Getto, *Paolo Sarpi*, pp. 223, 254.

10. Amelot de la Houssaie's translation into French, *Traité des bénéfices* (Amsterdam, 1685), was issued four times more within the century. There was also a Latin translation (Jena, 1681). In the "Dedicatio" of the latter the translator (Charles Caffa, S.T.D.) says of Sarpi and of his book:

Nec prorsus exiguus est libellus, quem Serenitati Tuae offero, nisi mole. Scitu enim summè necessariam continet historiam Viris praesertim Magnis, Caetusque fidelium Capitibus, nec alibi tam dilucidè, tam apertè, tamque sine ullo partium affectu propositam eam deprehendi, quàm in hoc Authore, italicè conscriptam, aliàs celeberrimo, Reipublicae Venetae olim Theologo, judicii acumine, solidâ rerum fidei, Ecclesiae, ac Status eruditione, Veritatis sincero amore atque candore, maximè conspicuo, F. Paulo Sarpi. Hic Vir, suae Religionis abusus publicos, publico hocce Scripto, simulque eorum originem, modum, occasiones, quibus irrepsere, omnibus ab oculos proponere voluit, ut per eosdem gradus ad pristinam primitivae Ecclesiae perfectionem sensim ascendere valeant miseriae profunditatem sensim descenderant.

11. The confusion and uncertainty concerning this title arises from the following circumstances: (1) the title page reads *The Free Schoole* . . .; (2) the running head on sig. B1 reads *The True Schoole*; (3) the running heads of sigs. B1 verso–H1 verso read *true Schoole*; and (4) the running heads on sigs. Hij verso–Kiij verso read *Free-Schoole*.

12. Sarpi, *The Free Schoole of Warre*, sig. A4 verso.

13. Shuckburgh, *Two Biographies of William Bedell*, p. 287.

14. I.e., in the same font and format as Bedell's *Interdicti Veneti Historia*, discussed above, chap. 6, p. 77.

15. Shuckburgh, *Two Biographies of William Bedell*, pp. 291–92.

16. To which his answer was, "Ask them in Rome. They know there who the author is."

17. Micanzio, *The Life of the Most Learned Father Paul*, sig. M7.

18. Venice, Archivio di Stato, Consultori in iure, filza XI. This is the MS used for copy-text in Gambarin's modern critical edition; see Sarpi, *Scritti giurisdizionalistici*, pp. 119–212.

19. Sarpi, *Scritti giurisdizionalistici*, p. 314.

20. Title transcribed from a copy in the British Museum, pressmark 200.a.4.(1.).

21. For Meietti (or the Meietti family) and his or their connection with Sarpi and the Venetian quarrel with Pope Paul V, see Dennis Rhodes, "Roberto Meietti e alcuni documenti della controversia fra Papa Paolo V e Venezia," *Studi Seicenteschi*, 1(1960): 165–74.

22. Sig. A3 recto and verso.

23. Edward Brown, translator of Sarpi's *Letters* (1693), Preface, p. xxvi, mentions a Latin translation of *The History of the Inquisition* by "*one* Dr. Andrew Colvius, that was a *curious Collector of the secret Papers and Letters of Learned Men.*" The work to which he refers, and which I have not seen, was *Historia inquisitionis P. Pauli, cui adiuncta est confessio Fidei, quam ex Italica lingua latinam fecit Andreas Colvius* (Rotterdam, A. Leers, 1651).

24. Edward Arber, *A Transcript of the Registers of the Company of Stationers of London, 1554–1640* A.D., 5 vols. (London and Birmingham, 1875–1894), 4:199.

25. Sarpi, *A Discourse upon the Reasons of the Resolution taken in the Valteline against the tyranny of the Grisons and Heretiques* (London, 1628), p. 4.

26. Pressmark 700.f.6.4. The collection (of about a dozen tracts) largely concerns Catholic persecution of Protestants in the Piedmont and in France. It throws considerable light upon the temper of Milton's tremendous sonnet "Avenge, O Lord."

27. Henry R. Plomer, *A Dictionary of the Booksellers and Printers . . . from 1641 to 1667* (London, 1907), p. 115.

28. [Paolo Sarpi], in Minucci, *La Repubblica di Venezia*, which reprints the *Aggionta* and *Supplimento* and prints the *Trattato di pace et accommodamento*, p. 455.

29. Ibid., pp. 424*n*, 457*n*.

30. Cf. the modern critical edition of *Su le immunità delle chiese* in Gambarin's collection of Sarpi's *Scritti giurisdizionalistici*, pp. 259–301. Getto, *Paolo Sarpi*, pp. 241–42, speaks of the *consulto* as expounding "in a clear synthesis all the history relevant to the right of asylum."

31. Sarpi, *De Iure Asylorum, liber singularis Petri Sarpi I.C.* (Lugduni Batavorum, ex Officina Elzeveriana, 1622), a small quarto of eighty pages. The translator, Augerius Frikelburgius, says in his preface, "Operae me pretium facturum existimavi, si, utcunque possem, Latine facerem, quae magnus vir Italice conscripsit: tum ut elegantissimum opus, ab iis etiam, qui Italice nescirent, legi & intelligi possit" (sig. A2). A later edition, published under a Meietti imprint (Venice, 1677) adds to Sarpi's treatise a collection of the writings of other learned men on the laws of asylum.

32. Sarpi, *Lettere italiane di Fra Paolo Sarpi . . . scritte . . . al Signor*

Dell'Isola Groslot (Verona [Geneva], 1673).

33. Sarpi, *The Letters of the Renowned Father Paul Counsellor of State to the most Serene Republick of Venice; And Author of the Excellent History of the Council of Trent. Written to Monsieur Del Isle Groslot, a Noble Protestant of France: The Learned Monsieur Gillot, and others; in a Correspondence of divers Years. Translated out of Italian....* (London, 1693).

34. Ibid., Epistle Dedicatory, pp. vii–viii.

35. Ibid., pp. xix–xxi. In transcribing, I have reversed the italic and roman types.

36. Ibid., p. cxviii. For further remarks concerning the *Life*, see above, chap. 7, pp. 87–88. A small manuscript tab in a roughly contemporaneous hand, inserted in the Folger volume (acc. 131628) which I have used, lists a number of controversial books, largely anti-Catholic. Among them is an entry for "The History of ye Venetian Quarrel by Father Paul publish'd by Wm Bedel Bishop of Kilmore in Latin & Dr. Potter in English."

37. See above, chap. 12, pp. 185–86.

CHAPTER 7

1. Sarpi, *Letters of Father Paul*, pp. xlvi–xlvii. In transcribing, I have reversed the italic and roman types.

2. Paragraph based principally on Thomas Seccombe's article in *DNB*.

3. Sir Roger Twysden, *An Historical Vindication of the Church of England in Point of Schism, as it stands separated from the Roman and was reformed I. Elizabeth* (London, 1657), British Museum pressmark 487.1.3.

4. Ibid., pp. 77, 126 *(bis)*, 148, 177, 179. Twysden gives references to both the 1619 and 1629 editions of the Italian text.

5. Ibid., p. 148.

6. Sarpi, *A Full and Satisfactorie Answer to the late unadvised Bull thundred by Pope Paul the Fift, . . .* (London, 1606), British Museum pressmark 4051.b.38.

7. *A Catalogue of the Duplicates and a considerable Portion of the Library of Sir John Sebright, Bart. . . . ,* British Museum pressmark 269.i.7.(1).

8. *DNB*, s.v. "Twysden, Sir Roger."

9. Sarpi, *Historia del Concilio Tridentino* (London, 1619), British Museum pressmark C.55.k.6.

10. These brackets are in the original.

11. See, for example, pp. 177, 420, 423, 549, 554, 574, and 589 of Twysden's copy of the 1619 edition of Sarpi's *Historia del Concilio Tridentino*.

12. Folger Shakespeare Library, *STC* 21760, Copy 2, formerly the Sir Thomas Phillipps copy of the 1619 edition of Sarpi's *Historia del Concilio Tridentino*.

13. Ibid., see, for instance, pp. 212, 315, 524.

14. Ibid., pp. 420, 423, 431, 739.

15. Ibid., pp. 423, 739.

16. Ibid., see pp. 35, 146, 524, 772.

17. Ibid., pp. 314, 572.

18. Ibid., from Book VI, p. 473.

19. James Howell, Δενδρολογια. *Dodona's Grove, or, The Vocall Forrest* (London, 1640), pp. 115–17. Howell relates a series of jests and repartees attributed to Gondomar. The Spanish ambassador also figures in Howell's *Epistolae Ho-Elianae. Familiar Letters Domestic and Forren* (London, 1645) and his *Proedria Basilike: A Discourse*

Concerning the Precedency of Kings. . . . (London, 1664).

20. Howell, *Dodona's Grove*, pp. 122 ff.

21. Ibid., pp. 91–100.

22. Ibid., p. 3.

23. Howell, *Epistolae Ho-Elianae*, Sect. I, pp. 6–7 (Gondomar and Raleigh); Sects. II–III (numbered together), pp. 49, 53, 69, 71–72, 79–80, 91–92, 114; Sect. IV, p. 12.

24. Ibid., Sect. IV, p. 30.

25. James Howell, *S.P.Q.V. A Survay of the Signorie of Venice, of Her admired policy, and method of Government, &c.* . . . (London, 1651), p. 8.

26. Ibid., p. 10.

27. See ibid., p. 94.

28. Ibid., pp. 163–65.

29. Ibid., pp. 135–42.

30. Ibid., p. 142.

31. Ibid.

32. Ibid., p. 147.

33. Ibid., p. 137.

34. Sarpi, *The History of the Quarrels of Pope Paul V. with the State of Venice*, pp. 42–44.

35. Howell, *S.P.Q.V.*, sig. CC1 (pagination badly confused toward the end of the volume).

36. Ibid., sigs. Ee1 verso–Ee2 verso.

37. Ibid., sig. dd4 verso.

38. The first two words of the title have been transliterated from the Greek.

39. Howell, *Proedria Basilike*, sig. C2.

40. Ibid., p. 119.

41. Ibid., pp. 127–28.

42. Sarpi, *The Historie of the Councel of Trent*, pp. 707–8.

43. Howell, *Proedria Basilike*, p. 130.

44. Sarpi, *The Historie of the Councel of Trent*, pp. 727–28.

45. William Denton, *Horae Subsecivae: or, a Treatise Shewing the Original Grounds, Reasons, and Provocations necessitating our Sanguinary Laws against Papists* (London, 1664), pp. 6–8.

46. Ibid., pp. 15–18.

47. Ibid., pp. 17–18.

48. Sarpi, *The History of the Quarrels of Pope Paul V. with the State of Venice*, pp. 139–40.

49. William Denton, *The Burnt Child dreads the Fire: or an Examination of the Merits of the Papists, Relating to England, mostly from their own Pens* (London, 1675), sig. B2 verso. Denton is using the Colvius *Historia inquisitionis P. Pauli* (Rotterdam, 1651).

50. Denton, *The Burnt Child*, p. 96.

51. Sarpi, *A Treatise of Matters Beneficiary by Fra Paolo Sarpi, the Author of the History of the Council of Trent. Newly translated out of Italian, according to the best and most perfect Copy Printed at Mirandola, Anno Dom. 1676. Wherein is Related with the Ground of the History, how the Almes of the Faithful were Distributed in the Primitive Church. The Particulars whereof the Table sheweth* (London, 1680).

52. Ibid., Dedicatory Epistle, pp. [iii–iv].

53. William Denton, *Jus Caesaris et Ecclesiae vere dictae. Or a Treatise wherein Independency, Presbytery, the Power of Kings, and of the Church, or of the Brethren in Ecclesiastical Concerns, Government and Discipline of the Church . . . are discoursed* (London, 1681).

54. Ibid., pp. 114–15; compare Sarpi, *The History of the Inquisition . . .* (London, 1639), pp. 12, 16–17, and elsewhere.

55. Denton, *Jus Caesaris*, pp. 195–97. *"Sparsim"* in *The History of the Inquisition*, yes; but see especially pp. 69–71.

56. Denton, *Jus Caesaris*, p. 199. Notice that the opening of the first statement embodies virtually the entire title of Potter's translation, *The History of the Quarrels of Pope Paul V. with the State of Venice.*

57. Denton, *Jus Caesaris*, margin, p, 212.

CHAPTER 8

1. Above, chap. 7, pp. 87–88.

2. Hacket, *Scrinia Reserata*, 1:14, 49, 81, 129, 206; 2:89, 160, 207.

3. Ibid., 1:159, 225; 2:34–35, 89, 189.

4. Ibid., 1:85, 186; 2:13, 77, 114, 127, 144, 181, 184, "our English Horace," 217.

5. Ibid., 2:53.

6. This is perhaps a trifle odd: Archbishop Williams owned a copy of *The Historie of the Councel of Trent*, Brent's 2d ed., 1629, which he annotated most copiously. The volume is preserved in the Cambridge University Library (pressmark Adv. a. 48. 4.).

7. Hacket, *Scrinia Reserata*, 1:14.

8. See Micanzio, *Life of Father Paul*, sig. D5 recto and verso.

9. Hacket, *Scrinia Reserata*, 1:16; Micanzio, *Life of Father Paul*, sig. M8. Between pp. 32 and 81 the pagination of the *Life* is incredibly confused. Reference to this part are therefore given by signatures.

10. Hacket, *Scrinia Reserata*, 1:16–17.

11. Ibid., 1:28.

12. Micanzio says that he was twenty-six.

13. Williams was Dean of Salisbury (1619) and of Westminster (1620). He was an outrageous pluralist.

14. Hacket, *Scrinia Reserata*, 1:57; Micanzio, *Life of Father Paul*, pp. 23–25.

15. Hacket, *Scrinia Reserata*, par. 110. (Pagination in this part of the volume is badly disordered; references are to the numbered sections or paragraphs.)

16. Ibid., 2:33; Micanzio, *Life of Father Paul*, sig. E2 recto. Micanzio's passage about Sarpi is worth quoting: Himselfe was in all his life time of very few words, but pithy and sententious, acute without scoffing, ye[t] he tooke great pleasure to make men speake and with a dexterity, like *Socrates* delighted to make discovery of the abilities that were in others. And this he called, to make them deliver themselves, or to help them to bring forth. And the dexteritie arose, not onely from being verst, but consummate, and made up in all sorts of learning, because he was able to follow every one, in his own element. Physitians in medicine, and Mathematicians in the Mathematiques, and so in all other things. And upon what subject the discourse fell, he that knew him not very well, went away perswaded that that subject was his principall profession and masterpiece.

17. Hacket, *Scrinia Reserata*, 2:64; Micanzio, *Life of Father Paul*, sig. D5 recto.

18. Hacket, *Scrinia Reserata*, 2:89. The quotation, slightly altered, is from Bacon's essay "Of Revenge."

19. Micanzio, *Life of Father Paul*, pp. 123–24.

20. The phrasing, however, is not

supplied by the translator. See Micanzio, *La Vita del Padre Paolo*, p. 167: "spirito di vendetta, ch'è una sorte di selvaggia giustitia."

21. Hacket, *Scrinia Reserata*, 2:92; Micanzio, *Life of Father Paul*, p. 84.

22. Hacket, *Scrinia Reserata*, 2:103.

23. Ibid., 2:104.

24. Ibid., 2:131; Micanzio, *Life of Father Paul*, sig. D3 recto.

25. Hacket, *Scrinia Reserata*, 2:227; Micanzio, *Life of Father Paul*, sigs. O5 verso–O6 verso.

26. I use the "modern" edition, edited by Mackenzie E. C. Walcott (London, 1865), of Thomas Plume's *An Account of the Life and Death of the Right Reverend Father in God, John Hacket, late Lord Bishop of Lichfield and Coventry*.

27. Plume, *Life of Hacket*, p. 27. The editor's footnote reads: "John St. Amand, probably Secretary to the Lord Keeper; M.P. for Stamford, 1623 and 1625."

28. We shall presently have occasion (see above, chap. 11, pp. 159–64) to observe the use to which Peter Heylyn put Sarpi in *his* part of this controversy.

29. Ibid., p. 109.

30. S. G. Deed and Jane Francis, comps., *Catalogue of the Plume Library at Maldon, Essex* (Maldon, Plume Library Trustees, 1959). It is arranged alphabetically.

CHAPTER 9

1. See above, chap. 4, p. 50.

2. George Carleton, *Directions to Know the True Church* (London, 1615), pressmark 3935.a.6.

3. Ibid., p. 110.

4. Sarpi, *Historia del Concilio Tridentino* (ed. 1619), p. 388.

5. Sarpi, *Petri Suavis Polani Historiae Concilii Tridentini libri octo, ex Italicis summa fide & accuratione Latini facti* ([London, Bill], 1620), pressmark C2.15. Th Seld.

6. In full title, *The Defence of Constantine: with a Treatise of the Popes temporall Monarchie. Wherein, besides divers passages, touching other Counsels, both Generall and Provinciall, the second Roman Synod, under Silvester, is declared to be a meere Fiction and Forgery. By Richard Crakanthorp, Doctor of Divinity* (London, 1621). Even this lengthy title is inadequate, for it does not mention the three sermons constituting 136 pages of the volume.

7. Crakanthorp, "Treatise of the Popes Temporall Monarchy," in ibid., p. 188, margin: "*Ant. Quirinus* dissertat. de iure Reip. Venet. pa. 61."

8. Margin: "Ibid."

9. Margin: "Ibid., pa. 62."

10. The reference in the final clause is to one of Sarpi's works, the *Trattato dell'Interdetto* (Venice, Meietti, 1606), the names those of two of the subscribing seven "Theologhi."

11. "*Fr. Paulus.* Consid. sup. Censur. Pauli 5."

12. Richard Crakanthorp, "A Treatise of the Popes Temporall Monarchie," pp. 188–89, in his *The Defence of Constantine*.

13. Robert Abbot, *A Hand of Fellowship, to help keepe out Sinne and Antichrist . . .* (London, 1623), p. 50.

14. See Sarpi, *The Historie of the Councel of Trent* (1620), p. 140.

15. Richard Bernard, *Looke beyond Luther: Or An Answere to that Question, so often and so insultingly proposed by our Adversaries, asking us;*

Where this our Religion was before Luthers time? (London, 1623).

16. Ibid., sig. G2, margin: "Protestants are not convicted of obstinacie."

17. Anthony Wotton, *Runne from Rome* . . . (London, 1624), sigs. A3 verso–A4 verso.

18. Ibid. In transcribing, I have reversed the italics and roman of the original.

19. I have consulted the version in Andreas Dudith, *Andreae Dudithi . . . Orationes in Concil. Trident. habitae. Apologia ad D. Maximil. II. Imp.* . . . (Offenbach, 1610), pp. 39–41.

20. William Lloyd, *Papists no Catholicks: and Popery no Christianity*, 2d ed., London, 1679; 1st ed., 1677.

21. Ibid., sigs. A2 verso–A3 recto.

22. Thomas James, *A Manuduction, or Introduction unto Divinitie:* . . . (Oxford, 1625), quarto; pp. [viii]+136+[viii].

23. Ibid., see pp. 6, 11, 28, 72, 81, 84, 89, 102, 107, 109, 115.

24. Ibid., p. 61.

25. Ibid., p. 65; marginal reference: "Hist. Conc. Trid. p. 169."

26. Ibid., p. 103, margin: "It was the office of Bishops to preach. Hist. Conc. Trid. p. 188."

27. Ibid., p. 119, margin: "Pietro Soave."

28. Ibid.

29. Ibid., p. 123. Dudith's letter, quoted above, confirms Sarpi's observations on the voting at the council, and both of them (as does James here) make use of the Holy Ghost–cloak bag figure, which became a standard Protestant taunt.

30. Alexander Cooke, *The Abatement of Popish Braggs, Pretending Scripture to be Theirs. Retorted by*

the Hand of Alexander Cooke (London, 1626).

31. Ibid., pp. 41–42.

32. Thomas Jackson, *A Treatise of the Holy Catholike Faith and Church* (London, 1627), p. 122, margin: "See this point excellently handled by father *Paul*, whose Apologie [i.e., *History of the Quarrels of Pope Paul V*] for the state of Venice, (as I now perceive) is translated into the English tongue."

33. Ibid.

34. Perhaps Jackson is here half remembering what Sarpi (*Quarrels of Pope Paul V*, p. 155) relates as a *papal* decree: "He forbade likewise them of *Romagna*, and the *Marquisate* of *Ancona* to have any cōmerce with the *Venetians*, which quickly after he was fain to recall, having learned by experience that the greatest damage herein would redound to themselves."

35. Jackson, *A Treatise of the Holy Catholike Faith and Church*, pp. 123–24.

36. In *A Censure of Simonie* (London, 1624), Henry Burton refers, once (p. 102), to a sermon as "Related by *Democritus* junior in his bookes of the causes of Melancholy p. 177."

37. Ibid., p. 27.

38. Ibid., pp. 107–8. The passage which I have placed in italics is quoted almost verbatim from Brent's *Historie*, p. 493.

39. Jackson, *A Censure of Simonie*, p. 48. See also pp. 110–12, where the expression "Let mee, not with *Gehazies* staff, but with *Elizeus* his spirit, prove if any life be fetcht againe out of it" is especially suggestive of *The Historie of the Councel of Trent* (ed. 1620), p. 493.

40. Henry Burton, *Truth's Triumph over Trent; or, the Great Gulfe be-*

tweene Sion and Babylon . . . (London, 1629); see sig. A1, pp. 9, 44, 83 ("Latina editio"), 219, 232–36 passim —this last being a sort of running summary.

41. Andreas Vega, Franciscan; Domingo de Soto, Dominican.

42. Burton, *Truth's Triumph over Trent*, sig. A1 recto, margin: "Hist. Concil. Trid. lib. 2."

43. Ibid., sig. A1 recto and verso.

44. Fuller, *The Church-History of Britain*.

45. In his two-part *Examen Historicum* (1659), Peter Heylyn devotes the first part exclusively to an ill-tempered answering of Fuller's "mistakes" —337 of them! The defense of de Dominis occurs on pp. 191–92.

46. It was in the Bodleian by agreement with the Stationers' Company; for Sion College, see John Spencer, *Catalogus Universalis Librorum Omnium in Bibliotheca Collegii Sionii apud Londinenses* . . . (London, 1650), p. 144.

47. Thomas Fuller, *The Historie of the Holy Warre*, 3d ed. (Cambridge, 1647), p. 112, margin. It should be noted that whereas the marginal reference gives the title in English as *History of Trent* and the page references fit Brent's translation (eds. 1620–1640), in the "Catalogue of Authours cited in this book" (sig. Dd5) the title is entered in an abbreviated Latin (or Italian) form: "Hist. conc. Trident."

CHAPTER 10

1. My texts are those of *The Complete Angler & the Lives of Donne, Wotton, Hooker, Herbert & Sanderson*, ed. Alfred W. Pollard, Library of English Classics (London, 1925).

2. Ibid., pp. 251, 254.

3. Ibid., p. 265.

4. Ibid., p. 266. The rest of the passage, concerning the manner in which *The History of the Council of Trent* was sent to England, has already been quoted above, chap. 4, p. 45.

5. Ibid., p. 471.

6. Henry Foulis, *The History of Romish Treasons & Usurpations* . . . *Carefully Collected out of a great number of their own approved Authors, by Henry Foulis, B.D. Late Fellow of Lincoln-Colledge in Oxford* (London, 1671). I might add that some of the authors from whom this "History" was collected were distinctly *not* "approved"—by the Romanists.

7. Ibid., Preface, sig. e1 verso.

8. Ibid., p. 36, margin: "Hist. of the Quarrels of Pope *Paul* the Fifth, with the *Venetians*, lib. I. pag. 96." The quotation is from the English translation (1626).

9. Ibid.

10. See above, chap. 10, pp. 131–32.

11. Foulis, *History of Romish Treasons*, p. 69, margin: quotes (in Italian) a brief passage as being from "*Anton. Bovio*, Risposta alle considerationi del M. *Paolo*, p. 69."

12. Ibid.

13. Ibid., pp. 150, 449–50, 635–38.

14. Ibid., p. 152, margin: "*Paolo*, pag. 507, 508, 530, 551, 623, 635, 604, 659, 661, 683, 566, 569."

15. Ibid., margin: "Id. p. 279."

16. Ibid., margin: "Id. p. 818."

17. Ibid.

18. Ibid., p. 404; margin reading: "Hist. Concil. of *Trent*. lib. I. pag. 86." The italicized portion is quoted verbatim from Brent's translation.

19. Ibid., p. 425, margin: "Hist. Council of *Trent*, pag. 279, 318."

20. Ibid., margin: "Id. *pag.* 167, 168, 507, 508, 530, 551, 566, 569, 635, 644, 659, 661, 683."

21. Ibid., margin: "Id. *pag.* 589."

22. Ibid., margin: "Id. *pag.* 660."

23. Ibid., margin: "Id. *pag.* 497, 703."

24. Ibid., margin: "Id. *pag.* 374."

25. Ibid., margin: "Id. *pag.* 374, 375."

26. Ibid., margin: "Id. *pag.* 366, 367."

27. Ibid., margin: "Id. *pag.* 254, 255, 256, 257."

28. Ibid., margin: "Id. *pag.* 267, 268, 269, 277, 278, 279, 281, 282, 283, 284, 285, 286, 300, 301, 302, &c."

29. Ibid. p. 426, margin: "Id. pag. 661, 719."

30. Ibid., margin: "Pag. 818."

31. Ibid., margin: "Id. *pag.* 165, 189, 259, 260."

32. Ibid., pp. 425–26.

33. A pretty picture! Only a Voltaire could do it justice.

34. In short, had Sarpi been living in England when Foulis wrote, he would doubtless have been one of the chief ornaments of the Royal Society.

35. Foulis, *History of Romish Treasons*, p. 637, margin: "vid. Ind. lib. Prohibit. *edit. Alexand.* VII pag. 98, 222, 226, 227, 272."

36. Ibid., p. 638, margin: "Spond. an. 1623. § 13. *Rob. Johnston* Rerum *Brit.* Hist. lib. 20. an. 1623. p. 638."

37. Ibid., pp. 635–38.

38. Edward Stillingfleet, *A Discourse Concerning the Idolatry Practised in the Church of Rome*, 3d ed. (London, 1672).

39. Ibid., p. 183, margin: "The History of the Council of *Trent*, l. 2. *p.* 237."

40. Ibid., pp. 182–83. The entire passage within the quotation marks is to be found in the Brent-Sarpi (1620) reference of the preceding note.

41. Ibid., p. 394.

42. Ibid., p. 395, margin: "History of the Council of *Trent*, l. 2. p. 138."

43. The brackets are in the original.

44. Stillingfleet, *Discourse Concerning the Idolatry Practised*, p. 395, margin: "P. 149." (of *HCT*, cited above). The italicized portion is quoted verbatim.

45. Ibid.

46. Edward Stillingfleet, *The Council of Trent Examin'd and Disprov'd by Catholic Tradition* (London, 1688), Preface, p. i.

47. Ibid., pp. 4–5.

48. Ibid., p. 30, margin: "*Hist. of the Council of* Tr. l. 2. *p.* 154."

49. Ibid.

50. Ibid., margin: "*Ibid. l. 6. c.* 11. *p.* 4."

51. Ibid., pp. 9, 31, 42, 61.

52. See above, chap. 9, p. 121.

53. William Lloyd, *The Difference between the Church and Court of Rome, considered in some Reflections on a Dialogue entitled A Conference between Two Protestants and a Papist. By the Author of the Late Seasonable Discourse* (London, 1674), a quarto pamphlet of 38 pages.

54. Ibid., p. 7.

55. Nathanael Vincent, ed., *The Morning-Exercise against Popery. Or, the Principal Errors of the Church of Rome Detected and Confuted, in a Morning-Lecture Preached lately in Southwark: By Several Ministers of the Gospel in or near London . . .* (London, 1675).

56. Joseph Glanvill, *The Zealous and Impartial Protestant* (London, 1681).

57. Vincent, *The Morning-Exercise,* sig. A3.

58. Ibid., p. 27.

59. Ibid., p. 47. In the margin: "Ecclesiasticks rightful Subjects to either Monarchs, Commonwealths, as was excellently and effectually asserted by the *Venetians* against *Paul* the 5th."

60. Ibid., p. 51.

61. Ibid., p. 59, margin: "History of the Quarrels between P.P. 5th and *Venetians,* Anno 1605"—Sarpi's account.

62. Ibid., pp. 59–60.

63. Ibid., p. 63, margin: *"Illud hercle pontificibus in more positum, de alieno corio ludere, & quod justis dominis auferre nequeunt, id ipsis Elargiri. Histor. Conc. Trident. l. 5."*

64. Ibid.

65. Ibid., p. 68–69.

66. Ibid., pp. 688 *(bis),* 689.

67. Ibid., p. 688, margin: *"Hist. of the Council, p. 813."*

68. Ibid.

69. Ibid., p. 689, margin: *"Histor. of the Counc. of Trent. p. 5."*

70. Ibid.

71. Ibid., pp. 776, 779–80, 797 *(bis).*

72. Ibid., pp. 854, 875.

73. Recorded also, twice, and with some asperity in Leonel Sharpe's *A Looking-glasse for the Pope* (London, 1616), first at sig. e4, and again at p. 299: "Baronius goeth farther, in the excommunication of the Venetians, to *Paul* the 5. There is a double ministery of *Peter,* feede and to kill, for the Lord said to him feede my sheepe, and hee heard a voice from heaven kill and eate."

74. John Bramhall, *The Works of the Most Reverend Father in God, John Bramhall D.D. . . .* (Dublin, 1676), Tome I, pp. 41–42.

75. Ibid., p. 64.

76. Ibid., Tome I, p. 73, margin: "Consid. *p. 49."*

77. Ibid., margin: "Oratio ad Paul. 5. *pro Rep. Venetâ."*

78. Ibid.

79. Ibid., Tome I, p. 117, margin: *"An. 1543. Pad. Paolo Apolog. pag. 405."*

80. Ibid.

81. Ibid., Tome I, pp. 119–21. The marginal citations of the Sarpi which had been read occur on p. 119: *"Pad. Paolo Historia Partic. l. 4. p. 141; Idem l. I. p. 24"*; and p. 120: *"Pad. Paol. Hist. part. l. 4. p. 145."*

82. Ibid., Tome I, p. 123, margin: "Hist. Con. Trid."

83. Ibid.

84. See ibid., pp. 249, 414, 991.

85. See ibid., pp. 123 *(bis),* 177, 228, 250, 281, 619 *(bis).*

86. Hippolite du Chastel de Luzancy, *Reflexions on the Council of Trent. By H. C. de Luzancy, Deacon of the Church of England, and M. of Arts of Christ Church in Oxford* (Oxford, 1677).

87. Ibid., Dedication, sig. a2.

88. Ibid., sig. B3 recto and verso.

89. Ibid., sig. B4.

90. Ibid., p. 27.

91. Ibid., p. 38.

92. Ibid., pp. 42–43.

93. Isaac Barrow, *A Treatise of the Pope's Supremacy* (London, 1680), p. 3. In the margin: *"di avertire, Che non si venga mai per qual causa si sia alla disputa dell'Autorita di Papa.* Concil. Trid. *lib.* 2 *p.* 159." The reference is to the original Italian edition (1619), where p. 159 (sig. O2) is misnumbered 145.

94. See ibid., marginal references to *HCT,* pp. 61, 24, 22.

95. William Sherlock, *A Brief Discourse Concerning the Notes of the Church* . . . (London, 1687), p. 232, margin: "Hist. Counc. Trent, l. 1."

96. Ibid.

97. Ibid., pp. 348–49, margin: "*Hist. of the Counc. of* Trent. l. 2. p. 149."

98. Ibid.

99. Slingsby Bethel, *The Interest of the Princes and States of Europe. The Second Edition with Additions* . . . (London, 1681). The first edition had appeared in 1680.

100. Ibid., "Advertisement to the Reader," sig. A7.

101. Ibid., sig. A7 recto and verso.

102. Ibid., pp. 36–37.

103. Abp. Thomas Tenison, ed., *Popery not Founded on Scripture: Or, The Texts which Papists cite out of the Bible, for the Proof of the Points of Their Religion, Examin'd, and shew'd to be alledged without Ground* (London, 1688–1689). 4to., 879 pp.

104. Ibid., p. 381, margin: "Vid. *Histor. Council, of* Trent. *p.* 546."

105. Ibid., pp. 380–81. The italicized portion reproduces the language of Brent's translation.

106. Ibid., p. 772, margin: "*History of the Council of* Trent, l. 5. [p. 460]." Again, the italicized portion represents Brent's wording.

107. Thomas Tenison, *A Discourse Concerning a Guide in Matters of Faith; with respect, especially, to the Romish pretence of the necessity of such a one as is infallible* (London, 1683).

108. Ibid., p. 20, margin: "H. Conc. Trid. l. 2."

109. *A Discourse*, p. 20.

110. David Abercromby, *Academia Scientiarum* (London, 1687), sig. N6 verso.

111. David Abercromby, *A Moral Discourse of the Power of Interest* (London, 1690), pp. 82–83.

112. Thomas Barlow, *Genuine Remains.*

113. An earlier form of this exists in manuscript in St. John's College, Cambridge (and in variant forms elsewhere). The St. John's manuscript has been recently published as '*A Library for Younger Schollers' Compiled by an English Scholar-Priest about 1655,* edited by, and with Bibliographical Index by, Alma Dejordy and Harris Francis Fletcher, vol. 48 of Illinois Studies in Language and Literature (Urbana, Ill., 1961).

114. Barlow, *Genuine Remains,* p. 28.

115. Ibid., p. 59.

116. See ibid., pp. 266, 271, 303, 385, 633—this last referring to the Latin edition of Leyden, 1622.

117. Ibid., p. 302, margin: "*Vide Interdicti Veneti Historiam, per Paulum Sarpium* pas. 4. & 58." The reference is to Bedell's translation.

118. Ibid.

119. Ibid., p. 308.

120. Michael Geddes, ed., *The Council of Trent No Free Assembly: More fully discovered by a Collection of Letters and Papers of the Learned Dr. Vargas and other Great Ministers, who assisted at the said Synod in Considerable Posts. Published from the Original Manuscripts in Spanish, which were procured by the Right Honourable Sir William Trumbull's Grandfather, Envoy at Brussells in the Reign of King James the First. With an Introductory Discourse concerning Councils, shewing how they were brought under Bondage to the Pope. By Michael Geddes LLD. and Chancellor of the*

Cathedral Church of Sarum (London, 1697).

121. Ibid., pp. 73–77.

122. Ibid., p. 77.

123. Ibid., p. 80.

124. Ibid. The account of these letters given here, and even the detail about their badly timed suppression as Sarpi's *History of the Council of Trent* was being first published, will be found repeated by Geddes's good friend Bishop Gilbert Burnet, in his *History of the Reformation of the Church of England*, 3 vols. (London, 1681–1753), 3:176.

CHAPTER 11

1. I quote from the "Columbia" Milton (*The Works of John Milton*, ed. F. A. Patterson, 18 vols. [New York: Columbia University Press, 1931–1938]), 4(1931):302.

2. Sarpi, *The Historie of the Councel of Trent* (ed. 1620), pp. 472–76.

3. Sarpi, *The History of the Inquisition*, pp. 68–84. Sarpi's other writings on the subject (cf. Gambarin, ed., *Scritti giurisdizionalistici*, pp. 213–31) would not have been available to Milton.

4. Milton's use of Sarpi in connection with the inquisitional surveillance of books is paralleled by Abraham-Nicholas Amelot de la Houssaie's *The History of the Government of Venice* . . . (London, 1677) and Luke de Beaulieu's *The Holy Inquisition* . . . (London, 1681), both discussed above, chap. 11, pp. 164–69, chap. 12, pp. 189–90.

5. Milton, *Of Reformation*, in *Works*, 3:46. The "judgement" to which Milton refers is in a letter to Leschassier, dated from Venice 3 Feb. 1609.

6. Ibid., p. 59.

7. James H. Hanford, "Milton's Private Library," in *A Milton Handbook*, 4th ed. (New York, 1946), app. D.

8. John Milton, *Commonplace Book*, in *Complete Prose Works of John Milton*, ed. Don M. Wolfe, vol. 1, ed. Ruth Mohl (New Haven, Conn.: Yale University Press, 1953), 1:344–513.

9. Ibid., p. 396.

10. British Museum MS Burney 368.

11. British Museum MS Sloane 874.

12. Johnston, *Historia rerum Britannicarum*. See above, p. 213n18.

13. Ibid., p. 638.

14. William London, *A Catalogue of the most vendible Books in England, Orderly and Alphabetically Digested. . . . London, 1657 [and 1658]* together with *A Catalogue of New Books, by way of Supplement to the former . . . London, 1660*—both reprinted in *English Bibliographical Sources*, Series II, No. 2 (London, 1965). My references are to these reprints.

15. Ibid., sig. T4 verso.

16. Ibid., sig. X2 verso.

17. Ibid., sig. Y1 verso.

18. Ibid., sig. X3 verso.

19. Ibid., sig. Y2 verso.

20. This paragraph is based largely on the *DNB* article on Heylyn (by Mandell Creighton).

21. Heylyn, *Microcosmus*. Strictly, Sarpi does not figure in this first edition, but makes his appearance in the second edition (1625).

22. Ibid. (ed. 1621), p. 163.

23. In one of the Folger Shakespeare Library's copies (Copy 1) of the third edition (Oxford, 1627) a seventeenth-century owner has taken the pains to transcribe into the margin the *Italian* text of the part which I have set off by asterisks.

24. Heylyn, *Microcosmus* (ed. 1625), p. 293. The passage is quoted from the Brent translation of the *The Historie of the Councel of Trent* (1620), p. 2.

25. Peter Heylyn, *Theologia Veterum: or the Summe of Christian Theologie* . . . (London, 1654).

26. See ibid., pp. 50, 98, 328, 476. Other passages from Ovid's *Metamorphoses* Heylyn may have translated himself.

27. Ibid., Preface, sig. B1 recto and verso.

28. Ibid., p. 12.

29. Ibid., p. 102.

30. Ibid., p. 384, margin: "Histor. Concil. Trid. l. I." The Latin "Article" is repeated in Heylyn's *Ecclesia Vindicata* (London, 1657), sig. a4 verso.

31. Heylyn, *Theologia Veterum*, p. 397, margin: "Hist. Concil. Trid. l." (*sic*).

32. Ibid., p. 398, margin: "Hist. Concil. Trid. l. I."

33. Ibid.

34. Heylyn, *Ecclesia Vindicata*, "A General Preface to the Reader," sig. a4 verso.

35. Ibid., p. 51.

36. Ibid.

37. Heylyn, *Historia Quinqu-Articularis* (London, 1660), preface "To the Reader," sig. Sss3 verso.

38. The order of discussion of these five points in Sarpi's *Historie* (Brent tr., 1620) is: original sin (pp. 161–71), justification (pp. 178–86), grace (pp. 186–94), free-will (pp. 194–97), and predestination (pp. 197–200).

39. Not to be misread. The word simply means "sober," thoughtful."

40. Heylyn, *Historia Quinqu-Articularis*, pp. 510–11.

41. Ibid., p. 514.

42. Sarpi, *The Historie of the Councel of Trent*, pp. 194–95.

43. See *Historia Quinqu-Articularis*, preface "To the Reader," sig. Sss3, where he defines "Compiler": "By which name the old Criticks and Grammarians used to call those men, who pilfering their materials out of other mens writings, did use to lay them close together as their own, to avoid discovery . . . So that a *Compilator* and a *Plagiary* are but two terms of one signification."

44. This paragraph is based on Gordon Goodwin's article on Luke de Beaulieu in *DNB*.

45. Beaulieu, *The Holy Inquisition*, pp. 116–17.

46. Ibid., p. 142.

47. Ibid., p. 164.

48. Ibid., pp. 175–76.

49. Ibid., pp. 205–6.

50. Ibid., p. 207.

51. Ibid., p. 228.

52. Ibid., pp. 213–14.

53. Ibid., p. 215.

54. Ibid., pp. 215–18; Sarpi, *The History of the Inquisition*, pp. 69–71.

55. Beaulieu, *The Holy Inquisition*, p. 219.

56. Ibid.

57. Ibid., p. 220.

58. Ibid., pp. 221–22.

59. Degory Wheare, *The Method and Order of Reading Both Civil and Ecclesiastical Histories. In which the most Excellent Historians are Reduced into the Order in which they are Successively to be read; and the Judgments of Learned Men, concerning each of them, Subjoin'd. By Degoraeus Wheare, Camden Reader of History in Oxford. To which is Added, an Appendix concerning the Historians of Particular Nations, as well Ancient as*

Modern. By Nicholas Horseman. Made English, and Enlarged, by Edmund Bohun, Esq; Author of the Address to the Freemen and Freeholders (London, 1685).

60. See Courtney's *DNB* article on Wheare, upon which this paragraph is based.

61. Wheare, *Method and Order*, p. 294, margin: "Sir Nathaniel Brent, *Kt. Master of* Merton *Coll.*"

62. Ibid., p. 295, margin: *"Sir* Adam Newton *Knight."*

63. Ibid., pp. 293–95.

64. William Temple, *The Works of Sir William Temple, Bart.*, 4 vols. (London, 1770), 3:488–89.

65. Gilbert Burnet, *The Infallibility of the Church of Rome Examined and confuted. In a Letter to a Roman Priest* (London, 1680), pp. 15–16.

66. Ibid., p. 22; cf. *HCT* (1620), p. 216. The two "Divines" were D. Soto and A. Vega.

67. Gilbert Burnet, *The History of the Reformation of the Church of England. In Two Parts. . . . The Second Edition, Corrected. 2. Volumes* (London, 1681). These first two early volumes cover the reigns of Henry VIII, Edward, and Mary. A Third Part (and volume), written thirty-three years later, was published in London (in the edition I use) in 1753.

68. Ibid., Vol. I, Preface, sig. (b). I have reversed the roman and italic type of the original.

69. Ibid., 1:135.

70. Ibid., 2:212–13.

71. See above, chap. 10, pp. 150–51.

72. Burnet, *History of the Reformation*, Vol. III, Preface, p. vii.

73. Burnet, *Life of William Bedell*, p. 5.

74. Ibid., p. 7.

75. Blount, *Censura*, pp. 608–9. The entire passage, partly quoted from Burnet and partly improvised, reads thus:

P. *Paulo* was a Man equally eminent for vast Learning and a most consummated prudence; and was at once one of the greatest Divines, and one of the wisest Men of his Age. But to commend the celebrated Historian of the Council of *Trent*, is a thing so needless that I may well stop; yet it must needs raise the Character of *Bedell* much, that an *Italian*, who, besides the Caution that is natural to the Countrey, and the Prudence that obligeth one in his Circumstances to a more than ordinary distrust of all the World, was tyed up by the strictness of that Government to a very great Reservedness with all People, yet took *Bedell* into his very Soul; and, as Sir *Henry Wotton* assured the late King, He communicated to Him the inwardest thoughts of his Heart; and professed, That he had learnt more from him in all the Parts of Divinity, whether Speculative or Practical, than from any he had ever conversed with in his whole Life.—P. *Paul* gave *Bedell* the unvaluable Manuscripts of the History of the Council of *Trent*, together with the History of the Interdict and of the Inquisition; the *first* of these will ever be reckoned the chief pattern, after which all, that intend to succeed well in writing History, must copy. Dr. *Burnet* in the Life of Bishop *Bedell*, p. 7, & 17.

Blount also quotes (*Censura*, p. 609) part of Sir Henry Wotton's letter (printed by Burnet in his *Life of William Bedell*) giving a "character" of

Sarpi, and, among other encomiums, quotes (p. 610) Daniel Georg Morhof's *Polyhistor*, where Sarpi is styled "sui generis Phoenix."

76. As may be seen from the preceding note, the portion of text between the supplied asterisks is repeated verbatim in Blount's *Censura*, p. 609.

77. Burnet, *Life of William Bedell*, pp. 15–18.

78. See above, app., pp. 201–3.

79. Burnet, *Some Letters Containing an Account of what seem'd most remarkable travelling thro' Switzerland, Italy, Some Parts of Germany, &c. in the Years 1685. and 1686* (London, 1724), p. 142. The *Letters* were first published at Rotterdam in 1686.

80. See above, chap. 11, p. 169, and p. 232n60.

81. Edmund Bohun, *A Continuation of the History of the Reformation to the End of the Council of Trent,* . . . (London, 1689), p. 86.

82. Ibid.

83. Sarpi, *The History of the Council of Trent* (ed. 1676), p. 443.

84. Bohun, *A Continuation*, p. 87. Sarpi's citing of this saying is on p. 465 of *The History of the Council of Trent* (ed. 1676).

85. Bohun, *A Continuation*, p. 89. Sarpi's notice of the election occurs on p. 589 of the *History of the Council of Trent* (ed. 1676).

86. Bohun, *A Continuation*, p. 90.

87. Sarpi, *The History of the Council of Trent* (ed. 1676), pp. 609–11.

88. Bohun, *A Continuation*, p. 96, marginal reading: "The censure of the Council."

89. Ibid.

90. Sarpi, *The History of the Council of Trent* (ed. 1676), pp. 1–2.

CHAPTER 12

1. James I, *Triplici Nodo, Triplex Cuneus,* in C. H. McIlwain, ed., *The Political Works of James I* (Cambridge, Mass., 1918), p. 101. James's note identifying the *Apologie* reads: "Apol. Pat. Paul. adversus opposit. Card. Bellar."

2. Osborne, *The Works of Francis Osborn Esq.*, sig. Dd5.

3. Thomas Pope Blount, *Sir Thomas Pope Blount's Essays on Several Subjects . . . The Third Impression; with very Large Additions. Besides a New Essay of Religion. And an Alphabetical Index to the Whole* (London, 1697), p. 82. Perhaps Blount had before him the passage quoted above, pp. 146–47, from Slingsby Bethel's *The Interest of the Princes and States of Europe.*

4. See Blount, *Sir Thomas Pope Blount's Essays*, pp. 37, 41–42, concerning auricular confession and clerical celibacy, respectively.

5. As, for instance, in the Cambridge University Library (Acton. e. 32. 11) and in my own collection.

6. Pseudo-Sarpi, *Opinione*, pp. 109–10. Original text in italics.

7. Zera Fink, *The Classical Republicans* (Evanston, Ill., 1945), pp. 141–42.

8. *The Papacy of Paul the Fourth* . . . (London, 1673), sig. A4 verso.

9. Sarpi, *The Historie of the Councel of Trent* (1620), pp. 389–416.

10. *The Papacy of Paul the Fourth*, sig. B1.

11. Sarpi, *The Historie of the Councel of Trent* (1620), p. 395.

12. *The Papacy of Paul the Fourth*, sig. B4.

13. Nathaniel Johnston, *The Assurance of Abby and Other Church-Lands in England to the Possessors, Cleared*

from the Doubts and Arguments Raised about the Danger of Resumption. In Answer to a Letter of a Person of Quality. By Nathaniel Johnston, Dr. of Physic, Fellow of the Royal College of Physicians in London. Published by His Majesty's Command (London, pr. by Henry Hills, 1687).

14. Ibid., p. 53, margin: "*Pietro Soavo Polano* Hist. of the Council of Trent, fol. 666." The pages cited here and elsewhere in the work indicate that Johnston was using the fourth edition (1676) of Brent's translation.

15. Ibid., p. 55, margin: "*Idem.* p. 667."

16. Ibid., p. 56, margin: "*Idem.* 739."

17. Ibid., pp. 53–57.

18. Johnston's second draft, compounded out of Sarpi and Burnet, occurs on pp. 170–73 of *The Assurance of Abby Lands*.

19. John Willes, "Abby and other Church-Lands, not yet assured to such Possessors as are Roman Catholicks; Dedicated to the Nobility and Gentry of that Religion" [1688?], p. 3, col. 2; p. 5, col. 1; p. 6, col. 1; pp. 6, col. 1–7, col. 1.

20. Johnston, *The Assurance of Abby Lands*, pp. 172–73.

21. The imprint reads Ratisbonne, Jean Aubri, 1677.

22. Sarpi, *Histoire du Concile de Trente*, trans. by Amelot de la Houssaie (Paris, 1683). Commenting on the difficulty of faithfully translating Sarpi, Amelot engages in a bit of sly suggestion: "*Diodati*, qui étoit Italien, & qui a traduit son Histoire du Concile en François, n'a peutêtre pas mieux entendu sa Langue, qu'il a parlé la nôtre. Et je m'assure, que ceux, qui confronteront nos deux traductions, croiront quasi, que nous avons traduit

deux diférens Auteurs," *Histoire du Concile de Trente*, 3d ed. (Amsterdam, 1699), Preface, sig. *****3 recto.

23. *Petrus Suavis Polanus, seu Paulus Sarpius Venetus, in auro contrà non charo Historiae Concili Tridentini Opere, adversus operosam, & Veram falsò inscriptam, Concilii Tridentini Historiam, P. Sfortiae Pallavicini . . .* (Curiae [V]ariscorum, Typis Minzelianis, 1686). The translator, probably the J. C. Layriz who signs the dedication, has rendered the entire preface into Latin, including the here irrelevant final paragraph—about the author's index!

24. *Histoire des Uscoques. De la traduction du Sieur Amelot de la Houssaie* (Paris, Chez la Veuve Loüis Billaine, 1682).

25. Sigs. ã5 verso–ã6 recto.

26. London, printed by H. C. for John Starkey, 1677.

27. Houssaie, *History of the Government of Venice*, p. 227.

28. See pp. 68–84 of Gentilis's translation of *The History of the Inquisition* (London, 1639).

29. Richard Simon, *The History of the Original and Progress of Ecclesiastical Revenues . . .* (London, 1685), sig. A3.

30. Ibid., p. 51.

31. Ibid., p. 89, margin: "*P. Paolo tratt. delle mat. benef.*"

32. Ibid., pp. 88–89.

33. Ibid., pp. 121–22.

34. Pierre Jurieu, *The History of the Council of Trent* (London, 1684), p. xci.

35. I.e., Camillo Olivo.

36. Jurieu, *The History of the Council of Trent*, "Historical Reflections on Councils," pp. xciii–xciv.

37. Ibid., p. cxvii.

38. Ibid., pp. cxvii–cxx.

Bibliography

The following selective list of works which are quoted or referred to in the text does not include certain well-known general collections or works of reference such as the *Dictionary of National Biography*, the *Calendar of State Papers*, the *Enciclopedia italiana* (Treccani), etc. These, when cited, are sufficiently identified in the notes. A number of titles, especially long ones, are given in abbreviated form; and with a few anonymous works the Pollard-Redgrave *STC* or the Wing *STC* number is given for ready identification. No effort has been made to preserve or to recognize the peculiarities of capitalization or type fonts on the title pages of early printed books. A few items, usually either anonymous or else used in particular exemplars, are identified by library pressmarks or call numbers; and except in the case of John Bill, King's Printer, the names of the printer-publishers of early books have generally been omitted. Unless otherwise indicated, the place of publication for British books may be assumed to be London; for American books, New York.

1. SARPI AND SARPIANA

Amelot. *See* Houssaie.

Bellarmino, Roberto. *Risposta ad un libretto intitolato Trattato et resolutione sopra la validità delle scommuniche.* Rome, 1606.

———. *Risposta del Card. Bellarmino al Trattato de i sette Theologi di Venetia, sopra l'interdetto della Santità di Nostro Signore Papa Paolo Quinto. Et all'oppositioni di F. Paolo Servita, contra la prima scrittura dell'istesso Cardinale.* Rome, 1606.

Bovio, Giovanni Antonio. *Risposta del P.M. Gio. Antonio Bovio da Novara Carmelitano alle considerationi del P.M. Paolo da Venetia sopra le censure della Santità di Papa Paolo Quinto contra la Republica di Venetia.* Rome, 1606.

Gerson, Jean. *Trattato et resolutione sopra la validità delle scommuniche di Gio.*

235

Gersone Theologo e Cancelliero Parisino. Translated by Paolo Sarpi. Venice, 1606.

Herrico (or Errico), Scipio. *Scipionis Henrici in Messanensi Academia Doctoris Theologi, censura theologica et historica adversùs Petri Soave Polani De Concilio Tridentino pseudo-Historiam* . . . . Dillingen, 1654.

Houssaie, Abraham-Nicholas Amelot de la. *Petrus Suavis Polanus, seu Paulus Sarpius Venetus, in auro contrà non charo Historiae Concili Tridentini Opere, adversus operosam, & Veram falsò inscriptam, Concilii Tridentini Historiam, P. Sfortiae Pallavicini* . . . . Translated by [J. C. Layriz?]. Curiae Variscorum, 1686.

Jurieu, Pierre. *Abregé de l'Histoire du Concile de Trente.* 2 vols. Amsterdam, 1683. (1st ed.: Geneva, 1682.)

——. *The History of the Council of Trent. In Eight Books. Whereunto is prefixt a Discourse containing Historical Reflexions on Councils, and particularly on the Conduct of the Council of Trent, proving that the Protestants are not oblig'd to submit thereto. Written in French by Peter Jurieu, Doctour and Professor of Divinity. And now done into English.* 1684.

Minucci, Minuccio. *Historia degli Uscochi scritta da Minuccio Minuci Archevescovo di Zara. Co i Progressi di quella Gente sino all'Anno M.DC.II. e continuata dal P.M. Paolo dell'Ordine de'Servi, e Teologo della Serenissima Republica di Venetia. Sino all'Anno M.DC.XVI.* Venice, 1676. (Sarpi's *Aggiunta,* pp. 169–319; his *Supplimento,* pp. 321–472.)

——. *Histoire des Uscoques. De la traduction du Sieur Amelot de la Houssaie.* Paris, 1682. (Sarpi's "Continuation," pp. 139–256, and "Supplement," pp. 257–385.)

——. *La Repubblica di Venezia, la casa d'Austria, e gli Uscocchi.* Edited by Gaetano and Luisa Cozzi. Bari, 1965. (Contents: Sarpi's *Aggionta* and *Supplimento* to Minucci, and his *Trattato di pace et accommodamento.*)

The Papacy of Paul the Fourth. Or, the Restitution of Abby Lands and Impropriations, an indispensable condition of Reconciliation to the Infallible See. 1673. (Wing *STC* S700; extracted from Brent's tr. of the *HCT.*)

Pseudo-Sarpi. *Opinione falsamente ascrita al padre Paolo Servita, come debba governarsi internamente et esternamente la Republica Venetiana, per havere il perpetuo dominio.* Venice, 1685.

——. *The Opinion of Padre Paolo, of the Order of the Servites . . . given to the Lords the Inquisitors of State. In what manner the Republick of Venice ought to govern themselves . . . to have perpetual dominion. Delivered . . . in the Year 1615.* [Translated by William Aglionby.] 1689.

Quorlius, Philippus. *Historia Concilii Tridentini Petri Suavis Polani ex Auctorismet assertionibus confutata. A Philippo Quorlio Sacr. Theol. Legumque Doctore. Nunc secundo edita per V.I.D. Josephum Crimibella, cum duobus posterioribus libris, qui desiderabuntur.* Palermo, 1661. (The first two "books" were printed at Venice in 1655.)

Raccolta delgi scritti usciti in istampa, e scritti a mano, nella causa del P. Paolo V. co'signori venetiani. Coire, 1607.

———. *Controversiae memorabilis inter Paulum V. Pontificem Max. & Venetos . . . Acta et scripta varia.* Villa Sanvincentiana [Coire?], 1607. (Latin version of preceding, with some differing inclusions.)

Risposta all'Historia della Sacra Inquisitione, composta già dal R.P. Paolo Servita. O sia Discorso dell'origine, forma, ed uso dell'Ufficio dell'Inquisitione nella Città, e Dominio di Venetia del P. Paolo dell'Ordine de Servi Teologo della Serenissima Republica. N.p., n.d.

Sarpi, Paolo. *Apologia per le oppositioni fatte dall'Illustrissimo, et Reverendiss.^mo Signor Cardinale Bellarminio alli Trattati, et resolutioni di Gio. Gersone sopra la validità delle Scommuniche. Del Padre Maestro Paulo da Vinetia dell'Ordine de'Servi.* Venice, 1606.

———. *An Apology, or, Apologiticall answere, made by Father Paule a Venetian, of the order of Servi, unto the Exceptions and objections of Cardinall Bellarmine, against certaine Treatises and Resolutions of John Gerson, concerning the force and validitie of Excommunication. First published in Italian, and now translated into English. Seene and allowed by publicke authoritie.* 1607.

———. *Concerning the Excommunication of the Venetians. A Discourse against Caesar Baronius Cardinall of the Church of Rome. In which the true nature and use of Excommunication is briefly and cleerly demonstrated, both by Testimonies of Holy Scripture, and from the old Records of Christs Church. Written in Latine by Nicolas Vignier, and translated into English after the Copie printed at Samur 1606. Whereunto is added the Bull of Pope Paulus the Fift, against the Duke, Senate and Commonwealth of Venice: With the protestation of the sayd Duke and Senate. As also an Apologie of Frier Paul of the Order of Servi in Venice.* 1607. (*STC* 24719.)

———. *Considerationi sopra le censure della Santità di Papa Paulo V. contra la Serenissima Republica di Venetia del P.M. Paulo da Venetia dell'Ordine de'Servi.* Venice, 1606.

———. *A Full and Satisfactorie Answer to the late unadvised Bull, thundred by Pope Paul the Fift, against the renowned State of Venice: Being modestly entitled by the learned Author, Considerations upon the Censure of Pope Paul the Fift, against the Common-wealth of Venice: By Father Paul of Venice, a Frier of the Order of Servi. Translated out of Italian.* London, John Bill, 1606.

———. *L'Examen de P. Paul Docteur en Theologie a Venise, Religeux de l'ordre de'Servi. Contenant la response aux Censures de nostre S. Pere le Pape Paul V. contre la Serenissime Republique de Venise. Traduit d'Italien en François.* N.p., 1606.

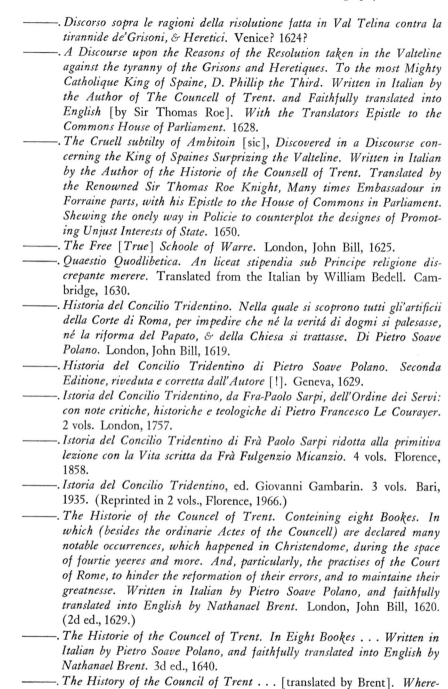

———. *Discorso sopra le ragioni della risolutione fatta in Val Telina contra la tirannide de'Grisoni, & Heretici.* Venice? 1624?

———. *A Discourse upon the Reasons of the Resolution taken in the Valteline against the tyranny of the Grisons and Heretiques. To the most Mighty Catholique King of Spaine, D. Phillip the Third. Written in Italian by the Author of The Councell of Trent. and Faithfully translated into English* [by Sir Thomas Roe]. *With the Translators Epistle to the Commons House of Parliament.* 1628.

———. *The Cruell subtilty of Ambitoin* [sic], *Discovered in a Discourse concerning the King of Spaines Surprizing the Valteline. Written in Italian by the Author of the Historie of the Counsell of Trent. Translated by the Renowned Sir Thomas Roe Knight, Many times Embassadour in Forraine parts, with his Epistle to the House of Commons in Parliament. Shewing the onely way in Policie to counterplot the designes of Promoting Unjust Interests of State.* 1650.

———. *The Free [True] Schoole of Warre.* London, John Bill, 1625.

———. *Quaestio Quodlibetica. An liceat stipendia sub Principe religione discrepante merere.* Translated from the Italian by William Bedell. Cambridge, 1630.

———. *Historia del Concilio Tridentino. Nella quale si scoprono tutti gli'artificii della Corte di Roma, per impedire che né la verità di dogmi si palesasse, né la riforma del Papato, & della Chiesa si trattasse. Di Pietro Soave Polano.* London, John Bill, 1619.

———. *Historia del Concilio Tridentino di Pietro Soave Polano. Seconda Editione, riveduta e corretta dall'Autore* [!]. Geneva, 1629.

———. *Istoria del Concilio Tridentino, da Fra-Paolo Sarpi, dell'Ordine dei Servi: con note critiche, historiche e teologiche di Pietro Francesco Le Courayer.* 2 vols. London, 1757.

———. *Istoria del Concilio Tridentino di Frà Paolo Sarpi ridotta alla primitiva lezione con la Vita scritta da Frà Fulgenzio Micanzio.* 4 vols. Florence, 1858.

———. *Istoria del Concilio Tridentino,* ed. Giovanni Gambarin. 3 vols. Bari, 1935. (Reprinted in 2 vols., Florence, 1966.)

———. *The Historie of the Councel of Trent. Conteining eight Bookes. In which (besides the ordinarie Actes of the Councell) are declared many notable occurrences, which happened in Christendome, during the space of fourtie yeeres and more. And, particularly, the practises of the Court of Rome, to hinder the reformation of their errors, and to maintaine their greatnesse. Written in Italian by Pietro Soave Polano, and faithfully translated into English by Nathanael Brent.* London, John Bill, 1620. (2d ed., 1629.)

———. *The Historie of the Councel of Trent. In Eight Bookes . . . Written in Italian by Pietro Soave Polano, and faithfully translated into English by Nathanael Brent.* 3d ed., 1640.

———. *The History of the Council of Trent . . .* [translated by Brent]. *Where-*

unto is Added The Life of the Learned Author: and the History of the Inquisition. 1676.

———. *Histoire du Concile de Trente.* Translated by Amelot de la Houssaie. 3d ed. Amsterdam, 1699. (1st ed.: Paris, 1683.)

———. *Petri Suavis Polani Historiae Concilii Tridentini libri octo, ex Italicis summa fide & accuratione Latini facti.* [London, Bill], 1620.

———. *Historia della Sacra Inquisitione. Composta gia dal R. P. Paolo Servita: ed hora la prima volta posta in luce. Opera pia, dotta, e curiosa: a' Consiglieri, Casuisti, e Politici molto necessaria.* Serravalle [Venice?], 1638.

———. *Discorso dell'origine, forma, leggi, ed uso dell'Ufficio dell'Inquisitione nella citta, e dominio di Venetia. del P. Paolo dell'Ordine de'Servi, Teologo della Serenissima Republica.* N.p., 1639.

———. *The History of the Inquisition: Composed by the Reverend Father Paul Servita, who was also the Compiler of the Councell of Trent. A Pious, Learned, and Curious Worke, necessary for Councellors, Casuists, and Politicians. Translated out of the Italian Copy by Robert Gentilis.* 1639. The edition of 1655 omits the name of the translator.

———. *Historia particolare delle cose passate tra'l Sommo Pontefice Paolo V. e la Serenissima Repubblica di Venetia gl'anni MDCV. MDCVI. MDCVII.* Lyons [Geneva?], 1624.

———. *Histoire des différens entre le pape Paul V et la république de Venise ès années 1605, 1606, et 1607. Traduite d'Italien en françois* [by Jean de Cordes]. Paris, 1625.

———. *The History of the Quarrels of Pope Paul V. with the State of Venice. In seven Books. Faithfully translated out of the Italian, and compared with the French Copie* [by Christopher Potter]. London, John Bill, 1626.

———. *De Iure Asylorum, liber singularis Petri Sarpi I.C.* Leyden, 1622.

———. *Trattato dell'Interdetto della Santità di Papa Paulo V. Nel quale si dimostra, che egli non è legitimamente publicato, et che per molte ragioni non sono obligati gli Ecclesiastici all'essecutione di esso, né possono senza peccato osservarlo.* Venice, 1606.

———. *Interdicti Veneti Historia de motu Italiae sub initia Pontificatus Pauli V Commentarius. Authore R.P. Paulo Sarpio Veneto. Recèns ex Italico conversus* [by William Bedell]. Cambridge, 1626.

———. *Istoria dell'Interdetto e altri scritti.* Edited by M. D. Busnelli and Giovanni Gambarin. 3 vols. Bari, 1940.

———. *Paolo Sarpi, Lettere ai Gallicani.* Edited by Boris Ulianich. Wiesbaden, 1961.

———. *Lettere ai protestanti. Prima edizione critica.* Edited by Manlio Duilio Busnelli. 2 vols. Bari, 1931.

———. *Lettere di Fra Paolo Sarpi raccolte e annotate da F.-L. Polidori, con prefazione di Filippo Perfetti.* 2 vols. Florence, 1863.

———. *Lettere inedite di Fra Paolo Sarpi a Simone Contarini.* Edited by C. Castellani. Venice, 1892.

————. *Lettere italiane di Fra Paolo Sarpi . . . scritte . . . al Signor Dell'Isola Groslot*. Edited by J. A. Portner. Verona [Geneva], 1673.

————. *The Letters of the Renowned Father Paul Counsellor of State to the most Serene Republick of Venice; And Author of the Excellent History of the Council of Trent. Written to Monsieur Del Isle Groslot, a Noble Protestant of France: The Learned Monsieur Gillot, and others; in a Correspondence of divers Years. Translated out of Italian* [by Edward Brown]. 1693.

————. *Scritti giurisdizionalistici*. Edited by Giovanni Gambarin. Bari, 1958.

————. *Trattato delle materie beneficiarie di Frà Paolo Sarpi. . . .* Mirandola, 1676.

————. *A Treatise of Matters Beneficiary by Fra Paolo Sarpi, the Author of the History of the Council of Trent. Newly translated out of Italian . . .* [by William Denton]. 1680.

————. *Traité des bénéfices*. Translated by Amelot de la Houssaie. Amsterdam, 1685.

————. *History of Benefices and Selections from History of the Council of Trent*. Translated and edited by Peter Burke. New York, 1967.

————. *Opere varie del Molto Reverendo Padre F. Paolo Sarpi dell'Ordine de' Servi di Maria Teologo Consultore della Serenissima Repubblica di Venezia*. 2 vols. Helmstat [Verona], 1750.

A True Copie of the Sentence of the high Councell of tenne Judges in the State of Venice, against Ridolfo Poma, Michael Viti Priest, Alessandro Parrasio, John of Florence the sonne of Paul and Pasquall of Bitonto: who of late most trayterously attempted a bloudy and horrible Murder upon the person of the reverend Father Dr Paolo Servite, Theologue of the common wealth of Venice. Faithfully translated out of Italian. 1608. (*STC* 24635.)

Vignier, Nicolas. *See* Sarpi, *Concerning the Excommunication,* . . . .

2. MANUSCRIPTS

Biblioteca Marciana (Venice). Sarpi, *Historia del Concilio Tridentino*, scribal copy with corrections in Sarpi's own hand: MS Marciana, Cod. it., V, 25.

British Museum. MS Additional 22,467: Sir Edward Dering's Journals, 1670–1673.

————. MS Burney 368: Meric Casaubon's miscellaneous papers.

————. MS Sloane 874: "Historical Collections of the Earl of Derby." Folios 16–88^v are headed, "Collections out of the History of the Councell of Trent 1645."

————. Sarpi, *Historia del Concilio Tridentino* (1619), the printed copy (B.M. C.55.h.6), with copious MS notes by Sir Roger Twysden.

Cambridge University Library. Sarpi, *The Historie of the Councel of Trent*, the printed Brent translation (2d ed., 1629), with copious MS notes by Archbishop John Williams. Pressmark: Adv. a. 48. 4.

Bibliography

Folger Shakespeare Library. MS V.b.297: Sir Edward Dering, Bart. 1598–1644, catalogue of books.

———. Sarpi, *Historia del Concilio Tridentino* (1619), the printed copy (Folger, *STC* 21760, Copy 2; formerly the Sir Thomas Phillipps copy), with copious MS notes by Sir Roger Twysden.

———. MS W.b.132: the Strozzi Transcripts, especially vols. 90, 91, 95, 98, 124, 128, 129, 140.

3. ORIGINAL PRINTED SOURCES

Abbot, Robert. *A Hand of Fellowship, to helpe keepe out Sinne and Antichrist. In certaine Sermons preached upon severall occasions.* 1623.

Abercromby, David. *Academia Scientiarum.* 1687.

———. *A Moral Discourse of the Power of Interest.* 1690.

Aquilini, Cesare. *De tribus historicis Concilii Tridentini.* Antwerp, 1662.

Atterbury, Lewis, ed. *Some Letters relating to the History of the Council of Trent.* 1705.

Barlow, Thomas. *The Genuine Remains of That Learned Prelate Dr. Thomas Barlow, late Lord Bishop of Lincoln . . . Publish'd from his Lordship's Original Papers.* 1693.

Baronio, Cesare. *Paraenesis ad Rempublicam Venetam.* Rome, 1606.

Barrow, Isaac. *A Treatise of the Pope's Supremacy.* 1680.

Beaulieu, Luke de. *The Holy Inquisition, wherein is represented what is the Religion of the Church of Rome: and how they are dealt with that Dissent from It.* 1681.

Bernard, Richard. *Looke beyond Luther: Or An Answere to that Question, so often and so insultingly proposed by our Adversaries, asking us; Where this our Religion was before Luthers time?* 1623.

Bethel, Slingsby. *The Interest of the Princes and States of Europe. The Second Edition with Additions . . . .* 1681. (1st ed., 1680.)

Blount, Thomas Pope. *Censura celebriorum authorum.* 1690.

———. *Sir Thomas Pope Blount's Essays on Several Subjects . . . The Third Impression; with very Large Additions. Besides a New Essay of Religion. And an Alphabetical Index to the Whole.* 1697.

Bohun, Edmund. *A Continuation of the History of the Reformation to the End of the Council of Trent, in the Year 1563. Collected and written by E. B. Esq.* 1689. See also Sleidan, John, *The General History of the Reformation of the Church.*

Bramhall, John. *The Works of the Most Reverend Father in God, John Bramhall D.D. Late Lord Archbishop of Ardmagh, Primate and Metropolitane of all Ireland. Collected into One Volume. In Four Tomes . . . .* Dublin, 1676.

Burnet, Gilbert. *The History of the Reformation of the Church of England.* 3 vols. 1681, 1753.

241

———. *The Infallibility of the Church of Rome Examined and confuted. In a Letter to a Roman Priest.* 1680.

———. *The Life of William Bedell, D.D. Bishop of Kilmore in Ireland.* 1685.

———. *Some Letters Containing an Account of what seem'd most remarkable travelling thro' Switzerland, Italy, Some Parts of Germany, &c. in the Years 1685. and 1686.* 1724. (1st ed.: Rotterdam, 1686.)

Burton, Henry. *A Censure of Simonie.* 1624.

———. *Truth's Triumph over Trent: or, the Great Gulfe betweene Sion and Babylon . . . .* 1629.

Carleton, George. *Consensus Ecclesiae Catholicae contra Tridentinos.* London, John Bill, 1613.

———. *Directions to Know the True Church.* London, John Bill, 1615.

Catalogus Bibliothecae instructissimae, Reverendi, Clarissimi, & Doctissimi Viri, D. Ludovici Gerardi à Renesse. Dordrecht, 1672. (B.M., 821.h.1.)

Chamberlain, John. *The Letters of John Chamberlain.* Edited by Norman Egbert McClure. 2 vols. Philadelphia, 1939.

Cooke, Alexander. *The Abatement of Popish Braggs, Pretending Scripture to be Theirs. Retorted by the Hand of Alexander Cooke.* 1626.

Coryat, Thomas. *Coryat's Crudities Hastily gobled up in five Moneths travells in France, Savoy, Italy.* 2 vols. Glasgow, 1905. (1st ed., 1611.)

Crakanthorp, Richard. *The Defence of Constantine: with a Treatise of the Popes temporall Monarchie. Wherein, besides divers passages, touching other Counsels, both Generall and Provinciall, the second Roman Synod, under Silvester, is declared to be a meere Fiction and Forgery. By Richard Crakanthorp, Doctor of Divinity.* 1621.

———. *Defensio Ecclesiae Anglicanae, contra M. Antonii De Dominis, D. Archiepiscopi Spalatensis Iniurias.* 1625.

Dalrymple, David (Lord Hailes). *Memorials and Letters Relating to the History of Britain in the Reign of James the First.* Glasgow, 1762.

A Declaration of the Variance betweene the Pope, and the Segniory of Venice . . . Whereunto is annexed a Defence of the Venetians. 1606. (*STC* 19482.)

de Dominis, Marco Antonio. *Concio habita Italice a Reverendo Patre Marco Antonio de Dominis, Archiepiscopo Spalatensi primo die dominico Adventus Anno 1617. Londini in Mercatorum Capella, coram Italis ibi commorantibus, & aliis honorificiis in illa Synaxi & Comvent . . . .* Leeuwarden, 1618.

———. *A Sermon Preached in Italian, by the most Reverend Father, Marc'Antony De Dominis, Archb. of Spalato, the first Sunday in Advent, Anno. 1617. . . . First published in Italian by the Author, and thereout Translated into English.* London, John Bill, 1617.

———. *A Manifestation of the Motives, whereupon the most Reverend Father, Marcus Antonius De Dominis, Archbishop of Spalato, (in the Territorie of Venice) undertooke his departure thence.* London, John Bill, 1616.

Another version (Edinburgh: Andrew Hart, 1617) is dated at the end Venice, 15 Sept. 1616.

———. *Papatus Romanus*. London, John Bill, 1617.

———. *De radiis visus et lucis in vitris perspectivis et iride*. Venice, 1610.

———. *De Republica Ecclesiastica*. 2 pts. London, John Bill, 1617–1620.

———. *The Rockes of Christian Shipwracke, Discovered by the holy Church of Christ to her beloved Children, that they may keepe aloofe from them. Written in Italian by the Most Reverend Father, Marc'Ant. de Dominis, Archb. of Spalato, and thereout translated into English*. London, John Bill, 1618.

———. *Sui Reditus ex Anglia Consilium*. Rome, 1623.

Denton, William. *The Burnt Child dreads the Fire: or an Examination of the Merits of the Papists, Relating to England, mostly from their own Pens*. 1675.

———. *Horae Subsecivae: or, a Treatise Shewing the Original Grounds, Reasons, and Provocations necessitating our Sanguinary Laws against Papists*. 1664.

———. *Jus Caesaris et Ecclesiae vere dictae. Or a Treatise wherein Independency, Presbytery, the Power of Kings, and of the Church, or of the Brethren in Ecclesiastical Concerns, Government and Discipline of the Church . . . are discoursed*. 1681.

———. *Jus Regiminis: being a Justification of Defensive Arms*. 1689.

Dudith, Andreas. *Andreae Dudithi . . . Orationes in Concil. Trident. habitae. Apologia ad D. Maximil. II. Imp. . . .* Offenbach, 1610.

Foulis, Henry. *The History of Romish Treasons & Usurpations . . . Carefully Collected out of a great number of their own approved Authors, by Henry Foulis, B.D. Late Fellow of Lincoln-Colledge in Oxford*. 1671.

Fuller, Thomas. *The Church-History of Britain; from the Birth of Jesus Christ untill the Year 1648*. 1655.

———. *The Historie of the Holy Warre*. 3d ed. Cambridge, 1647. (1st ed., 1639.)

Geddes, Michael, ed. *The Council of Trent No Free Assembly: More fully discovered by a Collection of Letters and Papers of the Learned Dr. Vargas and other Great Ministers, who assisted at the said Synod in Considerable Posts . . . .* 1697.

Glanvill, Joseph. *The Zealous and Impartial Protestant*. 1681.

Griselini, Francesco. *Memorie anedote spettanti alla vita ed agli studi del sommo Filosofo e Giureconsulto F. Paolo Servita*. 2d ed. Lausanne, 1760.

H., T. *Newes from Rome, Spalato's Doome. Or an Epitome of the life and behaviour of M. Antonius de Dominis, first Bishop of Segnia, afterwards Archbishop of Spalato; who about seven or eight yeeres since came from Venice into England; and from thence by the practise and perswasion of the L. Gundamar, departed to Rome: And of late was imprisoned in the Castle of Saint Angelo. Herein is contained the Reasons for which he*

243

was imprisoned, together with his miserable disastrous end. 1624. (Folger *STC* 7006.5, the Harmsworth copy.)

Hacket, John. *Scrinia Reserata: A Memorial Offer'd to the Great Deservings of John Williams, D.D.* 1693.

Harding, John. *A Recantation Sermon preached in the Gate-House at Westminster the 30. day of July 1620.* 1620.

Heylyn, Peter. *Ecclesia Vindicata: or, the Church of England Justified . . . .* 1657.

———. *Examen Historicum.* 1659.

———. *Historia Quinqu-Articularis,* 1660: See his *Historical and Miscellaneous Tracts.*

———. ΚΕΙΜΗΛΙΑ ΈΚΚΛΗΣΙΑΣΤΙΚΑ. *The Historical and Miscellaneous Tracts of the Reverend and Learned Peter Heylyn, D.D. Now Collected into one Volume . . . And an Account of the Life of the Author: Never before Published.* 1681.

———. *Microcosmus, or A Little Description of the Great World. A Treatise Historicall, Geographicall, Politicall, Theologicall.* By P. H. Oxford, 1621.

———. *Theologia Veterum: or the Summe of Christian Theologie . . . .* 1654.

Houssaie, Abraham-Nicholas Amelot de la. *Histoire du gouvernement de Venise.* Amsterdam, 1676.

———. *The History of the Government of Venice . . . Written in the year 1675, by the Sieur Amelott de la Houssaie, Secretary to the French Ambassador at Venice.* 1677.

Howell, James. Δενδρολογια. *Dodona's Grove, or, The Vocall Forrest.* 1640.

———. *Epistolae Ho-Elianae. Familiar Letters Domestic and Forren.* 1645.

———. *Proedria Basilike: A Discourse Concerning the Precedency of Kings . . . Whereunto is also adjoynd a distinct Treatise of Ambassadors, &c.* 1664.

———. *St. Pauls Late Progress upon Earth, about a Divorce 'twixt Christ and the Church of Rome, by reason of her dissolutenes and excesses . . . Rendred out of Italian into English.* 1644.

———. *S.P.Q.V. A Survay of the Signorie of Venice, of Her admired policy, and method of Government, &c. With a Cohortation to all Christian Princes to resent her dangerous Condition at Present.* 1651.

Jackson, Thomas. *The Raging Tempest Stilled.* 1623.

———. *A Treatise of the Holy Catholike Faith and Church.* 1627.

James I, King of England. *The Political Works of James I.* Edited by C. H. McIlwain. Cambridge, Mass., 1918. (Contains his *Triplici Nodo, Triplex Cuneus,* 1607.)

James, Thomas. *Catalogus librorum Bibliothecae publicae quam T. Bodleius in academia Oxoniensi nuper instituit.* Oxford, 1605.

———. *Catalogus librorum . . .* 2d ed. Oxford, 1620.

———. *A Manuduction, or Introduction unto Divinitie: containing a Confutation of Papists by Papists, throughout the important Articles of our Religion; their testimonies taken either out of the Indices Expurgatorii, or out of the Fathers, and ancient Records; but especially the Manuscripts.* Oxford, 1625.

Johnston, Nathaniel. *The Assurance of Abby and Other Church-Lands in England to the Possessors, Cleared from the Doubts and Arguments Raised about the Danger of Resumption. In Answer to a Letter of a Person of Quality. By Nathaniel Johnston, Dr. of Physic, Fellow of the Royal College of Physicians in London. Published by His Majesty's Command.* 1687.

——. *The Excellency of Monarchical Government.* 1686.

Johnston, Robert. *Historia rerum Britannicarum: ut et multarum Gallicarum, Belgicarum, & Germanicarum, tàm Politicarum, quàm Ecclesiasticarum, ab Anno 1572, ad Annum 1628.* Amsterdam, 1655.

Kidder, Richard. "The Sacrifice of the Mass," in *Popery not Founded on Scripture*, ed. Thomas Tenison.

Leti, Gregorio. *La Bilancia politica di tutte le opere di Traiano Boccalini.* Castellana, 1678.

Lloyd, David. *The Statesmen and Favourites of England since the Reformation.* 1665.

Lloyd, William. *The Difference between the Church and Court of Rome, considered in some Reflections on a Dialogue entituled A Conference between Two Protestants and a Papist. By the Author of the Late Seasonable Discourse.* 1674.

——. *Papists no Catholicks: and Popery no Christianity.* 2d ed., 1679.

London, William. *A Catalogue of the most vendible Books in England, Orderly and Alphabetically Digested . . . London, 1657 [and 1658]* together with *A Catalogue of New Books, by way of Supplement to the former . . . London, 1660*, reprinted in *English Bibliographical Sources*, Series II, No. 2. 1965.

Luzancy, Hippolite du Chastel de. *Reflexions on the Council of Trent. By H. C. de Luzancy, Deacon of the Church of England, and M. of Arts of Christ Church in Oxford.* Oxford, 1677.

Micanzio, Fulgenzio. *Confirmatione delle Considerationi del P.M. Paulo di Venetia . . . contra Gio. Ant. Bovio.* Venice, 1606.

——. *La Vita del padre Paolo.* Leyden, 1646.

——. *The Life of the Most Learned Father Paul, of the Order of the Servie. Councellour of State to the most Serene Republicke of Venice, and Authour of the History of the Counsell of Trent. Translated out of Italian by a person of Quality.* 1651.

Middleton, Thomas. *A Game at Chess.* Edited by R. C. Bald. Cambridge, England, 1929.

Milton, John. *Commonplace Book.* Edited by Ruth Mohl, in Yale *Complete Prose Works of John Milton*, general editor Don M. Wolfe, 1(1953): 344–513.

——. *Second Defence of the People of England*, in *Milton: Prose Selections*. Edited by Merritt Y. Hughes. 1947.

————. *The Works of John Milton.* Edited by F. A. Patterson. 18 vols. New York: Columbia University Press, 1931–1938.

Morhof, Daniel Georg. *Danielis Georgii Morhofii Polyhistor, Literarius, Philosophicus et Practicus . . . editio quarta.* 2 vols. Lubeck, 1747.

[Neile, Richard, comp.]. *Alter Ecebolius M. Ant. de Dominis, Arch. Spalatensis.* London, John Bill, 1624. (Latin version of next entry.)

————. *M. Ant. de Dñis, Arch-Bishop of Spalato, his Shiftings in Religion. A Man for many Masters.* London, John Bill, 1624.

Osborne, Francis. *The Works of Francis Osborn Esq: Divine. Moral. Historical. Political. In Four several Tracts. Viz. 1. Advice to a Son, in two Parts. 2. Political Reflections on the Government of the Turks, &c. 3. Memoires of Q. Elizabeth and K. James. 4. A Miscellany of Essays, Paradoxes, Problematical Discourses, Letters, Characters, &c. The Seventh Edition.* 1673.

Pallavicino, Ferrante. *Il divortio celeste, cagionato dalle dissolutezze della Sposa Romana, et consecrato alla simplicità de'scropolosi Christiani.* Villafranca, 1666.

Pallavicino, Sforza. *Istoria del Concilio di Trento scritta dal Padre Sforza Pallavicino della Compagnia de Gesù, ora Cardinale della Santa Romana Chiesa. Ove insieme rifiutasi con autorevoli testimonianze un'Istoria falsa divolgata nello stesso argomento sotto nome di Pietro Soave Polano. Nuovamente ritoccata dall'Autore.* 3 vols. Rome and Milan, 1717. (1st ed., 2 vols.: Rome, 1656–1657.)

Payne, William. "Celibacy of Priests, and Vows of Continence," in *Popery not Founded on Scripture,* ed. Thomas Tenison.

Porta, G. B. della. *Magiae Naturalis libri viginti.* Frankfurt, 1591.

Potter, Christopher. *A Sermon Preached at the Consecration of the right Reverend Father in God Barnaby Potter . . . Hereunto is added an Advertisement touching the History of the Quarrels of Pope Paul 5 with the Venetians; Penned in Italian by F. Paul, and done into English by the former Author* [Christopher Potter]. 1629.

Querini, Antonio. *Aviso delle ragioni della Serenissima Republica di Venetia, intorno alle difficoltà che le sono promosse dalla Santità di Papa Paolo V. Di Antonio Quirino senator venet:. Alla sua Patria e a tutto lo Stato della medesima Republica.* Venice, 1606.

A Relation Sent from Rome, of the Processe, Sentence, and Execution, done upon the Body, Picture, and Bookes, of Marcus Antonius de Dominis, Archbishop of Spalato after his Death. London, John Bill, 1624. (*STC* 7007.)

Roe, Sir Thomas. *The Negotiations of Sir Thomas Roe, in His Embassy to the Ottoman Porte, from the Year 1621 to 1628 Inclusive . . . Now first published from the Originals.* 1740.

Sandys, Edwin. *Relatione dello stato della Religione. E con quali dissegni & arti è stata fabricata e maneggiata in diversi stati di queste Occidentali parti del mondo. Tradotta dall'Inglese . . . in lingua volgare. Con*

Aggiunte notabili. [N.p.], 1625. The translation and additions are said to have been the work of Sarpi.

Scott, Thomas. *The Second Part of Vox Populi.* 2d ed. Goricum, 1624.

Sharpe, Leonel. *A Looking-glasse for the Pope.* 1616.

Sherlock, William. *A Brief Discourse Concerning the Notes of the Church. With some Reflections on Cardinal Bellarmin's Notes.* 1687.

Simon, Richard. *The History of the Original and Progress of Ecclesiastical Revenues: wherein is handled according to the Laws, both Ancient and Modern, whatsoever concerns matters Beneficial, the Regale, Investitures, Nominations, and other Rights attributed to Princes. Written in French by a Learned Priest. And now done into English.* 1685.

Sleidan (or, properly, Philippson), John. *The General History of the Reformation of the Church, from the Errors and Corruptions of the Church of Rome: begun in Germany by Martin Luther, with the Progress thereof in all Parts of Christendom, from the Year 1517, to the Year 1556. Written in Latin by John Sleidan, L.L.D. and faithfully Englished. To which is Added, A Continuation to the End of the Council of Trent, in the Year 1562. By Edmund Bohun, Esq.* 1689.

Spencer, John. *Catalogus Universalis Librorum Omnium in Bibliotheca Collegii Sionii apud Londinenses . . . .* 1650.

Squitinio della libertà veneta nel quale si adducono anche le ragioni dell'Impero Romano sopra la Città e Signoria di Venezia. Mirandola, 1612.

Stillingfleet, Edward. *The Council of Trent Examin'd and Disprov'd by Catholic Tradition.* 1688.

———. *A Discourse Concerning the Idolatry Practised in the Church of Rome.* 3d ed. 1672. (1st ed., 1671.)

A Survey of the Apostasy of Marcus Antonius de Dominis, Sometyme Archbishop of Spalato. Drawne out of his owne Booke, and written in Latin, by Fidelis Annosus, Verementanus Druinus, Devine: and Translated into English by A. M. [St. Omer?], 1617. (*STC* 7008. I have used the copy in Emmanuel College, Cambridge, pressmark 328. 5. 55.)

Tanner, Adam, S.J. *Defensionis Ecclesiasticae Libertatis Libri duo: contra Venetae Causae patronos, Joannem Marsilium Neopolitanum, et Paulum Venetum Servitam, &c.* Ingoldstadt, 1607.

Temple, Sir William. *The Works of Sir William Temple, Bart.* 4 vols. 1770.

Tenison, Thomas. *A Discourse Concerning a Guide in Matters of Faith; with respect, especially, to the Romish pretence of the necessity of such a one as is infallible.* 1683.

———, ed. *Popery not Founded on Scripture: Or, The Texts which Papists cite out of the Bible, for the Proof of the Points of Their Religion, Examin'd, and shew'd to be alledged without Ground.* 1688–1689.

Twysden, Sir Roger. *An Historical Vindication of the Church of England in Point of Schism, as it stands separated from the Roman and was reformed I. Elizabeth.* 1657.

Vincent, Nathanael, ed. *The Morning-Exercise against Popery. Or, the Principal*

Errors of the Church of Rome Detected and Confuted, in a Morning-Lecture Preached lately in Southwark: By Several Ministers of the Gospel in or near London . . . . 1675.

Walton, Izaak. *The Complete Angler & the Lives of Donne, Wotton, Hooker, Herbert & Sanderson.* Edited by Alfred W. Pollard. 1925.

Wheare, Degory. *The Method and Order of Reading Both Civil and Ecclesiastical Histories . . . By Degoraeus Wheare, Camden Reader of History in Oxford. To which is Added, an Appendix concerning the Historians of Particular Nations, as well Ancient as Modern. By Nicholas Horseman. Made English, and Enlarged, by Edmund Bohun, Esq.* . . . 1685.

Willes, John. "Abby and other Church-Lands, not yet assured to such Possessors as are Roman Catholicks; Dedicated to the Nobility and Gentry of that Religion." [1688?] Pamphlet.

Wilson, Arthur. *The History of Great Britain, being the Life and Reign of James the First.* 1653.

Wotton, Anthony. *Runne from Rome. Or, a Treatise shewing the necessitie of Separating from the Church of Rome.* . . . 1624.

4. MODERN STUDIES

Albertazzi, Adolfo. *Romanzieri e romanzi del cinquecento e del seicento.* Bologna, 1891.

Arber, Edward, ed. *A Transcript of the Registers of the Company of Stationers of London, 1554–1640* A.D. 5 vols. London, and Birmingham, 1875–1894.

Belvederi, Raffaele. *Guido Bentivoglio e la politica europea del suo tempo, 1607–1621.* Padua, 1962.

Bianchi-Giovini, Aurelio. *Biografia di Frà Paolo Sarpi, teologo e consultore di Stato della Repubblica Veneta.* 2 vols. Zurich, 1836.

Bouwsma, William J. *Venice and the Defense of Republican Liberty.* Berkeley, Calif., 1968.

Brown, Horatio. "Paolo Sarpi," in *Studies in European Literature, being the Taylorian Lectures 1889–1899.* Oxford, 1900.

Burke, Peter. *See* Sarpi, *History of Benefices*, above.

Campbell, Arabella Georgina. *La Vita di Fra Paolo Sarpi, Teologo-Consultore della Serenissima Repubblica di Venezia e autore della Storia del Concilio Tridentino.* Florence, 1875. (English original, 1869.)

Cantimori, Delio. "Avventuriero irenico," pp. 97–110 in *Prospettive di storia ereticale italiana del Cinquecento.* Bari, 1960.

Cantù, Cesare. *Les Hérétiques d'Italie. Discours historiques de César Cantú traduits de l'Italien par Anicet Digard et Edmond Martin.* 5 vols. Paris, 1869–1870.

A Catalogue of the Duplicates. . . . *See below*, under Twysden, Sir Roger.

Cessi, Roberto. *Storia della Repubblica di Venezia.* Rev. ed., 2 vols. Milan and Messina, 1968.

Chabod, Federico. *La politica di Paolo Sarpi.* Venice and Rome, 1962; reprinted in 1968.

La Civiltà veneziana nell'età barocca. Venice, 1959.

Cozzi, Gaetano. *Il Doge Nicolò Contarini.* Venice and Rome, 1958.

———. "Fra Paolo Sarpi, l'Anglicanesimo, e la *Historia del Concilio Tridentino,*" *Rivista Storica Italiana,* 68(1956):559–619. (*See also* under Minucci, above.)

Deed, S. G., and Francis, Jane, comps. *Catalogue of the Plume Library at Maldon, Essex.* Maldon, 1959.

Fink, Zera. *The Classical Republicans: An Essay in the Recovery of a Pattern of Thought in Seventeenth Century England.* Evanston, Ill., 1945.

Fiorentino, Francesco. *Scritti varii di letteratura, filosofia e critica.* Naples, 1876.

Froude, James Anthony, *Lectures on the Council of Trent.* 1896.

Fueter, Edward. *Storia della storiografia moderna.* Translated by A. Spinelli. 2 vols. Naples, 1943–1944.

Getto, Giovanni. *Paolo Sarpi.* 2d ed. Florence, 1967.

Hale, John R. *England and the Italian Renaissance: The Growth of Interest in Its History and Art.* London, 1954.

Hanford, James H. *A Milton Handbook.* 4th ed. New York, 1946.

Index Librorum Prohibitorum Sanctissimi Domini Nostri Gregorii XVI Pontificis Maximi. Rome, 1841.

Index Librorum Prohibitorum SS. mi D. N. Pii PP. XII. Rome, 1948.

Mattingly, Garrett. *Renaissance Diplomacy.* London, 1955.

Morozzo, Raimondo della Rocca, and Tiepolo, Maria Francesca. "Cronologia veneziana del Seicento," pp. 259–315, in *La Civiltà veneziana nell'età barocca.*

Newland, Henry. *The Life and Contemporaneous Church History of Antonio de Dominis, Archbishop of Spalatro.* Oxford and London, 1859.

The Oxford Dictionary of the Christian Church, ed. F. L. Cross. London, 1957.

Paolo Sarpi e i suoi tempi. Studi storici. Città di Castello, 1923.

Pascolato, Alessandro. *Fra Paolo Sarpi.* Milan, 1893.

Plomer, Henry R. *A Dictionary of the Booksellers and Printers . . . from 1641 to 1667.* London, 1907.

Plume, Thomas. *An Account of the Life and Death of the Right Reverend Father in God, John Hacket, late Lord Bishop of Lichfield and Coventry,* ed. Mackenzie E. C. Walcott. London, 1865. (1st ed., 1675.)

Ponti, Giovanni. *Paolo Sarpi.* Torino, 1938.

Quazza, Romolo. *La guerra per la successione di Mantova e del Monferrato.* 2 vols. Mantua, 1926.

Ragg, Laura M. *Crises in Venetian History.* London, 1928.

Rampolla Gambino, Adelaide. *Fra Paolo Sarpi. Studio storico e letterario.* Palermo, 1919.

Rhodes, Dennis. "Roberto Meietti e alcuni documenti della controversia fra Papa Paolo V e Venezia," *Studi Seicenteschi,* 1(1960):165–74.

Robertson, Alexander. *Fra Paolo Sarpi, the Greatest of the Venetians*. London, 1911.

Salvatorelli, Luigi. "Le Idee religiose di Fra Paolo Sarpi," in *Atti della Accademia Nazionale dei Lincei* (1954). Serie 8ª: Memorie. Classe di scienze morali, storiche e filologiche, 5:311–60.

———. "Venezia, Paolo V e fra Paolo Sarpi," pp. 67–95, in *La Civiltà veneziana nell'età barocca*.

Scaduto, Francesco. *Stato e Chiesa secondo Fra Paolo Sarpi*. Florence, 1885.

Scott, Mary Augusta. *Elizabethan Translations from the Italian*. Boston and New York, 1916.

Sella, Domenico. "Il declino dell'emporio realtino," pp. 97–121, in *La Civiltà veneziana nell'età barocca*.

Sells, A. Lytton. *The Paradise of Travellers: The Italian Influence on Englishmen in the Seventeenth Century*. Bloomington, Ind., 1964.

Seneca, Federico. *La politica veneziana dopo l'interdetto*. Padua, 1957.

Sestan, Ernesto. "La politica veneziana del Seicento," pp. 35–66, in *La Civiltà veneziana nell'età barocca*.

Shuckburgh, E. S., ed. *Two Biographies of William Bedell, Bishop of Kilmore. With a Selection of His Letters and an Unpublished Treatise*. Cambridge, England, 1902.

Smith, Logan Pearsall. *The Life and Letters of Sir Henry Wotton*. 2 vols. Oxford, 1907.

Stoye, John Walter. *English Travellers Abroad, 1604–1667*. London, 1952.

Tenenti, Alberto. *Venezia e i corsari 1580–1615*. Bari, 1961.

Toni, G. B. de. "Fra Paolo Sarpi nelle scienze esatte e naturali," in *Paolo Sarpi e i suoi tempi*.

[Twysden, Sir Roger]. *A Catalogue of the Duplicates and a considerable Portion of the Library of Sir John Sebright, Bart. . . . Also the very curious collection of Manuscripts . . . collected by Sir Roger Twysden and Mr. E. Lhwyd . . . which will be sold by Auction by Leigh and S. Sotheby . . . on Monday, April 6th, 1807, and Six following days (Sunday excepted)*. London, 1807. (B.M. pressmark, 269.i.7.1.)

Yates, Frances. "Paolo Sarpi's *History of the Council of Trent*," *Journal of the Warburg and Courtauld Institutes*, 7(1944):123–44.

Index

A., E.: 185–86, 199

Abbot, Robert: 118, 224*n*

Abbott, George, archbishop: his "character" of de Dominis, 32–33; his letters to Brent, 47–48, 51; on de Dominis's defection, 58; examines de Dominis, 60; residence of de Dominis with, 213*n*; mentioned, 29, 40, 44, 49, 57, 89

Abercromby, David: 148, 229*n*

Acosta, Jérôme (pseud.): *See* Simon, Richard

Acquapendente: *See* Fabrizio d'Acquapendente, Girolamo

Adam: 163

Adrian IV, pope: 113

Adriana (=Venice): 93

Aglionby, William: 85, 184

Albertazzi, Alberto: 212*n*

Albertino, P.: *See* Aubertin, P., Genevan printer

Albicocco, Fabio, printer: 80

Alexander VI, pope: 52

Amelot, Abraham-Nicholas: *See* Houssaie, Abraham-Nicholas Amelot de la

Ancona, Marquisate of: 225*n*

Andrewes, Lancelot: 50, 212*n*

Anglesey, Earl of: 150

Antonio da Viterbo, Fra: 133

Aquilini, Cesare: 144

Aquinas, St. Thomas: 114, 161

Arbe (modern Rab), town and island: 27

Arber, Edward: 220*n*

Arcangelo, Maestro: 9, 111

Areopagitica: 153

Armachanus: *See* Vauchop, Robert, titular archbishop

Arminianism: 50, 160

Asselineau, Pierre: 5

Ataide, Jorge de: 147

Atterbury, Lewis, editor: 46–48, 215*n*, 216*n*

Aubertin, P., Genevan printer: 78

Aubri, Jean: 234*n*

August, Duke of Brunswick-Lüneburg: 83

Augustine of Hippo, saint: 114, 147, 162

Bacon, Sir Francis: 27, 80, 107, 109, 111, 202, 223*n*

Bald, R. C.: 214*n*, 216*n*

Barberini, Maffeo: *See* Urban VIII, pope

Bargrave, Isaac: 128

Barker, Robert: 44, 51

Barlow, Thomas: 149, 198, 218*n*, 229*n*

Baronius, Caesar (Cesare Baronio),

251

Index

Buckingham, Duke of: *See* Villiers, George
Burby, Cuthbert: 24, 210*n*
Burgess, John: 112
Burke, Peter: 219*n*
Burnet, Gilbert, bishop: on de Dominis, 29; his opinion of Sarpi, 171–77, 199; Wotton's "character" of Sarpi in Burnet's *Life of William Bedell*, 201–3; his works cited, 210*n*, 211*n*, 212*n*, 213*n*, 216*n*, 230*n*, 232*n*, 233*n*, 234*n*
Burton, Henry: 124–25, 225*n*, 226*n*
Burton, Robert: 225*n*
Busnelli, Manlio Duilio: 208*n*, 217*n*

Cabassutius, Johannes: 150
Caffa, Charles: 219*n*
Calendar of State Papers: 212*n*, 216*n*
Calistini: 159
Calvin, John: 136, 156, 157, 165
Cambridge University: 126, 169, 201, 223*n*, 233*n*
Camden, William: 113, 155
Campo di Fiori: 68
Canaye de Fresnes, Philippe: 105
Canonical books (of Bible): discussed at Trent, 138–39
Cantimori, Delio: 218*n*
Caorle, bishopric of: 8
Capello, Marc'Antonio: 208*n*
Cappella, Gian Maria: 1, 2
Capuchins: 16
Caraffa, Carlo: 186
Carleton, Dudley: 29–30, 40, 49, 50, 56–57, 115, 212*n*, 215*n*, 216*n*
Carleton, George: 40, 50, 115–16, 118, 125, 216*n*
Casaubon, Meric: 154
Castellani, C.: 212*n*
Catarino, Ambrosio: 164
Cebes, Table of: 202
Cecil, Sir Robert: 21, 209*n*
Celibacy: 147–48, 158–59, 233*n*
Cervantes Saavedra, Miguel de: 39

Cervini, Marcello: *See* Marcellus II, pope
Cessi, Roberto: 207*n*
Chabod, Federico: 207*n*, 208*n*
Chamberlain, John: 212*n*
Charles (Charlemagne), emperor: 102
Charles I, King of England: 77, 100, 109, 111, 154, 157
Charles V, emperor: 143
Charles IX, King of France: 187
Chaucer, Geoffrey: 143, 154
Chemnitz, Martin: 125, 143, 158
Childibert, King of France: 102
Chiswell, Richard: 85
Christ Church, Oxford: 164
Church of England: Crakanthorp's defense of, 69; Twysden's *Historical Vindication* of, 88; Carleton on, 116; Heylyn on, 159; Burnet's *History* of reformation in, 172–74; mentioned, 60, 64, 118, 123, 126, 142, 218*n*
Cibo, Franceschetto: 141
Cibo, Maddalena: 141
Claudio of Piacenza, Maestro: 4
Clement VII, pope: 92
Clement VIII, pope: 8, 13
Clesel (or Cleyssel), cardinal: 61
Coire: 30
Coligna, Ambrose: 130
Colin Clout: *See* Spenser, Edmund
Collins, Samuel: 21, 201
Collisoni, Gabriele: 6, 8, 9, 112, 132
Colvius, Andreas: 103, 198, 220*n*, 222*n*
Communion, Holy: 119, 159
Commynes, Philippe de: 171
Condé, Prince of: 79–80, 202–3, 215*n*
Confession, auricular: 138, 214*n*, 233*n*
Contarini, Simone: 214*n*
Conversion, spiritual: 160
Cooke, Alexander: 122–23, 225*n*
Cordes, Jean de: 219*n*
Coryat, Thomas: 25, 211*n*
Council of Constance: 174
Council of Ten: 14, 15, 24, 209*n*
Council of Trent: decrees of, 5, 12; de

45–46; his interest in Sarpi, 87–92; mentioned, 22, 116, 221*n*
Twysden, Sir William: 87

Ulianich, Boris: 214*n*
Upsalensis: *See* Olaus Magnus (Stora)
Urban VII, pope: 6
Urban VIII, pope: 61, 93, 94, 129, 136, 142
Usher, James: 113
Uskoks: 12, 28, 64, 189, 207*n,* 212*n*

Vane, Sir Henry, the elder: 88
Vargas, Francisco: 150, 174
Vauchop, Robert, titular archbishop: 118
Vega, Andreas: 125, 226*n,* 232*n*
Vendramin, Francesco: 13
Venice: Sarpi's acquaintances in, 7; supports Sarpi for bishopric, 8; Wotton ambassador to, 11; quarrel with Paul V, 11–19, 95–97, 228*n;* behavior of clergy in, 15; resents attack on Sarpi, 18–19; Coryat's visit to, 25; English interest in, 78; admired by Howell, 93, 94–97; quarrel with pope related, 131–32; her policy praised by Bethel, 146–47; Sumner on "Venetian Controversy," 155; Heylyn on same, 159; books against heretics in, 165; and James I, 182; Blount on Venetian "policy," 183; slandered in *Opinione falsamente ascrita,* 183–84; English continuing admiration of, 188; Amelot on, 189–90; and papal conflict abstracted, 193; pamphlets on quarrel, 207–8*n;* pope forbids commerce with, 225*n*
Vergerio, Paolo: 178
Vignier, Nicholas: 23
Villiers, George, First Duke of Buckingham: 111
Vincent, Nathanael: 140, 198, 227*n*

Viti, Michiele: 24, 209*n*

Walcott, Mackenzie E. C.: 224*n*
Waltham-Abbey (Essex): 126
Walton, Izaak: 45, 127–28, 198, 215*n*
Ward, Samuel: 78, 79, 113, 176
Wheare, Degory: 169–71, 199, 231–32*n*
Whitgift, John, archbishop: 112
Wicelius, Georgius: 122
Willes, John: 188
Williams, John, archbishop: 36, 107–14, 128, 223*n*
Wilson, Arthur: 69, 213*n,* 218*n*
Winwood, Sir Ralph: 30
Wolfe, Don M.: 230*n*
Wood, Anthony à: 48
Works, doctrine of good: 138
Wotton, Anthony: 119–21, 139, 225*n*
Wotton, Sir Henry: first English ambassador to Venice, 11; his interest in Sarpi, 19, 20, 215*n;* his high estimate of Sarpi, 21; letters concerning Venetian affairs, 21–22, 209*n;* his residence center for visitors, 25; visited by Coryat, 25; David Lloyd on, 45; his Venetian embassies, 49; and Diodati, 53; proposed translation, 83; his "motto," 112; Walton's *Life* of, 127–28; and Sarpi's portrait, 153; his "character" of Sarpi, 197, 201–3, 232*n;* mentioned, 23, 175, 176, 198, 214*n*

Xavier, St. Thomas: 1

Yates, Frances: 215*n*
Yelverton family: 88

Zane, Matteo: 13
Zeno, Renier: 82
Zuliani, Eleanora: 211*n*
Zwinglians: 161